Modern Restaurant Service

Modern Restaurant Service

A manual for students and practitioners

John Fuller

Hutchinson

London Melbourne Sydney Auckland Johannesburg

Hutchinson & Co. (Publishers) Ltd
An imprint of the Hutchinson Publishing Group
17-21 Conway Street, London W1P 6JD

Hutchinson Group (Australia) Pty Ltd
30-32 Cremorne Street, Richmond South, Victoria 3121
PO Box 151, Broadway, New South Wales 2007

Hutchinson Group (NZ) Ltd
32-34 View Road, PO Box 40-086, Glenfield, Auckland 10

Hutchinson Group (SA) (Pty) Ltd
PO Box 337, Bergvlei 2012, South Africa

First published 1983
Reprinted 1983

© John Fuller 1983
Illustrations © Hutchinson & Co. (Publishers) Ltd

Set in Times

Printed and bound in Great Britain by
Anchor Brendon Ltd,
Tiptree, Essex

British Library Cataloguing in Publication Data
Fuller, John, *1916-*
    Modern restaurant service.
    1. Restaurant management
    I. Title
    647'.95'068   TX945

ISBN   0 09 146830 2 cased
           0 09 146831 0 paper

Contents

List of figures and tables

Tables

Preface

Modern Restaurant Service has its origins in *The Waiter*, which was published in 1947 under the auspices of the then National Council for Hotel and Catering Education as the first of a series of textbooks, and was based on contributions from practising restaurateurs and hoteliers. In 1965, with Mr A. J. Currie's help, we developed this material to more than twice its original length. Now, once more substantially expanded and updated, *Modern Restaurant Service* bears little resemblance to those earlier versions.

Since the 1965 augmented edition appeared both industry and readership have changed. *The Waiter* was originally used as a text by students taking waiting examinations of the Hotel and Catering Institute (now the Hotel, Catering and Institutional Management Association) but subsequent editions were used by a far wider range of students. Therefore, this book has been written to cover the needs of this wider readership and the changes in restaurant service.

Some textbooks dealing with theoretical and management-oriented topics must, by their nature, be of relevance and interest to a relatively narrow readership; but the practicalities of catering such as cookery and table service concern a wide readership group in industry and a broad band of students. Hence this book's forerunner was used by students from craft to higher level courses, and by operatives and managers alike. A few teachers may question whether different levels of students should use the same textbooks but I have long observed that, in practice, future managers need as much knowledge of food and beverage service as do craft students.

For practical elements of a course, whether higher TEC or even degree level, guidance in applied skills, that is, 'how to do things' is sought in a food and beverage service manual.

Hence *Modern Restaurant Service* has built on long-standing procedures which have been found useful over the years. Even some 'historic' material about formal 'brigades' in traditional restaurants is retained because awareness of the origins of practice, and understanding past evolution, helps today's readers appreciate current change and future possibilities. But to time-tested techniques have now been added newer methods and fresh encouragement to adopt a questioning approach.

Those working and training in food and beverage service need a guide to practice. This book describes how procedures may be carried out; even at the risk of being dubbed 'descriptive'. Necessary descriptive material dealing with the 'how' should not inhibit students or other readers from questioning 'why', for I seek throughout this book to stress the inevitability of social, economic and technological factors occasioning constantly shifting emphasis in service techniques, if not decisive change.

My hope is, therefore, that *Modern Restaurant Service* will meet the requirements of students following City and Guilds, ordinary and higher level TEC and degree courses and, in its comprehensive form, continue to be of use also to trainees and practitioners in industry itself.

Despite many years on the academic side of hotel and catering management, I recall with pleasure my time spent as a commis, demi-chef, chef de rang and sommelier d'étage in London, Switzerland and Paris. I found then that restaurant work can be enjoyable and, when well performed, can earn high repute. Great maîtres d'hôtels spring to mind as embodying high status in restaurant service. There are many others who never achieve fame but who, nevertheless, earn a good living, gain job satisfaction and achieve respected standing through the vocation of restaurant service.

Contact with customers and with other staff from restaurant service is also a valuable prelude to later responsibilities. A potential manager's ability to master table service will enable him to gain maximum benefit from restaurant work experience and in later years provide insight for managing the activities of others, supervising arrangements for functions and checking day to day table service. I hope this book will continue to set readers on that path.

John Fuller 1982

Acknowledgements

I acknowledge generous help and advice given by colleagues in teaching, in our industry and by suppliers to the industry.

I am especially grateful to Mr M. A. Hewens, FHCIMA, Head of Department of Hotel, Catering and Hairdressing Services, West Kent College of Further Education, for many pages of material most of which is incorporated, and whose suggestions were most valuable.

I am similarly appreciative of comments from Mr A. Willis, MHCIMA, and Mr A. Crawford, MHCIMA, Department of Hotel Management and Catering, High Peak College of Further Education, Buxton. Colleagues at Oxford Polytechnic, particularly Ms Valerie Flavell, Mr Frank Mieczkowski and Mr John Valentine have been most supportive and I also acknowledge past contributions in previous editions from Mr A. J. Currie of Strathclyde University's Scottish Hotel School.

I stress my indebtedness to Mr S. O. J. Willer, FHCIMA, who has kindly allowed me to use his device and his material for setting out the sequence of courses in menus in Chapters 7 and 8.

For supplying menus and promotional literature, I thank Trusthouse Forte Hotels, Grand Metropolitan Hotels and Anchor Hotels.

I am grateful for the kind contributions of: Mr Ted Oldfield, Director of the Cutlery and Allied Trade Research Association (for a substantial amount of material integrated in Chapter 5), Mr A. J. M. Price, President of the Federation of British Cutlery Manufacturers and Squadron Leader James Rush, AFC.

I thank the following companies and organizations for their help and for supplying material: Josiah Wedgwood & Sons Limited; Royal Doulton Ltd; Diversey Limited (D. M. Hillyard, Technical Services Manager); the Cona Coffee Machine Company; Comité National des Vins de France and SOPEXA; Food and Wine from France; Wines from Germany Information Services; James Rush & Company (Glassware) Limited; Hunters and Frankau Cigar Importers.

I am grateful to the following for their permission to reproduce illustrations: Gardiner & Co, pages 34 and 35; Arthur Price of England, pages 50, 52, 54 and 55; the Tea Council Limited (Mr Peter Haines, Catering Trade Adviser), page 62; the Cona Coffee Machine Company, page 65; Crypto Peerless Ltd, page 66; Miele Company Ltd, page 68; Anchor Hotels, page 92; Trusthouse Forte Hotels, pages 102, 207 and 269; Josiah Wedgwood & Sons Limited, page 132; James Rush & Company (Glassware) Limited, page 254; Grand Metropolitan County Hotels, page 96; American Express, page 183.

Every effort has been made to reach copyright holders, but the publisher would be grateful to hear from any source whose copyright they may have unwittingly infringed.

Finally, I thank my wife who has collaborated throughout the writing of this book and who prepared and typed the manuscript for publication.

Part One
Staff and Workplace

1 Restaurant service in catering context

Because so many people eat away from home, most people should have some notion of the nature of restaurant service and its broad purpose. Nevertheless, it is worth noting that those with responsibilities for the service of food have a vital role in hotel keeping and catering, Britain's fourth biggest industry in terms of numbers employed, and one which helps substantially to support the tourist and travel industry as a top earner of foreign currency. Good waiters are necessary to the success of this important hospitality industry (tourism, hotel keeping and catering), to business as well as to holiday travel and,

hence, to the well-being of society and its economic strength.

Waiting staff within catering constitute an important link in the chain of food production and selling which can be summarized as:

1 Food is grown by farmers; then
2 Shipped or transported to markets; to be
3 Sold by wholesalers to caterers; who
4 Prepare, cook and serve it to the public.

Figure 1 on page 14, further illustrates the nature of catering and the service staff's part in it.

Tradition and change

The modern waiter (wherever the word waiter is used in this book it refers also to waitresses, unless otherwise indicated) is aware that today more people eat away from home than in pre-World War II days when dining style was dominated by hotels and fine restaurants, and largely oriented towards the well-to-do. Many waiting practices and traditions were developed in those times.

Types of service
Today, food and beverage service is basically either:

* *Waiter/waitress service* Where food and drink is brought to a customer or guest.
* *Self-service* Where a customer collects his own food.

Both kinds of service may be found in profit catering (that is, hotels, restaurants, guest houses,

holiday camps) or in 'at cost' or welfare catering (that is, industrial (staff catering), or institutional (hospitals, schools, etc.)).

Types of restaurant
Because of the diverse styles and sizes of catering operations, the term restaurant can imply establishments ranging from luxurious to modest and include:

1 *Restaurants of large residential hotels,* probably licensed Music, dancing and other entertainments may be provided. Style may include (among others) table d'hôte dining rooms, à la carte (including gourmet level) restaurants, coffee shops. Styles may be formal or informal, popular priced or expensive and service may extend to functions, banquets, private parties, floor (room) service.

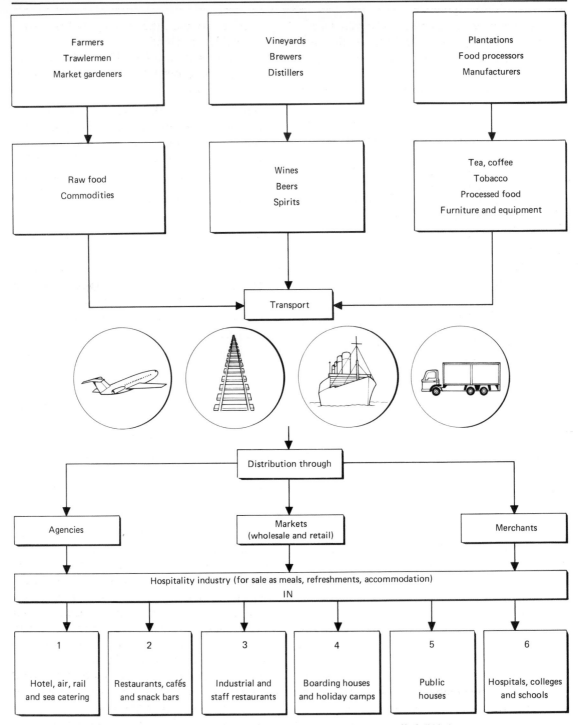

Figure 1   *Nature and structure of the hospitality industry*

2 *Dining rooms in smaller residential hotels, inns or guest houses* Licensed or unlicensed, with a range more modestly reflecting (1) above.

3 *Residential clubs* Also offer restaurant services.

4 *Other commercial restaurants with no residential accommodation* These establishments in traditional style may vary from 'up-market' establishments catering for the rich, open until late at night and offering a wide choice of dish (often French type) to those offering limited menus (steak houses or, perhaps, simple 'English fare') during business hours. Restaurants may also be found 'supporting' other facilities, that is, in department stores, concert halls, theatres and other places of entertainment.

5 *Other speciality restaurants* These may include vegetarian, health food, sea food, pizza and ethnic restaurants (Chinese, Indian, Italian, Greek, Kosher, etc.).

6 *Fast food restaurants and cafeterias* Whether individually owned, owned and operated under franchise, or operated by companies with a chain of identical operations, their pattern and style constantly change.
'Traditional' cafés and snack bars offering lighter meals service still persist but there are many variations, some offering waiting service others with self-service and take-away. Restaurants offering a fairly extensive meal service (as well as beverages and snacks) on a self-service basis are usually described as offering a cafeteria service.

7 *Outdoor catering* Racetracks (and other sporting events), garden parties and other alfresco functions.

8 *Travel catering* Rail, air and liner catering services both in transit and at terminals and stations.

9 *Industrial and staff restaurants* Serving from a small number up to several thousand employees daily. These provide employees with a choice of dishes. Preparation may be for large quantities but if cafeteria style, with customers 'helping themselves' at a service counter, the work of staff is correspondingly reduced.

10 *Institutional catering* Dining facilities in schools, colleges, hospitals, hostels and other institutions.

This list indicates the general, and changing, nature of restaurants. It is not exhaustive, for restaurants of other kinds are to be found because food service is commonly provided in a wide variety of settings. Moreover, the categories overlap or are affected by new developments as, for example, condominiums and self-catering for holidays emerge.

Type and style of operation has a bearing on what kind of waiting service, if any, is offered. Guidance about serving procedures outlined in this manual must always be conditioned by, and subservient to, policy and 'style of the house'. These vary considerably when food service operations comprise such diversity. Figure 2 on page 16 indicates the variety of food services.

Varying levels of service

We see that waiting services are provided at many levels; from luxury hotels to holiday camps and industrial catering dining rooms. Yet as more people eating away from home seek a dining service, traditional solutions cannot always solve catering problems. Lack of staff is just one reason which prompts caterers to devise new types of operation.

Today, many fast food outlets do not provide any waiting service at all, and in the USA experiments like a 'gourmet' take-away restaurant (such as the Handover-Fiste in Marina Del Ray, California) also eliminate the waiter. In Chicago, a computerized service drastically reduces waiter service using only 'captains' to take orders and 'runners' to bring dishes. Other restaurants at various price levels may offer not only take-away services but combine more traditional restaurant services with other activities such as selling delicatessen or other foods.

Because of staff shortage, waiting even in more conventional hotels may be provided by students on vacation (especially in resorts). These

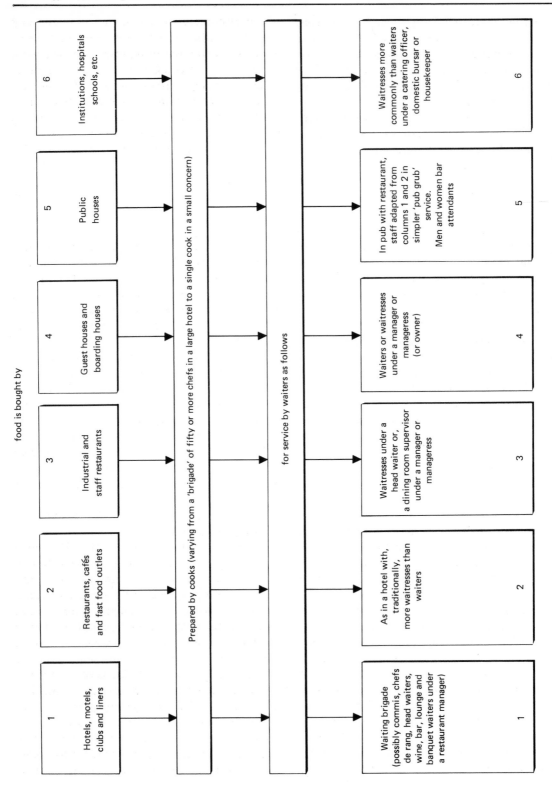

food is bought by

1	2	3	4	5	6
Hotels, motels, clubs and liners	Restaurants, cafés and fast food outlets	Industrial and staff restaurants	Guest houses and boarding houses	Public houses	Institutions, hospitals schools, etc.

Prepared by cooks (varying from a 'brigade' of fifty or more chefs in a large hotel to a single cook in a small concern)

for service by waiters as follows

1	2	3	4	5	6
Waiting brigade (possibly commis, chefs de rang, head waiters, wine, bar, lounge and banquet waiters under a restaurant manager)	As in a hotel with, traditionally, more waitresses than waiters	Waitresses under a head waiter or, a dining room supervisor under a manager or manageress	Waiters or waitresses under a manager or manageress (or owner)	In pub with restaurant, staff adapted from columns 1 and 2 in simpler 'pub grub' service. Men and women bar attendants	Waitresses more commonly than waiters under a catering officer, domestic bursar or housekeeper

Figure 2   *Food service in various catering operations*

are not necessarily students on catering courses, but students of all kinds. There is, therefore, a continuing trend for caterers to seek new ways of providing food and beverage service. This may even mean attempts to 'de-skill' the waiting task or to eliminate it.

In short, economic pressures cause a waiter's employer, the hotelier, restaurateur or caterer to change. In turn the modern waiter, too, must be adaptable and ready for change.

Adding value

Despite changes and the disappearance of many 'traditions', it is inconceivable that there will not continue to be a demand for trained waiting staff, especially in catering operations where a diner seeks relaxation and pleasure as well as nourishment.

Indeed, some sectors of catering are virtually in show business. Some customers eat out not merely to assuage hunger but for change, amusement, to see and be seen; in short, for entertainment. Thus, many customers see waiting service as adding value to their meal experience. They are spared chores which they may have to face when eating at home and they are also undergoing a pleasurable experience in which they are cossetted and made to feel wanted.

Thus, the training of modern waiters has to be directed towards social and personal skills as well as technical expertise. There are still catering operations throughout the Western World where there is a continuing demand for many traditional styles of service. These are by no means all 'up-market' operations but include guest houses (family pensions), hotel restaurants, 'classic' restaurants, ethnic restaurants (Chinese, Indian, Greek, Italian, for example) and restaurants catering for tourists (such as in Soho and other city and resort centres).

Wherever he works, an effective waiter will realize that his service should be seen by a customer to add value to the meal experience, and by management to aid meal sales.

The areas of hotels in which waiting staff serve (including restaurant, dining room, coffee shop, lounge and bedroom floors) are those in which customers are actually encountered and must be satisfied. They are revenue generating areas. In them a waiter represents management in customer contact. On him rests the main task of selling to, and satisfying, a guest. Waiting staff have similar functions in newer types of operations, some of them already well-established, such as coffee shops in hotels, snack bars, self-service, motorway restaurants and pub catering, as well as experiments and permutations already discussed.

Selling

A waiter not only serves food, but does, as later chapters show, play an important part as a salesman of food. He assists in merchandising a meal through its accompanying services. Waiters are 'sales staff' in a firm, just as a chef is its manufacturer, turning raw materials into palatable dishes.

A successful hotel, restaurant or café with waiting service is one which guests want to visit again, a place where they feel as comfortable as in their own homes. This pleasant atmosphere is produced by friendly courtesy, a welcoming attitude; well-cooked food; advice in selecting dishes; a knowledge of how dishes are prepared; and quiet, efficient, but unostentatious, service. By these amenities, both buyer and seller are satisfied and goodwill of the business increased.

But such amenities need not be 'classical' or 'conventional'. Professor Matthew Bernatsky of Cornell University has observed that 'Hotelmen once thought they could not dispense with old-fashioned, formal service in their dining rooms. Yet when they converted to speciality rooms, they gained patronage and made more money'. Professor Bernatsky realized that this change was partly prompted by a shortage of trained waiters capable of giving a silver service; but he thought it more important 'that most Americans, except on rare occasions, prefer quicker and less formal service'. This brought emphasis on buffets and smorgasbord and explained why service from trolleys caught on. Such switches of emphasis continue today, will continue to change tomorrow, and in countries other than America.

Co-operation and contact

Successful catering depends on a partnership between management, cooks and sales staff. All have different parts to play, but they belong to a team. All must have an interest in their work, pride in the concern and a sense of loyalty towards it. This positive attitude of mind helps eliminate any drudgery in the work.

One attraction of catering is, at a time when so many jobs are monotonous and packed with the same deadening routine throughout the year, that it offers a career of interest and variety. Sales staff (waiters for example) come into contact with a wide range of people, all with different interests; waiters are consequently prompted to develop tact and initiative, to keep their brains active and to develop and reveal their personality.

Because a waiter contacts, and often represents, the hotel or restaurant owner he contributes to the image and repute of the establishment. Much catering success, therefore, depends on a waiter's skills, interest and personal qualities.

Friendliness

While teaching in a hotel school in an American university, a colleague of mine conducted a survey which revealed that waiting staff thought that expert serving techniques were the most important features of their work. Their customers surveyed, on the other hand, indicated that what they valued most in a waiter was a smiling, agreeable, welcoming blend of social qualities. This does not mean that techniques are not important; for many guests who appreciate the result of techniques may not be fully aware that a skilful and unobtrusive waiter is practising them. However, it does mean that waiting staff in merchandising a 'meal experience' must cultivate friendliness, good manners and many other social qualities and skills.

One reason why relatively unskilled students (such as those on law or arts courses) are often successful as waiters, even on a temporary basis, is that their social abilities allow them to adjust readily to guests.

Thus, waiting is not only an important link in the chain of food preparation and service, but holds vast possibilities for the right person. Many restaurant proprietors started as commis or junior waiters.

Every restaurant manager is likely to have had long experience in waiting; for without knowledge and skill based on such experience he could hardly hold his position. There is no short cut to restaurant management. One cannot just 'drop into' this position. Today especially, it is worth trying to start a steady climb to it because a restaurateur can command a high salary and a respected status.

A waiter's efficiency reacts upon the success of the hotel, restaurant or other catering operation for which he works. His work, his attitude to those above him and to his fellows, how he deals with those who visit his restaurant (who may be referred to as 'guests', 'customers', 'patrons', or 'visitors'), have their effect in building up an establishment's reputation and thereby affect his own career.

Advancement

Nearly all posts of head waiter, maître d'hôtel, or restaurant manager, are obtained by those with years of service in waiting who have learned by training and experience how best to do the work which they organize and direct. This applies, also, to many of the most successful owners of catering establishments.

Good service is widely sought so that a good waiter has always an opportunity for promotion.

The changing nature of catering also changes career patterns. It was only in the late 1970s that food and beverage managers in this country formed an association which reflected the way in which management of food and beverage operations had established a new type of hotel post in Britain, that of the food and beverage manager (though such jobs have been long recognized in the USA). During the 1980s, posts advertised in the leading French hotel and catering weekly paper have included those with a job titled 'food and beverage manager' in

English. (This sought candidates aged 35 years, with a baccalaureate (a good GCE), a hotel school diploma and several years experience in de luxe restaurants.) A similar job in a four star luxe hotel in Paris has advertised for a chief hostess and an assistant chief hostess (with strong restaurant experience). Thus, even in the French heartland of traditional restaurant brigades, new-style posts and new job designations emerge.

Those who wait at table today may be career waiters or 'moonlighters' working part-time in catering, or catering students seeking experience in different departments. For all of them, experience gained through waiting is a valuable, if not essential, forerunner to a variety of opportunities in the catering business. Certainly, career waiters and waitresses will consider gaining qualifications through the technical education system, either full-time or part-time, and will tend to aspire towards food and beverage service specialization even when they advance to senior posts. In particular, they seek to become head waiters, maîtres d'hôtel, restaurant managers and food and beverage managers. Others who take advantage of what the technical educational system offers part-time may even move on to more general management in the industry.

Training opportunities

Courses of interest to waiting staff include those based on City and Guilds of London Institute schemes. These are provided in over 300 colleges and training centres in Britain and in many other countries. Schemes for both full-time and part-time attendance reflect recommendations of the Hotel and Catering Industry Training Board, evaluation of earlier courses and consultation with industry.

From many courses, the following are especially interesting to waiting staff:

707 Food and beverage service (707/1 Part I and 707/2 Part II)
For those training or employed in food and beverage service, Part I provides an introduction to hotel keeping and catering and to food service.

Specific educational qualifications are not required for entry to a course which may be a one term part-time day release or a ten week full-time course. On its completion, a person should be able to work effectively as a waiter.

Part II provides for development of skills particularly for more complex forms of food and beverage service. It also provides an introduction

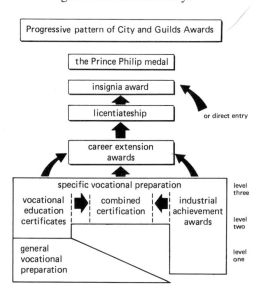

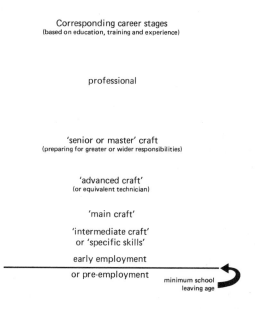

Figure 3 *Training opportunities for waiting staff*

to supervisory skills, so that with further practical experience the duties of a head waiter/waitress might be undertaken. Previous success at Part I or experience in industry is suggested for entry to a course usually offered as a twenty week full-time course, or over two or three terms on a part-time day or block release basis.

717   Alcoholic beverages
This course is intended for those responsible for sales and service of alcoholic beverages and is of interest to those who wish to broaden their knowledge as waiters or to specialize as wine waiters.

771   Organizational studies
A catering option in this scheme is intended for more able craftsmen, including waiting staff, training for positions of higher responsibility.

700   Specific skill schemes for the hotel and catering industry
These schemes are intended for those who wish to enter, or are already employed in, hotel and catering jobs requiring a limited range of special-ized skills. There are schemes for: short-order cooks, counter service assistants, food service assistants (waiters/waitresses), room attendants, wine waiters and bar staff.

Training may be arranged by industrial or educational establishments and undertaken by any mode of study. Trainees receive instruction and also undertake practical activities. Length of training programmes is at the discretion of an establishment. Assessment is primarily of practical work.

Training information and further possibilities
Pamphlets (for a small charge) are available from: Sales Section, City and Guilds of London Institute, 76 Portland Place, London W1N 4AA, but information on the *Specific Skill Schemes (700)* may be obtained from the City and Guilds of London Institute (S16A), 46 Britannia Street, London WC1X 9RG.

While City and Guilds of London Institute courses are those most directly related to food

and beverage service, ambitious restaurant staff can continue their education through part-time study (and even by full-time courses as mature students) in a variety of ways. For those who aspire to become food and beverage managers (or to qualify for more general forms of hospitality industry management) there are other schemes involving Technician Education Council (TEC) courses, and courses leading to the examinations of the Hotel, Catering and Institutional Manage-ment Association (HCIMA). Information about such possibilities is obtainable from the Hotel and Catering Industry Training Board, PO Box 18, Ramsey House, Central Square, Wembley, Middlesex, (or its regional offices), and from the Hotel, Catering and Institutional Management Association, 191 Trinity Road, London SW17 7HN.

Conditions of work

Government Acts controlling hours, wages and conditions exist in the catering industry. Wages Councils have been formed so that minimum rates of pay (and other conditions of service) may be regulated for the various sections of the industry. It is not appropriate to detail these regulations in this book, but the following notes indicate conditions that generally apply in the industry.

A waiter spends the greater part of his time in public rooms, which are well-lighted, carpeted, clean and comfortable. Food has to be brought from the kitchen to the restaurant. Where there are service lifts, or the kitchen is on the same floor as the restaurant, service can be straight-forward without strain to the staff. In some establishments food has to be carried upstairs or downstairs, according to kitchen layout. In any case, a waiter is nearly always on his feet, for he has to stand or walk for many hours every day.

Terms of employment

Hours worked vary according to the establish-ment. In a hotel open from early morning until late at night, some staff must be on duty (probably on 'shifts') at all the times necessary to prepare for and serve visitors. In staff catering or restaurants run for business people or in departmental stores and similar establishments, hours approximate to those of other callings, for example from 9 a.m. to 5 or 6 p.m., with a half-day free on Saturday, and all Sundays free.

Remuneration of waiters has for many years been considerably above that in most comparable occupations. Pay may be a regular fixed amount, as in staff catering, snack bars, etc., but in hotels and restaurants it is usually made up of a weekly guaranteed sum, with the addition of tips. These may be a share of all the tips paid to staff or just what the waiter may himself receive from his customers. In addition, he nearly always has meals free, or under specially favourable staff arrangements.

He may be non-resident or resident. In large hotels most men live out, but up to about two-thirds of women staff may live in. In small hotels and boarding houses, the proportion of men and women living in is greater. Staffs of canteens, departmental stores, snack bars, day restaurants and cafés, mostly live out.

Favourable and unfavourable aspects of working as a waiter are summarized in Table 1.

Vocational interest

It is hardly realistic to weigh advantages and disadvantages of the waiter's vocation against one another with mathematical precision. The fact is that many entrants retain a career-long interest in (indeed, a fascination for) the hotel or restaurant world, its customers and their colleagues. One thing can be said with certainty, the job of a waiter, if it is to be enjoyed and well-done, demands that he has this interest, liking, and even is fascinated by his job.

Seeking jobs

Hotel keeping and catering attracts many recruits. Such recruits should note the information about City and Guilds of London Institute and other courses on pages 19–20.

Table 1 *Aspects of waiting*

Advantages	Disadvantages
Warm, often luxurious environment	On his feet most of the day
Times when he can relax	May stand for long periods
Wages council control Tips can supplement wages Accommodation may often be provided	Wages can be poor
Free meals, uniform, laundry, accommodation	Wages reduced accordingly for meals, uniform, etc.
Work is seldom boring Allows for time off in the day Time off in uncrowded periods	Hours can vary day to day 'Unsocial' hours, for example shifts Working on bank holidays, Christmas
Good promotion prospects	Better prospects if prepared to move and to travel

For older as well as younger job seekers, the weekly trade papers *Catering Times* and *The Caterer and Hotelkeeper* (especially the latter) carry advertisements for vacancies in waiting. In London, there is a specialist, government-operated Employment Services Division, Hotel and Catering Job Centre, 3 Denmark Street, London WC2H 8LR for Southern England, the Midlands and parts of Wales. In the North, Leece Street Employment Exchange, Liverpool, and in Glasgow, the Central Employment Exchange have hotel sections. Private bureaux such as Alfred Marks Ltd., 8 Frith Street, Soho Square, London W1 5TZ, or the Burnett Bureau, 77 Dean Street, Oxford Street, London W1 may be tried. Daily and evening papers, especially the *Daily Telegraph* and London's *New Standard* also advertise jobs in catering. Many hotels and restaurants are glad to have enquiries from those seeking waiting posts and may be able to offer occasional jobs at functions if not a full-time opening. It is always worth enquiring if there are opportunities.

Applying for a post

When seeking a job it is customary to telephone the personnel department of a hotel or catering operation for an appointment to see the personnel manager.

Personal appearance and good manners are important when applying for employment. There is always a need for good waiters but, in attending for interview, the waiter is reminded to:

1   Be well groomed and quietly dressed
2   Call between meal hours: 10 a.m. is an excellent time
3   Use the service entrance
4   Take testimonials or any other documentation that may be needed

At the interview, applicants will find out the conditions of the post (wages, 'live-in' or 'live-out', etc.).

If applying in writing, a waiter should state briefly, in simple good English, the position he is seeking, his experience and the names of those who have given him a testimonial or to whom reference may be made. If no indication has been given of wages offered, he should state what wages he seeks.

2 Waiting staff and kitchen support

This book is concerned more with techniques and practices in selling and serving food and beverages than in organization of restaurants from a managerial standpoint. This chapter, therefore, does not attempt to develop any theory of organization. Nevertheless, all waiting staff should be aware that management will have an approach to organization which is concerned with, as one American writer put it, 'what people are supposed to be doing'. Thus, the organization of food and beverage service involves identifying necessary tasks, analysing and describing them, grouping them appropriately and fitting the right sort of people to them.

Organization

Unfortunately, organization within catering has a tendency to become static both in the production (the kitchen) and the service (restaurant) areas. Extremely elaborate kitchens were organized during the heyday of luxury hotels in the Edwardian period in order to produce meals of several courses and complex dishes. Such meals, both à la carte and table d'hôte, were for service to individuals and small parties but in rapid sequence for large numbers. Kitchens organized for this work were of French style. The different groups of tasks and work sections were thus called *parties* and that form of kitchen organization became known, and is still known, as the partie system.

A similarly elaborate form of waiting service and organization was arranged to match the varied and lavish menus that this kind of kitchen produced. There emerged, in effect, a 'partie system' in restaurant service though this term has not been applied in restaurants where the sections are called *rangs*. In food service, the designation brigade du restaurant or the restaurant brigade was employed. So that students may understand something of the background of hotel and restaurant business at its most elaborate, details of these traditional organizations are included in this book. Thus, the work of the partie chefs is touched upon in this chapter and the hierarchy and duties of the traditional French waiting brigade outlined.

However, it must immediately be said that as times change so do customers' demands on the catering trade. With different, often shorter menus, many old tasks in kitchens have disappeared. With new-style menus and forms of service, the organization and types of staff required in waiting brigades also alters.

Jobs and skills

Preconceived ideas of standard job descriptions for waiting staff are dangerous. Jobs vary according to need. Variations reflect different performance of tasks and house style prompted by factors such as consumer demand and labour costs. The 'traditional' nature of different waiting tasks has been indicated but it should be stressed that organizations will continue to be adapted (and probably simplified) according to consumer needs, menus and establishments. In turn, duties of waiters or assistant waiters will continue to be adapted to meet these changing needs. For example, it could be that in one type of restaurant, a waitress need not undertake duties which would involve a comprehensive knowledge of guéridon (side-table) service but she might be required, for meal merchandising purposes, to know how to dress a salad in front of a guest. Her job description and her place in the organization would be written and outlined accordingly. In short, it is possible within this book to identify many existing skills and many commonly encountered work patterns; but everyone must realize the inevitability of continuing change in the way they are grouped and used.

Types of operation

Figure 2, on page 16, indicates broad categories of catering operations within the various sectors of the hospitality industry. These broad categories persist for long periods of time; but within them there is continuing change (and change of emphasis). This can be rapid.

Modern management in today's varied catering circumstances plan catering staffing, including waiting personnel, according to real need of operations within this shifting pattern. Management identifies the nature of catering activity and what waiting style is appropriate to the menu and setting selected. Tasks are then grouped and staff allocated accordingly.

Managing food and beverage services

In the career possibilities noted in Chapter 1 we have seen how the post of the food and beverage manager has developed. His responsibilities in larger hotels (normally with more than fifty bedrooms) comprise stores, kitchens, restaurants, bars, cellars, and for service in lounges and

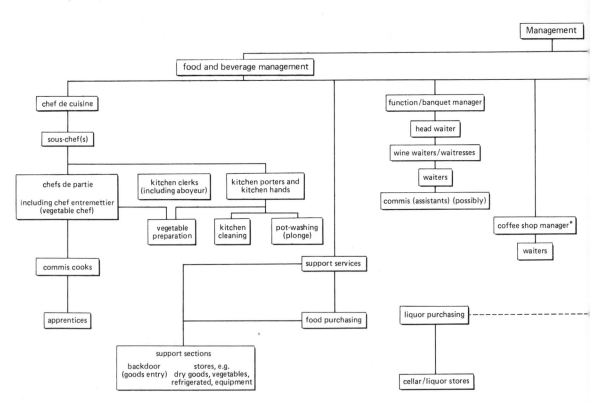

Figure 4   *Food and beverage operations within an outline of hotel organization*

floors; though precise coverage can vary according to an employing company's policy. A food and beverage manager looks after food and drink, menus and service style, ordering and planning. His ancillary interests naturally include staff and their training. Experience in several hotel departments (especially kitchens, stores and control) are clearly desirable if not essential for a food and beverage manager. Particularly relevant for him is experience in food and beverage service (waiting) in restaurants and other hotel service areas. It is not only acquisition of service techniques which is important but a better knowledge of customers and their need which waiting experience can provide.

When considering food and beverage service areas all the possible permutations of staffing for different operations could not possibly be covered in the notes which follow. Hence emphasis tends to be on more elaborate 'brigades' and more

traditional waiting jobs. These indicate the nature of waiting service at its finest and most complex. But it should not be thought that descriptions of jobs and samples of organizational structure in any way establish a 'standard'. See Figure 4. The needs of the consumer, the menu, and the style of the house are the final determinants of necessary tasks, who is to perform them and how they will be grouped in organization. In this, size and exclusiveness of the restaurant will be a major determining factor.

Traditional approach to organization

In a large restaurant, whether belonging to an hotel, a non-residential establishment, or within industrial catering, there must be one person in charge. Under him are principal assistants in charge of sections of the room and under each of the assistants come the general assistants.

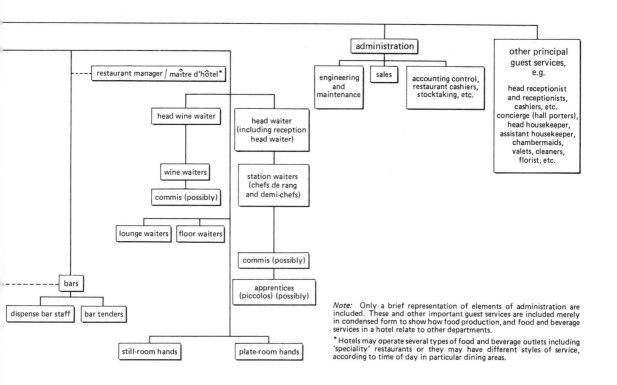

Note: Only a brief representation of elements of administration are included. These and other important guest services are included merely in condensed form to show how food production, and food and beverage services in a hotel relate to other departments.

* Hotels may operate several types of food and beverage outlets including 'speciality' restaurants or they may have different styles of service, according to time of day in particular dining areas.

A traditionally organized restaurant or dining room is controlled either by a maître d'hôtel, a head waiter/waitress or a restaurant manager/manageress who is directly responsible to management (possibly in a hotel through a food and beverage manager) for the running (including cleanliness and general maintenance) of his department.

Madame Prunier (of the Prunier Restaurant family), in writing of French restaurants in *La Maison* (Longman Greens, 1957), refers to the designation 'chefs de brigade' for the head waiters immediately below the maître d'hôtel or head waiter, and the restaurant director, observing that 'a competent waiter may hope for advancement to the rank of chef de brigade, in which he will have a brigade, or squad, of five, six or even ten waiters under him.'

The room is divided into sections called rangs or carrés. Each rang consists of five tables averaging four customers each, thus serving about twenty customers. The numbers of rangs or sections will be determined by the size of the room. The waiter in charge of such a section or rang is called a chef de rang. Two rangs may be grouped to form a station under the control of a head waiter. In large establishments with elaborate service styles, chefs de rangs are assisted by junior waiters (or commis). In most establishments, the maître d'hôtel or head waiter is responsible for showing guests to their tables and should have a personal table plan readily available. (Large restaurants may have such duties delegated to reception head waiters or 'hosts'.)

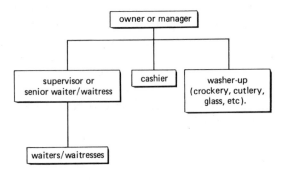

Figure 5   *Staffing in a small restaurant*

He is responsible for the smooth working of the stations and, if necessary, should be prepared to help should any of his stations be hard-pressed.

In small establishments, a head waiter often acts as a wine waiter. In larger organizations, a wine butler (sommelier) dealing exclusively with wines and drink orders has his own small team. One or more wine waiters are available, according to the size of the restaurant. A sommelier in a traditional operation was expected to look after eight to ten tables.

A waiting rang

It is not possible to lay down rigid or hard and fast 'rules' about waiting station size or how many covers a waiter can handle. Much depends upon the scope of the menu and the style of service. A typical 'rang' in a 'traditional' French-style service could vary from four to five tables (or ten to twelve covers) for a station waiter, or six to seven tables (or twelve to sixteen covers) for a station waiter working with a commis. Four tables with four seats at each is one example of a size; but even in restaurants with 'old-style' menus a waiter in charge of a station should be able to handle up to twenty guests.

An American restaurateur, Peter J. Robotti, writing in 1961, said (regarding America) 'In a well-staffed dining room, a captain generally is in charge of two waiters and one busboy to take care of five tables. This constitutes good service.'

At about the same time Mario Gallati writing of his restaurant in London (*Mario of the Caprice*, Hutchinson 1960) observed: 'at the Caprice we have forty tables with one waiter and a commis waiter for every four tables. There are also eight head waiters who supervise the room by dividing it into sections.' These days such staffing would be regarded as lavish even in a luxurious operation.

But many modern operations have, through rationalized menus and procedures, increased service staff productivity. Waiters and waitresses in some speciality restaurants or steak bars may serve up to fifty customers during a lunch or dinner period.

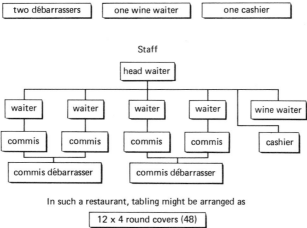

For an 'old style' seventy-two seater restaurant with lavish staffing there might be

| one head waiter | four waiters | four commis waiters |
| two débarrassers | one wine waiter | one cashier |

Staff

In such a restaurant, tabling might be arranged as

12 x 4 round covers (48)

12 x 2 square covers (24)

Figure 6 *Staffing in a traditional restaurant*

Hotel restaurant routine

A general indication of the waiting task is afforded by the routine in traditional hotels. Waiters reported for duty before breakfast at an agreed hour to ensure that tables and equipment were clean and ready for immediate use.

After breakfast table-cloths were changed, the room swept, service tables cleaned and tables relaid for luncheon service. Other chores included linen changing in the linen room, replenishment of cruets and cleaning of walls and lights. Assigning these duties was generally the responsibility of the head waiter.

There would be a break for staff lunch, and time for a wash before waiters reported back to check their laid-up tables, check their glass and silverware for cleanliness and (perhaps through a briefing) acquaint themselves with the menu.

After lunch, waiting staff generally went off duty, except for the lounge waiters. A similar procedure preceded the evening meal.

It was a head waiter's responsibility to see that the dining room or restaurant was left clean and tidy after dinner service and before waiters were released from duty for the night. Late meals in

dining rooms and restaurants were usually cold and served by a night porter or lounge waiter according to house custom.

Today, shifts are arranged with more consideration for staff, and hours are not so long, but broadly these are the kinds of activities that are included in a restaurant routine and which later chapters in this book further elaborate.

'Classic' brigades

In the largest and highest class establishments, waiting staff may still be organized in the French restaurant system as a restaurant brigade. Brigade types of posts have been widely established throughout the Western World and duties are similar in several European countries. This organization is likely today to be reduced or simplified but a classification of possible staff is as follows (variations in terminology for American staff are also indicated).

Restaurant manager (directeur du restaurant) He is responsible for all the restaurant service and is in general charge of all persons connected with it. He quotes prices for daily menus and, in addition (unless there is a separate banqueting manager), makes arrangements for banquets and private parties.

Lounge service outside the restaurant (for example lounge drinks, after-meal coffee, afternoon teas) traditionally comes under the head waiter, as does floor service (see *lounge waiter* and *floor waiter*).

Head waiter (maître d'hôtel)   He is in direct charge of either the whole of a small restaurant or part of a larger one. He supervises service, receives guests (either directly or from the restaurant manager) and seats them. He may take the orders from guests and pass them to the station waiters. In large establishments there may be subordinate or assistant head waiters, that is, second or third head waiters (deuxième or troisième maîtres d'hôtel) and/or reception head waiter (see below) to take telephone bookings and enter them in the reservation book, and to receive guests and direct them to a table.

Reception head waiter (maître d'hôtel de réception)   In some large restaurants, one senior head waiter is responsible for the reception and seating of guests which is otherwise undertaken by the maître d'hôtel.

Hostess or greeter   In American restaurants, the role of receiving may be dubbed 'greeter', if undertaken by a male. Often a woman may undertake guest reception duties as 'hostess'. Her responsibilities can include supervising service for one particular sales outlet (coffee shop or dining room) and be linked with the instruction and supervision of the department's personnel including rosters, dining room mise-en-place, greeting and dealing with guests' complaints.

Station head waiter (maître d'hôtel de carré)   He is responsible for a section of the restaurant carrying out similar functions in his own area to those of the maître d'hôtel. He helps with seating, taking orders and, if necessary, with service.

Captains   In American luxury restaurants, the member of staff who is most nearly the equivalent of a station head waiter is the captain, and he normally helps the customer select from the menu, and takes the order which he then passes to the waiter.

Station waiter (chef de rang)   He is in charge of a 'rang' or group of about five tables, to seat approximately twenty guests, and is responsible for taking guests' orders and serving them, for the cleanliness of his rang or station, and for ensuring the proper service of each dish in the right sequence.

Junior station waiter (demi-chef)   He has similar duties to a station waiter but normally works a smaller station and often without the aid of assistants or commis.

Assistant waiters (commis waiters)   There are several kinds of junior assistants known as commis, for example:

Assistant station waiter (commis de rang or commis de suite)   He assists the station waiter and is responsible for giving food checks into the kitchen, bringing dishes to side-tables, removing plates from guests' tables and returning used plates and dishes to the service area and by generally attending on the station waiter.

Trolley assistant waiter (commis de wagon)   He is a commis, an assistant waiter, assigned to a trolley (a voiture or wagon or, in America, a 'cart') usually of hors d'oeuvres or pâtisserie.

Busboys   In America, assistant waiters are called busboys. A busboy is similar to a commis de suite on a French brigade. They are usually youngsters learning to be waiters, or may be students preparing for other careers in the catering industry. Busboys clear away soiled dishes and replace used table-cloths. They may offer bread and rolls, even pour coffee at a meal service but otherwise are not expected to serve food to guests. They can assist by replenishing trolleys (dessert, hors d'oeuvres, etc.) and buffet tables (by bringing refilled trays). They help set up the dining room in advance, help lay covers, clear tables when the meal is over, and assist in cleaning.

Runners A term sometimes used in the USA to denote assistants to waiters fulfilling roles similar to busboys or clearing assistant waiters (see below).

Clearing assistant waiter (commis débarasseur) He is the most junior assistant, mainly clearing away used plates and dishes and simply 'fetching and carrying' under instruction. He holds this post only during a short period of early training.

Apprentices (apprentis) In apprenticeship, young waiters work up through the assistant posts. In Continental brigades, young waiters or apprentices are known as *piccoli* (literally 'little ones' from the Italian).

Wine butler or wine waiter (chef de vin or sommelier) He takes orders for wines, spirits, beers and soft drinks and serves them to guests. He, too, may have his own assistant wine waiter (commis de vin).

Specialist staff

Additionally, big restaurants may have other specialist staff such as:

Carver (trancheur) Wearing either chef's dress or white jacket, usually with an apron, a carver carves hot roasts from a trolley or stationary hot table plate, or cold joints from a buffet.

Special trolley service waiters Such as costumed servers for Turkish coffee or for the service of curries.

Other service staff

Working outside the restaurant itself but belonging to the food and beverage service team (usually under the control of the head waiter) are:

The floor waiter (le chef d'étage) Is normally responsible for a complete floor of bedrooms and suites (see Chapter 18 for further details). In some Continental hotels a floor waiter (whose duties may be primarily serving light meals and drinks) may be designated sommelier d'étage.

Assistant floor waiter (commis d'étage) Assists the floor waiter.

The lounge waiter (le garçon de (la) salle) Serves light refreshments, afternoon teas and drinks in lounges and other public areas of a hotel other than restaurants (see Chapter 18 for further details).

Ancillary staff

Restaurant cashier Sometimes waiters are responsible for making out bills but this can be the responsibility of a cashier, stationed either in a cash desk in the restaurant or in the service area. In any case, the waiter presents the bill to a customer (see Chapter 15).

Billing procedures are further referred to in Chapter 16.

Apart from managing the waiting services, a restaurant manager or maître d'hôtel normally controls the maintenance and washing of plates, cutlery and glasses. He ensures that all such service equipment is fit to be placed before, or seen by, guests.

Traditional dress

Chapter 3 indicates what is worn by men and women today on waiting duties, and stresses that old-style 'fracs' (long, black tails) and similar clothing are rarely encountered. However, it may be of interest to note the styling of traditional waiting dress, which also helped to identify grades of staff. (Rank or grading as Chapter 3 shows can be achieved today by other means.) Old dress was as follows:

Restaurant manager (directeur du restaurant) Managerial dress, that is: for day, morning clothes comprising black jacket (at one time the longer frock coat) and striped trousers; and for evening, evening dress originally of tails, white waistcoat and white tie, though latterly a dinner jacket.

Head waiters (maîtres d'hôtel) Sometimes the premier maître d'hôtel (the first or *the* maître d'hôtel) was regarded as the restaurant manager and wore managerial dress. Otherwise head waiters and subordinate maîtres d'hôtel wore tail coat, white waistcoat, wing collar and black bow tie for evening (dinner); and tail coat, black waistcoat, wing collar and black bow tie for day (luncheon).

Station waiters (chefs de rang)   Tail coat, black waistcoat, wing collar and white bow tie.

Junior station waiters (demi-chefs)   Dress as for station waiters.

Assistant waiters (commis)   Black 'café' jacket, that is, short, black jackets with accompanying black waistcoat, wing collar, white bow tie and long white aprons or alternatively white jackets in place of the black jackets.

Busboys   American assistant waiters traditionally wore white patrol-type jackets (that is, high military collar).

Wine waiter (sommelier)   Dressed either as a station waiter (though usually wearing lapel badges with grape design), or wore a special black uniform with chain and cellar key, and possibly black or green baize apron.

Waitresses   Traditional dress: black or dark dress, with launderable collar, cuffs and cap (usually white) and apron (also usually white); stockings and simple black shoes.

Kitchen support

Efficiency of restaurant staff is highly dependent upon that of the kitchen. In order to appreciate the nature of dishes and how they are produced, a waiter should understand how a professional kitchen is organized. This is especially important when a waiter is working in a high class restaurant of traditional French (or international 'classic') style. Today, kitchens are organized in a variety of ways according to differing levels of food and service, and the degree of reliance on convenience foods. Even restaurants aspiring to haute cuisine are not all structured on traditional lines nor do they all have all the parties or sections which were once taken for granted. For example, the work of the larder (garde-manger) may be greatly reduced by restaurants buying pre-portioned cuts of meat or fish; and today, the work of the pastry chef (pâtissier) seldom includes ice

cream making, for ices are usually supplied from outside.

Nevertheless, the following outlines of the work of kitchen staff organized on old partie lines may still help waiting staff to appreciate how tasks are interrelated.*

Traditional kitchen brigade

1   *The chef (or head chef)* (chef de cuisine (or maître chef))   Controls all the sections and the cooks in charge of them (parties and chefs de parties). Supervises preparation, cooking and service of food from the kitchen to all the dining outlets. Arranges the menus. Plans the timing for completing food production for the beginning of restaurant service. Checks food for flavour and seasoning by tasting. Supervises the servery (personally or by delegating to his deputy, the first sous-chef) giving dishes a final inspection before service, with attention to correct garnish and appearance.

2   *Sous-chef*   Literally under chef. Assistant to, or deputy for, a head chef.

3   *Sauce cook* (chef saucier)   Makes sauces for various savoury dishes and prepares entrées. He may also act as sous-chef.

4   *Larder cook* (chef garde-manger)   Is in charge of the 'cold kitchen' and the preparation of hors d'oeuvre, cold meats, canapés, sandwiches, salads, mayonnaise and dressings. He also prepares cuts of meat, fish, poultry and game for treatment by other appropriate chefs de partie (though fishmonger, butcher and poulterer may have separate 'shops' in big kitchens). The chef garde-manger may also act as sous-chef.

5   *Vegetable cook* (chef entremettier)   Cooks all vegetables, egg dishes and farinaceous dishes (for example Italian pasta) including vegetable garnishes.

6   *Soup cook* (chef potager)   Prepares and cooks soups.

---

* See J. Fuller, *Professional Kitchen Management* (Batsford 1981) for more information.

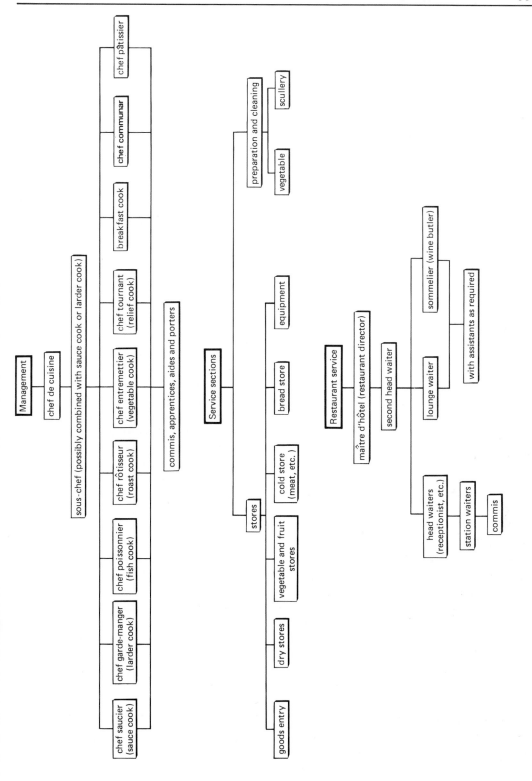

Figure 7 *Kitchen and service departments*

7   *Roast cook* (chef rôtisseur)   Roasts meat and poultry and prepares savouries. He is also responsible for grilling (though there may be a subordinate grill cook – chef grillardin) and for deep frying of potatoes.

8   *Fish cook* (chef poissonnier)   Prepares and cooks fish dishes and their accompanying sauces.

9   *Pastry cook* (chef pâtissier)   In charge of the pâtisserie where sweet dishes and desserts are prepared including pastry, cakes, jellies and ices.

10   *Relief cook* (chef tournant)   An experienced cook who relieves other chefs de partie when they are away on days off, sickness or holiday.

11   *Staff cook* (chef communar)   In charge of staff catering.

12   *Breakfast cook*   Early duty cook (often of limited training) who prepares breakfast dishes.

In a large restaurant such as that of a high class hotel, the principal cooks may have one or more assistants (commis), according to the size of the establishment.

Ancillary kitchen staff

The brigade of chefs is supported by kitchen porters, vegetable preparation assistants, pot-washer (plongeur) and kitchen clerks. Of the latter, the following come into contact with waiting staff.

- *Still-room staff*   Responsible for hot beverages, toasts, etc., are not usually regarded as part of the kitchen brigade but, like the silver and plate-wash, are usually supervised by the restaurant manager or maître d'hôtel. Still-room work is outlined in Chapter 5.

- *Announcer* (aboyeur (literally 'barker'))   The kitchen clerk who calls out to the kitchen the orders brought to the servery by the waiters.

- *Storekeeper* (l'économe)   In charge of commodity store.

The traditional kitchen brigade, as outlined, indicates the scope of kitchen activity at its most complex, but it must be appreciated that such brigades were originally organized for à la carte service from extensive menus in French style offering many choices. Modern trends towards shorter menus enable organization to be simplified and staff to be reduced. Similarly, in services of set menus (table d'hôte) of modest scope, including those featuring British or other ethnic forms of cooking, the same amount of specialization is not required. Cooks can combine duties to reduce the members of parties or sections.

Trends alter traditions

The traditional restaurant brigade, and older dress styles indicate the nature of waiting duties under a most elaborate system. This is not intended to demonstrate an enduring style of organization nor a permanent hierarchy.

The chapters which follow indicate where and when organizational changes and alterations in the nature of duties have occurred, and where they are likely to occur in future. For example, tea-making and other self-service devices on the floors of hotels limit or change the nature of room service. Simplified wine service systems in speciality restaurants or steak bars may reduce sommeliers' opportunities for future posts, but may give opportunities for waiters and waitresses to serve wine who in old-style operations might not have had the chance. New developments in mechanized restaurant accounting, for instance, may reduce the industry's reliance on restaurant cashiers but, on the other hand, would give more billing responsibilities to waiting staff.

Therefore, when interpreting the nature of restaurant service and the duties of waiters, present trends and future change must be used as a corrective to any impression of 'enduring tradition'.

This book is not about staff management, but it is worth reiterating that however much physical planning, equipment and decor contribute to a restaurant's ambiance and efficiency, its staff is its heart. It is through the people employed (from plate-washer to manager) that customers are pleased, goods and services sold, and an operation consolidates its character.

3 Conduct and appearance

Waiting at table involves close contact with customers and their food, and means that waiters are under constant observation. Chapter 1 stressed the importance of personal characteristics in discharging waiting duties, in 'selling', and in guest contact. This chapter seeks to indicate factors which are important in the personal characteristics, appearance and development of the waiter.

Clothing

A waiter or waitress is usually required to wear some form of uniform. At one time when dress was more formal at all levels of society, the reason for wearing uniform was to distinguish staff from customers. Chapter 2 has shown that, like military uniform, waiting dress was (and to a large extent still is) devised to indicate differences in rank in the restaurant.

Today, differences in waiting rank formerly indicated by variations in evening-type dress are marked by devices such as different coloured jackets, varied epaulets on white jackets or even stripes or bands on jacket cuffs.

Today's case for uniform

There are other more relevant reasons for wearing uniforms. Two important reasons are:

● Hygiene, encouraging the selection of suitable, protective, washable clothing, keeping the wearer cool and healthy, and enabling frequent laundering and changes of clothing.
● Aiding the merchandising and selling of a meal service by an appropriate integration of staff appearance into a restaurant's theme and decor.

Modern waiting dress for men, especially day dress, is often a neat jacket with epaulets or a blazer-type jacket, including 'themed jackets' to match the surroundings. Commis are likely to wear washable white jackets as their work is more likely to soil their clothes.

Modern dress for waitresses should also be washable. Uniforms are usually bright, attractively coloured and 'themed' with the decor. Waitresses rarely wear traditional uniforms of black dress with white aprons except in banqueting, and they seldom wear white caps with this outfit.

Neither men nor women waiting staff should appear in the public part of a hotel or catering establishment when not in uniform or when not wearing full uniform. Waitresses, for example, should put on aprons (and caps, if worn) in the dressing or locker room and not in the restaurant.

Manufacturers of hotel and restaurant uniforms have also noted the unisex dress trend and have introduced lines into waiting uniform which reflect it.

Informality

The informality and egalitarianism which increasingly characterizes modern society is also reflected in informal dress styles for waiting staff especially in 'informal' eating out establishments. Waiters in shirts (or shirts with coloured waistcoats), waitresses in dirndl-type skirts or trousers

Figure 8   (a) *Patrol (or tunic) style jacket*
A washable patrol type jacket is often favoured because it eliminates the need for collar and tie. Normally available in white drill with detachable buttons, other colour variants are possible. Epaulettes may also be added

(b) *Mess jacket style*
In white drill and with detachable link buttons is also seen in other materials and colours. It looks smart when well-fitting and in upright stance, but when a waiter bends to serve an unsightly gap can often open between jacket and top

are commonplace in today's coffee shops or informal restaurants. Whatever the degree of informality, cleanliness of uniform, frequent change and laundering need to be just as rigorously applied.

Head-dress

The former requirement for waitresses to wear caps has increasingly declined. One original intention was that caps would confine hair tidily and prevent loose hairs dropping into food. During a period when men's hair was frequently worn as long as women's, it seemed pointless to insist upon one sex wearing caps and not the other. With proper hair styling and grooming there does not seem to be such an insistent reason for head-dress to be worn by modern waiting staff.

Figure 9   *Shawl collar style*
This style in washable material, with collars and cuffs in contrasting colours, is a popular compromise between tradition and modernity, in that frequent laundering and coolness in wear is compatible with the 'dressed' appearance afforded by bow tie and collar

White gloves

As recently as the 1970s, there was correspondence in a leading trade weekly journal about the wearing of white gloves by waiters. Today, it is rare for white gloves to be worn by waiting staff, though in the Edwardian and certainly the Victorian periods, footmen, waiters and staff at banquets frequently did so.

Traditional dress

In the early 1970s, Nigel Buxton in the *Sunday Telegraph* was asking 'What has happened to the archetypal British waiter; the kind that *Punch* always used to have in starched dicky and black tails standing at loose attention with head slightly and respectfully bowed?

'. . . Vanished in the social revolution of the past half century.'

However, Buxton did say that the old-style waiter in traditional dress could still be found in a few London hotels, and 'here and there in some venerable hotels in the provinces'. To enable you to appreciate the evolution of waiting dress with waiting staff organization, 'traditional' dress linked with traditional job titles is outlined in Chapter 2.

Management are increasingly following the advice of designers. Hardy Amies observed that 'people should be able to enjoy wearing a uniform as a dress or suit in its own right'.

Rules of dress

- Make sure that your uniform is neat and clean, is kept in good repair and fits well.
- Change washable clothing frequently and wear freshly laundered. Linen should be immaculately clean.
- Keep suits and shirts (or dresses, skirts and blouses) well-pressed and free from spots. When clothing is not washable, regular sponging is usually necessary.
- Shoes should fit well (with ample room for toe movement), be of conservative design and kept clean, well-polished and always in a good state of repair. Avoid high or pointed heels, or badly supported shoes. Change tights or socks daily.

Although the waiter may be responsible for the supply and upkeep of his clothing, it is customary for many hotels and restaurants to arrange, at the establishment's cost, for laundering his linen.

Jewellery, earrings and rings (except wedding rings) should not be worn.

Good waiters are as proud of their uniforms as they are of their jobs. They show it by an upright stance and by walking erect.

Personal qualities .

The desirable personal qualities (as distinct from technical skills) of waiting staff may be considered under two broad headings: one largely concerned with physical matters and hygiene; the other related to attributes and attitudes including courtesy, honesty, co-operation and speech.

Hygiene

Waiting staff should have a positive attitude to hygiene, which is about the maintenance of health. (The word hygiene is derived from Hygeia, the Greek goddess of health; and hygiene is concerned not simply with cleanliness, important though that is, but with principles of health and sanitary science.)

A waiter or waitress needs abundant energy, should have a fresh, wholesome appearance and naturally must not spread disease. Part of this positive attitude to hygiene should involve taking care to eat and sleep properly, being temperate in relation to alcohol, taking proper exercise, sufficient outdoor activity and fresh air.

Because waiting staff deal with food, utmost cleanliness and good grooming is necessary at all times. This applies not only in high class hotels and restaurants but in every branch of catering, however humble customers may be. Guests are not likely to return to an establishment where they know the waiter or waitress is dirty. Indeed, whenever a guest enters a catering establishment, he judges standards of hygiene and cleanliness by his personal observation. This observation includes the waiters and waitresses.

A writer in the *Sunday Times* in January, 1980 remembered 'An otherwise charming waitress in a swish London hotel whose overpowering underarm odour put me off my food. But I didn't mention it to her. Cowardice'.

Whether or not it is cowardice, it should not be for a customer to have to make such failings known to waiting staff. First, it is for the waiter (or waitress) himself to ensure that he does not give offence and for head waiters (or head waitresses or other supervisors) to take such remedial action as will draw offending staff's

attention to the need for personal fastidiousness. The same article quoted a writer and broadcaster who walks out of restaurants when the atmosphere is adverse including 'The smell of stale bodies, stale sweat. If the waiter is spotty or his clothes are dirty I can't eat my food. Am I too fastidious?' Another consumer quoted 'Can't bear unclean finger nails'.

Everybody in the catering business has to remember that though not frequently expressed openly, all customers expect high personal standards from those who serve them food and drink.

Reporting ill health

Apart from aesthetic considerations of not offending by unclean appearance or unpleasant odour, waiting staff have statutory obligations in regard to health and hygiene. Any catering employee (including waiters and waitresses) suffering from, or a carrier of, certain illnesses must immediately inform their employer. Illnesses include: typhoid fever; paratyphoid fever, or any other salmonella infection; amoebic or bacillary dysentery or any staphylococcal infection likely to cause food poisoning. Many waiting staff may be unfamiliar with the nature of such illnesses; they should look for, and report to their employer such symptoms as:

● Diarrhoea or vomiting
● Septic cuts or sores, boils or whitlows
● Discharge from ear, eye or nose

In turn, employers take appropriate precautions including notifying the Medical Officer through the Environmental Health Department or Area Health Authority.

Rules for clean conduct

To prevent germs contaminating food observe the following rules:

● Ensure scrupulous cleanliness of hands, face and parts of the body which directly, or through touch, may come into contact with food; for example, hair, scalp and forearms (when short sleeves are worn). Avoid touching nose and lips while handling food. Wash hands frequently.

● Keep personal clothing and uniform clean.
● Cover completely (with a coloured, water-proof dressing) all open cuts and grazes.
● Never smoke, or use snuff, while handling 'open' food or while in a room where there is such food even when not on duty.

For aesthetic, as well as hygienic reasons, waiting staff should avoid touching their hair or face when on duty in the restaurant. Waiters should not, of course, sneeze or cough carelessly (ensure that this is done into a handkerchief). Though always carrying a clean handkerchief, a waiter should avoid using it in the restaurant unless it is absolutely necessary.

Further detailed guidance regarding clean practice is developed in later chapters on service techniques.

Care of the person

The following require particular attention:

Finger nails and hands Must be washed fre-quently. Always wash immediately before service and always following use of the toilet. Nails and cuticles should be neatly trimmed and kept clean by use of a nail brush. Waitresses should avoid nail varnish whether clear or coloured when on duty. Smokers must ensure that they remove all traces of nicotine from fingers (pumice and bleach are useful).

Body cleanliness Cleanliness of the whole body is essential. Any suggestion of odour or staleness is a most grave offence in a restaurant employee. A daily bath or shower should be the minimum standard for good waiting staff. Underclothing should be changed frequently and deodorants regularly used. Talcum powder for body and feet is acceptable but scent (even for a waitress) must be avoided and aftershave used sparingly.

Skin and complexion Clear skin and complexion depend on good health based on adequate exercise, sleep, diet and cleanly habits. Waiting staff should use their leisure for fresh air re-creation and should try to ensure that wholesome fresh foods such as vegetables, fruit, wholemeal bread and milk are featured in their diet. Wait-resses should use cosmetics sparingly and rarely and only as consistent with a fresh complexion.

Hair Hair should be kept neatly trimmed and shampooed frequently to avoid dandruff and odour. Hair should be well brushed as well as combed. Men as well as women should avoid styles which cause hair to fall over the eyes; for tossing hair away from eyes, especially by hand, is offensive to guests during food service. Wait-resses' hair should be no longer than collar length, and waitresses should adopt neat hair styles. Long hair should be tied up and tied back.

Reference has already been made to the decreasing use of caps worn by waitresses and this reflects social change and attitudes. Similar factors are involved in relation to men's facial hair, that is, moustaches, beards and sideburns. That famous restaurateur 'Oscar of the Waldorf' in New York was involved at the turn of the century in well-publicized brouhaha when the Waldorf Astoria's general manager decided 'I want every waiter in the Waldorf Astoria clean shaven'. This is reminiscent of the time (in the Victorian period for example) when beards and moustaches were sufficiently commonplace for them to be accepted in service staff. Yet towards the end of the Edwardian era, waiters were expected to be clean shaven. One of the demands of Paris waiters in a strike before World War I was for the right to wear a moustache. More recently there has been a reversion to the accept-ability of more facial hair (sideburns, moustaches and even beards) and longer hair on the head.

All that can be said with any certainty is that what is acceptable in restaurant staff reflects what is acceptable in society at large; but generally rather higher standards of trimness and neatness are looked for in a restaurant. Where waiting staff can be induced to abjure facial hair, and long hair on the head, then by and large more customers are pleased; for facial hair worn by food service staff still seems to offend many customers.

Teeth   Sound teeth and a clean mouth are vital both for appearance and a wholesome breath. Teeth should be kept clean by brushing at least twice a day – certainly morning and night. Inspection by a dentist is advisable twice a year and certainly not less frequently than once a year. Dentures, if worn, must similarly be kept clean.

Feet   Feet need care both for comfort and cleanliness. Keep toe nails trim and feet well washed. Corns and other painful blemishes may require treatment by a chiropodist; for more serious foot weakness, medical advice should be sought. (See *rules of dress*, on page 35, regarding shoes and stockings selection and change.)

Posture   Good stance is also important for the appearance, comfort and efficiency of waiting staff. To stand upright and walk erect is to give a good impression to guests and also to avoid the bodily stresses that accompany slouching. Waitresses who require support garments are advised to choose sound quality and properly fitting ones to aid posture and health as well as comfort and appearance.

Attributes and behaviour

The following personal qualities which a waiter should cultivate, or how he should behave, are in no particular order of importance. Indeed, some types of operation encourage emphasis on some qualities or some styles of behaviour as against others; but all the observations which follow are considered relevant.

Addressing guests

Innumerable market studies reveal that an important element in a customer's choice of eating place is friendliness, in welcome and in service. It is also well established that a customer is eager for recognition. He likes to hear his own name for that expresses and establishes recognition. Therefore, the use by restaurant staff of a guest's own name is welcomed by most customers.

Guests' names

During the 1930s and 1940s a reception head waiter's (and other waiters') greeting sometimes avoided the use of a customer's name in the belief that name usage verged on the familiar. Today, the reverse is true. Whenever a guest's name is known (through former custom or through pre-booking) it should desirably be used. Many modern restaurants are successful because in the total dining experience they feed a guest's ego as much as his appetite. Ways in which remembering a guest's name can be aided are

- Listen carefully to the name when it is given.
- Jot the name on a piece of paper (not in the guest's presence).
- Repeat the name mentally several times.

In addition to using a guest's name when greeting or re-greeting, use his name when asking him for subsequent orders or about his satisfaction with food and service. A modern waiter may have greater difficulty in adapting his mode of speech to modern requirements than did waiting staff in earlier generations. In former times waiters were expected to adopt a more formalized style with, for example, invariable use of 'sir' or 'madam'. Despite injunctions to staff that they should be respectful rather than servile, these older styles of speech did, in fact, tend to mark customer/staff distinctions in a way often less acceptable to both parties today.

On first welcoming guests, a waiter should address them by name, for example, Mr or Mrs Patron. But name usage should not be overdone and 'sir' or 'madam' is more appropriate during service period.

Speech is linked with courtesy. Style of speech and modes of manners change. A hotel columnist, Michael Archer, in *Catering Times* has warned against overdoing courtesy to the customer and the need for emphasis on friendliness. He suggests that a friendly smile and 'What would you like to drink?' is more in keeping with present day informality than 'May I offer you an apéritif?'.

The points about speech which follow here should be read against its general background: namely that a pleasant, friendly manner (but certainly without undue familiarity) is acceptable today at almost every level of restaurant operation. To achieve an ease and friendliness of manner without giving offence requires sensitivity from staff. From management it requires a lively policy of training in social skills during induction and ongoing training whether in college, hotel schools or 'on-the-job'.

A respectful manner of speech towards customers still remains appropriate. A waiter is not servile, for he is proud of his skill, particularly if he is a good waiter; but he is a technical salesman of his establishment and a good salesman should aim to please.

Clear speech

A waiter's voice should be clear, low in pitch and natural, if still somewhat formal. He should be able to pronounce words properly and to express his ideas. He should acquire a sound knowledge of good English and be able to converse easily, for customers like to hear a well-modulated, pleasing voice, with well-expressed answers to any questions they may ask.

A knowledge of a second language is a help, particularly to waiters who seek service in large hotels or restaurants in London or other tourism centres where there are foreign visitors. French is useful, for not only are menus still often written in French, but it is the language used in cookery books and in répertoires of dishes based on 'la cuisine française'.

Handwriting

A waiter does not need great skill in writing nor to be an accomplished penman, but he will have to write out orders (see Chapter 12). Such orders must be legible to the kitchen and billing staff. Therefore, clear handwriting is an asset to a waiter.

Courtesy

It is the hallmark of a good waiter to be courteous on all occasions. Indeed, a waiter must often go out of his way to be considerate or forebearing to a critical or ill-tempered person. He will certainly be courteous to customers, but should also carry these good manners through to the service room and the locker room. His manners should not be just a part of the 'techniques of the restaurant', but inherent in his nature and a sign of well-bred desire to please those with whom he comes into contact. The aim is to be friendly without being familiar.

Memory

Cultivation of memory (and using aids of memory) is essential if customers' likes and dislikes are to be noted and remembered. Sensitive awareness of what a customer wants should also be sought. Charles Ritz (son of the famed hotelier Cesar Ritz) has referred to 'table radar' to describe the characteristic that a waiter has of knowing just when something is required without hovering near his guest all the time. 'He answers before you call. No restaurant has more than one or two really radar waiters,' said Charles Ritz.

If a waiter studies his customers' preferences, even their 'fads', he will find that they will be delighted when they realize that their wishes are known and anticipated.

Honesty

In recent years an increasing amount of research has been undertaken into hotel keeping and catering. This has included work by sociologists, and others, into practices and attitudes of waiting staff. Some studies have revealed persistent instances of pilfering and 'fiddles'. Malpractices detailed in such studies will not be outlined here; but unfortunately there are still opportunities in some establishments for waiters to seek to defeat checking systems (adding up bills incorrectly against the customer) or to secure privileged treatment or serving over-large portions to guests so as to gain larger tips.

Some waiters fall into dishonest habits, such as taking food from the restaurant for consumption elsewhere in the establishment or to their homes, 'borrowing' silver or linen for similar purposes. All this is stealing and denotes at the very least that a waiter has not acquired a truly professional attitude to his work. Opportunity for dishonesty makes it doubly important for waiting staff to have high personal standards of conduct; and equally, when they reach supervisory levels to create conditions which reduce temptation and create a positive morale.

The waiter should take the greatest care of all equipment belonging to an establishment and never think he can deal with it wastefully or carelessly because it is not his own. A waiter must be scrupulously honest in all his dealings; with guests, colleagues and management.

Co-operation and reliability

A dedicated waiter accepts unsocial hours, enjoys service to others and is ready to work until tasks are finished. He should not, for example, hurry customers in an attempt to 'clear' his station in order to leave promptly and early. He aims to be a good timekeeper and to carry out his duties without fuss and with minimum supervision.

His personal qualities and his professional skills will all help a waiter to remain courteous, even-tempered, able to work under pressure and to summon up a smile even when tired, or under difficult circumstances.

Since an establishment's success depends on effective co-ordination of all staff, a waiter should aim to help his fellow-workers. This implies such conduct as: not being jealous if another waiter has customers who pay higher tips; taking his proper turn in the servery queue; learning and keeping to 'rules of the house' in spirit as well as to the letter.

The changing room can be an orderly place if each waiter keeps all his articles in his own locker and puts any unwanted paper, cloths, cigarette-ends,,etc., in the proper receptacles.

A co-operative waiter cultivates his ability to get on well with customers and colleagues alike and to further the policies of management.

Conduct in the restaurant

When not serving, a waiter should stand by his station sideboard, his service cloth folded on to his left forearm. (A service cloth should never be tucked under the arm or thrust into a pocket.) This applies whether there are customers on his station or not. (See notes on the waiter's service cloth on page 77.) He should not pass in front of a customer, and at all times give right of way to a guest.

A waiter should never run in the restaurant nor in the service. Apart from the undesirable impression created, running is a potential hazard. Waiters should adopt a way of walking which is brisk without appearing hurried, taking care to avoid knocking against diner's seats. Above all he should move quietly. Good service comprises many things but it is always quiet service.

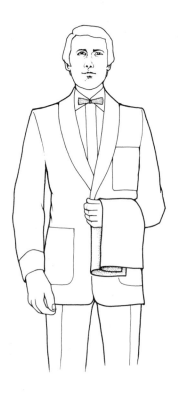

Figure 10   *Waiter's service cloth*
Regard this cloth as a tool and part of your dress. Use it only for its intended purpose – carrying dishes, polishing silver, etc., never inappropriately nor unhygienically, for example as a duster or for hand drying. Carry the cloth neatly folded over the left arm when not in use

A waiter must never eat on duty and this includes chewing gum. He must never use bad language either in the restaurant or in the dressing room. His pencil (ballpoint, etc.) should be carried in a pocket; never behind an ear or in the hair. When serving he should avoid breathing heavily. Singing, humming and whistling in or near the restaurant is, of course, forbidden.

Receiving gratuities

A waiter must never indulge in preferential treatment of customers according to, or in anticipation of, tips he may receive from them. Indeed, every customer, irrespective of his financial standing, should be treated alike. There should be no fawning on lavish tippers. Tips should be acknowledged graciously: if placed on the table they should not be removed until the customer has left and certainly never counted in front of a guest.

A waiter must never lean against the wall or sideboard, tables or other furniture. He must especially never lean on a chair back (above all not the customer's) when speaking with a guest. When addressed by a customer, a waiter should stand erect and steady.

Conversing

A waiter must not converse, far less argue, with other members of staff and emphatically never argue with guests. He should not interrupt a guest's conversation with an inquiry. If a customer enters into conversation with a waiter, the latter must answer politely and as briefly as possible. The waiter should ask to be excused at the first opportunity, but must use tact to avoid offending. He must never start a conversation with guests.

A waiter never discusses other guests with his customers nor must he give information regarding guests. A waiter must discipline himself not to listen to guests' conversation, whether it is carried out loudly enough for him to hear or not. If he has any complaints to make to the head waiter or to colleagues, a waiter must wait until service is over. There should be no quarrelling or horseplay on duty. Waiters should not, of course, talk among themselves or neglect guests by so doing.

Mistakes and complaints

If a mistake is made by the head waiter or by one of his assistants, a waiter should never remonstrate with or criticize him in the restaurant. First, he should remedy any fault (for example, bring the customer the dish he states he ordered). Any explanation that may be necessary to prevent an error recurring, or to apportion the blame for it, should be made outside the restaurant, preferably at the end of service. A waiter's capacity to deal with complaints is considered further in Chapter 15, but tact, courtesy and a sense of responsibility (informing superiors of complaints) must be brought to bear on complaints as in all customer contact.

Technical skill

In addition to cultivating social qualities and modes of conduct to support his sales function a waiter uses technical skills. He must be hungry for knowledge, know and like food and be eager to learn service methods. The skills and knowledge that a waiter needs are listed below, together with the relevant chapters.

1 Knowledge of the catering trade, of which he is an important member (Chapter 1).
2 Knowledge of foods that he will serve, menus and cooking times (Chapters 7 to 10).
3 Layout of restaurant or dining room and its preparation for the service (Chapters 4, 5, 6, and 11).
4 Actual method of serving, for example, generally on floors and in lounges, or in canteens and bars (Chapters 11, 12, 13, 14, 15, 17, 18).
5 Service of tobacco, cigarettes and cigars (Chapter 22).
6 Service of liquor (wines, spirits, etc.) (Chapters 19, 20 and 21).
7 A good groundwork, general education and attitude, ability to speak a foreign language or understand French terms used in catering (Chapters 2 and 3).

As Figure 11 indicates, an informed, knowledgeable waiter sells more.

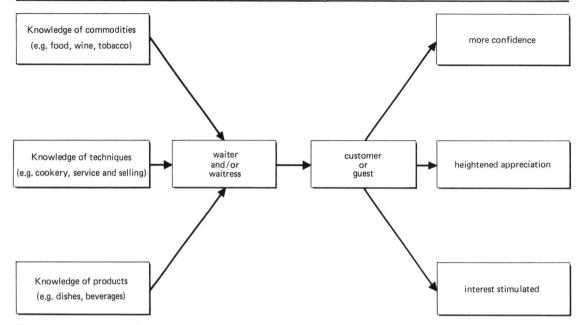

Figure 11   *An informed waiter sells more*
The more any salesman knows about the product or service he is selling the more he is likely to sell. The waiting team is the contact point between restaurant and customer. A waiter should be able not only to serve food competently and with respect, but also be able to: describe food; promote a restaurant's repute for quality by knowing how the dishes are made and what ingredients are used; impart such information with tact to customers

Personality and professionalism

A waiter's personality merges with, and is part of, his professionalism. He needs to integrate social skills and attributes with technical skills and knowledge. Many personal qualities have already been touched upon, and the technical skills needed have been indicated.

A waiter should be proud of his work and not treat it as an ordeal. He must always be in good humour, seeking to please and oblige customers without servility.

Developing personality and professionalism should involve: attitude, attentiveness, alertness leading to an ability to anticipate customers' needs and to be able to cope with customers and colleagues in varying situations. Waiters should avoid airs and mannerisms, but should certainly cultivate personality. This is particularly important for a head waiter. Reading, and an interest in current affairs, sport and constructive recreation can help. The waiter, it is re-emphasized, is

in essence a salesman, operating in a revenue generating sector. He is part of 'the show'. He is always during service 'on show'. His dexterity and skill controlled by a restrained personality can add to a guest's idea of value and also increase his enjoyment. Therefore, a waiter's 'showmanship' is positively useful.

However, in selling, simple skills and speed are as important as elaborate techniques. Speed is particularly important, for example, when serving hot food.

This chapter may seem crammed with encouragement to acquire or to develop qualities leading to almost 'unnatural goodness'; but most waiting staff do have a genuine desire to please. P. Harlow, the manager of the Civil Service Motoring Association's Eaves Hall Country Club, sent to the *Caterer & Hotelkeeper* in 1979 notes which an eighteen year old waitress of one year's experience had pinned on to the staff notice board 'for fun':

'What a waitress has to remember is to give her customers the service they deserve:

Make sure that everything is clean
Always look neat and tidy (apron and service cloth)
Always smile
Always give them good service
Always be as helpful as you can
Make sure everything lands on the plate – not the lap
Treat everyone the same
Don't serve them anything you wouldn't eat yourself
Talk to residents and make them welcome even if you don't like them
Try not to dive right in, just as they've put their knives and forks down
Never show them that you don't like them by giving them bad service and not smiling or by avoiding the table
Always treat them with respect
Take notice of this and you can't go wrong'
Janet Taylor

Though simply expressed and 'in fun' her notes show how the job of waiting can be intelligently tackled, and found rewarding by young entrants.

4 Restaurant and equipment

Remembering that the restaurant is a revenue-generating area, its design and its equipment are both important. A waiter's efficiency depends partly on his work behind the scenes; but it is in the restaurant itself during the time that meals are served that his effectiveness is really tested.

Design aims

Equipping a restaurant is a task for management and has to be consistent with the total concept for the operation and related to the consumer. A designer may be used in a consultant capacity and, in any case, an attempt will be made to relate space, decor, lighting, graphics for menus, waiting dress and other aspects into an integrated design. Service staff in the restaurant do not as a rule carry responsibility at this planning and design stage but should certainly appreciate what is involved.

Waiting staff may well be consulted about those design aspects which affect their activities and should always be ready to 'feed into management' suggestions based upon their close experience of working conditions. They should also be aware of how a design plan depends upon menu, service and atmosphere to achieve operational success so that their work style is in harmony with the plan.

Staff interest in design
Determination of plan details are for management, therefore, no attempt will be made here to outline them all. But factors of particular interest to waiting staff include:

1 The desirability of flexible arrangements. These include (a) the possible provision of divisions enabling unfilled areas to be shut off; and (b) the use of movable and stackable chairs and tables. (Service staff experience can help management anticipate the volume of business. Customers like a busy restaurant and the avoidance of empty spaces by screening off is sensible.)
2 Arranging working aisles not only for customer comfort but also for serving staff efficiency.

Within the restaurant itself waiting staff can help assure the efficiency of design by good arrangement of seating, effective and clean maintenance and efficient service.

Servery arrangements
Waiting staff are also concerned with 'behind the scenes' servery arrangements and must be ready to adopt rationalized procedures. Aims are:

- Minimizing walking by service personnel.
- Maximizing waiter self-service (to avoid long servery stints for kitchen production staff) by using pass-through refrigerators and pass-through facilities at hot tables and hot cupboards.
- Sensible sequence of servery collection points for picking up dishes, and with the minimum distance for hot foods to travel.
- Properly located and correctly swinging service or kitchen doors (or perhaps electrically controlled doors).

Furniture

Within the restaurant, furniture varies according to an establishment's nature. Floors may be covered with costly carpeting, polished wood or, in simpler restaurants, in linoleum or plastic floor covering. Chairs similarly vary in upholstery and covering according to the degree of luxury sought. Items such as curtains, other drapes, table lamps and other lighting fittings are similarly variable in quality and design.

Selection factors

Purchase of furniture is management's responsibility but a good waiter should be aware of general considerations affecting the selection of restaurant furnishing equipment. These include:

- *Style* Its appraisal and reappraisal in terms of customers, menu and forms of service.
- *Budget* That is, funds for initial purchase and subsequent upkeep and/or replacement.
- *Design features* Specifically functional qualities (fitness for task):
  - (a) durability
  - (b) ease of cleaning
  - (c) ease of storage (including stackability)
  - (d) colour suitability for restaurant 'themes'
- *Flexibility in use* For example cutlery size affording knives and spoons suitable for varied purposes.

Negative factors

Inappropriate designs may include:

- Ashtrays that are too shallow or are designed such that draught or movement may scatter ash (possibly over food).
- Confusing crockery design – badging on plate centres, for example.
- Plates without a rim may look fashionable, but often lack toughened edges with increased chipping risks and also do not afford waiters good handling.

Staff responsibility

In operations employing waiting staff, a waiter will normally be responsible for a section of the dining room, and its furniture and equipment, which must be made ready for service. The nature and market level of an establishment determines the restaurant's furnishings and also affects the extent of the waiter's responsibility for equipment upkeep and cleanliness.

In traditional establishments, a waiter was in charge of a large amount of furniture and equipment which he made ready for service. Waiters still have some responsibility for looking after the restaurant and its contents as indicated in Chapters 5 and 6. Waiters should also know how to keep furniture and equipment in good condition, clean, properly laid out and ready for service.

Emphasis in this chapter will be on those restaurants which are furnished and equipped for complete waiting service, on the assumption that a reader may modify 'downwards' for simpler establishments.

Tables and seating

Tables (and sideboards) as prime work points are of special interest to waiters; and for management they are, by their shape and size, relevant to the numbers to be seated.

Table height varies a little according to preference but does not usually exceed 760 mm (2½ ft). Many consider that a table height of 710 mm (2 ft 4 in) suits the average diner and enables him to control his cover setting better. Lower tables do, of course, present greater serving problems (necessity to bend lower) to a waiter.

Table tops may be of wood (plain or, as is more usual in good establishments, covered with baize), or in more popular-priced operations, covered with glass or plastic materials.

In order to adjust seating by removing or bringing in a table, it is desirable that tables should be both collapsible and stackable. Capacity to interlock is also useful. In any case, tables should be stable and with legs well-spaced to afford minimum interference to a seated diner.

In better class restaurants, each party of customers has its own table and two parties are never made to share. Round tables are favoured in such 'up market' operations. Larger round tables (for example, 1.75 m diameter) may be expanded by the insertion of a leaf. The table then becomes oval and suitable for seating larger parties of up to fifteen. (For notes on banquet seating see Chapter 17.)

In more popular restaurants, square or rectangular tables of a uniform size are generally chosen. These are not considered so intimate as round tables. Customers may in some establishments be requested to share one table which can accommodate four guests. An advantage of square tables is that two or more can be put together quickly during service to accommodate large parties who have not reserved a table in advance.

Cover space at tables

Table sizes should allow a length of at least 530 mm (1 ft 9 in) but preferably 610 mm (2 ft) per cover for simple plated service and up to 760 mm (2½ ft) per person for silver service. Wider spacing is not desirable as it tends to make a guest feel isolated.

Table sizes are by no means 'standard', and a round table for one guest may vary from 710 mm (2⅓ ft) to 760 mm (2½ ft) in diameter with similar tolerances for larger sizes. A table 760 mm square is considered to provide ample space for four guests in popular catering.*

Table 2 gives guidance on a generous scale for higher priced operations.

Chairs

From a serving point of view, a chair's styling is seldom important to a waiter (unless it has splayed out legs which obstruct him). But from a customer's standpoint, comfort (possibly with arms and without rough edges to catch ladies' tights) is important. Management, too, will be concerned with durability, ease of movement and stackability. A customary chair height (seat to floor) is about 450 mm (18 in).

Covers and seating should correspond exactly and chairs should be placed where covers are laid. Chairs should not be too near the table and should not touch nor press against the table cloth.

Wherever possible, chairs should be placed so that table legs do not obstruct seated customers. Figure 12 illustrates the aims and problems.

Sideboard (or station table)

For efficient service, each waiter needs his own sideboard (étagère) in the restaurant. This piece of furniture is also described as a dumb waiter,

*See P. Bertram. *Fast Food Operations* (Barrie & Jenkins. 1975).

Table 2   *Guide to table sizes and seating capacity*

Shape	Seating	Approximate size		
		metres		*feet*
Circular	1 person	700 mm to 750 mm diameter		2⅓ to 2½
	2 or 3 persons	900 mm to 1 m diameter		3 to 3¼
	4 persons	1 m diameter		3¼
	5 or 6 persons	1.25 m diameter		4
	8 or 9 persons	1.50 m diameter		5
	10 persons	1.75 m diameter†		5¾†
	12 persons	2.00 m diameter		8
Rectangular	4 persons	1.25 by 1		4 by 3¼
	6 or 8 persons	1.75 by 1		5¾ by 3¼
	8 or 10 persons	2.50 by 1		9½ by 3¼
	10 or 12 persons	3.00 by 1		9¾ by 3¼

† This size, seating ten, is popular for banqueting and functions but see Chapter 17 for further information on banquet tabling and seating.

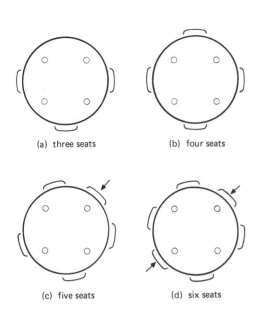

(a) three seats (b) four seats

(c) five seats (d) six seats

(a) and (b) In seating three or four people, each seat may be placed between table legs, thus guests are not obstructed

(c) When five guests are seated with equal spacing, one guest (shown arrowed) is inconvenienced by a table leg

(d) In seating six guests, table legs invariably inconvenience two guests

Figure 12 *Arranging seats at round tables*

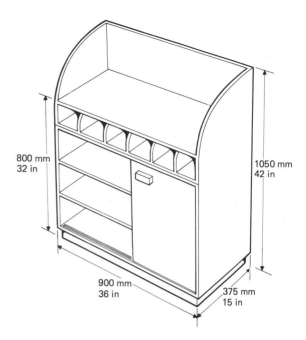

Figure 13 *A typical sideboard*

service console or station service table. It normally consists of an upper shelf on which a waiter effects all his preparations during service. Because of this usage, a clear space of good size is necessary. Often an electric or spirit-heated hot-plate may also be accommodated on this top surface.

Under the sideboard top are drawers or compartments, open or partially open at the front. All the spare table silver (cutlery) available is arranged here. (This arrangement is considered further in Chapter 11.) Below the cutlery compartment there is usually another shelf for storing plates of various sizes and usages, consommé and coffee saucers. Finally, on a second lower shelf is space for spare linen, including table-cloths, slip cloths (napperons), service cloths and napkins. There is sometimes built into the back or side of a station sideboard a cupboard with a slot or flap for temporary storage of used linen.

Sideboard shelves are usually covered with white cloths. These may be made from old table-cloths. Napkins or table-cloths should not be used to cover the service table.

The sideboard shown in Figure 13 is of a design commonly encountered in training restaurants. The divided compartment for cutlery below the top shelf is lined with baize to deaden sound, and can be slid in and out for ease of access to cutlery, and for cleaning. The cupboard on the right-hand side is especially useful for less sightly material.

Usually a small electric hot-plate is accommodated on right of the top shelf which otherwise is kept as clear as possible to cope with incoming and outgoing items during service. Mise en place is normally arranged uniformly on sideboards throughout the room, so that a change of station does not mean an unfamiliar operational centre, for the sideboard is indeed the focal point of service.

Cutlery stored in the compartments usually comprises, from right to left, table spoons and forks, dessert spoons and small forks, knives, small knives, fish knives and forks and any special cutlery or serving implements. Stacked under the cutlery compartments are the various plates required, and coffee saucers (cups will be obtained as required from the hot cupboard), finger bowls and clean linen.

In function service, a sideboard (or side-table) mise en place may be more limited, but on such occasions glasses and trays are usually required.

Reception desk

Normally, at the restaurant entrance is a high desk used by the reception head waiter. On it lies the book where table reservations are entered and also a telephone. It is customary to keep in the drawer of this desk the keys for linen cupboards, condiment lockers, etc.

Buffet

Many hotel restaurants (and other establishments) provide a modified form of self-service by providing a buffet. Buffets have wide application in modern service and may, when used for 'self-help', also accommodate hot dishes (kept warm on electric, bottled gas or spirit réchauds). Some such service may be a permanent feature at all main meal times; others may be on certain luncheon and dinner occasions, for example on Sundays.

In traditional restaurants it was usual to find near the entrance a long table covered with a large table-cloth draped right down to the ground. This was the cold buffet table, placed there so that incoming guests could see at a glance what cold dishes were available.

Such a buffet should be arranged just before lunch service. It must be made as attractive as possible, the most decorative dish being used as a centrepiece with other dishes placed on either side. Overloading must be avoided, as this could spoil the look of the buffet. Often a raised centre is created on the buffet by using specially made

shelves or with boxes covered with a white cloth. Today, many restaurants use trolleys to display and serve cold items of the day.

Other furniture and large equipment

A well-equipped restaurant carries other important items. Guéridons or service side-tables are required when high class service is offered as are trolleys (voitures) for hors d'oeuvre, carving, puddings, pastries and liqueurs. The use of such equipment is referred to in the following chapters.

An indication of what furniture and large equipment may be required is given in Table 3.

Table 3 *Guide to furniture for a 100 seater restaurant*

1 reception desk	10 guéridons
1 buffet table	1 refrigerated cabinet
40 tables (round or rectangular	2 hors d'oeuvre trolleys (possibly rotary type)
100 chairs (some or all with arms)	1 carving trolley
4 sideboards	2 dessert trolleys
4 electric hot-plates for sideboards	1 liqueur drinks trolley

Linen

Table-cloths, napkins and other textile items of tableware are usually described in hotels and restaurants as linen, whether or not they are actually made of linen. Indeed, despite the durability and beauty of damask, made from 100 per cent linen, it is used less frequently than before because of its high cost. Table linen may be of union material, mixed linen and cotton, or mixes of man-made fibres with cotton or linen. (Napkins with a high proportion of synthetic fibres resist fancy folding.)

Damask

Damask is a form of weaving in which the weft produces a self-pattern. Damask is traditionally, but not necessarily, white. The self-pattern can be simple (perhaps stripes or bands), elaborate (floral motifs) or even incorporate a restaurant's name or crest. Double or single damask are terms used to describe a difference in weave. In the former, use of finer yarn allows more threads in the weave. This closer weave makes double damask stronger and more hard-wearing.

Colour

Apart from pastel shades of damask, other coloured table linen is frequently used and in many cases constitutes an important element in a 'themed' restaurant. Some establishments may have different linen for different meals, for example, a simple, rustic style (such as a check pattern) for breakfast and a more glamorous and formal one for dinner. Careful rotation in laundering coloured linen is needed to ensure unformity in fading or 'washing out' of colours.

Linen sizes

Table-cloths

Table-cloths are available in a variety of sizes. For example old imperial measures were:

Square 36 in (915 mm); 54 in (1370 mm); 70 in (1780 mm); 90 in (2285 mm).
Rectangular 54 in (1370 mm) by 108 in (2740 mm).
Buffets and banquets 72 in (1830 mm) by 100 in (2540 mm).

Typical metric sizes of table cloths include:

Square 1000 mm (40 in); 1500 mm (60 in).
Rectangular 1500 mm (60 in) by 2000 mm (80 in).

Slip cloths/napperons

Napperons have a variety of dictionary definitions including slip cloth, tray cloth, afternoon tea-cloth or small table-cloth. It is this latter use for which the term napperon is chiefly employed in restaurants. They are used to cover table-cloths (especially when tables are relaid during service time) that are only lightly soiled on the surface. Common sizes for this purpose are:

Square 800 mm (30 in); 900 mm (36 in); 1100 mm (42 in).
Rectangle 800 mm (30 in) by 1300 mm (50 in).

Napperons may also be used as cloths for single or double tables.

Linen requirements are likely to be:

Napkins Varying from small (for afternoon tea usage) to large (for dinner usage) for example:

tea 300 mm (12 in) square
lunch 450 mm (18 in) square
dinner from 500 mm (20 in) to 600 mm (24 in) square

Table 4 *Guide to linen for a 100 seater restaurant*

1500 table napkins, dinner size	250 tea-towels
200 napkins, afternoon tea size	100 table-cloths 1500 mm square
150 runners (sideboards)	50 table-cloths (1500 mm by 2000 mm
200 glass cloths	300 slip cloths/ napperons (2 sizes square, 1 size rectangle)

Linen hire and disposables

Because of high laundry costs, some restaurants resort to linen hire rather than purchase their own. Speciality firms provide restaurants with a replacement service of laundered linen for a charge based on quantities used.

For similar reasons of economy, some establishments (especially those below luxury level) turn to disposable items instead of linen.

Napkins particularly may be of paper. A good quality three-ply paper napkin, thrown away after use, may cost less than laundering a starched linen one.

Disposable table coverings instead of linen table-cloths are similarly available in sizes of 900 mm (36 in) or 1200 mm (47 in) square. Banquet rolls in white (or other colours) of 1200 mm (47 in) wide are also obtainable in lengths of 40 and 100 metres (130 ft and 330 ft).

The extent to which disposables (linen substitutes as well as cups, plates and cutlery) are used is a matter for management decision related to consumer demand and style of establishment.

Equipment

Different types of equipment are briefly described and/or listed in the section which follows. This indicates the range of items with which waiting staff must be familiar and it also provides 'raw material' for check-lists which those assuming responsibility for function, party or outside catering find necessary.

Trays

Trays are chiefly used by waiters for breakfast or afternoon tea service when a rectangular type is appropriate. Wine waiters use salvers (or small trays) at all meals for the service of drinks served in glasses (whisky, gin, aperitifs, beer, minerals, etc.), and for removing dirty glasses from tables. A wine waiter's trays are round, in effect salvers, usually from 300 mm (12 in) to 450 mm (18 in) in diameter, the larger size normally being used for clearing. Salvers or large dinner plates, napkin-covered, are also used to carry cutlery (and other small items such as pepper-mills) to and from the table.

Square or rectangular trays are sometimes used for carrying food from kitchen servery to sideboard during meal service and also for clearing the dirties from the restaurant. In America there is increased use of trolleys for restaurant clearance.

Trays (or trolleys) used for carrying food and dishes should be covered with a clean napkin or slip cloth. Loading of trays is considered further in Chapter 18).

Silverware

Just as all table fabrics tend to be called 'linen' in restaurants, so 'silver' is habitually used to describe cutlery and metal flatware and holloware. In fact, restaurant 'silver' is often of stainless steel. Even when not stainless steel, cutlery and other items used are not made of solid silver, but

Figure 14   *Silverware cutlery*

of electro-plated nickel silver (EPNS). Use of stainless steel grows but 'hotel plate', that is, EPNS of heavy quality is still admired because of its appearance. Yet the plating on hotel EPNS is not as hard as stainless steel and can be scored and damaged if misused. Moreover, good quality hotel plate is relatively expensive and thus should be handled carefully.

Stainless steel is increasingly used instead of silver-plated items for reasons of cost and maintenance, for on the whole it is just as durable, and, unlike hotel plate, does not require replating. Its stain resistance is due to chromium being incorporated into the iron. Knife blades are usually made of a harder type than other stainless material and are therefore tougher and stain resistant. Other stainless steel items may be satin finished or mirror finished, and stainlessness is relative.

Cleaning of stainless steel and silver, and replating of EPNS, are referred to in Chapter 5. Irrespective of the actual type of metal, table silver consists of cutlery, serving dishes and a wide variety of other table and service appointments.

Cutlery

The principal items of cutlery and their uses are:

Soup spoons For soup when served in plates.
Fish knives and forks For fish and hors d'oeuvre.
Large knives and forks For entrée and main

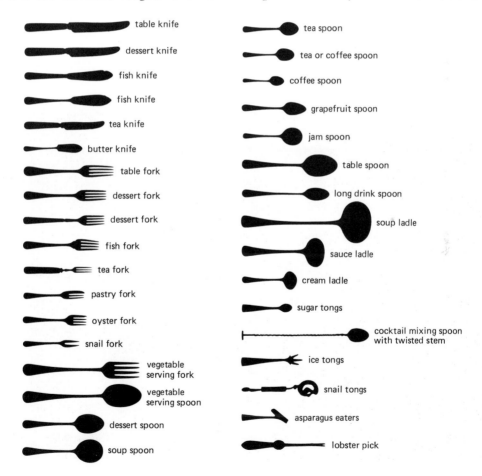

Figure 15 *Flatware item guide*

course (meat, poultry, etc.). Forks only for macaroni, gnocchi, etc. Fork with dessert spoon (or table spoon) for spaghetti.

Dessert or sweet spoons and forks   For all sweets served on plates and oeuf sur le plat. Spoon alone for soup served in cups, hot and cold cereals.

Small silver fruit knives and forks   For fresh fruit.

Small knives for side plates   For cheese and for savoury (used with a dessert fork).

Steak knives   With sharp or serrated edges (possibly with wooden handles, but these need hand-washing and need their handles oiled, and, therefore, present maintenance problems).

Teaspoons   For teas, fruit cocktails, ice cream served as 'coupes', grapefruit, oeuf en cocotte, etc. Grapefruit spoons may be provided, otherwise teaspoons are used.

Sundae spoons   May be provided for ice cream desserts.

Coffee spoons   For coffee.

Service spoons and forks   These are of larger size (tablespoon size) and are used for serving all food orders from the serving dish on to the plate.

Table 5   *Guide to cutlery for a 100 seater restaurant*

150 table spoons	250 small (side) knives
150 soup spoons	100 fish forks
250 large knives	100 fish knives
250 large forks	100 tea spoons
250 dessert spoons	100 coffee spoons
250 dessert forks	25 ladles

Another 'rule of thumb' giving an indication of cutlery required is:

soup spoons	1½ to 2 times the number of restaurant seats
knives	2 or 3 times the number of restaurant seats
forks	4 times the number of restaurant seats
teaspoons	4 times the number of restaurant seats

Figure 16   *Selection of silver pots for serving*

Silver table equipment

Also required when laying a table or for subsequent placing on are a number of other items. Usually of EPNS (or stainless steel) some of them may also be of china, glass or other material. See Table 6.

Special table items

Additionally required for customers' use with special dishes (in quantities according to the menu) are items such as:

asparagus tongs	lobster crackers
grape scissors	pastry forks (small,
nut crackers	two pronged forks
oyster forks	with one broad
corn on the cob	prong)
spears	pickle forks
lobster picks	snail tongs

Table 6 *Guide to table equipment for a 100 seater restaurant*

40 salt pourers	⎫
40 pepper pots	sometimes as sets
40 mustard pots (with	⎬ of cruets in stand
spoons)*	⎭
40 pepper-mills (can be of wood or partly wood)	
40 table numbers	20 sugar tongs
40 toothpick holders	75 ice cream coupes
75 ashtrays	40 flower vases
20 sugar bowls	60 finger bowls

*For French mustard, bone or wooden spoons are used because of corrosion from the vinegar.

Silver for serving

Tables 7 and 8 show a basis for food service equipment (these items are commonly 'silver' or stainless steel, but they may be of crockery).

Other equipment for such a restaurant, made in a variety of materials, including silver, in quantities varying according to the menu may include:

Soup tureens, double and large, individual soup bowls, soufflé cases (double), and hors d'oeuvre trays with fitted raviers.
Soup and sauce ladles (⅜ dl/⅛ pt).

Miscellaneous equipment
These include:

bread boats or baskets	fruit baskets
candelabra	fruit stands
casseroles; for prepared	gâteau slices
foods and sauces	lamps or réchauds
chafing dish	(gas or methylated
cheese boards	spirits) for prepar-
cheese scoops	ation of dishes in
crumb scoops	front of customers
epergnes (now 'dated'	tea strainers
and rarely used)	silver duck press

Table 7 *Guide to service dishes for a 100 seater restaurant*

60 oval dishes (with covers)	40 vegetable dishes (with covers and under-dishes)
80 round dishes (with covers)	10 sauceboats and trays
	75 hors d'oeuvre ravier's

Table 8 *Guide to still-room silver for a 100 seater restaurant*

20 coffee pots (3 dl and 5 dl (½ pt and 1 pt))
20 hot milk jugs (3 dl and 5 dl (½ pt and 1 pt))
20 teapots (3 dl, 5 dl and 8 dl (½ pt, 1 pt and 1½ pt))
20 hot water jugs (3 dl, 5 dl and 8 dl (½ pt, 1 pt and 1½ pt))
20 cold milk jugs (3 dl and 5 dl (½ pt and 1 pt))
20 cream jugs (0.4 dl, 1¼ dl and 3 dl (¹⁄₁₂ pt, ¼ pt and ½ pt))
30 toast racks (5, 7, or 9 bars)
20 egg cups
50 butter dishes

Figure 17   *Silver serving dishes*

Above: Figure 18   *Soup tureen and soup bowl*

Right: Figure 19   *Lamp and crêpe pan*

Figure 20   *Wine cooler and wine stand*

Wine service equipment

For details of wine service see Chapter 20. Silver required for serving drinks includes:

salver, for serving 305 mm (12 in) diameter (round)
salver, for clearing 610 mm (24 in) diameter (round)
ice tongs for all iced drinks
ice buckets and ice bucket stand
wine cradles
wine funnels

Glassware

Glasses are considered further in Chapter 22.

Requirements

In addition to glassware required for wine and liquor service the following glasses are among items usually required:

fruit juice glass (1¼ dl/5 oz)
water tumbler or goblet (2¼–2¾ dl/8–10 oz)
general beverage glass (2½ dl/9 oz)
iced tea glass (3¼ dl/12 oz)

In calculating requirements of glasses, a rough guide is:

large glasses   1½ times the number of restaurant seats

large goblets   3 to 4 times the number of restaurant seats

For special food services, cloches (dome-shaped plate covers in heat-proof glass) may be considered for dishes to be served 'sous cloche'.

Oven-proof ware

Because of breakage, oven-proof earthenware and glass is not used much in restaurants, but some silver serving ware is often replaced by enamelled cast-iron oven-proof dishes. Casserole and cocotte dishes can be brought to the table in the dish straight from the oven. Oval flats which are oven-proof, are ideal for service of gratinated dishes or glazed fish dishes.

China or crockery

Just as linen is used as a term to cover all textile materials used for table coverings, so is the term 'china' used for crockery whether bone china (fine and expensive), earthenware (opaque and cheaper) or vitrified (or metallized) ware. Members of the management team who are responsible for selecting crockery must contemplate several factors before deciding what quality at what price is appropriate.

Handling and stacking

All china must be handled with care and the following points regarding its nature will help waiters understand handling. Most of the crockery in a hotel is in fact of vitreous china (vitrified earthenware) which is strengthened and additionally fired to yield stronger and more chip-resistant crockery. Plates for restaurant use normally have a rolled edge, again to reduce the likelihood of rim chipping. It is desirable for all ware to be stackable including cups and even pots such as teapots (through sunken knobs on the lids). All lids should be of the same size irrespective of pot size so they are interchangeable. Gold rims (or other gold decorations) have a good appearance, but such decorations are often avoided because of the gold's tendency to wear away, and its inability to stand up to mechanized dish-washing.

Plates

There are several main types of plates used in the service of food.

Soup plate   Usually 230 mm (9 in) and used for all thick soups, pot au feu (unless a marmite is used), mussels and oysters, Irish stew, goulash and Lancashire hot-pot.

Entrée plates   Normally 216 mm (8½ in) and

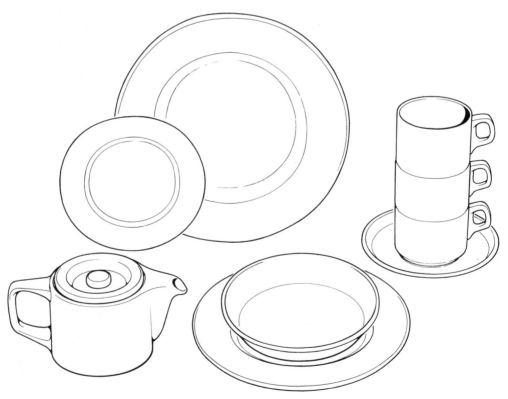

Figure 21   *Stackable crockery*

used for hors d'oeuvre, fish and entrées as subsidiary courses, as a soup under-plate, as a cover plate and service plate.

Meat or fish plate Usually 254 mm (10 in) for main course service.

Sweet plate For sweets and puddings (often the 216 mm (8½ in) plate is used).

Cereal plate 190 mm (7½ in) deep plate used for porridge and cereals at breakfast and, at other meals, for milk puddings or compôtes.

Dessert or fruit plates Often of different design, for example floral or fruit pattern. This change of pattern is possible because the table is completely cleared of other crockery before the service of dessert or fruit.

Tea plate For bread and butter, cakes, etc. This is usually of a floral pattern for afternoon teas.

Side plate 178 mm (7 in) size is used for cheese, bread and rolls.

Salad plate Crescent or half-moon.

Cups

There are four kinds of cups for use in the service of beverages:

Soup cup (two handles) 3 dl (½ pt).
Breakfast cup Plain pattern, 3 dl (½ pt).
Teacup 1½ or 1⅔ dl (¼ or ⅓ pt).
Coffee cup Demi-tasse, literally half-cup, ¾ or 1¼ dl (⅛ or ⅙ pt).

Some or all of the items above may be required but Table 9 provides a guide to basic stock.

Another way of roughly estimating crockery needs is:

dinner plates	2½ to 3 times the number of restaurant seats
small plates	3 to 4 times the number of restaurant seats
soup plates or bowls	2½ to 3 times the number of restaurant seats
tea (or coffee but *not* demi-tasse) cups	3 to 4 times the number of restaurant seats
saucers (for above)	2½ to 3 times the number of restaurant seats

Table 9 *Guide to crockery for a 100 seater restaurant*

150 soup plates	100 coffee cups
300 dinner plates	100 coffee saucers
300 dessert plates	50 teacups
120 side plates	50 tea saucers
50 salad crescents	
50 butter dishes	

Stocktaking

Some restaurant equipment, being easily portable, is particularly subject to loss. Therefore, the maître d'hôtel or restaurant manager seeks to control depredation by careful supervision and vigilance. He arranges stocktaking from time to time (not usually more than once a month). This involves (either before or after service time) setting out items on tables and sideboards in units of ten pieces for easy counting and checking against the restaurant inventory.

The inventory, with discrepancies noted, is passed to management for replacement and other action (tighter security, etc.).

Workplace and sales area

This chapter has indicated different aspects of the restaurant as a place of work, and of the equipment and furnishings within it, as tools of the waiting staff's trade. These elements should support both a waiter's technical skills and sales effort.

The care of the restaurant and its furniture is also the responsibility of the head waiter and his staff and is considered in Chapter 6. The restaurant itself and its equipment is supported not only by the kitchen but also by its own ancillary departments also under the maître d'hôtel's control. These sections are considered in other chapters, for example, the service pantry (Chapter 18) the still-room (Chapter 18), and the washing and care of crockery, glass and 'silver' (Chapter 5).

Campbell-Smith (in *The Marketing of the Meal Experience*, Surrey University 1967) recognized three basic elements in what consumers buy in restaurants. These are food, service and atmosphere. Several factors contribute to all three of them. A restaurant's design and equipment contribute to their effectiveness.

The physical design, decor and equipping of a restaurant is a complex entrepreneurial and management task involving many skills and factors such as ergonomics, economics, ventilation, lighting, etc., for which consultants are frequently required. As waiters acquire supervisory responsibility or progress to management they will, of course, seek to broaden their knowledge of such elements, but from his beginning a waiter should become familiar with the setting in which he works and with the 'tools of his trade'.

An *Encyclopaedia of Practical Cookery* published in Victorian times observed that 'good cooks deserve good service' and deplored the 'great error' made at that period in 'some of the best Parisian restaurants' of serving fine food on comparatively coarse plates'. The writer urged that 'the plates, and dishes off which we eat be as fine as our purses can afford.' Today, we must still remember also that fine table appointments must always demand the care of waiting staff in ensuring that they remain fine, clean and serviceable.

5 Ancillary sections and services

Apart from the restaurant itself, there are ancillary sections which, because they traditionally have been the responsibility of restaurant managers or maîtres d'hôtel, have special significance for service staff. These sections include service room or pantry, still-room, plate and crockery washes. All provide vital support services or products, not least are supplies of clean crockery, plates and some food and beverages not prepared by the kitchen.

Service rooms

Clean and orderly service room arrangements constitute an essential adjunct to an efficient restaurant. In large operations service rooms for mechanical dish-washing may be separated from other service rooms and a glass pantry may similarly be a separate unit staffed by those who are used to handling glassware.

The service room (or rooms) are normally sited between the restaurant and the kitchen. The latter is, of course, under the jurisdiction of the chef, the former is customarily controlled by the restaurant manager or maître d'hôtel with, in substantial establishments, a charge hand or foreman looking after, say, a plate-room.

Usually, two doors connect a service room with the restaurant: one to be used by waiters entering the restaurant from the service room; the other for their return. In well-regulated establishments, it is an offence to use the wrong door. By doing so, serious accidents and clashes can happen. The words 'In' and 'Out' will probably be marked on the doors.

Service pantry

A service room or pantry contains shelves or cupboards for stacking glassware, for example, a table (often of two or more tiers) to take the dirty plates and silver brought in from the restaurant, a box (or boxes) for dirty table silver, bins for rubbish, and sinks, with hot and cold water, and draining racks for washing glasses.

If a small service lift is used, then more shelves should be available alongside it to facilitate service during peak hours.

A large linen box (similar to a post box but with a larger 'mouth') should stand in one corner to receive used table napkins and table-cloths, etc. If this box has a flat top it can easily be used for extra service space.

A 'hot-plate' (a specially heated table-cupboard with a flat top, inside which a supply of hot-plates can be kept), forms an essential part of the equipment. Figure 22 illustrates a typical service room or pantry.

Waiter's procedures

A waiter leaving the restaurant with used materials puts the dirty plates, properly stacked (as explained in Chapter 4), on the table provided and the dirty silver in the appropriate boxes. (These tables and boxes should be near the exit door, and the service lift if there is one, in order to save fatigue and breakages.) The waiter then goes to the service table, in the service room or in the kitchen, to collect the next set of dishes ordered by the customer (as explained in Chapter

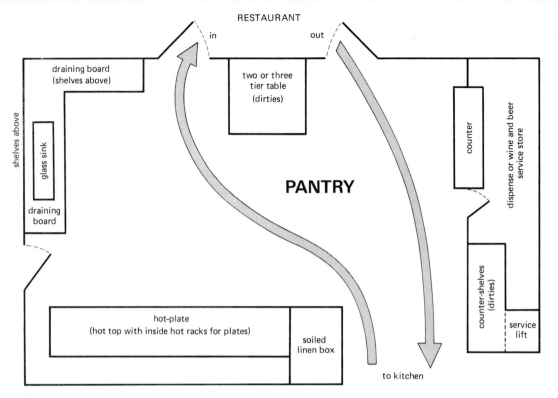

Figure 22   *A service room or pantry layout*
This layout is usual in a pantry although it varies according to the shape, size, plumbing, etc., of an establishment. Minimizing staff cross-tracking is important. If there is a small service lift, then additional shelving is required to cope with peak hour service

12), takes the plates from the hot-plate, and re-enters the restaurant.

Pantry maintenance
The pantry, including shelves, should be cleaned and the articles kept there (for example cruets and condiments) put in order for quick service.

Floor and shelves should be washed daily and sinks should be cleaned. The stainless steel (or aluminium) topped hot-plate also should be washed. Older steel tops requiring emery paper cleaning are now seldom seen. Walls, if tiled,

should be washed weekly. Larger establishments often employ a pantryman (or woman) who, during the rush hours when the waiters will be busy, can help to keep the pantry clear of dirty dishes and silver and thereby assist in service.

Dispense bar
Generally there is also a dispense bar or 'wine stores control' adjoining the pantry so that waiters or waitresses can collect orders for wines, beers, minerals, etc., ordered by the customers. (Chapter 21 deals with these arrangements.)

Still-room (cafetèrie)

Such items as coffee, tea, toast (plain and Melba), butter and preserves are prepared in a still-room. In many operations these are made or handled by a still-room maid or service counter-hand, and waiting staff are concerned only with serving these items.

A still-room functions from early morning to late coffee service including preparation of tea taken in the hotel lounge. Boiled eggs, porridge, sandwiches and a few other light food items (especially at the time of larder closure) may also be prepared in this section. Indeed, many requirements for breakfast and lounge service are met by the still-room.

Still-room equipment

A still-room is equipped with sinks, water boiling equipment and toasters. Space must be adequate to cope with returned equipment which cannot be immediately dealt with, and so that used crockery does not occupy working surfaces where food is prepared. Afternoon tea service, for example, needs a great deal of crockery.

Coffee and tea pots must be stored near the water boiler and sufficient toast racks available near the toaster.

Beverages

The service (and to some extent the making) of coffee, tea and other beverages are dealt with in Chapter 15 (coffee service) and in Chapter 18. Nevertheless, coffee and tea as important products of the still-room are considered further below.

Tea

Tea is an important beverage in Britain. Good caterers take care to make and serve it well.

Storing

Store tea in a dry, cool place away from strong-smelling commodities such as soap, fruit, cheese, spices and disinfectants which can affect its flavour.

If bought in packets, keep them in a box with the lid closed. If in a tea chest, keep it raised off the floor and away from walls to allow air to pass freely under and around it.

Quantities and brewing

The Tea Council Catering Advisory Service rules for quantities and brewing are shown in Figure 23.

Teapots

Tea should normally be made and served in teapots. Nothing else achieves the desirable standard. The best type of teapot is an earthenware pot, with a non-drip spout. Silver or plated pots are also suitable but clean and dry them thoroughly after use otherwise they tend to become stained and musty.

Large stainless steel pots may be used for quantity tea-making although bulk brewing of tea in urns may be necessary for rapid service to large numbers.

When teapots with separate lids are not in use, store them clean and dry, or if wet, store them upside down with the lids off so that moisture can drain away and so keep them 'sweet'. Those with hinged lids, such as silver teapots, should be cleaned and dried thoroughly and stored with their lids closed.

When large teapots are used and there is danger of tea 'standing' and becoming over-infused, use an infuser. This is made of monel-metal gauze or electrotinned copper, having the finest possible perforations (no fewer than 225 to every 645 mm^2 (1 in^2)).

Large-scale brewing

When a caterer has to supply tea to many hundreds of people at the same time, he may use urns or a multipot. A multipot is, in effect, a giant vacuum flask, enabling tea to be kept hot up to four hours. Tea can therefore be brewed in advance of peak demand. Multipots have linings of stainless steel which, if kept clean, do not affect the flavour of tea. They are lagged with heat-retaining materials and have an outer casing

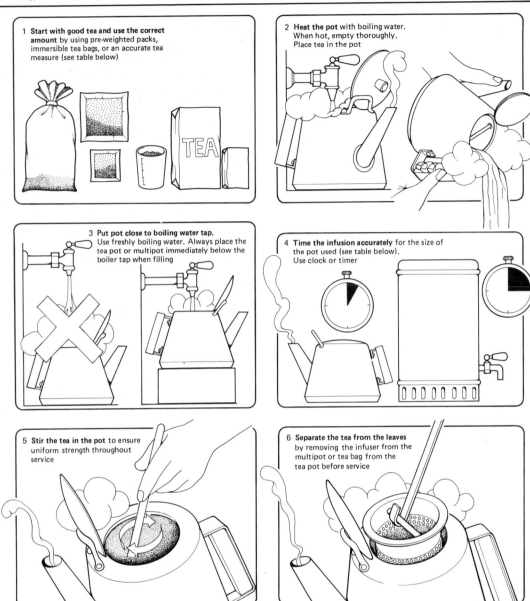

1 **Start with good tea and use the correct amount** by using pre-weighted packs, immersible tea bags, or an accurate tea measure (see table below)

2 **Heat the pot** with boiling water. When hot, empty thoroughly. Place tea in the pot

3 **Put pot close to boiling water tap.** Use freshly boiling water. Always place the tea pot or multipot immediately below the boiler tap when filling

4 **Time the infusion accurately** for the size of the pot used (see table below). Use clock or timer

5 **Stir the tea in the pot** to ensure uniform strength throughout service

6 **Separate the tea from the leaves** by removing the infuser from the multipot or tea bag from the tea pot before service

Table of tea usage and brewing times

Type of pot	Amount of tea	Brewing time	Type of pot	Amount of tea	Brewing time
Pot for one	6 grams	5 minutes	one-gallon pot	35 grams	5–7 minutes
Pot for two	10 grams	5 minutes	three-gallon multipot	95 grams	15 minutes from time filling
Half-gallon pot	18 grams	5 minutes	five-gallon multipot	160 grams	15 minutes commences

Figure 23   *How to make tea*

of polished stainless steel, chromium-plated copper or stove-enamelled tinned steel.

Like teapots, thoroughly warm them inside; put leaf tea into the perforated metal infuser supplied as part of the multipot. Fill completely with boiling water because air space left at the top lowers the temperature of the stored contents. Remove the infuser after ten to fifteen minutes, but before removing, agitate to ensure that all its contents have been infused with the boiling water. After withdrawal, tap the infuser gently by hand to dislodge any leaves. Do not bang the infuser as the metal dents easily.

Cup service

Wherever possible, tea should first be put in cups, then the milk added and customers allowed to take their own sugar. If, however, the whole mixture must be made in the urn, draw off some tea and add sugar to the rest in the form of a syrup. Add milk at the last possible moment. Whatever the pressures of fast service may be, never put milk in a teapot or urn. There are, of course, many customers who, when serving themselves, put milk first into their cups.

Urn care

Clean urns and multipots immediately after use. Clean taps daily. When not in use store the utensils upside down with their lids off and taps open.

Coffee

Coffee equals tea in importance in still-room procedures. Indeed, it is demanded after lunch and dinner when tea is seldom ordered. Because of still-room links with waiting staff, it is useful for the latter to understand the fundamentals of coffee-making. Moreover, coffee is often infused in the restaurant itself by filters, percolaters and other patent devices. If rules are adhered to, making good coffee is simple. The resultant coffee should be strong without being bitter, of a dark but bright colour, and full-flavoured with a pleasant aroma.

Beans and roast

Good coffee demands good coffee beans and suitable equipment for its making. The principal bean varieties are Arabica and Robusta. These determine a brew's flavour and cost.

Arabica, chiefly from South America, is both more flavoursome and usually more expensive. Robusta, mostly from Kenya and other areas of Africa, is more resistant to disease. Despite its name, it is less full in flavour but is normally cheaper. The better and more expensive blends are nearly always Arabica or contain a high proportion of such beans. Good coffee also comes from other areas, for example, Mysore in India, Java and Costa Rica. Mocha coffee has long enjoyed popularity for flavoursome after-dinner coffee. Hence the frequency with which it appears on menus as café Mocha. The bean comes from Arabia and Ethiopia.

Caffeine-free coffee

Brands of ground coffee from which the caffeine has been extracted may be requested by guests who believe coffee keeps them awake or that caffeine in other ways is unacceptable to them. Well-known brands are Sanka or Hag.

Consistent choice

The degree of roast of the bean is important. Breakfast coffee, often enjoyed 'milder' than after-dinner coffee, is more lightly roasted. Whatever the choice of bean and roast always use the same blend of coffee. Have the correct ground for the apparatus.

Coffee-making equipment

Coffee-making equipment is usually of the following kind:

Jugs Ground coffee simply infused in a ceramic or enamel jug in similar style to tea, then strained. Coffee bags extend jug method.

Vacuum infusion machines For example 'Cona' and other percolators using the principle of convection to send boiling water up to infuse a container of coffee above.

Filter equipment   Plumbed-in or for hand filling. Melitta filters and equipment are among those used in Britain.

Large scale filter systems and café sets   for urn coffee-making.

Pressure   In which boiling water is forced through a condenser into ground coffee. (Espresso machines extract coffee from the grounds by pressure.)

Still sets

There is a wide range of water boilers, milk heaters and coffee-makers constituting still sets for installation in still-rooms.

The appliance employed should always be thoroughly cleaned for coffee acquires other flavours easily. Therefore, good maintenance of apparatus is essential.

Coffee-making

To obtain a balanced coffee, make it freshly, never more than half an hour or so before serving. Coffee kept too long or reheated loses its bright, fresh colour and flavour.

Measured quantities

Guide lines in coffee-making are:

● Always weigh or measure ground coffee to balance with the amount of liquid coffee required. Guesswork can cause flavour to fluctuate from meal to meal and evoke complaints.

● An approximate guide is 225 grams (8 ounces) of medium ground coffee to 4.5 litres (1 gallon) of water.

No boiling

Never boil or simmer coffee when it is being made or when being kept hot. Boiling extracts the caffeine and other harsh qualities and causes coffee to become bitter. Although boiling water is used in making coffee, apparatus is designed so that the temperature drops to just below boiling (about 82°C (180 °F)) for service.

Quantity coffee-making

Large establishments may use coffee machines making 4.5 to 9 litres (1 to 2 gallons) at a time. This is usually made by a still-room maid, and if done correctly, such machines make appetizing coffee.

Modular coffee (and tea) preparation machines are available. Buffet installations (with optional control), mobile equipment and units capable of storing up to 70 litres (15⅓ gallons). Two to twelve cup capacity filter machines cope with hotel and restaurant needs for smaller operations.

Vacuum infusion method

The Cona machine is the best-known in Britain for this type of infusion. The way the machine operates is described in Chapter 15, in relation to service of coffee 'in the room'. Larger scale models are, however, available for use with electricity, gas or bottled gas.

Electric simmerstat method

Many establishments use a 1.5 litre (3 pints) machine with batteries in strategic positions in the room for regular supply of coffee. The machines work on the same principle as the table models but can be made ready slightly in advance of service and kept at the correct temperature by controlled heat.

Instant coffee

There are, of course, operations which may serve coffee made by dissolving instant coffee (that is, freeze-dried infused coffee or roller-dried infused coffee) with boiling water.

Individual coffee-making

Customers may like coffee made at the table to ensure a fresh infusion, or because they require a special type of coffee. There are various types of machine which are used.

Filter method

On the Continent, the method mostly employed for individual coffee is by the filter or drip method. There are various appliances, all basic- ally the same (see Figure 24). They consist of a

Figure 24   *Twin model Conacaf*
This model has a capacity per brew of 3.4 litres (6 pints) plus 3.4 litres milk or coffee

filter funnel in which the coffee is placed, which fits on top of the pot, glass, or cup and through which the coffee slowly percolates.

The one cup filter operated on the drip principle is assisted by the pressure of a plunger in the top section.

Cafetière
The word *cafetière* is simply the French word for coffee pot.

Plate and crockery washing

To support the service of food and beverages, arrangements for sparklingly clean crockery, glass and cutlery over and above a waiter's ménage duties are required. Methods must be established to clear dirty items from a restaurant, clean them, stack or store until required and then convey them back into the restaurant. As indicated previously, such washing up may be done in separate rooms. The methods are considered below.

Crockery care
Sections and equipment for food preparation and service should be laid out so that work flows progressively, minimizing return or cross-traffic. Cleaning of crockery and cutlery is a major element in the 'return line'. It should, therefore, take place near the service counter or doors but clear of the outward flow of prepared meals.

Any means of dish-washing is likely to be wet and steamy. Therefore, it ought not to be carried

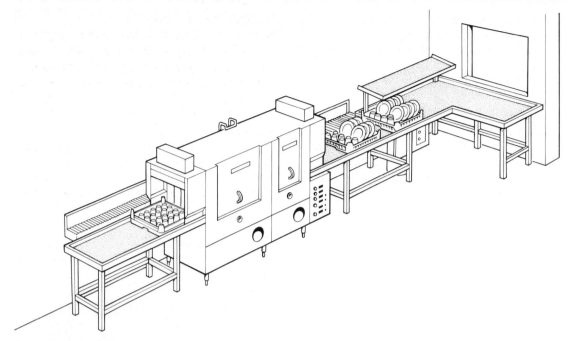

Figure 25   *A commercial dish-washer*

on in a room where food is prepared, though formerly still-rooms were used. Separate arrangements should be made if possible. The plate-wash is usually the responsibility of the restaurant (that is, under the restaurant manager). Whenever the size of operation justifies it, the washing process is mechanized.

Machine dish-washing

Dish-washing machines should be sited in an enclosed space which has mechanical ventilation and provision for floor and waste drainage.

A machine's capacity must relate to the work it has to do in terms of numbers of items to be dealt with, and time available for such a through-put.

In performance, a dish-washing machine must effectively scour and sterilize every part of every article put through it. Thermostatic water heating aids this, as does controlled cleaning, that is, where a moving belt feeds crockery through a machine and articles are automatically sprayed for the appropriate time.

Design of washers

Dish-washing machine designs should comply with the requirements applying to any sanitary fitting, that is, they should be made of smooth-surfaced, non-absorbent and non-corrodible materials. Machines should have no sharp edges or angles.

Rotating brushes are used less than before, but if they are used they should not be of organic material. They are unnecessary where the well-known 'difficult' smears (mustard, lipstick, fried egg) are not encountered, for example in school kitchens.

Where washing action depends on turbulence set up around immersed crockery, the protective shield placed over the impellor may obstruct cleaning of the machine. Types of machine where crockery is placed in a spinning basket may be considered.

Submerged projections and working parts are best avoided and jets which are overhead or placed fairly high at the side are least liable to obstruction.

Waste outlets should be positioned so that water used can be completely emptied away.

A spray or deluge-type washing machine is normally chosen.

Operating techniques

Staff responsible for washing up should be trained. Crockery washing should be prompt, that is, done before food begins to congeal. Before loading articles carefully into the washing machine receivers, food soil should be scraped off. In operating, proper stacking, detergent quantity and water temperature both for washing and rinsing are important.

Reducing breakage

Several basic rules can reduce tableware breakage. Two important rules are:
- The correct use of trays and racks when transporting large numbers of items; and
- Ensuring floors and work areas are clean, dry and tidy.

Research-based rules

Diversey Limited and Wedgwood Hotelware have sponsored a joint research programme investigating dish-washing that is effective but does not affect glazed decorations. The British Ceramic Research Association, who did the work, identified various factors affecting corrosion. The following material is based on their findings.

Water source

Hard water affects tableware more. Softened water should be used for washing.

Washing temperature

The correct temperature recommended by washing machine manufacturers is 60 –65°C (140 –143°F). Research confirms that optimum washing ability is obtained at this level. Temperatures outside this spectrum affect durability.

Contact time

Following recommended wash cycles of machine manufacturers adds significantly to long-term durability.

Detergent concentration

The correct amount of detergent is important. Insufficient detergent results in scum build-up, quickly detracting from tableware appearance. Excessive detergent concentration reduces design durability.

Abrasion

Tableware must be stored and racked correctly for dish-washing, as abrasion is a major factor in reducing design appearance. Tableware should not be allowed to vibrate together during washing.

Gold decorations

Research showed that gold decorations on metalized bone china have similar potential life-cycles to other in- and on-glaze decorations. The main factor reducing gold decoration durability is abrasion from excessive detergent concentration.

Metal marking

Small grey marks which can appear on tableware and detract from its appearance are normally due to scratching, caused by low quality cutlery which deposits some of the cutlery material on to the tableware glaze.

Procedure

Procedures in three stages are recommended by Diversey Limited and Wedgwood. These are: preparation, washing and close down. They involve:

1 Preparation
   (a) check that all curtains and scrap trays are in place.
   (b) Ensure that drains are closed.
   (c) Fill the dish-washer.
   (d) Turn the heater on when the machine is full.
   (e) Use correct temperatures, namely: wash 60–65°C (140–143°F); final rinse 82–88°C (180–190°F).
2 Washing
   (a) Pre-scrape – remove food scraps from plates and dishes, pour tea and coffee residues down sink.

(b) Stack knives, forks and spoons correctly in baskets.

(c) Rack all plates correctly according to size.

(d) Rack cups and glasses correctly over sink.

3   Close down

(a) When wash up is finished, turn off the dish-washer, including the heater.

(b) Empty the machine.

(c) Remove scrap trays and curtains and scrub.

(d) Finally, hose out the inside of the dish-washer.

Note: Ensure that racks are in good condition. Metal-framed racks should be replaced when their plastic covering becomes worn.

Final check and stacking

After draining and air drying, check dry articles carefully before stacking on shelves for any stains which might necessitate a rewash. Check especially for stubborn stains such as mustard and particularly distasteful stains such as lipstick. Organize storage of crockery carefully so that shelves are not over-loaded and piles not so high as to be unstable or to cause those lowest in the stack to crack.

Glass care

Care in handling glass is dealt with in Chapter 20 . The washing of glass is also a restaurant responsibility.

For hand-washing glasses and glassware use warm water (not too hot) and rinse in clean hot water. Some pantries may have a teak or a soft-metal sink or double sink for glass (the latter is particularly appropriate for the rinse procedure). Wood is softer than metal and helps prevent breakages but the softer type of metal sink is often chosen.

After washing and draining, dry the glasses with a linen cloth. A cotton cloth is not satisfactory as it leaves fluff on glass and does not absorb enough water to polish properly.

Water jugs may acquire a water line of chalk or other hard substances in water. This is removed in the normal way. If, however, the water jug has a 'neck' and will not allow the hand to enter easily, the method of cleaning is to use potato peelings, finely cut, or clean scraps of white absorbent paper swilled round the jug with water. Sometimes sand or shot is used for this purpose, but it has a tendency to scratch glass and should, therefore, be avoided.

Mechanical glass-washing

There is now a vast range of mechanical glass-

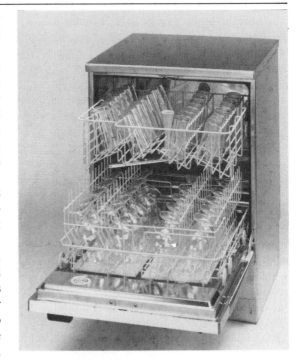

Figure 26   *A glass-washer*

washers from small appliances for use behind bars to more substantial ones for restaurants. They are selected on such factors as:

Hygiene Mechanical methods are usually more hygienic than hand-washed, cloth-dried glass-washing.

Appropriate load capacity That is, numbers and types of glass which can be accommodated per rack to meet an operation's requirement.

Installation costs Running costs related to the machine's usage, water pressure and energy costs; detergent consumption and cost (machine manufacturer's own brands may be more costly).

Silverware and cutlery

Restaurant 'silver' is usually silverplate known in the trade as A1 or hotel plate. Plating is thin but durable and with normal care lasts many years.

Silverplate is easily kept in good bright condition. Large silver dishes, covers, etc. (including stainless steel items) are attended to in the plate-room (usually under the jurisdiction of the maître d'hôtel), but cutlery and other special silver is often the responsibility of waiting staff.

Silver-plated articles

(The author is indebted to the Director of Research of the Cutlery and Allied Trade Association for the following notes of guidance on silver-plated items and their care.)

Silver-plated items consist of a base metal on to which a coating of silver is electroplated. The life of the silver coating depends mainly upon the thickness of silver which is usually quoted in micrometres (millionths of a metre) formerly known as 'microns'.

Table cutlery

British Standard 5577 for table cutlery, which covers other aspects of quality as well as silver thickness, specifies two grades of silver thickness: a 'restaurant grade' and a 'standard grade' which has a somewhat thinner deposit. Within each grade a thicker deposit is specified for place settings than for serving items as follows:

Restaurant grade	(*minimum thickness*)
place settings	33 micrometres
serving items	19 micrometres
Standard grade	
place settings	20 micrometres
serving items	12 micrometres

Some suppliers still quote in more traditional methods, for example pennyweights per dozen table spoons or grams per 24 square decimetres, the assumed area of one dozen table spoons plus one dozen table forks.

Approximate equivalents of these systems are:

1 gram per 24 square decimetres
    = 0.4 micrometres
1 pennyweight per dozen table spoons
    = 1.1 micrometres

or conversely:

1 micrometre
    = 2.5 grams per 24 square decimetres
1 micrometre
    = 0.9 pennyweights per dozen table spoons

Holloware

Because it is subject to less wear through handling, holloware is not normally plated with as thick a coat of silver as is cutlery, for example very heavy-duty hotel holloware would usually have an average thickness of 16 micrometres.

The base metal on to which the silver is plated is usually nickel silver (a copper zinc nickel alloy), brass or stainless steel. Stainless steel has the highest resistance to indentation when roughly handled but is more difficult to repair when damaged. Nickel silver is more tarnish resistant than brass – an advantage if the silverplate should eventually wear off through extended use or adverse conditions.

Tarnishing

Silver is highly resistant to corrosion and staining except in the presence of sulphides which cause tarnishing. Therefore, apart from normal 'dirtying', silverplating tarnishes and speed of tarnishing will vary according to foods in contact. Certain foodstuffs, particularly eggs, contain sulphides, therefore, silver-plated cutlery and flatware should be washed up as soon as is practicable after use. Sulphides are also present in the atmosphere and usually originate from the combustion of fuels, hence their concentration is normally much higher in urban areas than in rural areas. Restaurants in city and industrial areas suffer most due to sulphurous elements in the atmosphere. Moreover, waiters quickly learn which foods cause discolouration. Eggs, onions and sauces which contain onion are particular culprits. Obviously, silver-plated utensils should not be stored in a room heated by an open fire, or an oil or gas heater.

Routine washing of silver may be done through an ordinary washing machine. (See *silver washing*.)

Removing tarnish

There are three main methods of removing tarnishes:

- Ball-burnishing for a few minutes, for example in an Imperial silver burnishing machine (see also *silver washing*).
- Rubbing with a plate powder specially formulated for silver and using a grit-free soft cloth. Powders or pastes designed for cleaning other metals could cause scratches on silver. (Today, plate polishes and powders are seldom used in hotels and restaurants for cutlery because it is difficult to remove the cleaning agent.)
- Dipping the cutlery for a few seconds in a tarnish-removing solution, for example, Goddard's 'Silver Dip'. Such solutions should not be used on heavily tarnished silver because they can leave a dull finish. Chemical removal through using a proprietary dip, although speedy, needs careful control. Quick removal of the article and subsequent thorough rinsing and drying are necessary. For such reasons 'dipping' is not used much in catering operations. (Immersion of silver in a strong, hot solution of washing soda, in which there are pieces of aluminium, can also be used to remove tarnish.)

Storing and protection

Silver that is to be stored for a long period of time can be protected from the tarnishing effect of the atmosphere by wrapping it in polythene bags (preferably heat-sealed), or in heavy Kraft paper with an internal bitumastic layer.

Silver is a relatively soft metal which readily acquires a multitude of fine scratches that give it a characteristic white 'patina'. It is these fine scratches which cause the silver to appear much whiter than the brand new articles.

Nothing should be cut on a silver dish as the slightest cut will damage the silver.

Plate powders and polishes

Plate powder does keep a hard, bright shine on silverplate but its application is too time-consuming for cutlery. It is, however, used for large silverware or articles that cannot be cleaned by any other method. Typical items cleaned by powder are the silver parts of trolleys, réchauffé lamps, cruets, bread boats (or silver baskets).

Articles must be free from grease. Rub them briskly with a little moist plate powder (basically jeweller's rouge and whitening) and, when dry, brush evenly and firmly with a silver brush to remove all the plate powder, especially from any engravings, embossments or filigree work. Finally, give the silver a hard polish with a soft cloth, preferably of chamois-leather. Inspect the silver to make certain that the brush has done its work. If greasy black marks appear during brushing, it shows either that the article was greasy (this can be removed with a warm, moist cloth and the article re-brushed), or that the brush is dirty.

Aluminium with soda solution

The Polivit plate, for example, consists mainly of aluminium and is sometimes used for large pieces of silver such as flats, vegetable dishes and entrée dishes. These articles must be free of grease and food debris and must be completely submerged in boiling water containing a strong solution of ordinary washing soda and the aluminium plate. The combined action of aluminium and soda removes stains from the silver in a few seconds. Any silver treated in this way must be washed well afterwards and dried and polished while still hot and moist.

Safe methods
Some materials used to clean silver (and other materials) such as chemical solutions or salt and vinegar can attack the metal if not controlled in use.

Only under exceptional circumstances is silver harmed by washing up procedures, be they manual or automatic. Undissolved salt can cause black spots within a few seconds if it comes into contact with silver while it is immersed in hot solutions of certain detergents, particularly detergents intended for washing clothes rather than dishes or cutlery.

Mechanized silver washing
Automatic washers are generally satisfactory provided they do not cause silver to vibrate against other articles, in which cases local scratching can occur.

Burnishing machine
A common method of silver cleaning is by a metal-burnishing machine (as previously mentioned). It is more suitable for cutlery and small articles of silver. The machine consists of a revolving drum half filled with highly polished ball-bearings. The drum is lined with rubber to protect the silver during cleaning. The cleansing agent is detergent and hot water.

Rotating the drum or container polishes the silver's surface. It is then rinsed, dried and stacked. Training for and supervision of this job is necessary to avoid snags, for example:

● Ball-bearings should be kept submerged even when not in use to prevent rusting.
● Items need to be carefully positioned in the drum to prevent damage.
● Items which are not all metal, for example, those with wooden handles, may be damaged.

Cutlery washing

(The author is indebted to the Cutlery and Allied Trade Research Association for the following notes on washing cutlery.)

Stains
Staining on stainless steel is rare and in many cases is due to something firmly deposited on the steel, rather than to any attack of the steel itself. Probably the most common cause of staining is attack by one of the proprietary dip solutions used for removing tarnish from silver. Although excellent for cleaning silver and EPNS, these solutions should never be allowed to come into contact with stainless steel; they contain acids that etch the steel, first giving it an iridescent rainbow stain and ultimately etching it a dull grey. Even if care is taken to dip only the silver handle of a knife, it is so easy, when lifting it from the solution, to let drips fall on to the stainless steel parts of other cutlery that happens to be lying around.

All tap water contains dissolved mineral salts that would leave an extremely thin film on any article on which it was allowed to dry out without wiping. In most cases, the resultant stain will wipe off, but occasionally more vigorous treatment is needed, using a polishing preparation, such as Goddard's 'Stainless Steel Care' or Catercraft's 'Formula 9'.

A very few detergents leave an indelible rainbow stain on stainless steel if they are not rinsed off and are allowed to dry out on its surface.

Very hard water can deposit a chalky film on stainless steel, but this is only likely to occur in dish-washers that use unsoftened or incompletely softened water.

Very hot grease, fat or meat juices sometimes leave stubborn rainbow-coloured stains on stainless steel, but this is more likely to occur on meat dishes than cutlery, but again this does not mean there is anything wrong with the stainless steel and the articles will be as good as new after the stain has been removed.

Heat by itself will impart a rainbow-coloured heat tint to stainless steel, but this is only likely to happen if the cutlery is accidentally left on an electric hot-plate or gas cooker when the cause would be immediately obvious.

If stainless cutlery is placed in galvanized iron baskets or containers and then totally immersed in very hot water, zinc from the galvanizing dissolves and deposits itself on the stainless steel; if wiped off immediately no harm is done, but if left to dry, even for as short a time as ten minutes, an indelible stain will be left. This trouble is not uncommon in catering establishments.

Prolonged immersion in synthetic 'vinegar' (condiment) can stain stainless blades and chromium stainless steel or iron, but does not normally affect chromium/nickel stainless steels.

Sometimes rust-coloured stains occur. Wet fragments of steel wool that find their way on to cutlery may go rusty and leave indelible rust stains on the stainless steel. Other rust-coloured stains may come from corrosion pits in the cutlery, although the pits themselves may be so small as to be barely visible.

Most stains that resist ordinary rubbing with a soapy cloth can be removed with Goddard's 'Stainless Steel Care' or Catercraft's 'Formula 9'.

Finally, it must be pointed out that there may be other causes of staining that have not yet been identified.

Pits

When stainless steel corrodes, it does not rust all over like non-stainless steel but forms small pits that can be mistaken for pieces broken out of the steel – especially when they occur at the tip of a blade.

British spoons and forks are made from stainless steels that have such excellent corrosion resistance that they are virtually immune to pitting. For knives, however, the blade steel is selected to give a compromise between corrosion resistance and cutting properties. In order to achieve a lasting edge, a steel that is much harder but of lower corrosion resistance than spoon and fork steel is usually used. The corrosion resistance of this steel is strongly influenced by care in manufacture (thorough hardening and avoidance of overheating when grinding, etc.) but only marginal improvements are achieved by the selection of alternative steels, however, expensive. Constant research is being carried out in the search for significantly better steels and methods of treatment.

The strongest, neatest and most hygienic method of attaching hollow EPNS handles to blades is by silver soldering. At one time, the silver soldering techniques used seriously affected the corrosion resistance of the blade near to the joint – the heat needed to make the joint affected the structure of the steel. With modern methods, by minimizing the soldering time and temperature, this effect has been considerably reduced, but it is impossible to completely eliminate it, and the blades of all silver soldered knives have an area of somewhat lowered corrosion resistance on or near the bolster. However, such knives should give years of trouble-free service if attention is paid to the following points.

Prolonged contact with water is probably responsible for more pitting trouble than anything else. Knives have been made from stainless steel for such a long time that the highly corrosive effect of tap water, caused by the traces of mineral salts it contains is not appreciated. Why then do blades in one establishment last for years without trouble, while in others pitting becomes apparent within a few months? The answer lies in the length of time the blades are wet; knives that are left undried or actually immersed in water overnight can receive in this time as much exposure to the corrosive effect of water as three or four months' ordinary use, where they are in contact with water for only a few minutes each time they are washed.

Common salt and liquid bleaches or disinfectants are very corrosive and will greatly accelerate the corrosive action of water. Detergents, on the other hand, are normally harmless when fully dissolved – indeed they often inhibit corrosion by water. If, however, certain powder detergents are allowed to come into contact with blades in hot water before the detergent is fully dissolved, pits and/or stains can form within a few minutes. Undissolved table salt can have a similar effect.

If pitting does occur, a diligent inquiry into the washing procedure is recommended to find out whether the cutlery has been left in contact with water for a long time. Managers of catering establishments are not always aware of what really happens, for example, probably only the person directly involved may know that dirty cutlery is always left soaking in a bucket of water until someone has time to wash it, or that the last batch of knives to be washed in the early hours is left unwiped to dry overnight in a humid basement.

Washing cutlery in dish-washers

(Recommendations of the Federation of European Cutlery and Flatware Industries (FEC))

Dish-washing machines provide a welcome relief from the task of washing up but to maintain knives in good condition a few simple precautions are necessary. Special hardenable stainless steels are generally used for knives to give them a lasting edge but these steels can become slightly pitted if left repeatedly and for too long in contact with moisture.

1 Whenever possible, wash knives immediately; do not leave them wet overnight and do not subject knives to the 'rinse and hold' cycle.

2 As soon as the dish-washer has completed its cycle, remove the knives and wipe them dry. It is particularly undesirable to leave them overnight in the damp atmosphere of a dish-washer.

3 Observe the dish-washer manufacturer's instructions concerning the type and quantity of detergent used and the method of loading cutlery in the compartments provided.

4 Water with a high salt content is particularly corrosive to stainless steel. Dish-washers are often fitted with water softeners that must be regenerated with salt. After adding salt, make certain that the machine is put through the programme recommended by the supplier before washing knives in the machine.

5 Cutlery with non-metal handles should be washed by hand unless it is stated to be suitable for dish-washers.

6 If any stains are produced by hard water or by any other cause, they can usually be removed by rubbing them with a non-abrasive metal cleaning paste or liquid.

Waiter's responsibility

Dirty cutlery from tables is washed by the plate-room staff, but even with the care advocated above it sometimes may not always be satisfactory for immediate reuse. It may sometimes be necessary to dip silver in very hot water and give it a brisk polish while still hot and moist to ensure a good hard shine.

Hygiene and aesthetics

As indicated earlier in this chapter, the items and procedures which support food and beverage service greatly contribute to an operation's ambiance and success. Moreover, they are vital in maintaining hygiene standards necessary both for aesthetic and safety reasons. All sensible people involved in restaurant service realize the importance of well-maintained silver, stainless steel, crockery and glass and of those staff and sections concerned with them.

6 Preparing the restaurant

Apart from service at table, waiters also have other duties every day. These duties may vary from establishment to establishment. New ways of identifying and allocating tasks in hotels, restaurants and other catering operations may mean further changes and divisions for such work. Duties are affected by the nature of an operation, its degree of luxury, its style of appointments and furnishings.

Ménage

Preparation of the restaurant, cleanliness of furniture and equipment (including ancillary sections, such as the pantry, dealt with in Chapter 5), have long been a traditional responsibility of the waiting brigade. Such work is often referred to as doing the ménage – literally the housework. Modern conditions may change the amount of 'housework' and the way in which waiters do it; for example, hotel coffee shops may have a continuous twenty-four hour service, some establishments may have contract cleaning or 'in-house' night cleaners. Although job descriptions for a waiter's ménage cannot be regarded as unchanging, this chapter nevertheless describes much of what has been traditionally undertaken by waiters in higher class establishments on the assumption that some of these duties will still be carried out by waiters in at least some operations.

Ménage or housework is part of being ready for service. In restaurants (as in cuisines) equipment or food prepared in readiness for service is described as 'mise en place' (put in place). Hence, the work of preparing is itself called in restaurant jargon 'doing the mise en place'. What has been so prepared is also described as mise en place or as being 'en place'.

Organizing the mise en place

A head waiter (or waitress) of an establishment is usually responsible for the proper organization of mise en place and ménage duties. He should have sufficient experience and sufficient training, and understanding of, supervisory duties to identify and analyse the tasks required, and to allocate them to his staff. It is customary to assign one or more waiters to each of the ménage duties for a period (say a week at a time) on rota (see the example below). Thus, one waiter may be detailed to look after the cruets, another the glass, another the table linen, and so on. This, of course, is subject to 'house' custom and the supervisory management applied by a head waiter. In some restaurants, a station waiter is held responsible for all such duties concerning the tables that make up his station (or section).

A relief waiter takes charge of each section

when the waiter responsible has his 'day off'.

Subject to the comments already made about house custom and supervisor's discretion, the following indicates ménage routines.

Morning duties

On arrival in the morning, waiting staff first open all the windows so as to air the room thoroughly, clearing cigar and other smells. (This does not apply to enclosed rooms with air conditioning.) Each member of staff then attends to his particular duty as detailed by the head waiter. Such duties include:

1 Vacuuming the carpet or sweeping the floor (when not done by housekeeping staff).
2 Dusting furniture.
3 Polishing glass: mirrors, glass shelves, show pieces.
4 Cleaning certain articles of silver (in some restaurants all silver is cleaned by dining room staff).
5 Changing linen.
6 Restocking sideboards and dummy waiters.
7 Preparing the cold buffet table.
8 Sharpening knives (never done during service). Carvers may additionally be reset by contract.
9 Setting the tables for lunch.

When all such preparations are over (usually about an hour before service begins), windows are closed and the room allowed to reach comfortable warmth. The temperature of a dining room is around 19°C (64°F) (possibly higher, especially where American guests predominate).

Waiters then go to their dressing room to wash, tidy and clean their uniform. Normally, waiting staff have an early lunch and return to the dining room shortly before service in order to put finishing touches to their station, to attend to trolleys (for example, sweet dishes and plats du jour) and to place cold dishes on the buffet. Lunch is usually served between 12 p.m. and 2.30 p.m., in some cases, even later.

Evening duties

After service of the final meal of the day, a waiter's duties may include:

1 Clearing the restaurant (if breakfast is not served in this room).
2 Placing condiments (salts, peppers, etc.) on a table near the service doors.
3 Emptying mustards and wash liners.
4 Removing flowers to the flower room (or a cool place).
5 Folding clean table-cloths and piling them neatly on one table.
6 Chair design permitting, placing all chairs on tables (chair seats on tables).
7 Checking the safety of the room before leaving (for example, ashtrays emptied into bins, ashes doused, windows secured).

Duty allocation

Table 10 shows how ménage duty allocation may be presented on a staff notice board rather than to identify all tasks or exemplify a comprehensive system. It may be adapted to include commis by having two (or more) columns under each day.

Ménage tasks and methods

A waiter is responsible for ensuring that equipment used on his tables is spotless. He should not blame anyone else for dirty silverware, plates or glasses. He can easily rectify dullness, but if anything is not washed properly he should return it for rewashing. A waiter can make certain his 'mise en place' is always in perfect trim by:

Sweeping and vacuuming

Scrubbing floors, cleaning windows and walls are not part of a waiter's normal duties; this work is left to special cleaners. But he may need to vacuum or sweep the floor. If it is uncovered (for example parquet) a good hair broom and careful sweeping with minimum dust raising are all that is necessary, but occasionally an electric polisher should also be used.

In order to prepare a restaurant for sweeping, any cloths, silver, etc., remaining on tables should first be removed to the pantry and the chairs placed on top of the tables. If labour and time permit, the tables should be moved to one end of

Table 10   *Ménage duty roster*

	Monday	Tuesday	Wednesday	Thursday	Friday	Saturday	Sunday
Vacuuming and dusting	1*	2	3	4	5	6	C
Linen	2	3	4	5	6	1	
Cutlery layout	3	4	5	6	1	2	L
Glasses	4	5	6	1	2	3	
Wines and sideboards	5	6	1	2	3	4	O
Cruets and accompaniments	6	1	2	3	4	5	S E
Pantry and hot-plates	2	3	4	5	6	1	D

* The numbers relate to (1) Henri   (2) Hans   (3) Petros   (4) Arthur   (5) Luigi   (6) Manuel

the room, the chairs placed on top and the clear half of the room swept: the chairs and tables should then be moved to the clean half of the room to allow for the other half to be swept.

Rooms should be swept from the windows and outer edges of the room towards the service doors. When sweeping, a waiter should push the broom and not sweep dust towards himself. Dust will eventually pile up near the service doors and should be swept into a dust-pan. When sweeping is finished, tables and chairs should be placed in their proper positions and then be thoroughly dusted.

Most establishments use a vacuum cleaner for carpets. Before using a vacuum cleaner, remove all match ends, pins, etc., from the carpet otherwise the cleaner's mechanism is likely to be damaged.

Dusting

Walls and curtains should be dusted before a vacuum cleaner is used because dust may descend to the carpet. On the rare occasions when a carpet is swept with a broom, dusting should be done afterwards because brooms throw up dust which collects on walls and curtains.

Table cleaning

Tables should be cleaned. If they are glass-topped, a damp cloth should first be used, followed by a good rub with a dry polishing cloth. Sometimes when tables are stained a proprietary liquid cleaner (or other agents like vinegar and water, or ammonia and water) may be necessary followed by a rub with a dry cloth. Polished wood-topped tables may require a damp cloth to remove some marks, finishing when dry with a proprietary polish or wax polish. Formica and similar stain-proof surfaces usually need only a damp cloth to clean them.

Service tables and side-tables

Such tables, on which table silver, linen, etc., are placed for use during service, should be cleaned in the same way as other tables. (The method of stocking this type of table is outlined in Chapter 11.)

Chair cleaning

Chairs should be thoroughly dusted, not only the seat, but under the struts to clear crumbs or dust. Polished chairs should occasionally be wiped with a proprietary cleaner or vinegar and water.

Furniture glass

Glass of this kind may be cleaned with proprietary preparations. Otherwise mirrors should be polished with a dry polishing cloth.

Pastry and sandwich cases

These may need cleaning with vinegar and water, and finished with a dry cloth. (For the treatment of other glass see Chapter 20 .)

Flowers

Flowers need fresh water regularly and should be placed in clean vases. Flowers will be taken out of the restaurant to the pantry or a flower room at the end of the day's service. (Their arrangement is important in the layout of the restaurant and demands artistry. Some establishments employ a special person for this duty. Further comment on flowers is given in Chapter 11.)

Linen

Service staff have several responsibilities for linen before as well as during service.

Changing linen

Linen is changed at the linen room on a 'one for one' basis, that is, one clean for one dirty item. Counting soiled linen must therefore be done carefully. Usually a chef de rang and commis are appointed in rotation on a roster to be responsible for dining room linen stock, and for its change. Linen is changed daily once, twice or three times, according to a restaurant's size and quantity of stock.

It is a waiter's daily duty to collect, classify and count all soiled table napkins, table-cloths and slips.

Linen book

A waiter is usually required to record soiled items in a duplicate linen book. Soiled linen is bundled into 'tens' after being scrutinized for tears or burns. The waiter takes them to the linen room where they are checked by the linen maid in his presence. The amounts entered in the book being correct, the linen maid issues the same number of clean articles.

It is customary, once all the linen has been changed, for the waiter's linen book to be initialled. The top copy is retained by the linen room; the duplicate remains in the book. Any discrepancy must be recorded so that missing linen can be obtained later. Linen changing is an important duty and is allocated to a reliable person.

Pantrymen change linen in the same way. In large establishments waiters change their own waiter's cloths (and aprons if applicable) at the linen room. The linen room maid again gives clean items for soiled ones.

Handling linen

Care must be taken in handling clean linen. It is easily creased or soiled through carelessness. Waiters should learn to recognize which size cloths belong to which tables. Napkins should only be used for their correct purpose, that is, for the customer, and sometimes for clean service, such as on a plate carrying cutlery to and from the table. Used napkins, and other used table linen, should never be re-folded. If napkins are only slightly soiled they may get mixed with the clean ones and given to a customer by mistake.

On no account should napkins be used as drying cloths. It is usual to have various cloths for specific work. Kitchen cloths for drying and for polishing wet work; dusters (yellow) for dusting and dry polishing; and glass cloths. Linen is preferred for cleaning glasses because cotton cloths tend to leave fluff on the glass.

Service cloth

During service the waiter has a waiter's cloth which should always be clean. When a waiter is not using his cloth, it should be kept neatly folded over his left forearm. It should *never* be tucked under the arm or stuck in a trouser pocket. This cloth is used mainly to protect the waiter's left hand when placing hot plates and serving dishes in front of the customer (see Chapter 14).

Where a quantity of linen is held in reserve, care should be taken that it is used in rotation. Fresh stocks should be placed under those already in the cupboard.

Napkin handling

Table napkins may be folded in a number of different ways, but elaborate folding is not so common today, and is no longer considered to be in good taste. Customers realize that folding involves handling (perhaps excessive handling) by waiters. Therefore, today's managers are more likely to discourage decorative folding on aesthetic and hygienic grounds. Management may also be sceptical of the time and labour spent by restaurant staff on such tasks.

Nevertheless, there remains some demand and consequently use of decorative folds on place settings especially at functions (see Chapter 11).

Commodities

Commodities looked after by service staff 'in the room' chiefly comprise seasonings, bottled sauces, sugars and preserves.

Condiments, sugar and preserves

This somewhat old-fashioned term, condiments, embraces those things 'used to give relish to food' and normally includes salt, pepper, mustard, oil, vinegar and proprietary sauces. Loose usage of the word extends it even to sugar and preserves (jams, marmalade).

Cruets, bowls, bottles or other containers or holders of condiments and table commodities should be kept scrupulously clean.

Salt and pepper containers should be refilled and wiped daily, and emptied and washed weekly. (Complete emptying and change should be made, however, whenever the contents become lumpy or damp.) For weekly cleaning of silver or plated containers, clean the empty cruets (with a proprietary cleaner or plate powder), taking care to brush the screw joint well; refill and replace top. Wipe glass cruets daily and wash them once a week with a detergent. For stubborn stains try a small lead shot shaken with the detergent, or with a vinegar solution. Rinse well and drain, then place them sideways in or on a hot-plate to allow all the moisture to evaporate before refilling. Check carefully the metal caps of glass salt cellars for signs of verdigris.

Refill and wipe sugar bowls daily, and empty and wash weekly. Empty, wash and then replenish English mustard for each meal service. Between meal periods, other containers, for example proprietary brand bottles and French mustard pots, should also be wiped. Necks and mouths of chutney jars, bottled sauces and similar items should also be cleaned in this way.

After the day's service, remove any plated containers of preserves and sauces and their service spoons for cleaning.

Equipment during ménage

The care of restaurant equipment is considered in more detail in Chapter 4 and Chapter 6.

The total washing and maintenance of silver-plate (in modern restaurants there is an increasing use of stainless steel) is, for example, normally the responsibility of the restaurant manager or head waiter. The ancillary sections concerned with silver, stainless steel, crockery and glass washing are considered separately in Chapter 5. Here it may be observed that cutlery and other special silver is often the responsibility of the waiting staff.

Trolleys, réchaud lamps and other special silver
Items cleaned within the room by waiting staff
may include the silver parts of trolleys, cartridge
gas or methylated spirit lamps, cruets and silver
bread boats or baskets. The techniques of
cleaning are, however, considered in Chapter 4.
Voitures (trolleys or carts) should, in any case,
be cleaned daily. This includes those used for
carving, sweet dishes and cheese.

Réchaud lamps should also be cleaned and
filled before service. Normally this means checking gas cartridges rather than replenishing with
spirit, for spirit lamps, because of their smell,
tend to be replaced by gas models.

Trays
Metal trays are cleaned with metal polish. Silver
salvers are best cleaned with plate powder.
Stainless alloy trays only require a good wash
and dry polish. Wooden trays need cleaning with
a damp cloth and polishing with a dry cloth.
Formica trays, if stained, should be cleaned with
detergent solution. Great care must be taken
that aluminium alloy trays are never cleaned in a
soda tank or they will blacken.

Cutlery care
As dirty cutlery is washed by plate-room staff
(see Chapter 5), a waiter should ensure that the
silver or stainless steel placed upon the table, or
within the service table compartments, are
checked for cleanliness and given a final polish.

Glassware
Glass-washing is dealt with in Chapter 5 and care
in handling glassware is further referred to in
Chapter 20 . Wine waiters or waiters must,
however, ensure that glasses are well-polished
before they are placed on tables.

Chinaware
A waiter should ensure that his china is spotless.
Sometimes if crockery is not dried thoroughly
after washing, it becomes dull, spotted or streaky
from detergent washing powder residue. This
can be rectified by wiping the china with a warm
moist cloth and polishing (a dry cloth seldom
removes the marks). If the china still has food
particles on it, it should go back for re-washing.
Cups should similarly be carefully inspected to
ensure that there is no lipstick left on. Cracked
or chipped chinaware should never be used.

Ice
Where the staff does not include a special wine
waiter or lounge waiter, the duty falls to another
waiter to bring ice from the ice-making machine
for use in ice buckets, for iced water and for
cocktails. Ice from ice-making machines is used
as it is dispensed; but any block ice brought in
under contract may need to be rinsed or 'washed'
before being used in drinks.

Pantry and other duties
A waiter may be assigned responsibility for the
pantry which is usually under the supervision of
the head waiter (see Chapter 5).

Packed lunches may be required for picnics
and hot drinks prepared in advance. Some
suggestions are in Chapter 18 for preparing some
items of this kind, including safety and hygiene.

Conclusion

This chapter indicates the nature of ménage and
other duties involved in preparing a restaurant
for service. More detailed descriptions of tech-
niques for dealing with cleaning and maintenance
tasks will be found in specialist texts such as
Hotel and Institutional Housekeeping by D. A.
C. Gee (Hutchinson 1969); *Hotel, Hostel and
Hospital Housekeeping* by J. C. Branson and M.
Lennox (Edward Arnold 1976); and *Practical
Maintenance and Equipment for Hoteliers,
Licensees and Caterers* by D. Gladwell (Hutchin-
son 1974).

As waiters and waitresses advance into supervisory positions they should seek to increase
their understanding of all that is required to
prepare the restaurant for effective service.

Part Two
Meals and Menus

7 Menu trends and composition

Some chefs, caterers and maîtres d'hôtel still tend to regard menu making as akin to setting or solving a gastronomic crossword puzzle. 'Balance' in gastronomic terms is, of course, important on 'set' menus for functions, prearranged parties or fixed meals with little or no choice. But many menus are created from which customers make their own choice, in effect, do their own composing, when marketing and commercial factors are as relevant as gastronomic factors.

Economic realism

In all cases, menus must be realistic in economic terms. In commercial catering they must lead to profits. Whatever the type of food and beverage operation, an establishment's menu is a vital piece of sales literature designed to promote business. A menu epitomizes an operation's catering intentions as well as fulfilling many other roles.*

Therefore, composing menus is a managerial task of some complexity when marketing, profit and gastronomic criteria are all to be met. Executives to whom responsibility for menu making may be delegated include food and beverage manager, executive chef, restaurant manager and banquet manager. Waiting staff are interpreters and sellers of the menu rather than composers. Nevertheless, because they often help guests compose their own meal, service staff must understand the aims and principles affecting meals and menu making.

Variety of meals

The popularity of fast food outlets indicates the present tendency of customers to eat when hungry. Some meals are taken at times and in a style which do not fully accord with 'traditional' ones; for example, *brunch*, a meal halfway between an English/American breakfast and luncheon. Some meals (and their French designations) are:

Continental breakfast Café complet (or thé complet) that is, coffee or tea complemented (or completed) with rolls, butter, conserve. Today's Continental breakfast may include fruit juice.
Breakfast Petit déjeuner, the French term includes both Continental and English/American breakfasts. In the latter case, cooked items are preceded by fruit, fruit juices or cereals.
Brunch A meal between breakfast and luncheon.
Elevenses (or snack) Goûter (literally 'to taste'), the French term is used particularly for light food offered to children mid-morning (or late afternoon).
Luncheon Déjeuner.
Afternoon tea 'Le five o'clock'.
High tea A tea meal including hot or cold cooked items.
Dinner Dîner.
Supper Souper – less formal evening meal taken, for example, after the theatre.

*For more information, see J. Fuller, *Professional Kitchen Management* (Batsford 1981).

Breakfasts, beverages and informal meals

Breakfasts, hot beverages and light informal meals are not considered in detail in this chapter. Breakfast in hotels is an important service and breakfast menus, together with breakfast service and room and lounge service, are considered separately in Chapter 18.

Types of menu

Menus may be compiled to meet the requirements for all such meals. Modern waiters encounter many types of menus but they are usually variants of two main kinds: à la carte and table d'hôte. The former is a list of all the dishes within the resources of a particular restaurant's kitchen. From it a guest may select items to compose his own menu. The charge for the meal will be the total of the prices of individual dishes served to him.

The table d'hôte (literally and originally the host's or hotelier's own table) is a meal (usually divided into courses) at a fixed (inclusive) price with limited or no choice. A waiter may be asked by his guest for guidance in making choices from both kinds of menus.

Trends towards shorter menus may, however, result in shortened à la carte menus that resemble extended table d'hôte ones, while a 'selective menu plan' is also a compromise between à la carte and table d'hôte, where the price of the whole table d'hôte style menu is determined by the main course item selected by the guest.

Specialities and plats du jour

Some establishments each day carry on the à la carte menu an item called 'plat du jour' (dish of the day). This is frequently a main dish of the table d'hôte meal. When a dish is the plat du jour it is on the à la carte menu at a fixed price, often less than the price normally charged for it on other days. Potatoes and vegetables as a garnish are often included in the price. A plat du jour should always be a 'ready dish'. It is not a means of getting rid of kitchen left-overs. Specialities, however, may sometimes require pre-ordering.

A good waiter will be aware not only of the plat du jour or speciality of the day but also of seasonable dishes to recommend. Other factors to note in taking orders and, in effect, helping to 'sell' the food and service of the restaurant include:

● Knowing ready dishes, for quick service to guests in a hurry;
● Knowing items suitable for children;
● Salad, vegetable and potato suggestions for grills, roasts and main courses for à la carte guests;
● Suggestions for dessert courses when this stage is reached by à la carte customers.

Menu specifications

The menu is important to a catering operation because it gives practical expression to its catering policy and intention. Many leading hotel companies not only develop a menu, but in company manuals give additional information about it which ensures that dishes are appropriately served.

Menu specifications which guide food and beverage staff might take the form of three column instructions of which Table 11 is an extremely brief example of what would be a substantial listing.

Table 11   *Sample extract from a menu specification*

Dish	Served from	Service method
2 x 5 oz cream of tomato soup	Main hot-plate	Silver tureen and ladle. Waiter serves from guéridon on to 250 mm (10 in) soup plate with underplate
Coq au vin (half-chicken in red wine sauce, button onions, mushrooms)	Main hot-plate	Tin-lined copper casserole on oval flat
Butter	Still-room/pantry	From ice pail in room into butter dish

Visuals such as pictures and diagrams may also be used to support operational manuals to ensure that menu intentions are appropriately carried out.

Legal obligations

This chapter does not purport to provide comprehensive guidance in menu management, and therefore will not elaborate on legal constraints affecting menus. Nevertheless, legislation exists to protect the consumer. For example, it is an offence incorrectly to describe menu items, that is, butter must be butter if so stated on the menu and not be margarine.

Similarly, there are regulations regarding price marking. Waiters, especially when they are promoted to positions of responsibility, must ensure that they are fully aware of laws which condition menu descriptions and price display related to food and drink. Acts of Parliament (such as the Trade Descriptions Act) are also affected by statutory orders and instruments, for example, the price marking (Food and Drink on the Premises Order, 1979). As such orders may be added to by central and local government, hotels and restaurants must ensure that they keep abreast of legislation. Responsible serving staff should likewise make themselves aware of their legal and social responsibilites.

Approach to composition

A well-balanced meal satisfies the customer's appetite, pleases him and yet leaves him without any feeling of over-eating. Hence, the various dishes that constitute the meal should be balanced. Otherwise a series of dishes may be selected which are excellent individually, but collectively may make an indigestible meal.

Dish sequence

Gastronomic experience has led to an accepted order of dishes or courses in a meal. A banquet menu (in which there is seldom much, or any, choice) best exemplifies course sequence for this, the longest, most varied and perhaps most carefully prepared of the meals that a restaurant serves.

The order of dishes is from those that aim to stimulate appetite (hors d'oeuvre, soups, etc.), light food (such as fish with an appropriate sauce), followed by a light meat course (the entrée), on to a main dish (roast served with a salad or possibly, with vegetables and potatoes). The next dish is invariably a light sweet or ice to change the taste completely, followed by a choice of dessert, fruit or cheese. Finally, coffee is served.

Sequences of courses for lunch, dinner and supper are given on pages 88–97, but such sequences are not determined by rigid rules, simply by experience of what 'works well'. But gastronomic experience should not be lightly disregarded. Deviation should be undertaken only by those who appreciate the general gastronomic 'rules' and the consequences of breaking them.

Common sequence changes to menus today are, for example, service of cheese before sweet courses; or a 'fine' vegetable like asparagus either as an entremets de légumes immediately before the pudding course, or as the first or early introductory course; or a quiche Lorraine as a savoury at the end of a meal or an introductory course even before a soup. Great chefs and maître d'hôtels may, like great artists, depart from the rules and create menu masterpieces, but waiting staff will be wise to give due weight to the cumulative menu experience which has led to sequence patterns.

Chapter 21 explains that the service of wines follows the general order of stimulation of appetite; first the lighter wines (usually white) and then the heavier wines until the coffee is served, which, as it will be sipped at leisure, may be accompanied by a brandy or a liqueur to 'settle' the digestion.

A *dinner* (implying an ordinary meal of the

day, served usually in the evening) is seldom so elaborate as a banquet. Some of the courses mentioned above may, therefore, be omitted. Similarly *lunch* (the term for a meal served in the middle of the day) is lighter still. It may consist simply of three or, at the most four, courses, say hors d'oeuvre, fish, a roast or entrée and a sweet.

The courses

The number of courses offered at luncheon, dinner or supper varies according to the type of restaurant, numbers to be catered for and prices charged. The 'build up' from appetizer to heavier dishes has been indicated for the sequence of dishes. This applies no matter how long or short a menu may be.

At one time, a meal's quality tended to be judged by the number of courses served. In a multi-volume, American culinary work of 1904, the celebrated maître d'hôtel of the Waldorf Astoria, 'Oscar of the Waldorf' outlined a progression of ten courses for a dinner (with illustrations indicating table settings and service style for each). He named them

'Oscar of the Waldorf's' ten dinner courses:

1	Huîtres (oysters)
2	Potage (soup)
3	Hors d'oeuvre (dainty dish)
4	Poisson (fish)
5	Entrée
6	Rôti (roast)
7	Sorbet, punch
8	Gibier (game)
9	Dessert
10	Coffee

Modern service order

Today, the normal order in which dishes are served is:

Hors d'oeuvre
Soups
Eggs
Farinaceous (pasta, gnocchi, rice. At lunch these may also precede the rest of the meal as an opening course or be taken in place of the egg or fish course)
Fish
Entrée
Joint
Vegetables (some 'fine' vegetables, for example, asparagus or artichoke, may be served as a preliminary course)
Poultry or game
Salads
Sweets
Savouries (may be chosen by some diners to precede the sweet course. Some savouries may even be selected to open a meal)
Cheese (as in the case of savouries, may precede the sweet course)
Dessert
Coffee

At meals with many courses, a sorbet may be served between the entrée and joint, or between the joint and poultry. On shorter menus a sorbet is sometimes included after a fish course but this is regarded as both unnecessary and pretentious.

Alteration in fashion

Long ago different types of dishes or courses came together as one course. When the first services were 'removed' the next service of dishes was called the removes or relevées. Relevées still continue to appear on menus but whereas, at one time, a relevée might be served on the same menu as an entrée and a roast, it is now extremely rare to serve any but one of these three courses except at a most elaborate function.

Fashions in food change more rapidly than most people realize and it is only on ceremonial occasions that longer, 'old-fashioned' luncheons or dinners are served as banquets. Modern trends (conditioned by consciousness of aesthetics and health) are towards simplicity.

The following section summarizes the nature and sequence of possible courses but today a full dinner is seldom served. Three, or at the most four, courses usually suffice for a luncheon; four or five for dinner; two or three for supper; five or six for a banquet.

Nature of courses

Hors d'oeuvre This course is usually composed of tangy, salty dishes, aimed to stimulate appetite. Hors d'oeuvre varié applies to a variety of side dishes offered as appetizers such as potato salad, anchovies, prawns, olives, Russian salad, Bismark herring, gendarmes, sardines, cold egg dishes. Alternatively, an hors d'oeuvre may be a single item served as a preliminary appetizer course before the soup, for example dishes like melon, caviar, oysters, smoked salmon, salami, sausage, smoked ham.

Soup (potage) Two soups are usually featured on a table d'hôte dinner – one clear (consommé) and one thick (crème, velouté or purée). Only one is served with each meal. The clear soup is listed first on the menu.

Pasta (Italian and other pasta), rice (risotto) and Eggs Pasta (such items as spaghetti, gnocchi, nouilles) or risotto may be served as a preliminary course at luncheon, either in place of or following the soup course. Egg dishes (en cocotte, sur le plat, brouillés (scrambled), omelettes, etc.) may similarly be featured at this point on a luncheon menu. Egg or pasta dishes are usually taken in place of a fish course if hors d'oeuvre and/or soup have been chosen. They are seldom included on set dinner menus, but may be chosen as an early course from à la carte selections by guests taking less formal evening meals.

Fish Two kinds of fish are frequently offered on a table d'hôte dinner. One is invariably a poached fish served with a sauce mousseline or hollandaise or similar sauce. Plainly steamed or boiled potatoes are usually offered with this type of fish. For luncheon the fish course can be replaced by a hot egg dish such as an omelette or an 'oeuf sur le plat'.

Entrée This is the first of the meat courses. At dinner, it is usually complete in itself in that it is accompanied by its own appropriate vegetable or other garnish. It may be a dish like sweet-breads, garnished cutlets, vol au vent, tournedos and so on. (A luncheon entrée may be more

substantial and additional vegetables may be served separately.)

Remove or relevée Is a larger joint or 'pièce de résistance', poêlé rather than roast and may consist of a saddle of lamb, a cushion of veal, braised ham or even venison. Potatoes and one or two vegetables are served with this course.

The sorbet This course is intended to be a pause during a long meal. A sorbet was supposed to 'settle' dishes already served and stimulate the appetite. It is a water ice, usually flavoured with champagne or other delicate wine or liqueur and is served in a tall, small glass with a teaspoon. Cigarettes, usually Russian, are passed at this stage and ten minutes are allowed before the next course. With shorter menus, more disciplined appetite and better nutritional knowledge, the sorbet is less frequently included and its role increasingly questioned.

The roast (rôt) This course consists of poultry or game, such as chicken, duck, turkey, pheasant, grouse or partridge, served with their sauces and gravy. A dressed salad is served separately on a half-moon plate. Particularly for shorter dinners (that is without an entrée) it is nowadays possible that a fine meat roast such as a fillet of beef may be served.

Vegetables (légumes) The French customarily serve a finely dressed vegetable as a separate course (entremets de légumes), for example asparagus served with sauce hollandaise or beurre fondu. But at lunch time (or even at a simple dinner) some may choose this type of dish, that is, globe artichoke or asparagus as a preliminary course.

Sweet (entremets) This may consist of a hot sweet such as a soufflé or rum omelette, otherwise an ice (such as coupe, biscuit glacé, bombe glacée or meringue glacée). Petits fours (friandises or mignardises) are passed with this course.

Savoury A savoury course usually consists of a tit-bit on a hot canapé of toast or fried bread. Alternatively, a savoury course may be a hot soufflé (of, say, cheese or haddock) or a dainty savoury flan or ramequin. Many modern diners choose to take their cheese before a sweet course. One reason is that they can continue to drink a red wine (such as one selected for the main course) with the cheese.

Cheese (fromage) Alternatively, the cheese platter (particularly at luncheon) may be presented with biscuits, butter, celery, watercress as probable accompaniments.

Dessert This finale consists of a basket of fresh fruit (possibly also dried fruits and nuts). They are sometimes placed on the table as part of the decorations. Finally, coffee is served and liqueurs and brandy passed.

Menu balance
In selecting dishes from the range possible in the above courses, and in deciding the number of courses, a suitable menu is one that conforms to:

● Principles of digestibility.
● Customer's individual preferences.
● Season of the year and nature of the occasion.
● Resources of the kitchen staff and equipment and what it is possible to prepare in the time.
● Clear cost and price policy.
● Balance of foods not only nutritionally and for digestion but also in terms of varied but balanced flavour, colour, texture and consistency.

The composer of a menu need not be a chef or cook, but an appreciation of food is needed. Regular menus of the day are normally compiled by the chef, food and beverage manager, or caterer, in accordance with management's catering policy. But a menu for a pre-ordered party will usually be drawn up by a restaurant manager in consultation with the chef. The restaurant manager should know what customers desire, and the chef should know what can be prepared by his staff in the kitchen on the day in question and within cost limits allowed.

It would be of little use to compile a menu of dishes which could be prepared only with more kitchen staff than actually exist or which demand more knowledge or skill than is possessed by the chef and his assistants. There is a difference between compiling a menu for a busy restaurant which has to serve to capacity and at high speed during rush hours, and making one for a leisurely banquet.

Menu intentions
In catering, a menu is the food operation's marketing and merchandising in action. But in commercial establishments menus should be carefully costed to provide the appropriate ratio of profit. A menu should also provide:

1   A concise list of what is to be served to enable the diner to anticipate his meal and to enable him to choose his wine in advance.
2   A balanced meal as to colour and ingredients in proper sequence.
3   A meal planned so that it may be correctly served.

A menu compiler, where possible, clearly defines for the waiter the number of portions on each dish. The nature of garniture and vegetables should be related to the skills of waiting staff available and simplified where necessary. More elaborate dishes may need to be confined to small parties. For banqueting menus, eight portions (at the most ten) per service is regarded as satisfactory.

Menu factors
The following are among many points to be considered when compiling a menu:

1   For gastronomic reasons, a meal should not contain two dishes which are composed of the same ingredients, for example if an egg dish is on the menu then eggs should not form any appreciable part of the hors d'oeuvre. This applies to all other dishes, for example if the soup is crème Dubarry, which contains cauliflower as its base, then cauliflower should not be served later as a vegetable. Tomato soup should not appear on a menu with tomato sauce. If pie or pastry is served, for example vol au vent, then there should not be any starchy food served as sweet. Chicken base soup should not be served on a menu

containing chicken. Fried fish and fried fritters is another example of duplication.

2 Two white meats or two dark meats should never follow each other, for example pork should not be followed by veal, or beef by mutton. There are so many different dishes that this duplication of taste and nutriment can easily be avoided.

3 A light entrée should be followed by a heavier dish.

4 If the menu is long, dishes chosen should not be too heavy; for example, if a long banquet is being served, earlier dishes in particular, should be small and light. (Mention has already been made of the possibility of serving a sorbet or water ice.)

5 If a menu is short, more substantial dishes may be included to ensure that diners will have a sufficient meal.

Sequence of courses

The general nature and sequence of the different courses has already been considered. The following summarizes the situation in regard to principal meals and gives examples of menus.

Luncheon menus

Luncheon menus do not follow a pattern as strict as those for dinner. They are usually shorter, with fewer courses but offering more choice within each course. Emphasis is on stews, roast joints, grilled meats, cold buffet and hot puddings, all of which are seldom seen on dinner menus.

Many dishes served for lunch are considered to be less fine (cheaper cuts, ingredients or commodities) and, therefore, beneath the standard required for dinner. All dinner dishes may be served at lunch time though it is not usual to choose highly garnished classical ones. Luncheon is normally a more quickly served meal. Dinner taken more leisurely allows time to prepare more complicated à la carte dishes.

Table 12 shows the order of dishes for luncheon, and how they might be presented, on a menu. All dish categories, however, do not necessarily appear on all menus. Some dishes listed in the table are headed (a), (b), (c), etc. This indicates the accepted sequence of dishes as they appear within each course. Thus melon (1(b)) might be followed by smoked salmon (1(d)) before proceeding to the next course of, say, consommé (2(a)), followed by a thick soup (2(b)), and so on.

Table 12 *Luncheon – sequence of dishes*

Order of courses	Dishes available		Notes
1 First course	(a)	Cocktails: fruit or shellfish	
	(b)	Fruit: grapefruit, melon, fresh figs, avocado pears, fruit juices	
	(c)	Delicacies: caviar, oysters, seagulls' eggs, snails, potted shrimps	
	(d)	Smoked: salmon, trout, ham, salami, sausages	
	(e)	Hors d'oeuvre varié	
2 Soup	(a)	Clear soups: consommé, consommé based, broths	
	(b)	Thick: veloutés, flour base, creams, purées	

continued

Order of courses	Dishes available	Notes
3 Farinaceous	Pasta: macaroni, spaghetti and all other Italian pastes, gnocchis, risotto	Plain or garnished
4 Eggs	All varieties, excluding boiled. Omelettes	Usually garnished
5 Fish (hot)	(a) Steamed: poached (deep or shallow) but without complicated garnishes (b) Grilled and meuniére: prime fish, herring, mackerel and cod (c) Fried: prime fish, whiting, whitebait, scampi and cod (d) Shellfish: mussels and scallops, particularly scampi (less often crab or lobster)	Prime fish, skate and cod
(cold)	Salmon, lobster, crab, trout (Cold fish appears here only when there is one dish and when it is intended to be followed by a meat course. On à la carte menus it is featured with the cold buffet)	
6 Entrées	Stews and ragoûts: brown, blanquette, navarin, fricassé, hot pot, goulash, pilaff, oxtail, tripe, calves' head and feet Pies, puddings, vol au vents (rarely) Butcher's meats: boiled (fresh and salted), braised Sautés: veal collops and cutlets, lamb cutlets and noisettes, pork cutlets, calves' liver Réchauffé dishes: minces (including chicken), bitoks, etc. Braised game: jugged hare, salmis of game Served with: vegetables and potatoes	
7 Roasts	Mostly butcher's meats, rarely poultry or game. Served with vegetables and potatoes	
8 Grills	All the grilled meats, including chicken with garnishes, served with potatoes (often fried) and a vegetable or with a salad	
Vegetables and potatoes	Items under 6, 7, 8, will always be combined into one course with the vegetables printed at this point followed by potatoes. Omelettes (from 4) and fish (from 5) may similarly be sectioned as a main course and accompanied by vegetables and/or salad	
9 Cold buffet	Cold fish: salmon, lobster, trout, crab, prawns, aspic of fish, crayfish, etc. Cold meats: all the cold meats, joints, poultry, game, pies, terrines, etc.	Or see 5 above
Salads	With salads listed. Boiled (or other) potatoes may be offered	

Order of courses	Dishes available	Notes
10 Vegetable dish (entremets de légumes)	Hot or cold asparagus, globe artichokes, seakale, served alone as a course with the apppropriate sauces	A fine vegetable such as asparagus or globe artichoke is often also taken as an opening or early course
11 Soufflé	Savoury soufflés: cheese, spinach, mushroom, etc. served alone as a course by itself	
12 Sweet	(a) Hot puddings: steamed puddings, pancakes (though not as often as at dinner), fritters (b) Milk puddings (c) **Pies, tarts, flans, apple dumplings, savarin, babas, profiteroles** (d) Trifle, bavarois, mousse, jelly, fools, egg custards, charlottes (not apple which appears with hot puddings) (e) Fruit: stewed (compôte), baked, salad (f) Ices: various flavours. Coupes and sundaes (though more often featured at dinner) (g) French pastries, gâteaux	
13 Cheeses	(a) All varieties of cheeses, followed by (b) Celery, radishes, endive, followed by (c) Biscuits	
14 Dessert	All fresh fruits	Presented in a basket
15 Coffee	Coffee sometimes named after the country of origin	

Breakdown of courses within the luncheon menu depends upon the number required and choice desired. For example:

2 courses Choose from 3, 4, 5, 6, 7, 8, 9 and 12, 13.

3 courses Choose from 1, 2, 3, 4 and 5, 6, 7, 8, 9 and 12, 13; *or* from 1, 2, 3, 4, 5 and 6, 7, 8, 9 and 12, 13.

4 courses Choose from 1, 2 and 3, 4, 5 and 6, 7, 8, 9 and 11 and 12, 13; *or* from 1, 2, 3, 4, 5 and 6, 7, 8, 9 and 10, 11 and 12, 13.

5 courses Choose from 1, 2 and 3, 4 and 5 and 6, 7, 8, 9 and 12, 13; *or* from 1, 2, 3, 4 and 5 and 6, 7, 8, 9 and 10, 11 and 12, 13; *or* from 1, 2 and 3, 4, 5 and 6, 7, 8, 9 and 10, 11 and 12, 13.

There are many other combinations but these examples show the general application.

Dinner menus

Dinner, regarded as the principal meal, affords an opportunity for artistry in menu composition. At dinner guests have come for relaxation, to enjoy food, dining rituals and the atmosphere. Usually, with time to spare, customers can better appreciate a longer menu with a choice of more exotic or esteemed dishes. At dinner, dishes chosen may be classical. Menu language should be perfect. Menus will often be à la carte, but many will be compiled for functions. The same basic rules apply in composing a meal.

Table 13 indicates order of courses, and again where (a), (b), (c), etc., is used against dishes available, this is the accepted order in which they appear on menus.

APPETISERS

Prawn Cocktail	£1.25
Chef's Pâté with Hot Toast	£1.00
Egg Mayonnaise	80p
Soup from the Tureen	60p
Smoked Fillet of Mackerel Served with Horseradish sauce	£1.15
Chilled Melon	£1.05
Potted Shrimps	£1.50
Avocado Pear with Prawns or Vinaigrette	£1.55 £1.10
Spicy Crab Pâté	£1.05

ALL PRICES INCLUDE VAT

THE CARVING TABLE

Our Chef will carve you a generous helping from a choice of succulent roasts including **Prime Rib of English Beef** or a sumptuous cold buffet.

ADDITIONAL PORTIONS EXTRA

Please help yourself to a selection of freshly prepared vegetables or a variety of salads

A choice of sweets from the trolley including Gateau, Fruit Salad and Fruit Pie, all served with Fresh Cream

Dairy Ice Cream · various flavours

Cheese Board with Biscuits and Butter

£3.85
INCLUDING SWEET OR CHEESE
(Children £2.50)

Coffee with Cream (large cup)	35p

Figure 27   *An example of a carving menu*
At more modest price levels, carveries, carving tables and similar restaurants also operate the same menu for lunch, and dinner. This example is an Anchor Hotels and Taverns' carving menu

Table 13   *Dinner menu – sequence of dishes*

Order of courses	Dishes available	Notes
1 First course	(a) Cocktails: fruit, shellfish (b) Fruit: melon, fresh figs, avocado pears (c) Delicacies: caviar, oysters, seagulls' eggs, snails, potted shrimps, prawns, frogs' legs, foie gras, timbales (d) Smoked: salmon, trout, ham, salami, sausages, sprats (e) Hors d'oeuvre varié: hot and cold	General: formal dinners used to open with soup but single hors d'oeuvres and appetizers, especially the fine and costly ones, increasingly appear Traditionally these were not served cold at dinner, though recently appearing on menus
2 Soup	(a) Clear: consommé and consommé based, turtle, petite marmite, etc. (b) Thick: creams, veloutés, bisques	Including cold consommés
3 Fish	(a) Deep poached: salmon, turbot, blue trout (truite au bleu) (b) Shallow poached: prime fish, with classical garnishes and sauces (c) Hot shellfish: lobster, crab, crayfish, crawfish, scampi, scallops, (rarely mussels) (d) Meunière: sole, trout, salmon, red mullet (e) Fried: whitebait and, nowadays, scampi, sole (sometimes en goujon) (f) Grilled: lobster, sole, salmon, red mullet, turbot (g) Cold: salmon, salmon trout, trout, sole, usually in aspic	With garnishes (other fish appear rarely fried or grilled for dinner)
4 Entreé Lighter dinner dishes invariably garnished and usually individually portioned	(a) The sautés: tournedos, noisettes, cutlets, veal collops, etc. (not Viennoise), sauté of chicken, etc. Filets mignons, sweetbreads, kidneys, saddle of hare (b) Vol au vent, fried chicken (c) Hot: mousse, timbales, soufflés (meat) Where an entrée is followed by a relevé, vegetables and potatoes are not served separately	*Never* stews or ragoûts Served with a minimum of rich sauce
5 Relevé Larger dishes (not roasts, grills or the smaller entrées) which usually have to be carved	(a) The poêlés: chicken (casserole, cocotte, poêlé), saddle of lamb, veal, whole fillet, sirloin (usually boned as contrefilet)	Butcher's meat which, in classic menus, never appears as a roast at dinner, is poêlé to serve as a relevé. Normally garnished

continued

Order of courses	Dishes available	Notes
Vegetables Potatoes	(b) Braised: ham, tongue, duck, quail, pheasant, partridge (not 'au choux' or choucroûte), pigeons Usually served with one or more vegetables. Never cabbage and rarely root vegetables In finer style, for example château, Parisienne, etc. (seldom purée, plain deep-fried, sauté or plain boiled)	The term 'braised' is understood to include baked ham, etc., and the poultry and the game served 'aux raisins', 'aux olives', etc., in fact all the dishes other than roasts
6 Sorbet	A light sherbet ice, flavoured with a liqueur or champagne. Russian cigarettes offered. At a function, the first speech is sometimes given during this course	Perhaps an anachronism on modern, shorter menus but occasionally offered on long banquet menus
7 Roast Salad	Roasted: feathered and ground game and poultry served with all its adjuncts. Grouse, partridge, pheasant, snipe, woodcock, guinea fowl, wild duck, plovers, teal, widgeon, venison, saddle of hare, chicken, turkey, duck, goose The compound salads or a plain salad	*Never* butcher's meat, except perhaps a fillet of beef, saddle of lamb or veal. The roast is always served with a salad, never with vegetables and potatoes separate
or Grills on à la carte menus only	Served with a fried potato and salad and/or vegetable.	
8 Cold dish	Cold: mousses, mousselines, terrines, timbales, soufflés Foie gras: pâtés, aspics, parfaits, timbales Poultry: in aspic (sometimes) Cold: asparagus, seagulls' eggs	
9 Hot dish (entremets de légumes or special savoury item)	(a) Vegetable: asparagus, globe artichokes, seakale, aubergine, broccoli spears. (b) Truffles, bone marrow (c) Delicate savoury soufflés (sometimes)	
10 Sweet	Hot:soufflés, pancakes, fritters Fruit: condes, savarins, créoles, 'en surpise' liqueured, flambé Cold: soufflés, baked ice cream, bombes, biscuit glacé, coupes, accompanied by Petits fours, friandises, frivolities, etc.	Less common at formal dinners Often garnished with fruit

Order of courses	Dishes available		Notes
11 Savoury		Toasts and canapés: Baron, Diane, mushroom, haddock, Welsh rarebit, sardine, Scotch woodcock, etc.	All served hot
		Tartlettes: savoury fillings, quiche Lorraine, etc.	All served hot
		Fondues and fried cheeses	
		Savoury soufflés	
12 Cheeses	(a)	All types of cheese	Not usually offered
	(b)	with celery, radishes, endive, watercress	at formal dinners
	(c)	and biscuits	
13 Dessert		All fresh fruits and nuts	Often named and priced separately on à la carte menus
14 Coffee		Often named after the country of origin (for example Mocha) or method of infusion (filtré or double)	

Note

Grills, farinaceous and egg dishes

Grills above are indicated for à la carte menus only but farinaceous and egg dishes are excluded, yet all three are included in some à la carte dinner menus (particularly grills). This remains a matter of customer choice. But for formal dinners, such dishes should be disregarded entirely.

Entrées and relevés

There is often confusion about the difference between entrées and relevés. Entrées are invariably single portioned items and lighter than relevés which are larger pieces that need to be carved into portions.

Combination of courses

A dinner menu may consist of many courses (we have already noted Oscar of the Waldorf's ten), but is usually only four, five or six. Likely combinations are:

3 courses Choose from 1, 2, 3 and 4, 5, 7 and 10 .

4 courses Choose from 1, 2 and 3 and 4, 5, 7 and 10 , 11;

or 1, 2, 3 and 4, 5 and 7 and 10 , 11.

5 courses Choose from 1 and 2 and 3 and 4, 5, 7 and 10 , 11, 12;

or 1, 2 and 3 and 4, 5 and 7 and 10 , 11, 12;

or 1, 2, 3 and 4, 5 and 6 and 7 and 10 , 11, 12;

or/and 2 and 3 and 4, 5, 7 and 10 , 11, 12.

6 courses Choose from 1 and 2 and 3 and 4, 5 and 7 and 10 , 11, 12;

or 1, 2 and 3 and 4, 5 and 6 and 7 and 10 , 11, 12;

or 1, 2 and 3 and 4 and 5 and 7 and 10 , 11, 12;

or 1, 2 and 3 and 4, 5 and 7 and 8, 9 and 10 , 11, 12.

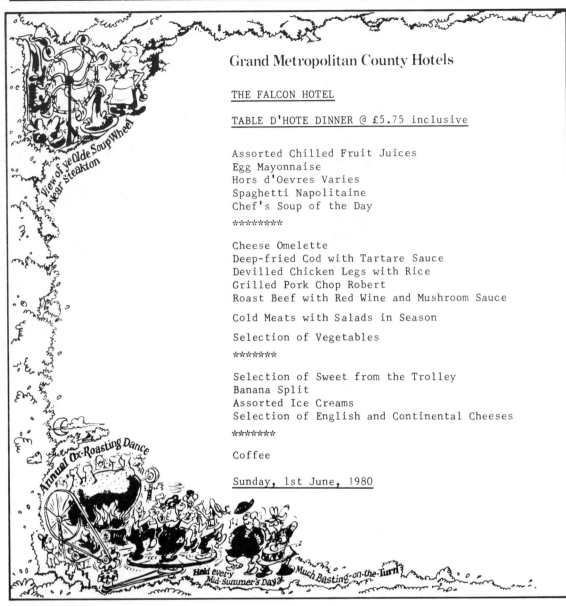

Grand Metropolitan County Hotels

THE FALCON HOTEL

TABLE D'HOTE DINNER @ £5.75 inclusive

Assorted Chilled Fruit Juices
Egg Mayonnaise
Hors d'Oevres Varies
Spaghetti Napolitaine
Chef's Soup of the Day
****

Cheese Omelette
Deep-fried Cod with Tartare Sauce
Devilled Chicken Legs with Rice
Grilled Pork Chop Robert
Roast Beef with Red Wine and Mushroom Sauce

Cold Meats with Salads in Season

Selection of Vegetables
****

Selection of Sweet from the Trolley
Banana Split
Assorted Ice Creams
Selection of English and Continental Cheeses
****

Coffee

Sunday, 1st June, 1980

An example of a dinner menu

Supper menus

Recherché suppers with carefully composed short menus are somewhat out of fashion. Suppers of that kind were a mixture of late dinner for those who had not yet dined and a lighter meal for those who dined early (for example, pre-theatre).

Today, supper menus are usually à la carte, with a customer choosing as many or as few dishes as desired. Only occasionally will there be found a set supper menu.

At suppers there are fewer courses. Dishes are lighter than those served at dinner (except, of course, at supper balls which are considered in Chapter 8).

Table 14 *Supper menu – sequence of dishes*

Order of courses	Dishes available	Notes
First course	(a) Cocktails: particularly shellfish (b) Delicacies: caviar, oysters, seagulls' eggs, snails, potted shrimps, etc. (c) Smoked: salmon, trout, ham, salami, sausage (d) Consommé and consommé base soups, particularly turtle and soupe à l'oignon	
Second course	Fish: deep poached: salmon and particularly smoked haddock dishes hot shellfish: the lighter dishes only fried: whitebait, scampi, sole (sometimes) grilled: kippers, salmon, sole (sometimes) Entrées: the sautés as at dinner (not hare) but with simpler garnishes. Calves' liver, minced chicken dishes Roasts: very seldom, and then the smaller birds like quail, woodcock, snipe Grills: all grilled meats including chicken and kebab and other skewered grills, kidneys	Crabs rather than lobster Kippers particularly in the early hours of morning Grills particularly featured at supper
Served with vegetables	Where applicable, but most supper dishes of fish, well-garnished entrées or grills do not require a dish of vegetables to accompany them	
and potatoes *or* Cold Buffet	Most varieties are served but frequently fried kinds for grills Cold fish: salmon, lobster, trout, crab, prawns Cold meat: all the cold joints and poultry, game, pies,	
served with salad	terrines Most varieties of salad	
Third course Sweets	Hot: soufflés, pancakes, fritters Cold: soufflés, bombes, biscuit glacé, fruit coupes (perhaps accompanied by petits fours, friandises, etc.)	
Savoury	All varieties served	As for dinner
Cheese	All varieties served	As for dinner
Dessert	As for dinner	
and Coffee	**Always served**	

Normally, set supper menus consist of three courses only, with many choices in the second or main course. (See Table 14.)

À la carte menus may include egg dishes (particularly bacon and egg) when 'informal' and consumed some time after supper meal time, towards the end of a floor show or during dancing.

To judge menus in a commercial context they should be regularly seen in actual hotel and catering establishments. For catering staff who are not able to seek out menus from other catering establishments in this way, there is a regular feature (and has been for many years) in the weekly trade paper *Caterer & Hotelkeeper*.

This provides a wide selection of menus each week. The feature includes informed editorial comment. Other trade papers also frequently reproduce menus of interest.

The few menus that are included in this section are intended merely to indicate the general shape and structure of different types of menus rather than to be regarded as comprehensive coverage of all menu-making possibilities.

Dating menus

A breakfast menu is usually dated only for special parties or events. Table d'hôte luncheons, dinners and suppers which change daily should always bear the date. This is usually printed or typed at the bottom right-hand corner.

The foregoing notes on menu making are intended to provide a basis for understanding the menu as a key element in catering and specifically to aid service staff in guiding guests as may be required. Chapters 9 and 10 , on cookery, food style and terminology, provide further details for waiters to support the fundamental factors involved in composing menus.

Notes on examples
Reproducing menus that are printed on large double cards (300 mm x 450 mm (12 in x 18 in or more when opened) pose printing problems in a book. Some of the operations from which samples have been taken earlier in this chapter have more elaborate menus of this sort. It is not thought appropriate to include a vast variety of menu examples for such reasons but also because prices in a period of inflation soon make menus appear dated. Menus from actual operations cannot be reproduced in the fashion in which they are originally presented, on cards, coloured covers, etc., but otherwise dish naming, typographical style (use of capital letters, accents, etc.) follow the original rather than reflect the author's own ideas.

---

8 Function menu making

Menus feature importantly before a function is sold (see Chapter 17). To achieve sales, costed and priced menus are prepared (constantly revised and replaced) and incorporated into function prospectuses or other sales literature mailed or handed to prospective customers. (Examples may be found on pages 201 – 3.)

Because they are fixed menus with little or no choice, function menus also illustrate the sequence and build-up of a meal and its courses.

Luncheons

Not all functions are banquets. Luncheons and suppers may be quite light, and luncheons frequently resemble a shorter and lighter dinner, for functions rarely, if ever, feature such dishes as pasta, eggs or the more commonplace midday entrées. A luncheon menu for a function could include the different courses which are listed in Table 15.

Table 15 *Luncheon dish sequence*

Order of courses	Dishes available		Notes
1 First course		Cocktails, fruit, delicacies, hors d'oeuvre, soups	As listed under luncheon*
2 Fish	(a) (b) (c) (d) (e)	Deep-poached salmon, turbot Shallow-poached prime fish Hot shellfish Meunière, fried, grilled Cold fish (for example aspic, chaud-froid)	 As at dinner** As at dinner As at dinner
3 Main course	(a) (b) (c) (d) (e) (f)	Entrées Butcher's meat, boiled Poêlés, braisés Game: salmis or roast Roasts: butcher's meat as well as those listed for dinner Grills (rarely)	As listed for dinner** Fresh or salted As listed for dinner**
Vegetables and potatoes		Served with the main course dishes as for dinner	
4 Cold buffet		As served for luncheons with the occasional cold dish listed at number 9 in the dinner sequence dishes	Served with various salads

continued

Order of courses	Dishes available	Notes
5 Vegetable dish or cold dish	As listed under lunch* As listed under dinner**	
6 Sweet	As listed for dinner** as well as those listed under lunch* with the exception of hot puddings and milk puddings	
7 Cheese	All varieties accompanied with celery, etc., and biscuits	
Dessert	Sometimes	
Coffee	As usual	

*See Chapter 7, page 89
**See Chapter 7, page 93

Table 16   *Dish sequence for seated and served wedding breakfast*

Order of courses	Dishes available
1 First course	Select dishes from the dinner** sequence (first course) and/or soup (2)
2 Second course and/or	(a) Select from any of the cold fish dishes (dinner**) (b) Select from the hot deep or shallow-poached fish or shellfish
3 Third course	(a) Select from cold meats and aspics (b) Select from dinner** entrées (4) though large numbers will preclude most of the sautés (c) Poêlés or braisés (dinner** 5) (d) Roasted poultry, sometimes game but seldom butcher's meat (e) Select from cold dishes (dinner** 8) Served with appropriate vegetables, potatoes and/or salad
4 Sweet course	(a) Select from dinner sweets with emphasis on fruit and ice cream dishes
5 Savoury or cheese	Seldom served
6 Coffee	

**See Chapter 7, page 93.

Wedding breakfasts

The term breakfast continues to be attached to the wedding meal though it is often simply luncheon. Menus are composed as for a served, seated meal but in less formal style than for banquets, and lighter and shorter than for dinner. Often a running buffet may be provided (see buffets on page 102).

When a buffet rather than a sit down meal is served, the menu is either of the same pattern as for light buffets, with perhaps a fork dish included, or as for supper balls.

A wedding cake is always centrally featured. Arrangements must be made to portion and distribute this quickly after the initial 'official' cutting. The wedding cake is not listed on the menu.

Apéritifs are served on arrival and sometimes (after nuptial mass) tea and coffee may be requested.

Meeting wedding demand

If a heavier wedding breakfast is required this may be based on the ball supper menu (see page 103) omitting hot soup (1), savouries (4), canapés (5) and soup on leaving (12).

In addition to general function order forms and prospectuses, a form specifically to agree menu and other details for a wedding reception may be devised. An example is included in Chapter 17 on page 205.

Thus for wedding breakfasts, most operators will offer a range of luncheon menus.

Buffets

Light, fork and supper or cold buffets may be provided for a variety of occasions. Light buffets can be displayed for self-service, or alternatively for guests served at tables.

Light buffet menu

Dishes need not be served all at the same time but can follow a sequence of:

1 *Hot savoury pastry* Patties (lobster, chicken etc.), sausage rolls and other savoury pastry.
2 *Hot sausages* Chipolata, bacon rolls, etc., served on sticks.
3 *Savoury finger toasts* To include any of the cold canapés.
4 *Sandwiches, bridge rolls* Always cut small with fillings such as smoked salmon, salad, ham, tongue, chicken, etc.
5 *Sweets* Charlottes, jellies, trifles, bavarois, etc. Fruit salad, fresh raw fruits (strawberries) with fresh cream. Ice creams (various flavours) but not as a rule coupes glacés. Pastries, gâteaux, biscuits.
6 *Beverages* Coffee, tea, fruit cup, punch bowl, iced coffee.

Fork luncheon

Fork buffets or fork luncheons permit individual pieces of fish, meat, game or poultry to be served providing they can be eaten by a guest (usually standing and holding a plate in one hand) with a fork only.

Most of the light buffet dishes listed can be included and soft items such as chicken or ham mousse, galantine, terrine, mayonnaise of fish, etc., cut up chicken and other meats accompanied by salads prepared in small pieces.

A fork meal may open with a fruit or shellfish cocktail, consommé en tasse (in a cup), followed by such luncheon items as, say, mayonnaise of salmon or hot savoury pastry, and then followed by a main meal course. Any sweets from those listed for light buffets may complete the meal.

Ball supper

Supper balls usually begin at a late hour. Dishes are not necessarily served by course nor taken in sequence when guests help themselves. Nevertheless, printed menus follow a pattern usually in the form shown in Table 17.

FORK BUFFET MENUS

MENU 1

Grapefruit and Tangerine Cocktail
Cold Leek and Potato Soup
*
Cold Wing of Chicken in Aspic
Mixed Salads
*
Syllabub and Lemon Ice
*
Coffee
_____

MENU 2

Prawn Cocktail
Grapefruit Cocktail
*
Cold Spring Chicken
Sugar Baked Gammon
Cold Roast Sirloin of Beef
*
Potato Salad
Mixed Salad   Beetroot Salad
Coleslaw, Sweetcorn
*
Sherry Trifle and Cream
*
Coffee
_____

MENU 3

Liver Pâté
Cheese and Bacon Flan
*
Hot Rib of Beef
Jacket Potato with Chive and Cream Dressing
*
Cold Lamb Cutlets in Aspic
Cornets of Ham
*
Mixed Salads   Salad Waldorf
French Beans, Tomatoes, Olives Salad
Potato Salad
*
Fruit Band with Fresh Cream
*
Coffee

MENU 4

Prawn Cocktail
Cold Asparagus Soup
*
Assorted Cold Meats
Mixed Salads
*
Profiteroles with Chocolate Sauce
Fruit Salad and Cream
*
Coffee
_____

MENU 5

Chilled Melon
Cold Clear Soup
*
Cold Salmon Mayonnaise
Mixed Salads
*
Raspberry and Redcurrant Compôte
Cream Caramel
*
Coffee
_____

MENU 6

Melon Cocktail
Potted Shrimps
*
Roast Turkey, Game Chips, Bread Sauce
Beef Wellington
*
Potato Salad
Beetroot
Mixed Salads
*
Chocolate Gâteau and Cream
Danish Pastries
*
Coffee

*These Menus are not interchangeable
unless by arrangement

Figure 28   *Examples of fork buffet menus*
These examples are Trusthouse Forte Hotel menus

Table 17 *Ball supper menu*

Item		Dishes available
1	Soup	Hot turtle or soupe à l'oignon or cold consommé (Madrilène). As it is the only hot dish served, soup is often offered as guests enter the supper room, or is served at tables by waiters. Other items are set on the buffet table for self-service
2	Appetizers	Melon, oysters, prawns
3	Fish appetizers	Smoked salmon, trout, ham, eels, etc.
4	Savouries	Chicken, lobster, crab, salmon patties (seldom included), chipolatas, bacon rolls, etc.
5	Canapés	Canapés Moscovite, savoury finger toasts
6	Fish	Cold or mayonnaise of lobster, salmon, dressed crab, aspics of turbot, blue trout, fillets of sole, etc.
7	Meats	Aspics, chaudfroids, decorated or cold chicken, turkey, ham, galantine, duck, game, tongue, beef, cutlets, etc. Raised pies, mousses, cornets, etc., foie gras
8	Salads	Lettuce, Russian, potato and a variety of mixed salads
	Bridge rolls	When filled bridge rolls are served (which is seldom), they are printed here. Rolls served with butter as an accompaniment to the meal are not, of course, listed
9	Cold sweets	Charlottes, jelly, trifle, bavarois, creams, mousse, condés, flans, French pastries, gâteaux, fruit salad and raw fruits
10	Ices	Various bombes, biscuit glacé with or without fruit. Petits fours, friandises
11	Beverage	Coffee, tea, iced coffee and tea, punch bowl, fruit cup
12	En partant (on leaving)	Most popular of several possible items is hot soup served on leaving. Service may be in the foyer where guests already dressed to go home may sip hot double consommé or turtle soup.
		Soupe à l'oignon (probably the most popular of the three soups), may be served at tables because a soup spoon is needed. Other dishes on leaving are simple breakfast items like bacon and egg or kippers.

Dinners

Grand dinners with several courses afford opportunity to compile menus which take gastronomic principles into account including colour and flavour balance, building to a climax, matching food with wine, and the other fundamentals outlined in Chapter 7. Nevertheless, while menus of this kind can be constructed to meet customers' requirements, and in consultation with them, many dinner menus can be pre-selected to meet commercial as well as gastronomic criteria and suited to an operation's own labour force and physical resources.

The possibilities in dinner menu compilation were indicated in Chapter 7.

BANQUET IN THE GRAND STYLE

les huîtres impériales
ou
les joyaux de la Volga en barquette
Persryba - Malossol

———

Gewurztraminer-vieille chapelle
1937
le bisque d'écrevisses

———

les oeufs "Zingara"

———

la truite de la Lesse aux amandes grillées

———

château Calon Ségur, mise
du château, 1939
le médaillon de veau à la Chimay
pommes Dauphine

———

les primeurs de lamines flots d'or

———

Musigny 1939   le délice de foie gras de Strasbourg au porto

———

magnum Pommery brut,
1929
les oranges glacées, givre de la citadelle

———

la tarte namuroise

———

le moka "Casino"

An example of a grand dinner menu

Menu pricing

Although some of the sample menus have prices integrated, inflation and commodity, labour and other cost fluctuations can quickly make quotations outdated. Hence a common device is to code menus by numbers or letters and append a separate price list.

A menu's link with service

As an important part of an operation's sales literature menus are integrated into function sales leaflets, brochures or packs.

Menus are not only part of the offer or a feature of a function department's 'shop window' but also a blue print for production and service. Examples have been chosen from real operations. Many more could be and should be sought out by readers, as was suggested in Chapter 7.

Moreover, this chapter, with the few samples included, should be read in conjunction with Chapter 17 in which other aspects of function catering and service are considered.

9 Food and menu terms

Composing menus is, as Chapter 7 indicates, a managerial task of enormous commercial significance. Whether or not chefs, food and beverage managers or maîtres d'hôtels are involved in drafting a menu, they must all regard an operation's menus in policy, profit, marketing and operational terms.

From an establishment's menu, guests make their own personal choice. Customers, therefore, are involved in composing their own menus whether for a meal in a restaurant for one or two, or when arranging a private party or function for many more. It is in counselling during customer selection, and in helping to merchandise a menu that head waiters and waiters as sales staff are especially important.

Terminology

Whatever the type of menu (à la carte, table d'hôte, etc.), a waiter should be familiar with all the dishes on it, know their composition and should have memorized them. He should have an appreciation of how courses are linked and combined in order to make acceptable suggestions to guests if required. Moreover, he will often be required to comprehend (and then explain to customers) menu expressions, particularly French ones. Words for food and methods of cookery included, and menu jargon listed, in this chapter are intended to constitute a basis for this knowledge.

However, some aspects of food and cookery knowledge have little to do with fashion or style. For instance, a waiter should know how much time will elapse between ordering a particular dish and when it is served; when certain foods are in season; basic modes of cooking and the meaning of more common French menu terms. The most essential words are those for the commonest items of food (for example, meats, cuts, vegetables, etc.), chief styles of cooking (boiled, grilled, etc.) and modes of dressing or garnishing.

Chefs in naming dishes now in the 'classical' répertoire were themselves French or were influenced by the fact that professional cookery of the Western World evolved in France. The traditional culinary code is fundamentally a French one. Some kinds of preparations may be simple peasant style (à la paysanne), others bourgeois (à la bourgeoise) or linked with the hunting field (chasseur). Many dish styles were named after particular people, kings, artists, etc. (for example Henri IV, Rossini, Melba); others for kinds of people, à la reine (queen), à la princesse (princess); after places (perhaps where the food flourished, for example Argenteuil (for asparagus); after battles (Marengo and Crécy); or even after the inventor chefs or their places of work (for example Reform (from the Reform Club) or Carême (after the great Regency chef)). Further examples are listed in Chapter 10 .

Designation

Whatever the language in which it is written, a menu's description provides at least some information of a dish such as:

Cut (of meat, poultry, fish, etc.)   For example fillet, cutlet, shoulder.

Main commodity   For example beef, pheasant, turbot, etc.

Form   For example rolled, boneless, diced, sliced.

Cooking style   For example roast, grilled, poached.

Quality or grade   For example prime, young, spring.

Origin   For example Southdown (lamb), Tay (salmon), Pauillac (lamb).

Essential, important or key ingredient/garnish   For example 'with mushrooms'.

Presentation or service style   For example 'en brochette' (on skewer), individual (for example chicken pot pie).

If a menu is in French, then knowledge of the following kinds of French words is needed:

Basic food   For example boeuf (beef), merlan (whiting), potage (soup).

Cuts, joints, form   For example filet (fillet), épaule (shoulder), émincé (minced).

Cooking style   For example sauté ('jumped' in shallow fat or shallow fried), frit (fried), à l'huile (with oil), au beurre (with butter).

Garnish, shape and cut   For example macédoine (dice), julienne (fine strips).

National style   For example à la française (French style), à l'anglaise (English style).

'Association' words   For example santé (health, that is, purée vegetables in soup), cultivateur (again vegetables from 'the cultivator of the soil'), including regional, geographic associations: Périgord (truffles), Chantilly (whipped cream), Florentine (spinach).

Chefs' names   For example Carême, Vatel, Escoffier.

Historical association   For example Marengo (chicken and crayfish dish invented after the battle), Crécy (carrots).

Patrons   For example Tallyrand (patron of Carême), Melba, Bernhardt, La Belle Otéro, (ladies after whom Escoffier named dishes). Or gourmets like: Colbert, Richelieu. Writers, artists, composers or other notable people honoured by dishes named for them like: Arnold Bennett, Rossini, Meyerbeer.

'House' speciality   À la maison (in the style of the house), au façon du chef (in the chef's style) or in the style of particular and famous chefs or particular establishments such as Reform (club), Waldorf, Delmonico.

An English example of a simple informative menu style is, therefore:

Roast sirloin of Aberdeen Angus beef with Yorkshire pudding.

A French example is:

Filet de plie frit à l'anglaise, sauce tomate (fried fillet of plaice English style (egg and crumbed) with tomato sauce).

Cookery style

The style of cooking (for example roast (rôti), grilled (grillé), etc.) is an important element in the menu description of a dish, but for convenience, cooking information for waiting staff is covered in Chapter 10.

Menu language

Many menus in English speaking countries today are written in English. This is sensible when dishes and their range are of our own tradition. The various tourist boards in Britain encourage the development of menus written in our own language and it is likely that the practice will continue to spread. Moreover, even when menus are written in French (or feature dishes in other foreign languages) many establishments provide an English translation or explanation.

Nevertheless, waiters still encounter French menus especially in higher priced operations. The other chapters in Part Two indicate some of the complexities in using French on menus. There are also several textbooks providing aid in the use of French in catering generally and on menu terminology in particular.

The information which follows is not intended to replace such textbooks but rather to enlarge a waiter's menu understanding. The vocabulary sections include words likely to be encountered by waiters in high priced restaurants.

Courses considered

The following items are listed course by course, section 1 listing the foods encountered. Sections 2, 3 and 4 indicate the styles of presentation.

Hors d'oeuvre or appetizer course

1 Names of items
Anchois Anchovies.
Anguille fumée Smoked eel.
Artichauts (fonds d'artichauts) Globe artichokes (artichoke bottoms).
Betterave Beetroot.
Canapés à la russe Russian canapés, that is, assorted dainty open sandwiches: round, rectangular, diamond shaped, etc. of for example, caviar, foie gras, sardines, smoked salmon.
Cantaloup frappé (au porto) Chilled cantaloup melon (with port wine).
Caviar The slightly brined roe from the sturgeon, from three types of fish: Beluga, largest grain from dark grey to pale bluish; Ocietrova (the true sturgeon) smaller steel-grey grain; and Sevruga, smallest grain of dark-green to black. To all three may be added (when correct) the term malossal, meaning best quality.
Céleri-rave Celeriac.
Champignons Mushrooms.
Charcuterie Cold sausage, smoked ham, etc.
Cornets (De jambon fumé, de saumon fumé, etc.) Cornets (of smoked ham, smoked salmon, etc.) usually filled.
Cornichons Pickled gherkins.
Crevettes grises Shrimps.
Crevettes roses Prawns.
Délices à la russe Assorted pastry barquettes (oval tartlets) filled with cold, dressed meat and fish preparations.
Escargots Snails.
Foie gras Goose fat liver: *au nature* – plain, untruffled (used in cooking, for example for tournedos Rossini); *pâté de foie gras en croûte* – pâté of foie gras cooked in pastry (usually with truffles when designated pâté de foie gras truffée en croûte); *suprême de foie gras truffée* – the liver in aspic with truffles; *terrine de foie grass (truffée)* – prepared as pâté in earthenware terrine (with truffles).

Harengs, filets de Herring fillets. *Bismarck* – pickled in white vinegar; *au vin blanc* – pickled in white wine; and *fumé* – smoked packed in oil.
Huîtres Oysters.
Jambon Ham.
Jambon de Bayonne, de Parme Bayonne ham and Parma ham are varieties of smoked ham.
Pamplemousse Grapefruit.
Pâté Paste, hence pâté de foie gras, goose liver paste or pâté maison, pâté in 'the style of the house'.
Radis Radishes.
Riz Rice
Rollmops Herrings pickled in white vinegar, rolled and skewered.
Salami Italian variety of sausage.
Saucisson Cold sausage
Saumon fumé Smoked salmon
Thon Tuna or tunny fish.
Tomates Tomatoes.
Truite fumée Smoked trout.

2 Styles and terms in hors d'oeuvre course
À l'huile With oil.
Barquette Boat-shaped pastry tartlet often filled with savoury items such as fish roe, mousse, etc.
Bouchée Small puff paste case usually with savoury filling.
Canapé Small bread slice, toasted or fried, garnished with savoury items served hot or cold (also at savoury course when hot).
Carolines Small choux paste buns with savoury filling.
Grecque, à la Greek style (that is, rice with pimento, raisins).
Strasbourgeoise Strasbourg-style (for pâté de foie gras).

Soups (potages) course

1 Names for soup items
Bisque Thick soup, normally fish especially shellfish.
Bortsch Russian (or Polish) broth served with soured cream, beetroot juice, pirogs (little

dumplings).

Bouillabaisse   Stew-like fish soup from South of France.

Bouillon   Broth.

Chowder   American potato soup, normally incorporating fish.

Consommé   Clear soup.

Crème   Cream soup.

Croûte   Crust.

Croûte au pot   Clear soup garnished with croûtes.

Croûton   Sippet of fried bread.

Fausse tortue   Mock turtle.

Minestrone   Italian, tomato-flavoured broth, heavily garnished with vegetables, Italian pasta. Served with grated Parmesan cheese as accompaniment.

Petite marmite   Small earthenware pot which gives its name to the clear, strong garnished consommé served in it.

Potage   Any thick soup, for example potage de santé (health).

Pot-au-feu   Beef and bone broth with vegetable garnish in the French style.

Purée   Soup thickened by its vegetables being sieved.

Soupe à l'oignon   Onion soup.

Tortue   Turtle.

Velouté   Alternative designation for cream soup.

Waterzoi   A stew-like fish soup.

2   Styles and forms of soups

Bonne femme, potage   Leek and onion soup.

Brunoise, consommé   Clear soup, garnished with finely diced vegetable.

Célestine, consommé   Clear soup garnished with fine strips of pancake.

Crécy, crème   Cream of carrot soup.

Faubonne, crème   Butter bean soup.

Jackson, crème   Cream of potato soup.

Julienne, consommé   Clear soup, garnished with fine strips of vegetables.

Palestine, crème   Cream of Jerusalem artichoke.

Parmentier, potage   Potato soup.

Princesse, velouté   Cream of chicken soup.

Vichyssoise   Cold cream potato soup, flavoured with chopped chives.

Luncheon preliminary courses

Italian pasta and rice

1   Names of types

Canneloni   Stuffed type of Italian paste.

Fettucine   Strip-type Italian paste.

Gnocchi   A small paste 'dumpling' of semolina (Italian) or choux paste (French) or potato paste.

Lasagne   A form of Italian noodle.

Macaroni   Tubular forms of Italian paste.

Nouilles   Noodles.

Pilaff   Rice, usually cooked in stock with light garnish.

Ravioli   Stuffed form of Italian pasta.

Risotto   Cooked rice dish, usually accompanied by garnish.

Riz   Rice.

Spaghetti   Finer tubular form of Italian paste.

Tagliatelli   An Italian pasta.

2   Examples of pasta, rice, etc., styles

Bolognaise   With minced meat sauce.

Italienne   Dressed with butter and grated cheese.

Milanaise   With tomato sauce, julienne of ham and tongue.

Napolitaine   With tomato sauce and grated Parmesan cheese.

Parmesan, au   With Parmesan cheese.

Eggs (oeufs)

1   Names of types of cooked eggs

À la coque   Soft boiled in the shell.

Brouillés   Scrambled.

Cocotte, en   Cooked in a small fire-proof dish.

Dur   Hard boiled.

Mollet   Soft boiled without shell.

Omelette   Omelet.

Poché   Poached.

Sur le plat   Baked and served in the same dish.

2   Examples of egg styles

À la reine   En cocotte with cream and diced chicken.

Argenteuil   Soft boiled, shelled with creamed sauce and asparagus tips (Argenteuil denotes asparagus).

Bercy (sur le plat)   With grilled chipolata sausages, tomato sauce.

Chasseur (sur le plat)   With chicken liver and chasseur sauce (q.v.).

Chimay   Hard boiled, duxelle stuffed, coated with Mornay sauce and glazed.

Florentine   On spinach, coated with Mornay sauce and glazed.

3   Omelette garnishes and styles

Aux champignons   Mushrooms.

Aux fines herbes   With chopped herbs (usually parsley predominates).

Aux rognons   Kidneys.

Clamart   Stuffed with peas à la française.

Espagnole   Spanish omelette (served plate-shaped, flat) with onion, tomato, pimento. Garnish, half stoned olive and anchovy strips.

Fish course

1   Names of fish

See also fish listed under foods in season in Chapter 8 and hors d'oeuvre above.

Barbue   Brill.

Blanchaille   Whitebait.

Brandade   Dish of salt cod.

Coquille St. Jacques   Scallop.

Fruits de mer   Literally 'sea fruit', usually denotes an assortment of shellfish.

Goujons   Gudgeons, small fish (see 'cuts' below).

Homard   Lobster.

Laitance   Soft herring roe.

Langouste   Crawfish, spiny lobster.

Limande   Lemon sole.

Merlan   Whiting.

Morue   Salt cod.

Moules   Mussels.

Plie   Plaice.

Rouget   Red mullet.

Scampi   Dublin Bay prawns.

Sole de Douvres   Dover sole.

2   Cuts of fish

Côtelette   Cutlet, a steak of fish cut on the bone (alternative term for tronçon (q.v.)).

Darne   Finest straight cut through middle (usually of salmon and similar large fish) with bone.

Délice   A fillet (of sole or similar fish) folded in two.

Filet   Fillet. Lightly flattened and cooked flat.

Filet en tresses   Fillet (of sole or similar) cut into three but left attached at head and plaited (for frying may be pané (breadcrumbed) for poaching left plain).

Goujons   Cut as gudgeons, that is, thin strips of fillet, usually panéed or flour coated and rolled as cigarettes.

Goujonettes   As goujons but even finer.

Médaillon   A round-shaped portion cut from a large fillet.

Mignon   Fillet of sole (or other fish) triangularly folded as a cornet.

Paupiette   Flattened fillets (of sole or similar fish), rolled up bone-side out with tail on top (often with stuffing inside).

Plié   Fillet folded head and tail under.

Rubané   Ribboned, that is, a large goujon (q.v.) tied in knot.

Suprême   Fillet from large fish e.g. salmon cut into portion pieces.

Tronçon   As côtelette (q.v.).

3   Fish preparations

Colbert   For sole. Whole, skinned, opened and spine extracted, panéed, deep fried.

Colère, en   For whiting, skinned, trimmed of eyes and gills, curled with tail in mouth, pané and deep fried.

Colette   As en colère but with tail through eyes.

4   Examples of fish styles

À l'anglaise   Egg and crumbed and deep fried.

Au beurre noir   With black butter.

Au beurre noisette   With butter heated to nutty stage.

Au bleu   Method of poaching (particularly trout) to give skin a blue tinge.

Bercy   Poached in white wine and fish stock with chopped shallots and parsley, liquor reduced, enriched with butter and glazed.

Bonne femme   In velouté sauce with mushrooms.

Carapace, en   (Of lobsters) in the shell.

Colbert (sole)   Sole slit on one side, with fillets then folded back, crumbed, deep fried and maître d'hôtel butter placed in slit.

Coulibiac (de saumon)   Special dish of salmon cooked in paste.

Dugléré   With white wine sauce, tomato.

Florentine   Poached, dressed on leaf spinach, coated with Mornay sauce and glazed. For example suprême de sole Florentine.

Hollandaise   Plainly poached, served with hollandaise sauce and boiled potatoes. For example darne de turbot hollandaise.

Maître d'hôtel   With maître d'hôtel butter (lemon and parsley, butter).

Meunière   Shallow fried on both sides, garnished with slice of lemon, coated with nut brown butter, lemon juice and parsley, for example filet de sole meunière. (Belle meunière indicates addition of soft roes as garnish.)

Mornay   Poached, coated with cheese sauce and glazed.

Newburg   For shellfish (usually lobster pieces) tossed in butter, flamed in brandy, cohered with cream and egg yolk. Garnish, truffle. Serve with pilaff rice.

Orly   Deep fried and served with tomato sauce, for example filet de sole a l'Orly.

Otero   Paupiette of sole Mornay sauce coated and glazed, served in half baked potato shell.

Saint-Germain   Filleted white fish dipped in butter, bread-crumbed, grilled, served with Béarnaise sauce and noisette potatoes.

Thermidor   For lobster. Served in mustard-flavoured cheese sauce in half-shell.

Véronique   Velouté sauce, garnished with peeled grapes.

Vin blanc (sole, etc.)   In white wine sauce.

Meat course

1   Names for meat, game and poultry and their cuts

(a)   Butcher's meat

Agneau   Lamb. Cuts include: *carré d'* – best end of lamb; *côtellette d'* – *cutlet; épigramme d'* – pressed breast cut into slices; *gigot d'* – leg of lamb; *noisette d'* – boneless small cut equivalent to boned loin chop or cutlet; *selle d'* – saddle of lamb.

Andouille, andouillette   Sausage of pork chitterling type.

Baron of beef   Double sirloin.

Baron of mutton (or lamb)   Saddle with legs attached.

Bifteck   Steak.

Bitok   Minced meat, shaped as tournedos.

Blanquette   White stew of white meat.

Boeuf   Beef. Cuts include: *aloyau de* – sirloin, with bone; *côte de* – rib; *filet de* – fillet of beef.

Boudin   Type of sausage (boudin noir, black pudding).

Carbonnade de boeuf   Type of stewed steak with beer as ingredient.

Carpetbag steak   Large steak (usually double entrecôte) split, stuffed with oysters and sewn.

Cassoulet   Braised dish of meats (usually pork, goose or sausage) with haricot beans.

Cervelle   Brain.

Châteaubriand   Double portion, thick fillet steak cut from 'head' or thick end of beef fillet.

Coeur   Heart, Also used to describe dainty cut of fillet beef, for example coeur de filet.

Côte à l'os   Rib cut beef steak (equivalent to a large cutlet).

Entrecôte   Sirloin steak.

Entrecôte minute   Thin, flattened entrecôte steak.

Escalope   Thin collop of meat usually veal or pork.

Filet mignon   Fillet from saddle of lamb or mutton.

Foie   Liver.

Fricassée   White stew of white meat or chicken.

Hanche de venaison (haunch, of venison)   Half-saddle with leg attached.

Jambon   Ham.

Langue   Tongue.

Médaillon   Medallion, name for smaller collops of meat such as veal or pork.

Mouton   Mutton (see agneau for cuts and joints).

Navarin   Brown stew of lamb or mutton.

Porc   Pork. Cuts include: *cuisse or cuissot de* – leg of pork; *longe de* – loin of pork; *pieds de* – pigs' trotters.

Porterhouse steak or 'T' bone   Prime sirloin steak on bone from the large end of the loin.

Pré salé   Mutton or lamb raised on pasture near sea.

Queue de boeuf   Oxtail.
Ragoût   Stew, usually rich and well-seasoned.
Ris de veau   Calf's sweetbreads.
Rognons   Kidneys.
Rognonnade de veau   Saddle of veal complete with kidneys.
Rosbif   Roast beef.
Saucisse   Sausage.
Tête de veau   Calf's head.
Tournedos   Small round, fillet steak.
Venaison   Venison.

(b)   Poultry and small game
(See also poultry and game listed under foods in season in Chapter 10 .)
Canard   Duck.
Caneton   Duckling.
Civet de lièvre   Jugged hare.
Crapaudine   Split whole (spatchcock) chicken, grilled and dressed to resemble a toad.
Cuisse de poulet   Leg of chicken.
Dindonneau   Young turkey.
Gibier   Game.
Lapereau   Young hare.
Lapin   Rabbit.
Perdreau, perdrix   Partridge.
Pintade   Guinea fowl.
Poussin   Chick.
Salmis   Stew of game.
Volaille   Fowl.

2   Main course styles and garnishes
Alsacienne   With sauerkraut.
Américaine   With grills – bacon, tomato, straw potatoes.
Boulangère   With roast lamb joints – sliced onions and potatoes.
Bouquetière   With mixed, turned (that is, shaped into small olives) vegetables.
Bourgeoise   (With braisés) turned carrots, larddons, and button onions.
Clamart   Artichoke bottoms stuffed with purée of peas, château potatoes (Clamart always denotes peas).
Dubarry   Denotes cauliflower. With, say, noisettes of lamb – cauliflower topped with Mornay and sauce Madère.
Duxelle   A basic preparation of finely chopped shallots and chopped mushrooms used for stuffed vegetables and other purposes.

Favorite   Asparagus, slices of foie gras, slices of truffle. (For noisettes and tournedos.)
Favorite   Quarters of artichoke bottom, celery, small château potatoes (for large joints).
Henri IV   Pont-neuf potatoes and watercress. (For noisettes and tournedos.)
Holstein   Breadcrumbed veal escalope: fried egg, lemon sliver, anchovy fillets.
Jardinière   For joints. Carrots, turnips, French beans, peas and cauliflower coated with hollandaise sauce.
Kiev   For chicken. Suprême stuffed with butter and fried.
King, à la   Diced chicken in cream sauce.
Louisiana   Creamed sweet corn, rice, sweet potatoes, fried bananas. (For chicken.)
Maryland   Segmented fried chicken (egg and crumbed) with banana fritters, sweetcorn pancake, tomato, bacon, croquette potato, horseradish cream.
Milanaise   Julienne of tongue, ham, mushrooms and truffles mixed with spaghetti covered with tomato sauce, grated cheese and butter. (For escalopes.)
Mirabeau   Anchovy fillets, stoned olives, anchovy butter. (For grilled meats.)
Moussaka   A Balkan dish of aubergines stuffed with minced lamb.
Niçoise   With French beans, tomato, château potatoes.
Opéra   (For noisettes and tournedos.) Tartlets filled with sauté chicken liver slices in Madeira sauce. Croustades of duchesse potatoes filled with asparagus heads.
Petit-duc   Tartlets filled with chicken purée mixed with cream, asparagus heads, slices of truffle.
Polonaise   For poussin, stuffed and poêlé-d, topped with chopped egg, buttered breadcrumbs.
Portugaise   Stuffed tomatoes, château potatoes.
Printanière   With mixed spring vegetables garnish.
Provençale   Prepared with a gravy of meat stock, herbs, shallots, mushrooms and, usually, garlic.
Rossini   With tournedos, topping of foie gras collop, truffle slice and Madeira sauce.

Soissonnaise   (For braisés) with haricot beans.

Washington   With poultry, eggs. Sweet corn.

Zingara   Julienne of ham, tongue, mushrooms, truffles, Madeira and tarragon essence (for escalopes).

Vegetables

1   Names of vetegables (légumes)
(See also vegetables listed under foods in season in Chapter 10 .)

Aubergine   Egg plant.

Boutons de Bruxelles   Tiny Brussels sprouts.

Carottes   Carrots.

Champignons   Mushrooms.

Chou   Cabbage.

Choucroûte   Sauerkraut.

Chou de mer   Seakale.

Choufleur   Cauliflower.

Courge (courgette)   Vegetable marrow. (Young marrows, zucchini.)

Cresson   Watercress.

Epinards   Spinach.

Flageolets   Kidney beans.

Laitue   Lettuce.

Macédoine de légumes   Mixed vegetables.

Navets   Turnips.

Navets de suède   Rutabagas, swede turnips or swedes.

Oignons   Onions.

Poireaux   Leeks.

Pommes de terre   Potatoes (see below for modes of serving). Usually abbreviated to pommes, for example pommes château.

Salsifis   Salsify.

2   Place names associated with vegetables
The name of districts where foods are renowned are often used on menus. For example, the following areas within Ile de France give an indication of the presence of a particular vegetable:

Argenteuil   Asparagus (asperges).

Arpajon   Cauliflower (choufleur).

Bagnolet   French beans (haricots verts).

Clamart   Peas (petits pois).

Crécy-sur-Morin   Carrots (carrottes).

Laon   Asparagus (asperges).

Soissons   White beans.

Versailles   Lettuce (laitue).

3   Styles of presenting potatoes
There are well over a hundred methods of cooking potatoes. The following are often found on menus:

Allumettes   Match size, deep fried.

Anna   Sliced, pressed and baked in mould.

Au four   Jacket baked. Cut with cross incision before service.

Berrichonne   Turned and cooked in consommé with chopped onions, bacon and chopped parsley.

Berny   Balls of duchesse (q.v.) incorporating diced truffles, dredged in chopped almonds and deep fried.

Boulangère   Sliced, with sliced onion, stock moistened and baked.

Byron   As macaire but sprinkled with a little cream and grated cheese and gratiné.

Cendrillon   Shaped as a sabot (wooden shoe). Crumbed and deep fried.

Château   Turned to olive size, blanched then roasted in butter.

Chips   Fine round slivers fried in deep fat (as commercial 'crisps').

Crème, à la   Diced potatoes (usually from raw) cooked in milk and butter.

Dauphine   One part choux paste (sugarless) two parts duchesse potato. Shape with oval spoon, deep fry.

Dauphinoise   Sliced raw potatoes, cooked in the oven with milk and grated cheese.

Delmonico   Raw diced potatoes cooked in milk and browned with breadcrumbs.

Duchesse   Purée with egg yolk, then 'piped' through forcing bag.

Elizabeth   Same as duchesse (q.v.) but centre filled with spinach.

En purée   Mashed.

En robe de chambre   Boiled or steamed in jacket.

En robe de champs   Alternative designation (literally in field dress) for en robe de chambre.

Flamande   Shaped as château (q.v.) cooked with small onions and carrots in white stock.

Fondantes   Large egg shaped, cooked in butter and stock with upper surface thus glazed.

Frites   Deep fried or 'French' fried.

Gaufrettes   Lattice-cut, deep fried.

Hongroise Paprika flavoured roundels of potatoes with sweated, chopped onion cooked in consommé. Chopped parsley finish.

Lyonnaise Sautéed with onions.

Macaire Purée from jacket potatoes, shaped like fish cakes and shallow fried.

Maître d'hôtel As à la crème with chopped parsley.

Marquise As duchesse (q.v.) flavoured with tomatoes.

Nature Plain boiled.

Paille Finely cut like straw, deep fried, chiefly for garnishing grills and other dishes.

Parmentier Shaped into cubes, blanched and roasted.

Persillées Steamed or boiled potatoes, tossed in butter with chopped parsley.

Pont-neuf Thick-cut, deep fried.

Provençale Sauté with garlic.

Rissolées Browned in fat.

Soufflées Rectangular slices deep fried twice in order to 'balloon' them.

Vapeur Turned to 'château' (q.v.) size and steamed.

4 Some styles with other vegetables

Au beurre fondu With melted butter.

À la moêlle With poached beef-bone marrow.

Farcis Stuffed, for example tomatoes, artichoke bottoms, etc., (usually with duxelle).

Vichy Carrots cooked in Vichy water and butter until complete evaporation and natural glazing.

5 Salads

A selection of 'classic' salads (with recommended dressings) is included in Chapter 15.

Sweet and dessert course

1 Fruits

Abricot Apricot.

Ananas Pineapple.

Cantaloup Type of melon.

Citron Lemon.

Fraises du bois (fraises des bois) Wood or wild strawberries.

Goyave Guava.

Letchi or litchi Lychee.

Marrons, purées Purée of chestnuts.

Marrons, glacés Candied chestnuts.

Pêche Peach.

Poire Pear.

Pomme Apple.

Raisin Grape.

Reine claude Greengage.

Tutti frutti Italian term for mixed, candied fruits (usually chopped) often served in or with ice cream.

2 Sweet and dessert items

Baba au rhum Yeast leavened light sponge soaked in rum.

Bande de fruits Long, narrow type of fruit flan.

Bavarois Bavarian cream; a cream and egg dessert set with gelatine.

Beignet Fritter.

Bombe (glacée) Bomb or shell shaped ice.

Cardinal With strawberry ice cream and raspberry sauce, sliced almonds for example as in fraises cardinal.

Chantilly Whipped and lightly sweetened fresh cream.

Charlotte russe Bavarois type cream set in mould lined with sponge fingers.

Compôte Stewed fruit, hence compôte d'abricots (stewed apricots).

Coupe Silver or glass stemmed dish for service of composite ice cream dishes.

Crème Cream.

Crème au chocolat Chocolate cream.

Crêpe Pancake.

Eclair A French choux pastry filled with cream or crème pâtissier.

Gâteau Cake.

Kirsch, au With Kirsch liqueur.

Marrons glacés Chestnuts boiled in syrup to become glazed.

Melba, sauce Raspberry purée sauce. Hence pêche or pear Melba – the fruit served with ice cream, Melba sauce and cream.

Meringues (glacées) Sugar and egg white confection with ice cream.

Millefeuilles, gâteau Gâteau of puff paste.

Moka Coffee flavoured, for example glace Moka.

Mousse Similar to bavarois mix with further aeration.

Nesselrode   Denotes presence of chestnuts.

Normande   With apples, for example, crêpes Normande.

Panaché   Mixed, for example glaces panachées, ices of mixed colours and flavours.

Pâtisseries   Pastries.

Poire Hélène   Pear on ice cream with hot chocolate sauce.

Puit d'amour   Ice cream and fruit salad served in timbale (usually topped with spun sugar).

Savarin   Similar mix to Baba but shaped as hollow ring.

Singapore   Denotes presence of pineapple.

Suchard   Denotes the presence of chocolate.

Sucre filé   Spun sugar (boiled sugar, sprinkled to form threads).

Tarte   Tart.

Tourte   Pie (fruit).

Further common menu terms

To complete the waiter's ability to interpret a French menu or understand restaurant jargon he should also be familiar with other words in common menu or restaurant usage, such as:

à la   After the style, or fashion of, for example à la française (French style), à la russe (Russian style), also with (or dressed in) for example à la crème (with or in cream).

à la carte   On the menu (literally card): implies many dishes at different prices for the guest's choice. Normally cooked to order (as distinct from table d'hôte, q.v.).

au   Masculine form of à la (q.v.).

Biscotte   Rusk.

Café   Coffee.

Café au lait   Coffee with milk.

Café double   Double strength coffee for lunch and dinner.

Café noir   Coffee without cream or milk, that is, black coffee.

Carte du jour   Menu of the day.

Chauffe-plats   Sideboard hot-plates.

Couvert   Cover or place setting.

Déjeuner   Lunch.

Demi-tasse   Literally, half-cup, small coffee cup.

Dîner   Dinner.

Entrée   A composed, garnished dish served before the roast or main meat course (or, at luncheon, served as main course).

Entremets   Sweet course (formerly entremets sucrés; as an entremets de légume, separate vegetable course was equally frequently served).

Fromage   Cheese.

Guéridon   Side-table (for service), nowadays may be a wheeled table or cart.

Mise en place   Literally 'put in place' to waiters implies pre-preparation of sideboards, table, restaurant, etc.

Petit déjeuner   Breakfast.

Plat du jour   Special dish of the day.

Réchaud   'Lamp' or small spirit stove for restaurant reheating or cooking.

Souper   Supper.

Table d'hôte   A set meal, usually of several courses, at a fixed, inclusive price.

Timbale   A round deep dish of straight sides.

Vol au vent   Puff pastry case usually filled with diced chicken, fish, etc., dressed in sauce.

Voiture   Carriage or trolley; for example for hors d'oeuvre or pastries.

Wagon   Alternative name for voiture.

Examples of proper names given to dishes

Dishes have been named after hundreds of personalities and the list is being continually extended. The following brief selection is intended only to exemplify the approach to dish naming and to identify a few of the more commonly encountered 'names' attached to dishes which have tended to survive.

Agnès Sorel   Lady favoured by the fifteenth-century King of France, Charles VII.

Albuféra   Spanish town, scene of a French victory in 1812.

Argenteuil   District near Versailles famed for asparagus culture.

Bagration   Russian general killed in the battle of Moscow, 1812.

Béchamel, Marquis de,   Financier and household steward to Louis XIV.

Belle Hélène   Title of Offenbach's light opera.

Bercy   Wine merchants' district of Paris.

Boistelle   Napoleon's chef.

Bourdaloue   A Jesuit preacher of the seventeenth century.

Brillat-Savarin   Eighteenth-century, French gourmet, author of *Physiology du Goût*.

Carême, Antonin   Famed French chef (1784–1833).

Cendrillon   Cinderella, from Perrault's fairy tales.

Chambord   A Loire château, former royal French residence.

Champeaux   A Paris restaurant.

Chantilly   A district in the Oise department of France.

Chateaubriand   French statesman and writer.

Chaucat   Paris restaurant.

Choron   French composer.

Clamart   Market garden district near Paris.

Colbert   Famous financier minister of Louis XIV.

Crécy   District reputed for carrot cultivation.

Dauphine   Title of the wife of the heir to the French throne.

Demidoff   Famous gourmet.

Diane   Goddess of the chase.

Dieppoise   Relates to Dieppe (and its fishery).

Doria   Name of an old Genoa family.

Dubarry, Comptesse   Louis XV's favourite.

Dugléré   Chef of Napoleonic period.

Esau   Jacob's elder brother who in the Bible story sold his birthright for a bowl of soup (hence linked with lentils).

Foyot   Paris restaurant.

Henri IV   King of France (1589–1610) who wished all his subjects to be able to have a 'chicken in the pot'.

Holstein   Nineteenth-century German statesman.

Jackson   Nineteenth-century President of USA.

Jean Bart   French pirate.

Joinville   French prince of royal blood.

Judic   French actress (1850–1911).

Livournaise   From the Italian town (Livourne in French).

Lucullus   Roman general and gourmet.

Macédoine   From Macedonia.

Marengo   Scene of Napoleon's victory in 1800.

Marguery   Paris restaurant.

Melba   Nellie Melba, the Australian-born singer.

Meyerbeer   German composer (1791–1864).

Mirepoix, Duc de   An eighteenth-century Marshal of France.

Montreuil   Seine region famed for peaches.

Mornay   Nicknamed 'Pope of the Huguenots' (1549–1623).

Nantua   Ain district whose streams yield crayfish.

Nimrod   Famed hunter who joined the Babylonian empire.

Nesselrode   Russian statesman of nineteenth century.

Omar Pasha   Turkish general of the Ottoman Empire.

Orly   Former commune in the Seine district.

Parmentier   Agriculturist who introduced potatoes to France in the eighteenth century.

Pompadour   Louis XV's favourite.

Régence   Regency period (in France during Louis XV's minority).

Romanoff   Russian royal family name.

Rossini   Italian composer and gourmet (1792–1868).

Saint-Hubert   Patron saint of the chase.

Saint-Germain   Château near Versailles, centre of market gardening (pea production).

Soubise   Marshal of France in reign of Louis XV.

Thermidor   Name of a month during the French Revolution.

Turbigo   District in Lombardy, Italy.

Viroflay   District in Seine-et-Oise.

Waleska   Polish countess, mistress of Napoleon.

Communication not confusion

The inclusion of the menu terms in this chapter is not intended to imply support for menus written in French but merely recognizes that service staff may still find such information useful. Straightforward menus in English may well 'sell the restaurant product' more effectively than the use of foreign terms or technical jargon. The aim of the menu must always be to communicate, to sell and not to confuse.

10 Cookery as product knowledge

The summary of a chef's work in Chapter 2 indicates how complicated professional cookery may be. To become a competent chef, years of training and experience are required. Service staff in the restaurant itself are not expected to have the same mastery of kitchen and culinary practice as do chefs.

Knowledge and selling

A waiter does, however, as a salesman need to have product knowledge. To support that product knowledge he must understand how his skills as a waiter may be applied to food so as to merchandise it in the best possible way.

In short, waiters should understand those elements of food and cookery that affect their work. This is expressed diagramatically on page 42.

In simpler operations, waiters may never encounter French cooking nor menus written in French. Even in high class hotels, many speciality restaurants no longer offer meals in classic or traditional character. Nevertheless, Western dining has been so influenced by France that the long-standing international restaurant style (which was fundamentally French) persists in many establishments. Waiting staff, therefore, should understand the fundamentals of French service but remain flexible in approach, ready to adapt to new demands both of today's customers and management.

Cooking methods

Experience and study helps a waiter to expand his knowledge of dish designations and food jargon. As a basis, a selection of information about foods, cooking times and terms is provided in this chapter, but readers must appreciate that modes of dressing dishes as codified in the repertoires of 'classic' cookery number many hundreds. A waiter's product knowledge rests on an appreciation of food commodities and how they are cooked.

Common modes

Styles of cooking usually appear on menus in the form of a past participle describing a noun; for example rôti (meaning roasted) is the past participle of rôtir, to roast. It describes gigot (meaning leg) in the phrase: gigot d'agneau rôti. Gigot is a masculine, singular noun, but when rôti has to describe a feminine noun it will change, as French adjectives normally do, by the addition of an e for feminine and s, or both es, for femine plural. Hence, pommes rôties for roasted potatoes.

There will inevitably and correctly be such changes in spelling of such words on menus, but for simplicity, the participles below have been rendered in the simple masculine singular.

Braiser To braise, by oven cooking in enclosed pot. Hence braisé (braised).

Bouiller To boil by immersion in boiling water, stock or other liquid. Hence bouilli (boiled).

Étuver To stew by gentle simmering (often in the food's own juice or a little added liquor). Hence étuvé (stewed).

Frire To deep fry by immersion in hot fat or oil. Hence frit (fried).

Griller To grill or broil, similar to true roasting but for smaller cuts, that is, cooking on gridiron over clear fire (often charcoal, gas or electric radiants). Hence grillé (grilled or broiled).

Pocher To poach by gentle cooking in boiling liquid. Hence poché (poached).

Poêler To pot roast in covered pan on bed of roots. Hence poêlé (pot roasted).

Rôtir To roast, cooking by radiant heat before or over a clear fire. (Today, food is often 'roasted' in the dry heat of an oven.) Hence rôti (roasted).

Sauter To shallow fry (literally to jump or toss) in pan with a smaller quantity of fat or oil. Hence sauté (shallow fried).

En vapeur To cook in steam. Hence vapeur or en vapeur (steamed).

Other styles of cooking or serving
Derivative from the basic styles in the foregoing list are further modes of cooking expressed by French terms.

Ail, à l' With garlic.

Anglaise, à l' In English style, that is, plainly roasted, boiled or fried with simple English accompaniments.

Aspic, en Cold in aspic or jelly.

Broche, à la On the spit, that is, roasted.

Brochette, à la On a skewer, that is, grilled or broiled.

Casserole, en Braised or stewed within an enclosed fire-proof dish.

Cloche, sous Under glass, presented under heat-proof glass dome or bell.

Cocotte, en Cooked in a small oven-proof, glazed dish.

Coquille, en Cooked in shell (usually in a scallop shell).

Croquette Minced, shaped as large corks and fried.

Croustade, en In pastry.

Daube, en Braised and often served in a daubière (covered braising dish).

Diablé Devilled, highly seasoned.

Emincé Minced.

Farci Stuffed.

Fines herbes With finely chopped herbs.

Flambé Flamed (in ignited brandy or other spirit).

Frappé Chilled.

Fricassé White stew of white meats (for example, veal, chicken). Unlike blanquette meat may be left on the bone.

Froid Cold.

Fumé Smoked.

Garni Garnished.

Gelée, en In jelly.

Glacé Glazed or iced.

Gratin, au Breadcrumb-topped and glazed.

Hachi Minced.

Jus, au With its natural juice or liquor.

Maigre, au Without meat, lenten fare.

Meunière Shallow fried (fish) in butter, finished with beurre noisette and squeeze of lemon, garnished with chopped parsley-dabbed sliver of lemon, thread of demi-glace.

Naturel, au In simple or natural style.

Orly, à l' Fried in batter (tomato sauce separately).

Panaché Mixed, for example salad panachée or glace panachée.

Papillote, en Cooked in envelope of greased paper.

Purée, en Mashed or puréed.

Rafraîchi Lightly chilled.

Réchauffé Reheated.

Tasse, en In cup (of consommé).

Terrine, en In earthenware dish (usually a pâté).

Vert-pré With watercress (usually grills).

Common sauces

Garnishes and other elements that affect dish designation are considered later in Part Two.

Cookery is a fundamental element in such garnishing and assembling. Yet perhaps the most important factor in many fine courses is matching the food with an appropriate sauce. A sauce may 'support' food in many ways, for example giving piquancy or sharpness to food (apple sauce with roast pork); or richness (fattiness) to foods lacking fat, for example sauce hollandaise with poached fish, or maître d'hôtel butter (a 'hard' sauce) or sauce Béarnaise with a plainly grilled fillet steak; or elaboration of a dish's flavour through the main ingredients' 'fumet' or essence being blended with wine to give subtlety. Whatever their function, sauces are important elements in cuisine.

Therefore, in higher class establishments waiters need to be familiar with the leading sauces, to understand their function in the menu and how this affects menu designation over a wide range of courses. Table 18 indicates the principal characteristics or ingredients of some of the sauces served with meats, poultry, fish and vegetables.

There are hundreds of sauces in professional cookery but most are from a mere handful of basic or 'mother' sauces.

Table 18   *Basic sauces*

Basic	Secondary basic	Examples of derivatives
Espagnole	Demi-glace	Bordelaise, Robert, charcutière, chasseur, diable, piquante, Madère, Lyonnaise, Périgueux, Reform
Béchamel		Mornay, Soubise
Velouté	Allemande	Hongroise, poulette
Velouté de poisson		Bercy, Normande, vin-blanc
Tomate		Portugaise
Hollandaise	Béarnaise	Mousseline, Choron
Mayonnaise		Tartare, remoulade

Some sauces are clearly destined for service with a particular type of food, for example sauces made from fish stock or fish velouté are to partner fish. Most 'meaty' sauces from Espagnole or demi-glace bases accompany meat or savoury items, but a 'thread' of demi-glace may be used to circle a dish of fish cooked meunière. Thus, divisions are not absolute. Moreover, some sauces, for example hollandaise and its derivatives; mayonnaise and its derivatives can both be used freely with meat, poultry, vegetable, egg and fish dishes.

The groupings below do not imply a rigid pattern, but a common or usual pattern of usage. (Sweet sauces, except those normally accompanying savoury dishes, are dealt with in the section on sweets, puddings and desserts.)

Brown sauces and gravies

Used with meat, poultry and game dishes, these sauces are chiefly derived from espagnole, demi-glace or jus lié (thickened gravy).

Berçy   Chopped shallot and white wine reduction with meat glaze, enriched with butter.

Bordelaise   Demi-glace incorporating red wine, chopped shallot, peppercorn reduction with meat glaze, chopped bone marrow and butter.

Bourguignonne   Demi-glace with Burgundy, chopped shallot, peppercorn reduction. Monté au beurre.

Bigarade   Orange juice and zest blended with jus lié (usually from braised and poêléd ducks).

Bretonne   Non-derivative. Reduction of onion, garlic, white wine with tomato concassé.

Champignons, aux   Demi-glace with mushrooms.

Charcutière   Sauce Robert (q.v.) with gherkin julienne.

Chasseur   Demi-glace with a little tomato sauce garnished heavily with tomato concassé and sliced mushrooms.

Châteaubriand   Demi-glace with white wine reduction, flavoured with mushrooms, tarragon. Maître d'hôtel butter enriched.

Demi-glace   Half-glaze. Refined espagnole (q.v.). The common basic brown sauce.

Diable Derived sauce. Demi-glace with wine vinegar, shallot and peppercorn reduction and added cayenne.

Diane Poivrade (q.v.) with cream.

Espagnole Basic brown sauce, used as 'mother' for others rather than as an accompaniment.

Financière Madère (q.v.) with truffle essence.

Glace (de viande) Glaze (meat). Meat stock reduced to a thick, dark brown, sticky consistency. Other stocks are reduced to produce glace de volaille (chicken glaze), glace de gibier (game) and glace de veau (veal glaze).

Grand veneur Reduction of poivrade (q.v.) and game stock or poivrade thickened with game blood (some cream).

Italienne Demi-glace and tomato sauce with deuxelle and chopped ham.

Jus Juice or gravy hence jus rôti (roast gravy).

Jus lié Thickened gravy.

Lyonnaise Demi-glace with white wine/wine vinegar reduction. Heavily garnished with sliced onion.

Kari Curry sauce.

Madère Demi-glace with Madeira wine.

Marchand de vin Chopped shallots and wine reduction with meat glaze.

Périgourdine Demi-glace with foie gras purée.

Périgueux Sauce Madère (q.v.) with truffle flavouring, garnish chopped truffle.

Piquante Diable (q.v.) with chopped gherkin, capers and fines herbes.

Poivrade Demi-glace with added mirepoix pepper and herb flavouring, red wine reduction. Enriched butter and meat glaze.

Porto, au Port wine-flavoured demi-glace.

Portugaise Non-derivative. Sweated onion, tomato concassé, garlic in veal stock.

Provençale Non-derivative. Oil-sweated chopped shallots and garlic, white wine reduction blended with tomato concassé, fines herbes and enriched with meat glaze and butter.

Régence Truffle flavoured demi-glace.

Reform Blended of poivrade and demi-glace with red wine reduction, red currant jelly. When used with lamb cutlet Reform incorporate julienne of ham, tongue, gherkin, eggwhite, beetroot, truffle.

Robert Demi-glace with white wine reduction, chopped onion, mustard flavour, enriched with meat glaze and butter.

Rouennaise Bordelaise (q.v.) with duck liver pâté.

Salmis Demi-glace with flavouring from game bones, truffle and mushroom essence for use with game.

Tomate Tomato sauce. A non-derivative sauce made from white stock, thickened with blond roux with mirepoix flavouring as base for tomato.

Tortue Tomato flavoured Madère (q.v.) with infusion of turtle herbs.

Venaison Grand veneur (q.v.) with red currant jelly.

Zingara Tomato flavoured demi-glace with julienne of ham, tongue, mushroom and truffle.

White and pale sauces

Savoury white sauces are chiefly made from veloutés (including fish veloutés but see separate list for fish sauces) and Béchamel bases.

Albert Sauce au beurre with grated horseradish, vinegar and mustard.

Albufera Sauce supreme (q.v.) enriched with meat glaze to ivory colour (also called sauce ivoire).

Allemande Reduced veal velouté (q.v.) enriched with mushroom-flavour, egg yolks and cream.

Apple sauce (Sauce aux pommes). Non-derivative. Unsweetened (or very lightly sweetened) apple purée.

Aurore Velouté (usually chicken) tinged with tomato sauce and cream.

Bâtarde* Velouté enriched with egg yolks and butter.

Béchamel Basic white savoury sauce. Onions, clove and bouquet garni infused milk thickened with white roux.

Beurre, au Roux-thickened, seasoned milk enriched with added butter, egg yolk and cream.

Bonnefoy Velouté (chicken) with white wine reduction. Enriched with butter and chopped tarragon.

Bread sauce   English sauce of onion and clove infused milk thickened with white crumbs. Added butter.

Capres, aux   Caper sauce. Mutton velouté with capers and cream. (If for fish use fish velouté or Béchamel.)

Champignons   With mushrooms.

Crème   Béchamel with added cream.

Egg Sauce   Béchamel garnished with chopped hard-boiled eggs. Cream.

Hongroise   White wine and onion and paprika reduction, blended with velouté, strained and enriched with cream and butter.

Ivoire   See Albufera.

Mornay   Béchamel enriched with egg yolks, grated Parmesan and Gruyère and finished with cream. (When used with fish, fish glaze may be added.)

Moutarde   Mustard sauce. Sauce au beurre (or Béchamel) flavoured with English mustard.

Oignons, aux   Onion sauce. Nutmeg flavoured Béchamel heavily garnished with sweated onions.

Paprika   Onion-flavoured veal velouté with paprika and cream.

Persil   Parsley sauce. Butter sauce with chopped parsley added.

Poulette   Allemande (q.v.) with lemon juice, chopped parsley, mushroom liquor and butter.

Smitane   Onion and white wine reduction in tomato-flavoured demi-glace. Cream finished.

Soubise, sauce   Onion purée blended with Béchamel.

Soubise (au riz)   Blend of rice and onion purée, finished with cream and butter.

Soubise tomaté, sauce   Soubise sauce flavoured with tomato and paprika.

Suprême   Chicken velouté enriched with mushroom liquor, cream and butter.

Villeroy   Sauce Allemande with ham and truffle essence.

Fish sauces

Américaine   Tomato sauce blended with lobster butter.

Anchois   Cream sauce anchovy-flavoured.

Berçy   Butter-sweated chopped shallots, white wine reduced and blended with fish velouté.

Cardinal   Fish (lobster) velouté enriched with lobster butter and cayenne butter.

Marinière   White wine fish sauce with fines herbes.

Matelote   As Bordelaise (see brown sauces) with fish glaze and anchovy flavour in place of meat glaze.

Newburg   Butter, cream, egg yolks, sherry.

Normande   Fish velouté with mushroom essence, egg yolk liaison finished with butter and cream.

Vin blanc   At least four styles of preparation but usually fish velouté, white wine reduction finished with egg yolk and butter.

Hollandaise and derivatives

These butter and egg emulsion sauces are widely used with meat (steaks), fish and vegetables. They are served warm *not* hot. Never attempt to make them hot on the lamp or réchaud.

Béarnaise   Hollandaise with tarragon in the vinegar reduction. Garnished with chopped tarragon and chervil.

Béarnaise brune   As above, tinted with meat glaze.

Choron   Béarnaise with added tomato purée.

Divine   As mousseline (see below).

Foyot   Béarnaise with added meat glaze. Top with thread of meat glaze on serving.

Hollandaise   Egg yolk beaten into peppercorn, lemon juice and vinegar reduction with melted butter. Serve warm.

Maltaise   Hollandaise with blood orange juice and grated orange zest.

Mousseline   Whipped cream folded into hollandaise.

Noisette   Hollandaise enriched with beurre noisette.

Paloise   As Béarnaise, substituting mint for tarragon.

Valoise   As Foyot.

The butters

Warm butters
As sauce-like accompaniments with warm dishes.

Beurre fondu Melted butter with the whey strained off and a drop of lemon juice.

Beurre noir Butter well-browned in pan. Add a drop of vinegar, lemon juice and chopped parsley.

Beurre noisette Browned, 'nutty' stage with lemon juice added.

Beurre meunière As noisette with a little chopped parsley.

Cold butters

Used as hard sauces with warm dishes, these compositions are moulded into cylinders of about 25 mm in diameter, chilled and sliced into roundels. Served in sauce boat on mound of broken ice.

Beurre Berçy Blended with chopped shallots and white wine reduction, with diced bone marrow, lemon juice, meat glaze, chopped parsley.

Beurre Colbert Maître d'hôtel with meat glaze and chopped tarragon.

Beurre diable With cayenne, paprika and curry powder.

Beurre échalote With chopped blanched shallots, lemon juice and cayenne.

*Beurre d'homard** Pounded lobster coral, lobster eggs and its creamy material sieved and combined with butter.

Beurre Madras Pinch of curry powder, chopped mango chutney and a pinch of cayenne.

Beurre maître d'hôtel Chopped parsley and lemon juice (hint of cayenne).

Moutarde, de Mustard, cayanne and lemon juice.

Montpelier Purée of blanched parsley, spinach, tarragon, chives and chervil with anchovy fillets.

Cold sauces

The following include cold sauces served with hot dishes as well as those employed with cold buffet items.

---

*Other fish, for example anchovy, smoked herring, soft roes can be similarly made into butters.

Airelles Cranberry sauce. Purée of lightly sweetened cranberries or compôte of cranberries (may also be served hot).

Chaud-froid (white) Velouté or Béchamel with aspic. For coating cold items.

Chaud-froid (brown) Demi-glace with aspic. For coating cold items.

Cumberland English sauce of red currant jelly, port wine, orange and lemon juice, blanched chopped shallots, mustard and julienne of orange.

Raifort Horseradish. Whipped cream blended with grated horseradish with drop lemon, salt and pepper and mustard. (May be extended with white crumbs soaked in milk, squeezed and blended in.)

Ravigote Vinaigrette (q.v.) with chopped shallots, capers, tarragon, chervil, chives and parsley served with hot dishes such as calf's head.

Menthe, à la Mint sauce. English. Chopped mint in slightly sweetened vinegar with lemon juice.

Vinaigrette A basic dressing. Oil, vinegar, mustard, pepper and salt mix. Also used with hot dishes, for example calf's head.

Mayonnaise and derivatives

Mayonnaise is the basic element in the following cold sauces.

Aioli With finely pounded garlic.

Andalouse With tomato purée and chopped pimento.

Cambridge Chopped hard-boiled egg pounded with anchovy fillet, chopped chives, chervil, tarragon blended with mayonnaise, with a chopped parsley finish.

Chantilly Mayonnaise with whipped cream.

Gloucester With sour cream and fennel.

Gibriche Thin tartare (q.v.) often with chopped hard-boiled egg.

Mayonnaise A basic cold emulsion sauce from oil whisked into egg yolks, vinegar, salt, pepper and mustard. Lemon juice finished.

Remoulade Chopped capers, gherkins, anchovy fillets (or anchovy essence) and Dijon mustard added to mayonnaise.

Tartare   Chopped gherkins, tarragon, capers, chervil, chives and parsley in mayonnaise. Common accompaniment to fried and grilled fish.

Tyrolienne   Chopped garlic and shallot sweated in oil with tomato concassé; sieved, cooled and added to mayonnaise. Garnish with chopped parsley.

Verte   Green sauce. Blanched and sieved spinach, watercress, tarragon, chervil and chives blended with mayonnaise.

Vincent   Equal parts sauce verte and sauce tartare.

Common terms for degrees of cooking

The following terms apply especially to grilling:

À point   Medium grilled, just done.

Bleu   Very underdone, that is, charred outside and raw or 'blue' inside.

Bien cuit   Well-cooked.

Flared   As bleu.

Rare   Underdone.

Saignant   Underdone.

Cooking times for à la carte service

Earlier reference has been made in this chapter to the importance of the waiter having an appreciation of how long dishes take to prepare and cook. Many factors (of skill and equipment, for example) may alter time but the following gives some guidance.

Table 19 shows the approximate times that elapse between giving an à la carte order and when it is ready for service to a customer. Both columns (average preparation and time to allow for service) are approximations.*

---

*For further guidance on times and procedures see J. Fuller and E. Renolds, *The Chef's Compendium of Professional Recipes* (Heinemann 1979).

Table 19   *Examples of à la carte dish service times*

Item	Preparation style	Average preparation and cooking time (minutes)	Time to allow for service (minutes)
Soups: consommé (clear) crème (thick)		variable	10
Eggs	au plat or omelette		5– 8
	cocotte		6–12
	fried, fried with bacon	5	10
	scrambled		8–12
Fish	fried, grilled meunière	10	10–15
	poached (portions; not whole large fish such as salmon or turbot)	15	15–20
Grills:	according to thickness and degree of cooking:		
	underdone	7	10
	medium	12	15
	well-done	15	20
lamb cutlets (côtelettes d'agneau)		5	10
lamb chops (chops d'agneau)		10–12	15

Item	Preparation style	Average preparation and cooking time (minutes)	Time to allow for service (minutes)
mutton chops		10–15	15–20
steaks, rump or point		5–10	15
steaks, fillet		5–10	15
steaks, Chateaubriand		15–20	25
pork cutlet (côtelette de porc)		15	20
veal cutlet (côtelette de veau)		15	20
Sautées:	again according to thickness and degree of cooking		
calf's liver (foie de veau)		10	15
escalopes, noisettes, sautées (dry shallow fried)		10	15
kidney sautés (finished in sauce or jus)		15	20
Poultry:			
spring chicken (poussin)	roast	15–25	30
poulet de grain (small two-portion chicken	roast	20–30	35–40
chickens (larger)	roast	60 (up)	75
	grilled	20–25	25–30
	en cocotte	35	40
	wing fillet (supreme de volaille)	15	20
duckling 1⅓ kg (3 lb)	roast	50	60
duck 1¾ kg (4 lb)	roast	60–75	65–85
guinea fowl	roast	45	55
Game:			
wild duck	roast	15–20	20–25
	for à la presse		12
pheasant	roast	35–45	50
grouse	roast	20–25	30
partridge, young	roast	15–25	20–30
quails	roast	10	15
snipe	roast	10–15	15
Pasta:			
spaghetti	in butter or tomato sauce		15
macaroni			
Potatoes	fried (pommes frites): blanching	5	
	finishing	1	2
	mashed (pommes en purée)		18
	sautées		20
Soufflés	cooked only (mixture ready)	20–25	25–30
Tomatoes	grilled	6	8
Omelettes surprise:			
omelette norvegienne	cooked only (mixture ready)	5–7	
baked Alaska	setting/browning	2	10

When microwave ovens, infra-red or radar range equipment is installed the cooking times given do not apply.

A customer ordering à la carte often states his requirements well in advance of the meal so that the kitchen has adequate time in which to prepare the dishes.

Foods in season

The statement that certain foods are 'in season' implies that they are served only at that time of the year, for example in Britain grouse is first shot on 12th August and the oyster season opens on 1st September. Development of deep freezing and cold storage facilities, however, have considerably lengthened seasons for many foods.

Fish

Oysters (huîtres)	September–April
Mussels (moules)	September–April
Mackerel (macquereau)	April–October
Salmon, Scotch (saumon d'Ecosse)	
	February–August
Salmon (English)	March–September
Salmon trout (truite saumonée)	
	March–September
River trout (truite)	April–September
Sole (sole); cod (cabillaud); whiting (merlan); haddock (aigrefin (alt. aiglefin)); herrings (harengs); turbot (turbot); halibut (flétan), etc.	
	All the year

Poultry

Duck, chicken, capons (canard, poulet, chapon)	
	All the year
Turkey (dinde)	All the year
Gosling (oison)	April–September
Goose (oie)	December

Game

Snipe, woodcock (bécassine, bécasse)	
	October–March
Quail (imported), (caille)	All the year
Wild duck (caneton sauvage)	
	In autumn and winter
Venison (venaison)	July–February

Pheasant (faisan)	1st October–February
Grouse (coq de bruyère)	
	12th August–December
Hares (lièvres)	August–February
Partridges (perdreaux)	1st September–February
Plovers (pluviers)	October–March

Vegetables (fresh)

Artichokes (artichauts)	November–June
Jerusalem artichokes (topinambours)	
	Autumn–winter
Asparagus, natural (asperges)	May–August
Celery (céleri)	September–March
Sprouts (choux de Bruxelles)	September–March
Seakale (chou de mer)	December–May
Marrow (courgette)	July–October
Broad beans (fèves)	June–August
French beans (haricots verts)	June–September
New peas (petits pois)	May–July
Truffle, fresh (truffe)	Autumn–winter
Chicory (endive)	October–March

Fruits

Cherries (cerises)	May–July
Green figs (figues vertes)	In autumn
Strawberries, forced and natural (fraises)	
	In summer
Raspberries (framboises)	In summer
Gooseberries and currants (groseilles à maquereau and groseilles)	In summer
Tangerines (mandarines)	November–June
Melon (melon)	All the year
Plums (prunes)	July–October
Rhubarb, forced and natural (rhubarbe)	
	January–June

Conclusion

As indicated at the beginning of this chapter, a waiter need not aspire to a knowledge of cookery anything like as comprehensive as a chef's. But the more a waiter knows about commodities and culinary methods the better he will understand his own service tasks. Useful books for further information are J. Fuller and E. Renold, *The Chef's Compendium of Professional Recipes* (Heinemann 1979) and J. Fuller, *Professional*

Kitchen Management (Batsford 1981). There are many other texts on food and cookery which a waiter, who wishes to advance his understanding of the kitchen, may profitably study.

In concluding Part Two, it is again stressed that information about traditional menu style and terminology is not intended to express the desirability of perpetuating either menu formats or French terminology in British or American menus. It reflects simply what is still found in many up market operations. Moreover, it is believed that understanding established practices may help waiters to understand better the developments and changes which may stem from them.

Part Three
Main Meal Service

11 Preparing for service

When the restaurant is clean and generally 'en place', as indicated in Chapter 5, a waiter must then turn more particularly to his own station to prepare for service. Although some of the following instructions apply to more elaborate services, many are appropriate to good waiting anywhere. This chapter deals primarily with preparation for main meal service. Preparing for breakfast is considered in Chapter 18.

Sideboard (or service station side-table)

Before the customers are due to arrive, the sideboard should be 'en place'; that is, everything (all the equipment that may be required during service) arranged 'in place'. This equipment should be laid out according to a recognized plan or sequence. All sideboards should be stocked and arranged in the same, uniform fashion so that there is no confusion when waiters change stations or are relieved on days off.

Mise en place items

Items commonly required on the sideboard for luncheon and dinner service include:

Ashtrays
Bread baskets
Bottle openers*
Butter dishes
Condiments: Worcestershire sauce, Tabasco sauce, tomato ketchup and other proprietary sauces, pickles, horseradish sauce, chutney, etc.
Corkscrew*
Cruet: salt, pepper, oil, vinegar, mustard (French and English)

Cutlery: soup, dessert, sundae and tea spoons, fish knives and forks, table knife and fork, side knives, coffee spoons and special items as required, for example oyster forks, lobster picks
Doyleys
Fingerbowls
Glassware: water jugs
Linen: napkins (serviettes), slip cloths (napperons), table-cloths
Matches*
Order (check) pad
Pencil*
Service cloths*
Service equipment: tablespoons, forks
Trays

Waiters must make sure before service that their sideboard has all that will be required during service, particularly an adequate supply of silver (especially a sufficient supply of service spoons and forks), cold joint plates, fish plates, side plates and coffee saucers. The waiter must also see that hot-plates are switched on about five minutes before service is due to begin, that sugar bowls are filled, and a supply of finger bowls are ready for use (half-slices of lemon ready for the edge of the bowl).

*Items commonly carried by the waiter.

Linen

Linen having been obtained from the linen room in the manner described earlier in Chapter 5, a waiter should check the number and sizes of all the pieces given to him to ensure that they are all in serviceable condition. The linen should then be sorted according to sizes and neatly stacked on the side-table.

Sideboard cutlery arrangement

Silver should be obtained from the plate-room (silver pantry), care being exercised that every piece is clean. These should be sorted into knives, forks, spoons, etc., and placed in the respective compartments or the drawers of the side-table, the handles being kept towards the outer part of the drawer, the prongs of forks and spoons facing sideways.

The order in which cutlery is placed varies according to the number of sideboard compartments available, but it should always conform to a pattern. The items normally placed at the left of a cover when setting a table should similarly be placed to the left in the sideboard. Cutlery placed at the right of a cover should similarly be placed to the right in the sideboard. This sequence should be observed in the same way in all the sideboards in the room.

Placing of more than one item in one compartment should be avoided; but if a limited number of compartments makes this necessary then logical pairing must be observed; for example, pair service spoons with service forks and fish knives with fish forks. It is also advisable not to pair items that are stocked in large numbers such as meat knives or forks.

Other items

Other items such as ice bowls, rolls of bread, butter, water, doyleys, the supply of which will depend on the kind of establishment, should also be obtained from the appropriate room and placed in readiness on the side-table.

Note: Butter should be kept fresh and cool, on ice, or in ice and water.

Preparing tables

Table laying is usually a group exercise for a brigade of waiters. Each waiter will take an allotted task throughout the room. However, the procedures involved in laying the cloth and setting the covers are outlined below.

Table-cloth or mats

Catering establishments offering waiting service usually fall into two main classes: those which use dining tables covered with a cloth; and others using tables, generally polished, on which plates are placed with or without an undermat.

The waiter first obtains the cloths, or mats (usually from the linen room). If mats are to be used they should be placed on the table exactly where the plate, bowl, glass, etc., are later to be set.

Table steadiness and silence

Before laying the cloth make sure that the table is in its proper place, in line with other tables, that it is correctly angled and that it is steady so that you do not have to handle it once the cloth is on. A small round cork is useful for steadying the short leg of a table.

When tables are to be covered with a cloth they should be of the type fitted with baize or felt. This is to:

● Deaden noise of plates, cutlery and glass placed on them.
● Keep the cloth in position, to hang evenly without slipping.
● Cushion the guests' wrists from sharp edges of the table.

If they are not so fitted, then a loose silence cloth (of baize or felt) covering the table-top (less in area than the table-cloth) must be used. Such an undercloth can be kept in position with clips or cord.

Checking the cloth

The table-cloth should be the right side up; this side is always more highly laundered and the hem is always on the underside of the cloth. The folds should be centred on the table with the points at the corners so that the cloth hangs evenly over the table legs.

Table-cloths are normally screen folded (that is to form a W) with the face side (more glossily laundered) outside. This facilitates putting on the cloth. The aim in laying a cloth is to cover the four table legs with the four corners hanging about 8 or 10 cm (3 or 4 in) from the floor.

When laying the cloth, care must be taken to avoid creasing it as this greatly spoils the general appearance of a table.

Steps in laying a table-cloth

The following are steps to be taken in cloth laying:

1. Check that the table is correctly positioned and firm.
2. If a felt is not already fitted, place felt over the table.
3. Choose the correct size of table-cloth.
4. Stand centrally between two legs of the table.
5. Place the folded cloth on the table with the open edges towards you and the main folds facing away from you.
6. Open the cloth across the table so that its woven edges (the selvedge edges) and its inside double fold lie facing you and with the two double folds facing away from you.
7. With thumbs uppermost, take the top flap of cloth between your thumbs and first finger and take the central folds between the first and second finger.
8. With arms spread out the width of the table, move the cloth to the far edge of the table away from you.
9. Release and drop the bottom flap (which is lying loose) over the far edge of the table.
10. Allowing the rest of the cloth to lie on the table, release your hold on the centre folds

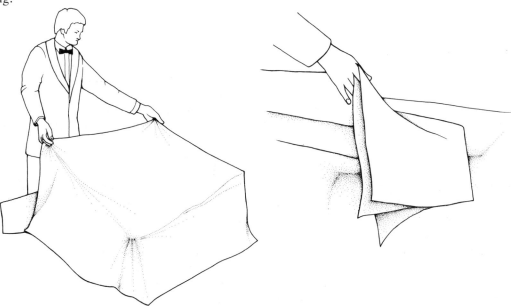

Figure 29   *Laying a table-cloth*

and gently unfold the cloth, drawing it across the table towards you until the table-cloth is opened and the table covered.

11 Inspect to see that the drop is even all round and that the cloth corners drape the legs.

12 To adjust the cloth, stand squarely between the table legs and with arms outstretched, pull square.

Note: On square and rectangular tables, mitre the corners where the table legs are.

13 The chairs should then be placed in their correct positions.

(For changing a table-cloth when guests are present see Chapter 14.)

Laying the covers
Having covered all the tables with cloths, the general table mise en place begins. These tasks of laying the covers are normally done *en masse* during the 'closed period'. Therefore, a waiter will usually deal with only two items throughout the room.

Tables are laid according to the requirements of the establishment. In à la carte service a minimum is usually put on the table beforehand and the waiter places the necessary cutlery in position after the order has been taken and he knows the customer's requirements. He does not, as a rule, lay them all in advance but only as required for each course and at the time of service. In table d'hôte service the table is laid in advance to cover all the principal courses, for example soup, fish, meat, sweet.

The tables should be laid neatly and geometrically. Remember it is the first thing a customer sees when sitting down. First impressions can make or mar his opinions as to the service he can expect. A tidy table usually means a conscientious waiter; an untidy table, an untidy and careless waiter.

The cover

Plates
First, 'show plates' (entrée plates) are placed at

each cover about 5 to 10 mm (¼ to ½ in) from the edge of the table (according to house custom) and central to the chairs. Plates must be checked and polished at the sideboards; cracked plates must never be put on the table. If plates are badged, always place them so that the badge is uppermost facing the guest (at 12 o'clock position) when he is seated.

Cutlery
The silver can now be laid. Clean polished cutlery should be carried on a salver covered with a clean cloth when guests are present during service. In preparing the room before service they may be, and usually are, carried in a clean service cloth in one hand (never in bare hands). Handling only at the base, place the cutlery at the correct position round the table (see Figure 31). It is laid in accordance with the following:

1 Knives on the right, forks on the left with space between them determined by the 'show' entrée plate.

2 Cutlery is set in the order in which items will be used. The first to be needed by the guest are laid in the outer position.

3 Place knives with the sharp edge turned to the cover plate (or space for a plate if the 'show plate' is not used).

Figure 30   *Place setting by Wedgwood*

4 Place forks with prongs turned up away from the cloth.

5 If a 'show plate' is not used, the distance between the inside knife and fork should be a good 250 mm (9 in).

6 Sweet or dessert silver (spoon and fork) when set, are laid horizontally at the top of the cover and should also be about 250 mm from the table's edge (but see point 10).

7 Thus, the plate space should be about 250 mm square.

8 Those knives, forks and spoons set at the right and left side of the cover should be near one another but without actually touching, and about 10 mm (½ in) from the edge of the table (except for fish forks on table d'hôte covers as indicated below).

9 Soup spoons at one time were set horizontally at the head or top of the cover. Now they are generally placed on the right of the first knife to be used (unless an hors d'oeuvre knife and fork are laid. However, except at functions a knife and fork for hors d'oeuvre is not usually laid on the table; but brought on a napkin-covered plate as required).

10 Dessert spoons and forks are set for table d'hôte service and functions and are then placed horizontally at the head of the cover. Otherwise, the same practice of bringing them as required (as for hors d'oeuvre cutlery) applies.

11 No knife, fork or spoon should be laid unless the meal requires it, that is, do not lay covers until the menu has been studied.

12 Table ware should not be spread out. Cutlery should be grouped closely.

While these points have general application, broadly two kinds of covers can be set. These are often determined by the category of establishment; for example, popular priced restaurant offering table d'hôte service or a more costly one giving à la carte service.

Table d'hôte

As a table d'hôte setting is intended to cover all or several of the principal courses, for example soup, fish, meat and sweet, it was customary to place all the necessary cutlery (that is, as required by the menu) on the table in the order indicated below. In modern cost-conscious and labour-conserving operations the general rule is to set only cutlery (and other silver) that is needed. This saves time in laying and clearing, saves cost in reducing wear and helps keep sideboards stacked en place.

Begin with the joint knife on the right of the entrée or 'show plate' 10 mm (½ in) from the edge of the table, then a fish knife and then soup spoon. To the left of the 'show plate' a joint fork is placed and then a fish fork. The fish fork is placed up a little, so that the top of the prongs is in line with the tip of the joint knife.

In front of the plate a sweet fork is placed, with the handle towards the left of the cover with a dessert spoon above it in alignment but with handle towards the right. Place a side plate to the left of the cover. Place a side knife on the plate. A water goblet or wine glass, turned upside down, is then positioned just above the tip of the joint knife at the top right-hand side. A folded table napkin is placed on the 'show plate' (see section on napkins below). Finally, a cruet set (salt and pepper only) and an ashtray are placed in the centre of the table.

Note: Layouts are basically the same everywhere but there are slight differences in various restaurants, so a waiter must adapt himself to the method employed.

Figure 31 *Table setting*
Basic single cover for luncheon or dinner with single glass. Note the position of the water or red wine glass which is always above the tip of the meat knife

Figure 32 *Table setting*
A similar basic cover showing additional wine glasses.
Three glasses may be laid diagonally as shown but if
six different glasses are to be laid they should be
arranged in a triangle (with the sherry glass at the
near point to the guest and the wine to be used first
on the right of the triangle, the others to the left)

À la carte
À la carte service requires only that the minimum of silver is placed on the table, just an hors d'oeuvre cover or a fish knife and fork suffices. Other cutlery when put on course by course as the meal progresses is brought to the table by the waiter on a napkin-covered service plate. This napkin-covered plate is used for every article placed or removed from the table. This kind of à la carte lay-up procedure is frequently used in fashionable restaurants whether they are dealing with a table d'hôte menu or an à la carte menu or both. Other than the covers, the rest of the à la carte table lay-up is the same as for table d'hôte service.

General
On a round table the covers are always placed between the legs. On a long table a space of 650 to 750 mm (26 to 30 in) should be allowed per cover.

For a prearranged party the complete cover is usually set up with the exception of the sweet fork and spoon. The silver on the outside must always be what is required for the next course.

Salt and pepper cruets are always neatly grouped on the table; in the case of a long table allow one set for each two covers. Mustards, sauces including those in bottles or jars are not left on the table. They must be passed by the waiter at the appropriate time for the course for which they are required. They are removed immediately after this course has been completed.

Shortly before the guests are due to arrive, the waiter turns up glasses left upside down during mise en place and gives them a final polish.

Flowers and table decoration
In the morning about half an hour before lunch, the vases of flowers are collected from the flower room and placed round the room, and on tables.

Traditionally, especially on the Continent, many head waiters learned the fundamentals of flower arranging (and even such extensions of arranging as petal patterns for table centre pieces). Today, flowers may be provided from the hotel florist, from external contract or from the housekeeping department. Waiters, certainly in the early stages of their career, may not be required to involve themselves in flower care or flower arrangement.

In laying a table, however, every item should be considered from a design point of view. Small, low cut vases or flower holders do not interfere with a guest's vision, tend to balance better with other items on the table and are economical in the use of flowers. Small, single-stem vases and placing single flower heads in brandy balloons or wine glasses are other possibilities. In any case, flower containers should be of glass, silver or the restaurant's style china and, in order to give prominence to the flowers, should be of inconspicuous style. However, as observed, it is generally recognized that further training and experience is desirable in the arrangement and care of flowers.

Napkins

In Chapter 5 it was noted that elaborate napkin folding is less fashionable than it used to be. The main reasons are:

● Guests' dislike of excessive handling.

- Customers' general taste for simplicity rather than complexity in table decoration.
- Management's reluctance to countenance unnecessary use of restaurant staff's time and labour.

But fashion rather than rules determines napkin folding practice and there remains some demand for, and consequent use of, decorative folds for napkins especially at functions. As fashion is fickle, a waiter, as he becomes more experienced will, as a matter of prudence, be able to fold napkins in at least one or two different designs.

Folding is undertaken for two principal reasons:

- To 'present' the guest's own personal table napkin at the cover and thus enhance the table.
- To aid in the presentation of food, for example gondola shapes, possibly made with more than one napkin and with stiffened card (white menus) inserts in which to set for presentation oval dishes of, say, fish. Rose or petal folds similarly are used to present smaller timbales or bowls.

Factors in folding

Some general points can be made.

Firstly, modern napkins tend to be smaller than in Victorian times so that old designs may be difficult to achieve without a full-size 66 cm (26 in) square. The 'classic' mitre is one fold requiring a large napkin.

Secondly, square is the operative word. If a napkin is not square then one of the long sides should be folded back so as to achieve one, for virtually all fold designs are based on the assumption that one starts with a square.

Thirdly, napkin folding is best achieved with well-starched linen (or linen and cotton union material well-starched). It is almost impossible to fold into retentive shapes, napkins of man-made fibres.

Simplicity favoured

Modern tastes favour napkins simply folded, set on the cover plate to reveal any monogram or design in the damask. Simple folds include merely folding in half for a triangle or into one or more simple rolls. A simple single roll remains an effective way of placing and presenting a napkin (see Figure 30).

Range of folds

The Encyclopaedia of Practical Cookery published in the last century listed about forty styles of napkin folding. Among more recent books, J. Ginders, *A Guide to Napkin Folding* (Northwood 1978) and M. Von Bornstedt and U. Prytz, *Folding Table Napkins* (Oak Tree Press 1974) both describe a similar number.

Examples of folds

It is not necessary here to do more than indicate two or three possibilities as a base from which waiting staff may develop an appropriate range. Moreover, in so many waiting activities, napkin folding is, in any case, best learnt by practice rather than through instructional notes in a book. For such reasons, only a small sample from the large range of possibilities is included.

Cornet (cone or pointed cap)

The cornet is popular on the Continent for its shape is useful for giving 'height' and 'importance' to a table (especially when table floral decor is a low posy bowl). This (and the lunch fold, an alternative to the cornet) requires a well-starched napkin to be effective.

For the cornet, open a square napkin on the table. Fold it in half away from you then re-fold in half lengthwise so that the selvedge edges are at the top. Fold the sides to touch in the middle (Figure 33 (a)).

Fold under the right and left-hand corners as indicated by the dotted lines shown in Figure 33(b). From the top right-hand side, point A, turn and roll towards the centre as shown in Figure 33(c). Repeat this roll on the opposite side (from point B). Press the rolled part into place so that the napkin will stand up.

Bishop's mitre

Mitre folds were once widely used for functions. They often had a dinner roll placed inside them.

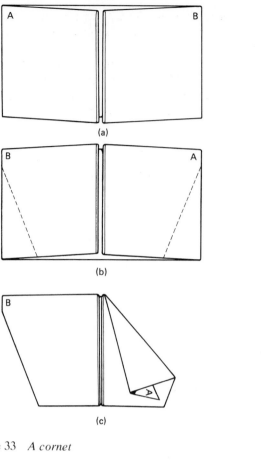

(a)

(b)

(c)

Figure 33   *A cornet*

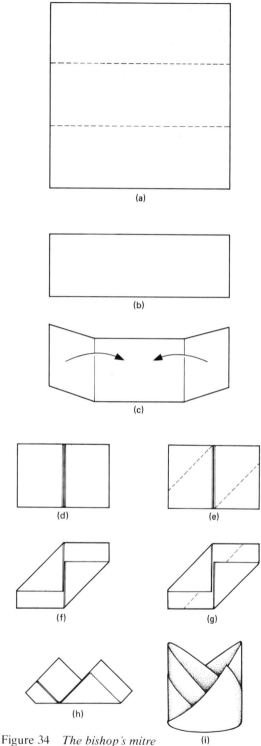

(a)

(b)

(c)

(d)

(e)

(f)

(g)

(h)

(i)

Figure 34   *The bishop's mitre*

Today, this practice is not universally approved as the roll is not always noticed by guests and may be dropped during unfolding.

For a bishop's mitre, first crease the square napkin into three as indicated by dotted lines in Figure 34(a). Fold the lowest third over the middle one. Turn the top one inwards and insert it between the first two. The resulting fold of three thicknesses is a rectangular shape as shown in Figure 34(b). Crease this strip equally into four parts. Open them out so that they are lying flat on the table so as to enable the two end sections to be lifted and folded over. Figure 34(c) shows these end sections lifted up. Figure 34(d) indicates how they are folded over so that the original ends of the strip have been brought together and now lie touching at the middle.

Next grasp the strip firmly to prevent it gaping and so that the corners are creased, as shown by dotted lines in Figure 34(e). Now fold them over as illustrated in Figure 34(f).

Crease the napkin diagonally along the middle, as indicated by the dotted line in Figure 34(g).

Now fold the napkin along the crease so that the two triangles emerge outwards and are not turned inwards. The napkin should now appear as shown in Figure 34(h) (the bottom line in Figure 34(h) being the dotted line as shown in Figure 34(g)).

To complete the design, grasp the farthest point on the left (see Figure 34(h)), and bring it up with a circular action so that its ends can be tucked into the pleats of the triangle seen towards the right. This provides the left-hand edge of the mitre.

Next, take the farthest point on the right as shown in Figure 34(h), and in the same way fold it into the pleats of the left-hand edge. This completes the mitre so that it should appear as in Figure 34(i).

The rose
This is mainly used for presenting round dishes or timbales.

With the square napkin open flat on the table, fold the corners to the centre (Figure 35(a)). Repeat this folding (Figure 35(b)). Repeat a

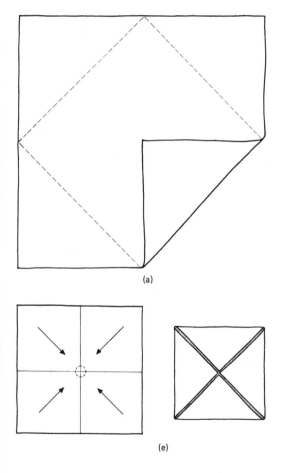

(a)

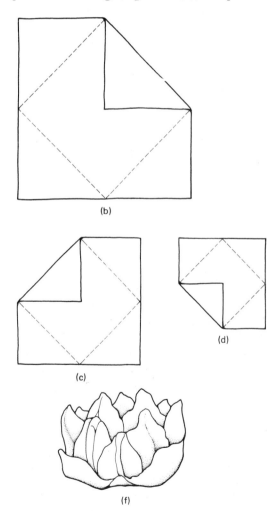

(b)

(c)

(d)

(e)

Figure 35   *The rose*

(f)

third time (Figure 35(c)). Turn the napkin over so that it faces downward and, again, fold all four corners to the centre (Figure 35(d)).

Using a small cup or simply the fingers, hold the centre firm (Figure 35(e)). Now pull up the twelve corners from underneath so that a petal appearance (Figure 35(f)) results.

In restaurant usage, corners are usually folded only twice to the centre before turning the napkin over. One set of corners is then pulled up, the napkin reversed again and the single corners turned.

The fan

For this Victorian 'period piece', take a well-starched napkin and fold it in three lengthwise.

Pleat half of it evenly to the centre. Then pleat from the other side also to the centre so that the pleats face each other. Firmly flatten them down. Holding it firmly, insert into a wine glass, fanning it out at the top (see Figure 36).

Additions to the table

Promotional material

Restaurant staff may also be required to include on tables 'table tents', that is, folded paper or card announcements (advertising restaurant or hotel services), or candles, decorative lamps, or other material. In all cases, the aim should be to group neatly, avoid cluttering and observe the simple design principles that apply to flowers.

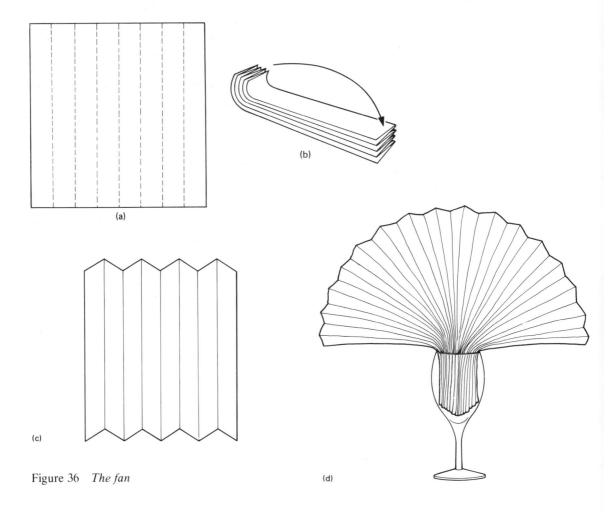

Figure 36   *The fan*

Bread, toast and butter

Toast Melba and butter may be placed on the tables before the beginning of the meal but never before the customer has occupied his table, whether reserved or not. If bread or rolls have not been placed on side plates as part of the cover, they should be passed at the beginning, and during the meal as required.

American-style covers

As many hotels in Britain and elsewhere are under American management or influence, it should be noted that in America there are broadly three styles where waiting service is offered: for French, Russian or American service. These services are considered further in Chapter 13, but the general nature of American covers is summarized below:

French service

A 'show plate' (hors d'oeuvre size) bearing folded napkin. To its right: joint (or dinner) knife, soup spoon (for set table d'hôte menus when it is known soup will be served, otherwise the spoon is brought as the customer's order demands).

To the left of the show plate: joint (or dinner) fork, side plate and side knife (in America it is called a butter plate and knife).

Above the show plate: dessert fork and/or spoon (for a set or table d'hôte menu otherwise appropriate silverware may be brought when a guest's dessert order is made).

Russian service

Covers are laid to match a menu as for American-style French service or in similar fashion to British table d'hôte.

American service

Without a centre 'show plate', the cover usually comprises a side (bread and butter) plate. Cutlery as for simple French style with glass. A napkin may be placed between the cutlery or on the side plate, and a sugar bowl in addition to salt and pepper shakers and ashtray.

Coffee cups and saucers (not demi-tasses) are also often included especially at group or function occasions.

Checking a laid table

When the table is laid, check that everything on it is scrupulously clean and arranged well. Covers should face one another across the table when four places are set. When only two covers are set, they must be facing towards the centre of the dining room and not facing a wall or a door. Flowers, cruets and other items should be in the correct position to balance the table setting.

Preparing oneself for service

Finally, you should ensure not only that you, yourself are neat, clean and generally physically ready for service but that you are mentally ready also. Study the menu, ensure that you know the nature of all its dishes. In this way you will be able to check that you have the proper accompaniments for service and can explain to guests, when necessary, the details of the menu.

12 Guest reception and orders

Earlier chapters have indicated changing trends in catering and waiting. Social changes are closely reflected in restaurants and in waiting procedures.

Guests' requirements

Courtesy naturally remains important. So too does a degree of formality, especially in up market operations, but more effort is now made to create a relaxed, welcoming atmosphere. Customers dining out seek warmth, friendliness and satisfaction in service in addition to politeness. Waiting staff, in direct contact with guests can and must provide these elements.

Many waiting staff in the Western World (this is especially true in America and Britain) are joined by part-timers or seasonal staff. Students other than catering students are among this number. Guests relate to such waiting staff in a way quite different from the older formality in the days when it was the 'done thing' virtually to ignore waiting staff.

Staff response

Today's customers, even those wealthy enough to use the highest class establishments may still not have many, or any, serving staff in their own homes. Service is being 'taken for granted' less and less, but it is still sought. There are few guests today who will not appreciate management's concept of hospitality being reflected in the greetings and sustained pleasantness of waiting staff.

Moreover, waiters themselves will respond to the slogan 'Business goes where it is wanted and stays where it is appreciated'. American operations were quicker than those of most countries to help motivate catering staff by such notice board reminders. Others, like 'It's up to us to please', 'Customers are always in the driver's seat' and many similar ones may be trite but they help remind us that our job is all about satisfying guests. Pleasing depends heavily on good first impressions, on the way guests are received.

Reservations

Allocations of tables, particularly in busy and successful restaurants, starts before guests arrive. This is because many guests reserve their seats, usually by telephone, in advance. Reservations are normally registered on a 'diary' basis, that is in a page in a foolscap-size register reserved for the day's lunch and/or dinner seating. In such cases, regular customers, or those making reservations who are known to the restaurant, are likely to be given priority and to have their wishes met in regard to their seating. It is vital not to let new guests or less favoured guests be aware of any priority accorded to others.

Erwin Schleyen, famed restaurateur of Mayfair's Mirabelle, was reputed to separate 'sheep and goat' guests by passwords: 'les convertis' for the fashionable part of the restaurant; for those less acceptable, 'le Congo Belge'. But the art of receiving and seating is to avoid giving any guest the feeling of being exiled to 'the Belgian Congo'. In New York, Oscar of the Waldorf was credited with the introduction of the red plush rope barring entry to a restaurant and which the ability to pass through seemed to confer a mark of distinction but there are hazards in manipulating such devices which can cause irritation and distrust in customers.

Table allocation

Where a guest is seated in a restaurant is important to him. Why certain positions or types of seats are liked or disliked has been the subject of considerable study, including research at universities. This book does not seek to explore all seating motivations but simply to stress that how a guest is received, and the table to which he is led is an initial procedure important to him.

Some problems are obvious; those of seating single customers so they do not feel self-conscious; or allocating unpopular tables, for example those too close to an entrance, to service door or to music. Customers, especially those on their own, tend to like 'back protection', that is, have their back to a wall, a corner or an alcove. Others seek tables with 'status' or amenities, that is, with views by windows or in raised alcoves. While this book does not explore behavioural patterns, it is never too soon for a waiter who wishes to succeed to realize the psychological significance of table allocation.

Actual allocation depends on whether a table is pre-booked. Otherwise it is conditioned by the number of vacant places at the time of entry, the size of the party and, as far as possible, the wishes of guests themselves. As already stated, some customers may prefer quiet corners, others to be near an orchestra or by a window. A good head waiter ascertains the wishes of guests or gauges them. He also uses his discretion, so that guests who are well-mannered and pleasing in appearance may have more conspicuous places than those who might appear to have undesirable qualities or to be not well-groomed. This 'sizing up' of guests and their wishes is acquired by experience

A group of guests who wish to sit together should not be placed at different tables. Therefore, if a restaurant is busy the waiter should know just when suitable places will become vacant or be ready to extend and prepare a table to accommodate a larger number.

Reception procedure

However management and staff may seek spontaneity and friendliness certain rituals (and training to achieve appropriate standards in them) still support a guest's reception. They start when a guest enters a restaurant and when he or she should be received and shown to a suitable seat usually by the head waiter.

Today, guests in many restaurants are first received at the entrance to a restaurant's cocktail bar or lounge. Here an aperitif is taken and the meal and accompanying wines may be selected. Flexible interpretation of the procedures which are outlined below must take this possibility into account.

Who receives

Previously, in large first class establishments, there were usually one or more head waiters exclusively engaged in receiving guests and they took advance bookings and entered them in the restaurant reservation book.

Many restaurant operators today question the desirability of 'tying up' a fully-trained head waiter on the reception task and modern brigades may increase the responsibilities in all directions of the section waiter (or captain in the USA – see page 28). In America, a hostess or greeter, may be assigned restaurant reception work on the basis of personality, intelligence and aptitude rather than skill in head waiter-type duties.

But, whoever receives customers at the door does so with a courteous greeting in a clear and affable tone of voice.

Greeting on arrival

Only a stranger need receive the old, traditional greeting: 'Good morning (or afternoon, or evening), Sir (or Madam). How many are there

Figure 37   *The correct stance of a waiter when taking an order*

Figure 38   *Unsuitable conduct of a waiter in front of a guest*

in your party, please?' Where guests' names are known they may be used.

Greeting phrases may, of course, be varied to suit the occasion. Having received an answer, the head waiter leads the way to a suitable table – if he gestures towards a table or to indicate a direction he should do so with open palm to avoid any impression of pointing. He then helps the ladies to be seated and calls the head wine butler and section head waiter to attend to the guests.

Greeting at table
A station waiter acknowledges customers with a smile and greeting: 'Good morning (or good evening) Mr Brown (or Sir, or Madam)'. After the first use of a guest's name he should be addressed as 'Sir' unless it is clear from the established relationship that he prefers his own name to be used. A waiter aims to make sure that guests feel welcome and gain the impression that staff are glad to look after them.

In America, a captain or station waiter customarily introduces himself by name saying, for example, 'I'm Arthur and I'm your captain (or

waiter) for tonight'. Sometimes, indeed, an American introduction of this kind can be most informal such as 'Hi! I'm Tom from Missouri and I'm your waiter for tonight'.

In Britain and on the Continent such informality is not yet widely practised, but social conditions today make anything acceptable provided it makes guests feel welcome, and that they are aware that a waiter is pleased to receive them and look after them.

However, a waiter should be guided by management and his supervisor before developing informality.

Arrival at table
On arrival at table, the head waiter helps the ladies (or gentleman, if it is a single party) to be seated, that is, he slightly draws the lady's chair from the table and as she is about to seat herself, slides the chair gently forwards. He also ensures that the station waiter has already come forward to help do this. Therefore, seating of a party of two or more people is usually done by both head and station waiter.

Where evening dress is worn, ladies should be

assisted in removing their wraps or stoles, which they might want placed over the chair back. If touching the floor, the wrap ends should be slightly tucked under the sides of the chair. (At the end of the meal, when ready to leave, ladies should be assisted again with their wraps and their chairs should be pulled back.) In a party of several people a waiter attends first to lady guests – unless the gentlemen accompanying them do so.

If any guest is smoking, ensure that an ashtray is placed on the table.

Adjusting covers

It may be necessary for a cover or covers to be added to, or taken from, a table. Any cutlery or other table items brought or removed should be so moved on a napkin-covered plate or salver. In such cases, the table usually requires total adjustment. For example, a table originally set for three covers might well have a flower vase where a fourth cover would normally be laid. The vase would thus need to be centred, with suitable adjustment made also to the position of the cruet, if a waiter needs to add a fourth cover.

Ordering procedure

Aperitif order

When aperitifs have been taken in an adjacent cocktail bar, lounge or anteroom, and the meal and wines have already been selected there, it may only remain for station waiters and wine waiters to greet the customers and initiate service. When food and wine orders remain to be taken at table, the head wine butler comes first and after giving the appropriate greeting, will enquire if an aperitif is required.

Handing a menu

Unless a meal has been pre-ordered, as soon as guests are seated the menu should be presented. If the station waiter is busy with other guests, he should apologize to the new customers for not being able to attend to them immediately, and he should assure them that he will do so as soon as possible. He should *never* ignore them or forget them.

When the aperitif order has been given, the section head waiter approaches the host from the left, unfolds the guest's napkin and offers it to him, places menus in front of him (and other guests) and allows the guest time to study it. Note that the menu is placed on the table before the guest and not handed to him.

Purpose of the order

Obviously, the first purpose of a guest's order is to make his choice of dishes known. In writing down this order, the waiter (or head waiter) records the instruction and provides the chef de rang with an aide memoire at the service table, transmits the order (possibly via a commis) to the kitchen and provides the raw material for billing to the cashier. (These elements and consequences of the order are dealt with in Chapter 16.) When taking orders from customers on a busy station, apply the principle of first come, first served, but reassure, rather than ignore, waiting guests.

Awaiting the order

When the menus (table d'hôte and à la carte) are long and varied, customers may require a few minutes before making their order. A waiter can, during this time, be offering bread rolls and send his commis, with appropriate checks, to the still-room for butter and, if used, Melba toast. Indeed, in good class restaurants, when guests are just received and considering their requirements, it is customary for a waiter to place fresh butter on the table, pass bread rolls and fill water glasses. In more modest establishments and where, for example, butter is not included with the cover, but only as a charged item, then this procedure may be modified. As noted previously, it is usual for a waiter to assist by unfolding table napkins, offering or helping to place them for guests if this has not already been done by the head waiter.

A waiter should not position himself so near to the table as to inhibit the host's discussion with guests of the menu, nor should he ever lean over the table. He should be, of course, near enough to respond to queries.

How to take an order

Having given guests time to study a menu, a waiter will approach the guest from the left. He should inquire 'May I have your order, sir (madam)?'. He should wait patiently, facing the guests, until (after any necessary advice has been given) the order is completed as far as and including the main course. When it is apparent that there is a host, take his instruction first, otherwise receive orders as guests are ready.

While taking an order it may be necessary for a waiter to inquire about such dishes as grilled steaks and chops, 'How do you like them cooked, sir – rare (underdone), medium or well-done?' He should inform a customer when a cooking time must be allowed for dishes ordered and the timing of service of the first course may need appropriate adjustment. For table d'hôte meals, or when no cooking time need be allowed, the first course should be served as soon as possible.

How to record orders

In recording an order, a waiter should fold his serving cloth into a neat pad on which to rest his book.

He should write in the corner of the next unused sheet of his order pad the number of the table being served. He then records (using abbreviations) the dishes that are ordered. The writing must be clear for it has to be read by other people. Many waiters' books are made out in duplicate, the original being given to the kitchen clerk before he will transmit the order to the chefs or parties concerned. The carbon copy is retained as the waiter's own record (that is, number and kind of meal served). It may even serve additionally as the bill that will be presented to the customer at the end of a meal (see Chapter 16 for further details of systems). Sometimes two carbon copies are made out, the original for the kitchen clerk, one as a basis for preparing the customer's bill and the other for the waiter.

Information normally required on an order includes: waiter's code number or his station number, table number, number of guests and the date as well as details of dishes, price and type of meal ordered.

Identifying orders with individuals

So that a waiter does not forget which person orders which particular dish it may be prudent for him to link first orders with individuals by brief aide memoire notes, for example host, blue shirt, moustache, etc., or, better still, to give each seat a number. If in any doubt, repeat an order back to a guest to avoid error. Orders for sweets, desserts and cheese are taken in similar manner when guests have completed their main course.

The wine order

By the time the food order has been taken, the wine butler has normally attended to and served the aperitifs. If wines were not pre-ordered in the cocktail bar or anteroom, the wine butler then returns to the table. He presents the wine list to the host from the left, remaining at hand ready to answer any queries and, if required, advise the customer on choice of wines to match food ordered. Part Five deals with wines and their service.

Passing food orders to the kitchen

A waiter knows the order of service of dishes that his customer has ordered. Therefore, he will go (or send his commis) to the appropriate part of the kitchen where he will give in the order (stating it in a clear voice) to the kitchen clerk (aboyeur in French because he 'barks out' the orders) or whoever is accepting the orders, handing over to him the check he has made out. The aboyeur calls out the order, then files the waiter's check on his series of spikes where it remains until the order is completed.

The chefs de partie on hearing the order from the aboyeur respond by calling out equally loudly to acknowledge their acceptance of it.

Kitchen commands in French

Kitchen language is often French in hotels and restaurants. Thus a series of various orders and acceptances might be a mix of French jargon and even odd English words as follows:

Aboyeur's order: Faites marcher deux lunch table d'hôte – deux potage du jour – deux. (Put in order: two table d'hôte lunches – two soups of the day – two.)

Response (by chef potager): Entendu. (Understood.)

Aboyeur: Rôtisseur, deux boeuf rôti – deux. (Roastcook, two roast beef – two.)

Response (by chef rôtisseur): Oui. (Yes.)

Aboyeur: Entremetier, deux pommes et légumes – deux. (Vegetable cook, two potatoes and vegetables – two.)

Response (by chef entremetier): Oui. (Yes.)

Aboyeur: Pâtissier, une meringue glacée – une. (Pastry cook, one meringue ice-cream – one.)

Response (by chef pâtissier): Entendu. (Understood.)

Such calls continue throughout service time and at the peak of business the flow of shouts is almost continuous.

In due course a waiter's order will pass to the servery, be checked by the chef (or sous chef) and will then be given to him.

Sequence of service

In order not to keep customers waiting, the first dish on a menu is usually one ready for immediate service, for example soup or hors d'oeuvre. This dish can be taken and served to a customer immediately, unless dishes following are likely to require lengthy preparation. In this case, timing may be adjusted.

Meanwhile, dishes that are to follow are immediately put into preparation. These dishes, such as fish, poultry or meat may require to be fried, roasted or grilled or cut from the joint.

The final course is usually a sweet course and will come from the pastry section of the servery or the pastry department itself. It may already be prepared (for example cold dishes which will need only to be apportioned) or (in high class restaurants) it may be prepared for each customer and take up to, say, thirty minutes from the time the waiter first placed the order.

Executing wine orders

Customers' wishes regarding the timing of wine service should be observed (that is, a host may not wish a red wine to be poured until the service of the main course), but the aim is to have the appropriate wine presented with (or immediately before) the course it is to accompany and most guests wish to see their first wine brought quickly (see Part Five for wine service detail).

Co-ordinating orders

Having served one course, a waiter (or his commis) goes to the kitchen for the next course, which he brings to the side table in time to take away a customer's used plates and to serve his next course.

He should check other tables at his station before leaving the restaurant for the kitchen or service area to ensure that no other guests are trying to attract his attention.

When a waiter has several separate customers to attend to at one time, he must have a clear memory and service skills to obtain and serve the various dishes promptly and correctly.

Timing courses

Since each course of the meal takes time to be eaten a waiter has, in the meantime, about five to ten minutes to serve a course to other guests. As he may have up to sixteen or more customers, it may happen that at any one time during service, some customers will be at first course stage, others the second, while others are at the third or final course. A waiter must co-ordinate his journeys to the kitchen to obtain the next courses that are required for each of these.

Attending to the order

If a waiter is busy and cannot attend to a customer at once, he should inform him that he will attend to him immediately or 'in a moment'. Customers may become impatient if they cannot 'catch the waiter's eye'. They may rightly be annoyed if a waiter apparently ignores them or passes them without giving some indication that he is aware that they have not been attended to.

Aiding other stations

This often happens when a busy waiter from a different station is passing an occupied table not on his station. He should stop and acknowledge the call, but say politely, 'I will send your station waiter to you, sir'.

Waiters should remember that they are a team and assist one another whenever possible to keep a constant contact with all clientele. Co-operation between staff is an essential part of a smoothly running restaurant, but waiters should not 'ordinarily overlap' other stations or they may cause confusion.

Table priority

A waiter must also be careful when two tables are occupied at approximately the same time that he takes the order of the first party first. Customers are apt to note with annoyance any failure to observe the 'first come, first served' rule (already advocated earlier in this chapter).

A good waiter will always either suggest an aperitif or a wine at table, or ensure the early attendance of the wine waiter to take these orders.

Checking the cover

If a table is laid for service of both soup and hors d'eouvre or fish and the customer has not ordered any of these dishes, the waiter should now remove the corresponding silver. When anything on the table is no longer required it should always be removed on a plate covered with a serviette.

Order of serving guests

In a party of two, a lady and gentleman, serve the lady first.

In a party of four consisting of two ladies and two gentlemen, serve the lady on the right of the host first, then the lady on his left, the gentleman opposite the host and finally the host.

In a party of six, three ladies and three gentlemen, the host and hostess will sit facing each other. The lady on the right of the host is served first, then the lady on the left, then the hostess. Next, the gentleman on the right of the hostess is served, then the gentleman on the left of the hostess and finally the host.

In a large party, but with a host rather than a chairman, the guest of honour, who is sitting on the right of the host is served first (in a mixed party this is usually a lady), then the guest on his left, then the host himself. The other waiter on the top table of a large party of this kind starts with the first guest on the right of the guest of honour. The hostess is served last in a party of **ladies and the host last of anybody.**

The exception to this rule is in banqueting, where each waiter serves his station in order of seating irrespective of precedence. (For order of **function service see Chapter 17.**)

To summarize, the sequence of serving guests is:

1 The guest of honour is served first.
2 A lady in a party takes precedence over a male guest of honour.
3 A lady in the company of men is served first.
4 Older people precede younger.

Delays in fulfilling orders

During the service, if there is any undue delay in obtaining an order, the customer must be informed by the head waiter who will offer a suitable excuse.

Finally, waiters should remember that however important the procedures and technicalities may be for receiving customers taking orders and fulfilling them, these are to support warm hospitality and lead to satisfactory service and are not mechanical rituals. Guest reception and order **taking are vital first stages in merchandising meals and service.**

13 Forms of service

Restaurant traditionalists are often unaware of how frequently over the years forms of meal service have changed. Whether eaten at home or eaten out, the time of when principal meals have been taken, and the style of waiting service that accompanies them have constantly altered. Therefore, nothing that is described in this chapter should be regarded as advocating unchanging procedures. Without detailing all present influences it is apparent that nouvelle cousine, speciality ethnic restaurants, health food and fast food operations are but some of the types of catering that prompt changes in forms of service.

Trends

One persistent trend is, however, the elimination of unnecessary staff and hence pruning rituals that are labour-consuming unless they add positively to meal merchandising and consumer satisfaction and thus 'pay their way'. Forms of service which demanded large and elaborate brigades of staff with many commis are now less frequently encountered. Nevertheless, some 'old style' services must be outlined in a work of this kind, for even if not all techniques and styles are used all the time, some of them can still be used selectively.

The different forms meal service can take are indicated in Table 20.

Restaurant styles

Some of the forms shown in Table 20, such as fast food and cafeteria services require few, if any, waiting skills. Hence in this chapter it is the main forms of restaurant service that will be considered further.

Table 20 outlines several forms of restaurant service from simple 'plated' meals (that is, food portioned directly on to customers' plates in the kitchen or servery) to elaborate forms of guéridon (side table) service. The principal types of service may, however, be adapted, simplified or elaborated to conform with the 'house style' of a restaurant. Moreover, names given to various forms of service tend to differ from one country to another, these are now summarized.

French service

In France itself, service à la française is derived from that used in bourgeois households and is found in both family pensions and in banqueting, where the dish (accompanied by its lid) is presented to the left of each guest who serves himself.

Thus, a fundamental element of true French service is that it affords guests an opportunity to help themselves.

For small parties up to three guests, dishes may be placed directly on to the table. The main dish (possibly on a table réchaud, perhaps of the 'night light' type) is positioned before the guest expected to be served first. The plates are placed

Table 20 *Service styles summarized*

Types of service	Principal uses	Advantages	Disadvantages
Plate: simplest form of service; food assembled in the kitchen on plates	American service; guest houses; platter meals; breakfasts; cafés; set **menus; design-conscious up-market service**	Rapid turnover and fast service. Labour saving. Fewer waiters needed. Costs minimized. Easy **to understand. Preserves chef's presentation**	Increased kitchen time and labour. Food can cool on hot-plate. Presentation can be poor e.g. over-loaded appearance
Silver (or English): food served by waiter with spoon and fork from flats, etc. (see page 149 for English service)	Good-class establishment; banqueting, directors' dining room, cruise liners and other travel catering	Dishes look good. Chef shows skill. Waiter can show skills. Conveys impression of high class service	Needs skilled staff to do well. Costs more. Food can cool. Service can be slow. Extra washing-up.
Semi-silver: combining plate and silver service. Main food item plated. Vegetables, etc., served by waiter	Good medium-class establishments; department store restaurants	Quicker than full silver service. Reduces wash-up. Customers decide amount of accompaniments taken	Kitchen assembly time, otherwise as for plate service
Family: plated main course and vegetables on table for customer self-service	Banqueting; clubs; institutions	Fewer and less-skilled staff. Customer decides his vegetable portion. Quite quick. Reduces service time. Enables more covers to be served	Customer can spill or burn himself. Poor presentation. Customer can feel neglected
Traditional family (English): host serves main course (or carves joint), then as for family service	Country houses; family	Readily understood. Food can be served without fuss. Suits informal occasions	Food can go cold. Depends on customer's attitude
French: food to be pre-carved, cut or portioned on dishes, passed (left). Customers help themselves	Highest standard; small banquets; royal functions; (see page 147 for French family service)	Good presentation. Personal	Possible poor portioning. Only suitable for small numbers of covers
Guéridon: using side-table or trolley, waiter shows his skills, e.g. carving, cooking, flambage.	House specialities; top-class establishments; night clubs	Personal service. Ideal for à la carte. Pampers guests. Good for sales	Expensive to run. Heavy staff costs. Difficult to organize. Food can go cold
Russian: similar to silver service (see page 150)	Functions and private parties	Good presentation	As silver service
Gannymede: heated pellet in a plate keeps food hot	Hospitals	Food kept warm. Can travel and stay hot. Good when service times vary	Expensive to install. Good hygiene essential

Types of service	Principal uses	Advantages	Disadvantages
Call order: orders called to kitchen, thereafter plated	Fast food operations; snack bars	Cheap to run. Minimum staff required. Quicker service. Good for certain trades	Pressure on 'caller'. No record of orders. Noisy to run
Cafeteria/Counter: customer collects tray then takes items from counter, finally paying cashier	Motorway services; institutions (schools, etc.)	Visually good. Economical on staff. Clean	Food can cool while customers wait. Dependent on good back-up and cashier
Prepaid counter: goods paid for at cash desk. Chits handed in at the counter for goods	Service areas; caféterias, etc.	Better quality food. No queuing. Effective control	Larger food stocks. Difficult for customer to understand. Clear menu essential
Single: items in a vending machine sold singly. Possible reheating in adjacent microwave	Industrial canteens; travel termini (bus stations, etc.)	Twenty-four hours food service. No service staff cost	Machine breakdowns. Cleanliness vital. Can frustrate customers
Buffet service: includes cafeteria style modified for hotels	Hotel self-service; functions	Low staffing. Customers please themselves	Possible queue delay. Erratic food control
Fast food: quick cooking of popular goods for take-away or eating on the premises from disposables	Chain and franchise operations	Fast turnover. High profits. Low staff costs	Quality control essential. Expensive to install. Dependence on convenience foods. Can wane in popularity

conveniently near the dish. (Dishes on the table or 'family service' is widely practised in 'pensions de famille' in France.)

For larger parties, certainly for tables of four or more, a guéridon or side table should be used. In this case, the waiter brings plates and dishes to the guéridon, sets the plates at guests' covers and then presents the dishes to guests to help themselves.

Often, of course, some preliminary treatment of portioning or carving may be required from the guéridon. Thus elaborated, French service can also enable guests to see food 'finished' by their table, for carving and portioning and salad mixing may be effected in front of them. Refinements or simplifications internationally depend on the grade of the restaurant.

Basic French service, as practised in France, has advantages in that it demands relatively few staff and does not require great skill, but it can be slow and less 'sure', because of possible guest ineptitude in serving themselves.

Although this is called French service in France, Switzerland and elsewhere on the Continent, some British people think that the custom of guests helping themselves from offered dishes typifies an English form of service because this style survives in private houses in this country when dishes are passed by servants.

English service
On the Continent service à l'anglaise is used especially in function service, fixed price table d'hôte and in travel catering (rail and ship). In

this style, the dish is presented to the left of the guest and served by the waiter. It is thought to have originated in the British tradition of the 'master' or family head carving or portioning and serving all at the table. In restaurant English service, the waiter fulfils this role, that is, the fundamental element is that he serves and at the same time, in effect, decides the portions as distinct from the guest taking his own. Again, refinements or simplifications depend on the grade of the restaurant.

Generally, English service is also a 'silver' service with portioning largely effected in the kitchen so that food, particularly when it involves a varied or complicated garnish, may be easily separated and served by the waiter.

The waiter brings plates and dishes to the sideboard, places a plate before each guest at his own cover, presents the main dish to the host or guests and then passes round the table serving each customer.

English service has the advantage of conveying a stylish or up market impression with relative speed and efficiency but it does require skill from staff. It is, for example, difficult to apply successfully to fragile food, for example fish fillets, omelettes.

This form of service also can be (and in high grade establishments is) effected from the guéridon. In this case, the waiter places the dishes (a lamp or réchaud is needed – at least for the main dishes) with the required number of plates on the guéridon. He serves by completing one plate at a time which is immediately placed before the guest. Guéridon service is greatly facilitated by the use of an assistant waiter to aid in passing the completed plates.

Just as there are some misconceptions about French service so there are in the case of English service. On the Continent (certainly, the French and the Swiss and their hotel schools where techniques are taught) know the foregoing as service à l'anglaise (English service) or service à l'ànglaise avec guéridon (English service with guéridon) as appropriate. Unfortunately, some in America especially and also in Britain (including even restaurateurs) are confused by elements such as silver, guéridon or the numbers of waiters involved. Such misconceptions lead to English service being dubbed 'French' service – or at its most refined from the guéridon as 'service à la Ritz'.

Russian service

A Victorian household manual, *Facts and Hints for Everyday Life* (Cassells) briefly described dinners à la russe as requiring tables laid as if for dessert only. Moreover, the role of the waiter (or footman) was enhanced, for according to L. Davidoff, *The Best Circles* (Croom Helm 1973), 'the new system of dinner à la russe, first observed in the 1820s, required the footman to carve at a side table and serve the food to each guest in turn. Guests no longer poured wine for each other but waited for footmen to do it'. The same author observed that this style grew rapidly in the middle of the century and was widespread by 1901.

The Russian style introduced during the nineteenth century, meant that each individual dish was served to guests from a sideboard and removed when finished. Thus separate 'courses' based on each dish were established. This contrasted with former dining style when many dishes of diverse kinds were placed simultaneously on the table rather in the way in which Indian meals are served today.

In France (possibly because of the sideboard or side table connection), service à la russe is guéridon service in that dishes are served garnished on the guéridon and then placed before the guest at table.

In Russia itself, appetizers (Zakouskis) or hors d'oeuvre were served outside the dining room in an ante-room close by.

Russian service doubtless derived from the old Russian style of having large joints, whole fish or birds, often decoratively treated on dishes with elaborate garnish, on the sideboard, visible to guests before being served. In Russian service these items were then carved, portioned, placed on platters and passed for guests to help themselves.

The great waiting authority of the Edwardian

period, J. Rey (author of *Guide du Maître d'Hôtel* and *The Modern Caterer's Encyclopaedia*) described service à la russe as 'serving the dishes one after the other, "piping hot" straight from the kitchen, without letting the guests wait for anything'.

But course and style later became integrated into French and English forms. of service – particularly English.

Indeed, Russian service can be confused with both French and English service but its distinguishing feature is that in England and America, the moveable side table or guéridon (as distinct from sideboard) is not used. Russian service survives today in the sense that in 'silver' service, preportioned food is passed by waiters to guests. Thus for banquets or functions Russian service (though often with French and English adaptations) is still applied.

American service

Fundamentally, this simplified form of restaurant service evolved more recently than French, English and Russian services. It depends on pre-plating and the pre-setting of tables with silver needed throughout the meal. Plated food is brought by waiters from the kitchen by tray which is then placed on a tray stand by the guest's table (an elementary form of guéridon). American service may be slightly elaborated by fine table equipment (double coupes for shellfish cocktails for example) and by ancillary serving procedures such as dispensing by separate waiters of hot rolls and trolley or 'cart' service for salads and so on.

American service is, therefore, plate service adapted to restaurant usage. Its advantages lie in its economy of equipment (sparing of dishes and silver), speed and simplicity. Hence it can be learnt easily by inexperienced staff.

Plate service

In this style the customer is served in the simplest manner with food already placed on the plate. Such service is used in canteens, many boarding houses and restaurants, where more personal silver service cannot be given. It is also used in up-market operations when chefs wish to ensure fine plate presentations.

In some higher class operations otherwise using silver service, grills may be served on plates. This is to speed service and ensure that they are hot when served *direct* from the grill without unnecessary manipulation.

Plating food requires care and supervision. For example, the plate should be the right size for the food item and adequate to accommodate its garnish and accompanying vegetables. In arranging the food, colour and consistency should reflect a chef's artistry or when done by service staff should aid or recreate such artistry.

In implementing plate service in popular style operations, metal plate rings enabling food to be stacked one plate on another may be used. Vegetables are not always 'plated' or pre-served but may be offered separately in a vegetable dish placed on the table, with its serving spoon (and possible fork) for guest self-service.

Trays are used by waiting staff for this type of service (see Chapter 14 for tray loading and carrying guidance).

Cafeteria service

Industrial and institutional catering make widespread use of cafeteria service. The basic principles of cafeteria food service have remained relatively stable. Food is set out on one or more counters with heated, unheated and refrigeration sections. Customers pick up a tray at the entry to a service line, and pass along the line selecting food as required. Cutlery and paper napkins are at the end of the line (or sometimes set on tables in the dining room) next to a cashier who receives payments. This may not be required in some institutional services where meals are pre-paid.

Commercial cafeterias may augment service by having staff at each station to assist or provide call-order service for grills, breakfasts or toasted sandwiches, etc.

In institutional catering where meals are pre-sold through an 'en pension' charge to students or other types of institutional customer, dishes are usually set up on the counter in order of consumption from soup through to sweet.

In cafeterias, where each dish is individually priced the servery line is arranged with merchandising and maximizing sales in mind. Thus an attractive salad display, hors d'oeuvres or side dishes might be first in line, for hungry customers are more likely to be tempted with such extra items when they are seen before main dishes.

Buffet service

Modern hotel operations increasingly adopt a buffet service which involves guests' self-service (and is thus an adaptation for hotels and restaurants of cafeteria approach). Guests help themselves to most items and these can include hot dishes. Carveries are a form of buffet service.

For buffet service, food is arranged on a buffet table in trays, on chafing dishes, oval flats, entrée dishes, etc. Plates, hot or cold (as applicable), are stacked at the head of each line or table. Napkins and silverware are normally located at the end of the buffet line.

A qualified member of the waiting or kitchen staff is available to deal with carving or portioning and is in attendance even in self-carving operations.

Cold buffets are usually embellished with decorative dishes such as ham or chaudfroid, salmon and poultry but centre-pieces can be of flowers, ice carvings, butter mouldings or company insignias or other relevant feature. Spot-lighting a buffet table is an effective finishing touch especially when highlighting a centre-piece.

U-shape, L-shape or V-shape and other shapes of table arrangement can be assembled to accommodate the food to be served and the numbers to be catered for. Some items, for example soup or beverages, are often set up separately so as not to cross the regular buffet lines and to increase traffic flow speed.

Silver service

In assessing the foregoing styles of restaurant service we can identify three forms in use today. These are:

- Silver service (including French, Russian, English and guéridon styles).
- Plate service.
- Cafeteria service.

Silver service is, in effect, what has emerged from restaurateurs blending together elements of French, English and Russian service.

Today, in silver service food is placed on or in appropriate silver plated dishes in the kitchen by the chef for presentation for service by waiters. The term 'silver' embraces stainless steel and also fire-proof enamel dishes, china or earthenware. These latter dishes are normally presented on oval 'flats' of silver or stainless steel. Fish, for example, is frequently so served.

Sometimes silver service has been called 'Continental' service in England.

In America four major service styles are thus recognized as:

- French service – guéridon service.
- English service – silver service.
- American service – pre-plated service.
- Russian service – silver service.

Guéridon service

The most elaborate form of silver service in restaurants today is called guéridon. In this case a side table (or guéridon) is exploited to the full. This side table can also be on wheels (in trolley form), and in America it usually is mobile.†

Advantages and disadvantages

Advantages claimed for guéridon service is that it helps merchandise meals and foods of all levels in an up market or high class restaurant because it is soignée, 'classy' and can be spectacular. A handed service is also safe (from spillage and accidents) and there is little or no risk of a napkin or clothing touching food.

But among its disadvantages are that it is labour and time-consuming. It may also tempt waiters to overserve guests and give them more than they require.

---

†For details of carving, flambage and other procedures see J. Fuller, *The Restaurateur's Guide to Guéridon and Lamp Cookery* (Hutchinson 1975).

Adaptations to brigades

In high class restaurants, a brigade of waiters used to be organized on the basic idea that one waiter (the 'chef de rang' or station waiter) was in charge of four, five, six or more tables with assistance from one or more 'commis'. This was fundamental to the original concept of good silver service, English or French style, (especially English silver service from the guéridon). With commis to bring dishes from the kitchen and to do the 'fetching and carrying', a chef de rang waiter could attend to the finer points of actual service to the guest. Some adaptations to the system of commis support have to be made in periods of high staff costs, staff scarcity and other manning difficulties.

Tradition and change

All the forms of service listed, and variants of them, are conditioned by general rules of serving, and the preceding notes are intended merely to outline their basic forms.

Restaurateurs, prompted by guests' demand for convenience, and tempered by common sense and good manners, have formed service styles in order to smooth or facilitate a meal's progress. In the restaurant business these customs and styles are affected also by staffing and cost considerations so that restaurateurs constantly seek to adapt style to modern needs and realities.

Despite the reservations already expressed regarding large brigades and costly labour usage, silver service (and adaptations of silver service) have long been accepted in Britain and the rest of the Western World as the standard of good waiting practice. Therefore, change is likely to be evolutionary rather than revolutionary.

Having covered the forms of service of a meal, Chapter 14 considers basic forms and techniques involved in main types of restaurant service.

14 Procedures and techniques

Techniques and waiting procedures for main meals have emerged over the years for convenience, both in meeting customers' needs and in aiding waiters to operate productively and profitably and to merchandise meals.

In explaining customary practices there are two dangers. One is that readers may come to regard practices as 'holy writ', while the other is that they may be dismissed as old-fashioned rituals. In fact, sensible meal merchandising blends tradition and innovation, so that forms of service best orientated to guests' needs are established. What follows should be read in this context, and, more importantly, should not be read in isolation from the book's other sections.

Here, general techniques are considered but information about specific dishes and courses dealt with in other chapters must be regarded as supplementing this information.

Conduct and technique

Above all, waiters must not become obsessed by techniques or procedures. Technical slips will either be unnoticed by guests or will be readily overlooked if a waiter's conduct is in other respects agreeably attentive.

In applying techniques, a waiter must not forget to be courteous and tactful with difficult customers and above all, he must never exhibit impatience and short temper. A waiter should never openly, or by implication, denigrate the quality of food he is serving. If he believes dishes are not satisfactory he should refer to his head waiter (or other superior) before serving it so that a decision may be made about its return to the kitchen.

Remember the importance of establishing good communication and relationship with guests, notify them of unavoidable delay, explain why, and avoid blaming others. All other rules of conduct, previously touched upon in Chapter 3, should be observed and, in particular, that waiting service should be conducted quietly (avoiding rattling and banging), and expeditiously.

General practice during service

During meal service, keep your service station tidy. Do not allow dishes to accumulate. Never put anything on the floor, or on tables.

Use of sideboard

If you find your sideboard is too small for all the things you want to put on it, change your layout and your method of work. Probably it is how you use your sideboard that is wrong, not its size.

Be 'method study' minded and organize your journeys (and your commis) to the kitchen and other ancillary departments, that is, when used dishes are awaiting clearance, do not leave the restaurant empty handed.

Dropping items on the floor

Pick up immediately any articles of silver dropped on the floor for return to wash-up. They must not be used at the table.

Never put back any food dropped on the floor on the dish with the rest of the food; pick it up immediately, put it on a plate and take it right out of the restaurant. Do this with due regard to cleanliness and delicacy, for example use a discarded menu as a scoop so as to make it clear that the dropped food will be thrown away. This is important as a customer is likely to watch to see what you are going to do with it.

Cracked and chipped items

Never lay a chipped glass or plate, and avoid serving from any such imperfect article. Take anything dropped on the floor to the side table for replacement, and then take it to the wash-up. This applies not only to food but to any article (knife, etc.) that may be dropped on to the floor.

Items not to be carried

Articles such as teaspoons, menu cards or lumps of sugar should never be kept in a waiter's pocket. The menu card should be on the table or the side table. It should never be carried in a waiter's pocket or tucked inside a waiter's shirt front.

Handling and handles

Handle all equipment as quickly as possible, with as little noise as possible. Pick up all equipment by their handles, never by the 'eating' or 'drinking' part. When serving a beverage, keep the jug or pot handle away from a customer but the handle of the cup, etc., from which he will drink should be turned to the customer's right. This means that service of coffee, etc., is always carried out from the right of the customer.

Place items such as sugar, cream, etc., to the right of the customer within easy reach.

Sides for service

It might be thought that the matter of which side of the guest a waiter should operate to serve or to clear would have been resolved long ago; but this is not the case.

Once it was widely accepted that food service should be from the left and food clearance from the right; with drink and glass service and clearance from the right. Many now believe that clearing food plates from the right is hazardous to glasses on the table and awkward when guests are drinking. Hence procedure tends to vary according to different establishments' ideas of efficiency and convenience.

In Europe there are broadly two main styles with deviations in some establishments often occurring in each case. There is the traditional Continental style, and the style which has been adapted in Britain.

This chapter outlines basic waiting procedures used in silver service and, indeed, in all forms of good waiting. At relevant points an indication is given of whether plate placing, serving or clearing should be from the right. However, for convenience, basic procedures of both the Continental and English practices may be summarized as follows:

Continental tradition

The main rules are:

- Place clean plates and glasses from the guest's right.
- Place coffee cups and saucers (with underplate) from the guest's left.
- Serve food from the guest's left.
- Serve drinks (including wine and coffee) from the guest's right.
- Clear all used items, that is, plates, cups and glasses, from the right.

These rules conform with conventional styles observed in most establishments in Europe, particularly France and Switzerland, and are the basis of teaching in most Continental hotel schools.

English adaptation

The main rules are:

- Plates or utensils for food are placed from the left.
- Food is served from the left.
- Used food plates are cleared from the left.
- Glasses are placed from the right.
- Drink is served from the right.
- Used glasses are cleared from the right.

The word English is used advisedly because in Scotland there is, perhaps, more conformity with Continental custom, but in many English restaurants and training centres, Continental style in regard to clearance is adapted as above.

There should be no feeling of inferiority regarding British styles of table service or waiting. The traditional British butler and the service standards of English clubs have long been regarded as worth emulating by other countries. Urbain-Dubois, the great French chef de cuisine, wrote of English table conduct as 'the one most observed and practised in the higher circles of society, the English enjoying, in this respect, a European reputation'.

Conforming with house custom

Rules or customs of the house as determined by the restaurateur or maître d'hôtel should be followed. Either right-hand or left-hand clearance may be regarded as correct and this book does not take up a rigid nor didactic attitude.

Guidance which follows should, therefore, be interpreted and conditioned always by the application of the 'house' rules of any particular restaurant as to which side of clearance shall be adopted. But once a decision is taken, observance of it should be total.

There should never be a mixture of right or left-hand clearance in any one restaurant, except when, as notes below indicate, guests' convenience is involved. (This means, for example, that a waiter must not interrupt a conversation in order to effect service nor force his way between a wall and the back of a customer's chair.)

Drinks and coffee service sides

Drinks are served from the right but further detail regarding wine service is contained in Part Five.

Coffee cups (on saucers and underplates), sugar (unless it is on the same salver as the coffee itself) and bread are also placed before or offered to the guest from the left. Because coffee, as other beverages, is served from the right some people consider it illogical to place coffee cups and saucers from the left. But, again, it is adopting one practice and sticking to it that is important. Coffee service is detailed on page 180.

Tools for service

Waiters may use many gadgets and pieces of equipment but their service cloth and service spoon and fork are aids and tools most often employed. Before turning to methods of service observations about these aids are outlined below.

Waiter's service cloth

Use your waiter's cloth only for the purposes intended. Note particularly the use of the service cloth in presenting a dish, as mentioned previously, and in putting on plates, as described on page 160. Moreover, *only* service cloths should be used, never table napkins (especially, for obvious hygiene reasons, those previously used by customers).

Service cloth use includes polishing glasses, cutlery, plates, etc.

Note: (When polishing, hold a cloth in both hands so that fingers do not touch glass or china.) Polish both sides of a plate. Wipe plates as they are taken from the hot-plate (never at table). (The bottom plate of a pile from a hot cupboard can pick up greasy dirt from the cupboard shelf and should be especially checked.)

Other service cloth use includes:

Wiping spillage from a plate or cup rim.
Wiping the underside of a dish before placing it on the table.
Handling dishes, hot or cold (always use a service cloth for this purpose).
Carrying dishes and trays when the neatly folded service cloth as a pad protects the hand from what is being carried.
Wiping fingers, to avoid slipperiness, before clearing.
When not in use (when standing at the sideboard), carry the service cloth neatly folded on the **left forearm (see Figure 10, page 40). Never tuck it under the arm.**
Never misuse the service cloth. (Especially do not use it to dust furniture, wipe service tables, clean shoes or flick crumbs off tables.)

Do not allow service cloths to get too dirty; if a cloth gets stained or soiled during the service, discard it at once and take a clean one from the service table. This applies also to napkins used for crumbing the tables or for covering the service plate.

Serving spoon and fork

Do not regard one-handed manipulation of service spoon and fork as a holy ritual. Some items such as small boiled potatoes, peas or some other vegetables, are served better using only a spoon and, as observed below, fragile sole fillets, for example, may be transferred better using two splayed-out forks.

Some 'modernists' have scorned 'spoon and forkery' and urged 'rationalization' of serving techniques. Yet the skill required to manipulate a spoon and fork is quickly acquired (most achieve dexterity in minutes rather than hours).

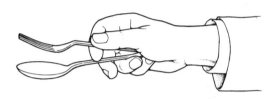

Figure 39 *Holding the serving spoon and fork*
Note the position of the first finger, which is inserted between the spoon and the fork, giving initial leverage and enabling the food to be firmly held. The spoon is supported by the second finger. Handles of both spoon and fork rest in the centre of the palm, where they can be kept 'locked' with ease

Figure 40 *Using the serving spoon and fork*
In using the serving spoon and fork to serve a round object such as a potato, the fork is inverted to follow the shape of the food. The serving dish is correctly positioned low down, almost touching and slightly overlapping the guest's plate

Alternative tools such as tongs add to silver inventories and would not always be available as readily as is a simple spoon and fork.

When using a service spoon and fork:

Take a clean set of service spoon and fork for each dish.
Do not use them again to serve another table.

Do not use a fork without a spoon (except in rare instances, that is, in serving smoked salmon, cucumber salad).
Never use two spoons.
Never use the same spoon and fork for both potatoes and green vegetables.
In lifting food, take care that the portion does not slip from the dish on to a customer's plate.

Serving from silver

In the following paragraphs the term 'silver' may be taken to include stainless steel. Similar techniques also apply when serving in this style from copper, oven-proof crockery or other ware.

Ensuring order accuracy

Always check carefully yourself the food you are about to serve and make sure:

● It is the right order.
● Portions are adequate.
● The dish is neat and clean.

Sequence of hot and cold dishes

If at any time you have to serve some customers with hot dishes, and others with cold dishes, serve cold dishes first.

Presenting a dish

Present each dish at table prior to serving from it. First show it to the host for his approval and to confirm it is the one ordered. If it is not visible to the rest of the party, present it also at the other end of the table.

When presenting a dish, lift its cover so as to avoid condensation dripping on to the carpet or table-cloth. At the sideboard invert the cover to avoid marking the sideboard cloth.

In high class service, deep dishes are not regarded as complete in themselves but are always presented on an underdish or liner.

Carrying a dish

Carry an oval dish lengthwise on the palm of the hand. Protect your hand with a service cloth folded into a neat pad. Do not handle dishes, hot or cold, without a service cloth.

For large dishes, stretching out the fingers affords better control. For extremely large and heavy dishes which are by no means easy to hold, it may help to allow one end of the dish to rest on the wrist, gripping the other end with the fingers.

Serving from a dish

With food already portioned on a silver dish, place on it a spoon and fork for service. Stand on the guest's left, feet together, with the dish on the palm of your left hand (protected by the pad of folded waiter's cloth).

Advance your left foot forward, bring the dish down to the level of the guest's plate just over the rim; the dish being perfectly level. (Most beginners do not lower the dish sufficiently.) Take the spoon and fork in your right hand to serve food on to the plate. The way the spoon and fork is held is shown in Figure 39. Basically, food should be lifted with the spoon, with the fork gently keeping it firm. Only occasionally is it necessary to use the spoon and fork as pincers, and then the leverage should be firmly gentle. Skill in spoon and fork usage, avoiding breakage or dropping food is readily acquired with practice.

Serving from large flat silver

When serving from a large flat dish remember to:

● Ensure that guests' plates are hot and clean.
● Protect yourself and the plates with a service cloth when carrying a pile of hot-plates.

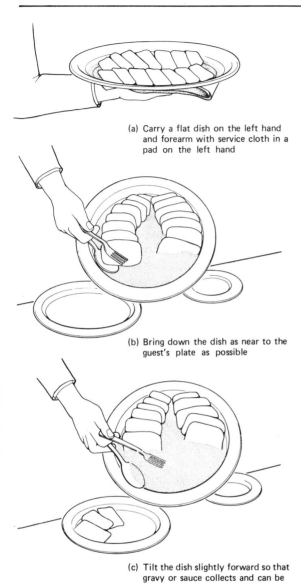

(a) Carry a flat dish on the left hand and forearm with service cloth in a pad on the left hand

(b) Bring down the dish as near to the guest's plate as possible

(c) Tilt the dish slightly forward so that gravy or sauce collects and can be served

Figure 41   *Serving from large flat silver*

- Stand on the guest's left.
- Serve with care to avoid spilling gravy or sauce on the plate's rim.

Serving from deep holloware

When serving from a deep dish (such as a cocotte or vegetable dish) remember to:

- Check that the dish is on an underdish.
- Ensure that guests' plates are hot and clean.
- Protect yourself and the plates with your service cloth when carrying a pile of hot-plates.
- Serve with care and avoid spilling on to the rim of the guest's plate.
- Use a separate spoon and fork for each dish (or each half of a divided vegetable dish) and avoid mixing the contents.
- Bring down the dishes as close to the guest's plate as possible.
- When there is more than one dish on your underliner, turn the underliner as necessary to bring each dish in turn, in line with the plate.

Serving large items

Should a fish portion be too big for easy service with spoon and fork, sever it across the middle with the spoon. When serving an omelette cut off the extreme tips with the spoon before serving. (Two fork serving is acceptable for certain dishes such as large sole fillets meunière or omelettes fourrées.) If an omelette, large fish fillet or other item has to be cut into several portions, check beforehand exactly how many, to avoid unequal portioning.

Positioning food on the plate

Arrange food appetizingly when placing on the plate. Generally, fish or meat is served lower centre with vegetables one side and potatoes the other; separate sauces and/or accompaniments at the top right-hand side (2 o'clock). When serving sauce, do not pour it over the food without ascertaining a guest's wishes. Arrangement on the plate should seek to reproduce the effect achieved by a chef on the silver dish. In the kitchen he aims to make dishes attractive; but his work can be spoiled by indifferent rearrangement by a waiter resulting in uninteresting and unappetizing food (see also Chapter 13).

Guéridon service

In more elaborate guéridon services (service from side table or trolley), entailing filleting of fish (particularly Dover soles), carving birds, and finishing dishes such as pancakes, remember that after presentation, the dish should not leave the customer's sight.

Such work is performed on a small service table or trolley with a réchaud (hot-plate) or spirit lamp (for cooking) in front of the customer. Where no guéridons are provided, portioning must be done at the waiter's sideboard.*

Using lamps (réchauds) and hot-plates
Sideboards are often equipped with electrically heated (or other forms of heated) hot-plates. These may be used as necessary to keep plates and dishes warm.

Use lamps or réchauds with caution. Dishes that have already been cooked may become over-cooked if excessively heated on a réchaud. An important use for a réchaud is in cooking and finishing certain dishes 'in the room'. Another use is to keep food hot during service. On some spirit models (today models tend to be bottled-gas heated) there may be two flames. One flame is used for keeping dishes hot and two flames (a double flame) are used for flambé dishes such as crêpes Suzette. This emphasizes the need to keep flames controlled and to avoid over-cooking.

Using a salver
Salvers may be used to serve vegetables, to clear glasses and to serve drinks.

Lay a cloth on the salver to stop slipping and prevent conduction of heat thus avoiding burning the palm of the hand.

Carry clean cups, glasses, etc., on a salver and lift them by their handles or stems and not by putting your fingers inside them.

---

*For detail regarding carving, flambé cooking and more advanced techniques see J. Fuller, *The Restaurateur's Guide to Guéridon and Lamp Cookery* (Hutchinson 1975).

Glasses
Remove dirty glasses on a salver and not by hand.

Do not allow glasses to knock against one another, making a noise – some guests are superstitious about this. (For notes on glasses see Chapter 20.)

Laying and using a tray
In a restaurant do not carry bottles of wine or mineral waters on trays except in the case of wine bottles in cradles or wine coolers. Lounge waiters, however, often carry split size minerals on salvers or small trays.

In restaurants in America, a large tray was used by busboys for fetching and clearing but today, trolleys tend to replace trays.

If trays are used during service, load them safely and correctly. Do not risk over-loading. Place the heaviest article in the middle to aid balance. Do not carry glasses on a tray containing dishes. Apart from the risk of toppling, there is also the possibility of their being smeared with gravy, grease or sauce.

Carrying trays
Trays in hotels are used mostly for room service and possibly for afternoon teas (see Chapter 18).

Trays in popular catering
The procedure for loading and carrying trays applies to all branches of catering. Many cafeterias, cafés and canteens bring food courses to guests on trays, and place the tray on the table in front of a guest. Some hotel coffee shop services also have individual trays already laid up at each guest cover. Arrange trays in conformity with hotel 'bedroom' service (see Chapter 18), and in accordance with the general guidance indicated above.

Plate handling

Before placing, check temperature and cleanliness of plates before they reach a table rather than wipe them in front of guests; though to wipe the underside before placing is prudent. For hot courses plates must be hot; for cold courses cold.

Putting on plates (silver service)

Hold a pile of plates on the left hand (not between thumb and fingers) which is covered with one end of the waiter's cloth. On approaching the right (or left) of the customer, gently wipe the top plate with the other end of the cloth, then pick up the plate with the tips of the thumb and fingers of the right hand. Keeping the plate horizontal, lower it into position. Continue this procedure, finishing with the host.

Plates are usually placed from a guest's right side in Continental service but in Britain most operations favour placing them from the left.

Underplates

Table etiquette and presentation style established the use of underplates for hollow items such as soup plates, coffee cups and saucers and butter dishes. In addition to aiding 'presentation', underplates help avoid drips and, in the case of soup, contact with soup and waiter's hand. An example of underplate service is that of clear soup in a consommé cup, on a saucer, on an underplate. For some food in coupes or similar containers (for example grapefruit, ice cream), place a doyley and an underplate under the container.

Plate and dish clearance

Clear used plates either from the left or the right, according to an establishment's rule, but the whole room must work in the same way.

Removing plates

Collect plates when guests signify that they have finished by putting knife and fork together across the plate.

Remove used plates directly all the party is finished (but not before) leaving the host until last. Priority should be given to clearing plates first to keep a table tidy and, secondly, to keep from a customer any impression that he is forgotten.

Clearing cutlery with plates

To remove plates with cutlery correctly, pick up the plates with the right hand and transfer them to the left. Hold the first plate by the thumb lying along the edge of the plate pointing across the body, and the first two fingers underneath, slightly spread. The third and fourth fingers stand up outside the plate – the tips level with the thumb (see Figure 42(a)).

Place the used fork with the curve upwards. Put the used knife under the curve of the fork and at right angles; this is the technique known as the 'first plate'.

Place the second plate on your forearm with the under rim behind the thumb joint and on the two extended fingers. In this way the plate cannot slip forward and the main weight is supported by your forearm (see Figure 42(b)).

Then pick up the knife and fork and gently scrape any remains of food on to the first plate. Then place them with the other cutlery on the first plate, fork with fork and knife under forks, as before. Continue round the table in this manner until it is cleared. You should be able to clear eight places comfortably in this fashion (see Figure 42(c)).

By this method, you have a neat stack of plates which do not wobble and are not top-heavy. When you go to the side table, you can take the first plate out of your left hand (using your right hand) and place it on top of the pile so that the whole pile is completely steady.

Shift food from one plate to the other as far as possible out of guests' vision. The angle of cutlery on the first plate should be such that should anything fall it will do so towards you and not the customer.

This routine ensures that dishes are cleared properly without food remains or cutlery between plates. Curiously, such a procedure is not considered de rigueur in England's stately homes. The butler of one noble lord was quoted in the *Radio Times* (August, 1980) as instructing ` . . . *never* to pile the plates up. Only waiters do that!'.

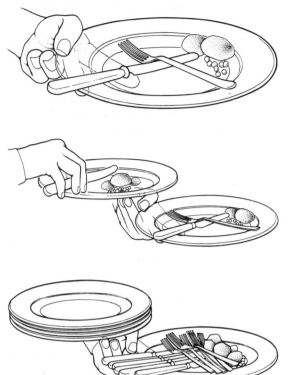

(a) Removing first plate
This is transferred to the waiter's left hand. Note the position of thumb, little and third finger on top; other two fingers below. The used fork is placed prongs upwards and the knife put at right angles under the bridge part of the fork. An alternative (favoured on the continent) is to reverse the fork's position, i.e. with prongs downwards thus forming a larger bridge under which to slide the knives. Both methods are acceptable. Some waiters find it more secure if the first fork is held by the thumb holding the cutlery plate

(b) Second plate stage
The second plate is balanced on three points formed by the knuckle of the thumb, tips of little and second finger and lower part of forearm (the wrist itself should not be in contact with the plate). Next step is to transfer knife from second plate to first plate alongside the first knife. Then any food remains on second plate are gently scraped with the fork on to the first plate. Carry out this procedure at a safe distance from guests and, certainly, never over the table

(c) Stack of cleared plates
Having cleared as outlined above, the waiter now has a neat stack of plates, which do not wobble and are not top-heavy. Finally while returning to the sideboard, the waiter will place the first plate (with the cutlery and remains of food) on top of the stack

Glass plates have been drawn to reveal hand positions. Service cloth, normally draping left forearm, is omitted for clarity.

Figure 42   *Clearing plates*

At wash-up, clear cutlery from soiled plates and place in the appropriate receptacle.

Clearing dishes
If any dishes have been left on the table for guests to serve themselves, return any which contain food to the kitchen.

Clearing vacated tables
Clear used items immediately from a vacated table. Replace cruets, flowers and clean ashtrays at the same time. If a cloth is soiled, and needs changing do so at once. Reset covers as soon as possible. Check that chairs are clean and free from crumbs when you are cleaning the table.

Table-cloth during service

Table linen will also require attention when guests are 'in the room'.

Changing the table-cloth when guests are present
When a soiled table-cloth has to be changed during service, the following method should be adopted. Any articles on the table should be cleared to the side-board, *never* placed on chairs or on the next table. The soiled cloth should be brushed, if necessary, on to a crumb tray or plate. The routine below aims to ensure that the felt-covered top of the table is not exposed during cloth changing.

Figure 43 *Changing the table-cloth*
Note that the soiled table-cloth is drawn towards the waiter who at the same time pulls the clean cloth across the table so that the table top is always covered

Steps in changing a table-cloth during service

1 Select the correct size table-cloth.
2 Stand as for laying a cloth (see page 131).
3 Place the new cloth on the far side of the table in the same way as for laying a cloth.
4 Open the new cloth and hold it as previously described (see page 131).
5 Stretching across the table, hold the loose flap of the table-cloth clear of the far edge of the table.
6 Release the lower flap and release the double fold held between the thumb and first finger. This allows the cloth to fall lightly (usually on to the chair on the far side).
7 Without relinquishing hold of the clean one, pinch the soiled cloth at the outer edges of the table between the palm and fingers to pick it up.
8 Draw the soiled cloth towards you, gently shaking the clean cloth over the table.
9 Inspect the clean cloth for correct drop and alignment.
10 Place the soiled cloth away in the dirty linen receptacle.

Dealing with spills

Water, wine, sauce or similar moist matter can be spilled on the cloth. For such spills as sauce, take a small plate with a knife or spoon to the table and remove the sauce by scraping. When the sauce is removed, cover the stain with a piece of white paper or menu card (in some cases slip a card also beneath the cloth). This prevents any marking of the clean slip cloth (napperon) or table napkin (if the stain is very small), which should then be neatly unfolded and laid over the card or paper.

Using a napperon (slip cloth)

Thus, when a table-cloth is only lightly stained, it may (as a measure of economy) be covered with a napperon (or slip cloth). This may often allow the same cloth to be used several times during one service.

In using a napperon for this purpose check that its folds correspond to those of the table-cloth underneath. If a napperon has to be changed in the presence of a guest then it should be done swiftly and neatly using the same sort of technique as applies to changing a table-cloth during service.

When the table is vacated a clean table-cloth or slip cloth must be laid before the table is offered to another party.

Relaying covers during service

The flowers, cruet and other items are replaced on the table and the table laid with the cutlery, one cover at a time, from a cloth-covered salver.

During service, cutlery should never be carried in the hand, even in a cloth, but always on a salver or large plate which has been covered with a napkin to deaden any noise.

The relay silver should be arranged neatly on the salver with the spoons and forks tucked underneath at right angles on either side. This facilitates handling, allays noise, possible accident, and looks neater.

Moving a laid table

When moving a laid table, fold back the hanging drape of the table-cloth so that you grasp the table itself, thus avoiding creasing the cloth.

Progressing the meal

Observe the meal's progress. Train yourself to notice right away what is missing from a table and to 'keep an eye' on guests (without staring which makes guests uncomfortable) so that customers can attract attention readily.

Seek a customer's permission before removing sauces, cruet or any other item from his table when required for another table. Remember to:

● Check that a customer can reach required items like salt and pepper.
● Check whether the butter dish contains butter.
● Pass rolls again each time a guest has finished the one on his plate or check that the plate or dish containing toast Melba is never empty.

Accompaniments
Make sure during service that all dishes are completely served, that is that all sauces and condiments required are passed with a dish and that a customer has the correct cutlery.

Finger bowls
A finger bowl is served with certain dishes particularly foods which a guest may handle, for example, asparagus or fresh fruit. Half fill the finger bowl with lukewarm water (in which a lemon sliver, rose petal or similar embellishment may be dropped) and place it on the left of the customer.

When served at the end of a meal, place the finger bowl in front of the guest after the dessert dish has been removed. After a finger bowl has been used, a high class establishment may present a fresh table napkin.

Adjusting covers
A waiter brings cutlery beforehand as may be required for the dish ordered. Similarly, he removes unwanted items.

Always carry out adjustment of a cover without delay removing or adding cutlery with a 'service plate', a medium sized plate (fish plate) with a folded napkin. Having the table thus ready for subsequent service helps to avoid serving confusion later for it makes clear which guest will be taking dishes selected.

Additionally, as soon as any course is finished, remove any unwanted items (cruets, sauces, etc.).

Crumbing down
Remove the cruet from a table at the end of the meat course, just before the sweet is served. Similarly, remove other remaining items such as unwanted cutlery and empty bottles. This is preparatory to 'crumbing down', for always remove crumbs and bread from a table before serving a sweet or dessert course. Use a neatly folded table napkin as a brush to bring crumbs to the table edge. From the edge they can be brought gently on to a medium-sized plate. A crumb scoop is nowadays rarely seen.

Adjusting the cover for sweet service
After crumbing down, if dessert spoon and fork have been laid across the top of the cover, move them down to right and left of the guest cover without stretching your arm in front of him.

A napperon after the sweet course is seldom used today. For this, a waiter used to unroll the smaller cloth gradually over the table, replacing glasses in their proper place. Coffee and liqueurs were then served on a clean table.

Courses and dishes
Procedures involved in serving courses and dishes from hors d'oeuvres to cheese are given in Chapter 15.

Coffee and the bill
The service of coffee (or tea) and the presentation of the bill are considered in Chapter 15.

Purpose of procedures
Techniques and procedures are prompted by the needs of guests. The way in which waiters wait at table has to do with merchandising the service product, with selling it and with selling themselves. The latter is, in turn, associated with techniques that are, as it were, good table manners in action. Never allow the technicalities of table service to degenerate into meaningless or mechanical rituals. Rather, let them reflect warmth and consideration for your guests.

15 Serving courses and dishes

During meal service, there are several points to observe at each course. This chapter gives guidance about service procedure but makes no attempt to detail the full intricacies of guéridon service, carving, salad and dressing-making and flambé work.* Indicated in this chapter, however, are fundamental points concerning the service of different courses, salads, other accompaniments and some special dishes.

Accompaniments

Many dishes have separate accompaniments and as they are not always mentioned on the menu a waiter must know them. Always have any accompaniments ready for service at the right time. Hot adjuncts come with the dish from the kitchen, but cold sauces are often to be found at the buffet or sideboard. Serve them directly with a dish to which they belong.

Serving sauces

The stance for service is the same as for a main dish. Except in certain instances (mentioned later), serve them from the guest's left on to the top right of his plate (not on the rim). When serving from a sauceboat carry the boat on an under dish or small plate, on the palm of the left hand. In serving, point the sauceboat lip towards the guest's plate. Pass the spoon or ladle over the lip of the sauceboat. Do not pour sauces from the boat.

Accompaniments are summarized below (but see also Part Two for further food information). French words for main items are given after the English to aid menu recognition.

*For these more advanced techniques see J. Fuller, *The Restaurateur's Guide to Guéridon and Lamp Cookery* (Hutchinson 1975).

Soup (potage)

Thick soup

When serving soup use an underlayer plate. Hold the underplate in the left hand, place the soup plate on it and then serve the soup from the tureen using a silver soup ladle. This is normally done from the sideboard. Should any soup be spilled on the soup plate's edge, wipe it with the service cloth before serving to the customer (from his left). (See Figure 44.)

Serving soup from a tureen

When ladling from a soup tureen:

- If brought really hot from the kitchen, use of a lamp or réchaud should not be necessary (overheating can spoil the soup).
- Ensure that soup plates are hot and clean.
- When carrying a pile of hot plates protect yourself and the plates with your service cloth.
- Stir and ladle with care to avoid drips on plate rims. The lid should be inverted when removed to avoid drips.
- Serve plates of hot soup on underplates with great care to avoid spillage on plate rims. The underplate also prevents any possibility of soup contacting a waiter's thumb. Its use is

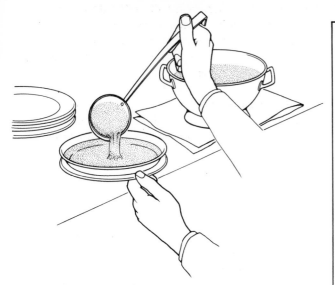

Figure 44   *Serving soup from a tureen*
With ladle in right hand, stir soup gently and serve

Table 21   *Examples of soup services*

Soup	Accompaniment	Cutlery and crockery
Artichoke	Chopped chervil and croûtons	Soup spoon and soup plate
Bortsch	Sour cream	Soup spoon and soup plate
Bouillabaisse	Toast	Soup spoon, fish cutlery and soup plate
Consommé cold, en gelée	Lemon wedge	Cup and dessert spoon
Consommé hot, en tasse	Pain grillé or paillettes	Cup and dessert spoon
Green pea	Croûtons	Soup spoon and soup plate
Minestrone	Grated Parmesan cheese	Soup spoon and soup plate
Onion	Flutes and grated cheese	Soup spoon as for marmite
Petite marmite	Flutes, grated cheese	Served in earthenware individual marmites with dessert spoon
Turtle	Buttered brown bread and lemon (formerly accompanied by small glass of cold milk punch)	Cup and dessert spoon (when en tasse) or soup plate and soup spoon
Vichysoisse (cold)	Toast Melba	Cup and dessert spoon

even more important when soup is plated in the kitchen and has to be carried a distance by the waiter.

Service from individual bowls
Alternatively, individual portions of soup may be presented in silver soup bowls. In this case, set soup plates and underplate before the guest. From the left, carefully tilt the silver bowl to transfer the soup, away from the guest, into his soup plate. For many soups, croûtons, grated cheese and flutes, are then separately passed. Serve them from sauceboats using a ladle or spoon.

Service in cups (en tasse)
Clear soup (consommé)   This is usually served in consommé cups, that is, a cup with two handles. A dessert spoon is used by the guest for clear soup en tasse instead of a soup spoon. The en tasse set consists of an entrée plate as the underplate, a saucer and a cup. Serve all three at one time. Serve the soup from the tureen into cup with a silver soup ladle and place the complete set from the left.

Thick soups are not usually served in cups (en tasse) unless cold (for example Vichyssoise).

Soup from a side table
Soup service is also often carried out from a guéridon which has been placed near the cus-

tomer's table. A spirit lamp is sometimes used to keep soup hot while it is being served. Take care not to over-heat certain thick soups on the lamp or réchaud as they may 'turn' or curdle if boiled.

Soup accompaniments
Croûtons (sippets)   Sprinkled over soup.
Croûtes (flutes)   Sprinkled over soup.
Fromage râpé (grated cheese)   Sprinkled over soup.

Lemon wedge   Served on the left side of the underplate with certain clear soups.
Paillettes (cheese straws)   Served on a bread plate and, having been proffered, any remaining are left on the table.

Clearing soup plates
When removing soup plates, both plates (that is, soup plate and underplate) must be lifted at once.

Hors d'oeuvre

Hors d'oeuvre variés are presented on a trolley, each variety being in a 'ravier' or similar dish. A separate service is used for each variety.

Wheel the trolley to the customer's table and place it near the person to be served. Remove the hors d'oeuvre plate (fish plate) from the customer's right-hand side with the right hand and place in your left hand.

Use your service cloth to hold the plate while serving the hors d'oeuvre according to the customer's instruction. When service is completed, place the plate before the customer from the left.

Wheel the trolley round to the next person to be served and repeat the routine until all guests have been served.

On certain occasions, when a smaller variety (say six) is offered on a set menu, a special tray or dish containing several compartments may be used. Again a separate item is placed in each compartment. This tray is carried by the waiter to serve hors d'oeuvre. Serve from the tray directly on to the plate in front of the customer, revolve the tray on your hand until you have offered each variety to the guest.

Hors d'oeuvre accompaniment
An oil and vinegar cruet must be put on the table when hors d'oeuvre variés are served.

Single hors d'oeuvre
The following 'single' items are also served as opening courses:

Caviar   Usually served in the original container buried in a silver timbale filled with crushed ice. It is served with a dessert spoon. The cover required is a fish plate and a side knife (or caviar knife if available).

Caviar accompaniments   Blinis, a type of hot pancake or, alternatively, hot toast (breakfast thickness) and slices of brown bread are passed. Also offered are half lemons wrapped in muslin, finely chopped onions and chopped parsley. In some restaurants, sieved egg white and egg yolk are also offered. Place a pepper-mill and cayenne pepper on the table. Set finger bowls at each corner after the caviar has been served.

Oysters (huîtres)   Serve oysters on a round silver flat or soup plate if individual portion) covered with broken ice and set on an underplate. Oysters are opened in the larder a few minutes before being served. The oyster is placed in the deep half of the shell, care being taken to remove the black ring (beard) around the edge of the shell. A half lemon is served with each portion. The oyster fork is placed across the tip of the joint knife at an angle of forty-five degrees.

Oyster accompaniments   Brown bread and butter or thin brown bread and butter sandwiches are passed with oysters. An oyster cruet consisting of chilli vinegar, Tabasco sauce, a pepper-mill and cayenne pepper is passed or placed between two guests. Lemon is an essential adjunct. Normally a half lemon is served with the individual portion. A finger bowl, half filled with tepid water is placed on a side plate covered with a small napkin. This is served to the guest, that is, set a little to the left above the cover, as he finishes.

Terrine de pâté de foie gras   For the cover, set an entrée plate and a side knife. The pâté is served in its original container (terrine) buried in a bed of crushed ice. A jug of hot water and a dessert spoon are all that is required for serving. Dip the spoon into hot water and scoop a portion (roughly a spoonful) from the terrine with the spoon and put it on the entrée plate. Dip the spoon again into hot water before serving the next guest.

Pâté de fois gras accompaniments   Serve hot brioche and/or hot toast (trimmed of crust and slightly thinner than for breakfast service) with fresh butter separately.

Plover (or gull's) eggs (oeufs de pluvier)   Serve cut brown bread and butter, spiced (oriental) salt and a finger bowl.

Potted shrimps   Cut brown bread and butter and cayenne pepper. Segment of lemon.

Prawns in shell   Prawns are arranged unshelled round the rim of a stem-glass. Place this glass on a medium-sized doyley-covered plate. Pass buttered brown bread and place a finger bowl (containing a thin slice of lemon) on the table. Alternatively, shelled prawns are sometimes served on a bed of lettuce. Accompaniments are the same.

Prawn cocktail   Shelled prawns enfolded in a dressing (usually of mayonnaise thinned with tomato juice/sauce and spiced with Worcestershire or Tabasco sauce) is presented on a bed of shredded lettuce in a stemmed glass on a doyley-covered small plate with teaspoon and small fork. Brown bread and butter and lemon are accompaniments. If an unpeeled prawn is hung on the glass's rim, a finger bowl may also be set. Other seafood cocktails are similarly presented.

Smoked eel (anguille fumée)   Buttered brown bread, wedge of lemon, pepper-mill and cayenne pepper.

Smoked salmon (saumon fumé)   This is usually cut (importantly in very thin slices) in the dining room in front of the guest, and placed directly on the plate. For functions it is cut in the kitchen and the slices arranged on a silver flat. It is then served by the waiter with a fork only. Roll the slivers round the prongs and unfold them onto the guest's plate. The cover required by the customer is a fish knife and fork with service on to a medium-sized (fish) plate.

Smoked salmon accompaniments   Place pepper-mill, cayenne pepper and a bottle of chilli vinegar on the table. Pass half lemons wrapped in muslin cloths. Also pass buttered brown bread, with the crust trimmed off.

Smoked trout (truite fumée)   Remove skin, head and tail. Serve buttered brown bread, wedge of lemon, sauce raifort (plain or flavoured and coloured with finely grated raw beetroot), pepper-mill and cayenne pepper.

Fruit and juices

Juices
Juices are served chilled in a stemmed glass on a doyley-covered plate with teaspoon for stirring.
Tomato juice   Worcester sauce should be on the table.
Fruit juices   For other fruit juices ensure that the caster sugar sifter (or similar dispenser) is available if required. Other juices commonly served include: orange, pineapple, passion fruit, pomegranate.

Fruit appetizers
Avocado (avocat or poire de coing)   Accompaniments include: vinaigrette; shrimps with sauce Marie-Rose; or lemon wedges and caster sugar.

Table 22   *Examples of hors d'oeuvre and appetizer services*

Item	Accompaniments	Cutlery
Artichoke, hot	Hollandaise sauce, beurre fondu	Dessert (side) knife and fork, finger bowl
Artichoke, cold	Vinaigrette	Dessert (side) knife and dessert fork, finger bowl
Asparagus, hot	Hollandaise sauce or beurre fondu	Dessert fork (or asparagus tongs), finger bowl
Asparagus, cold	Vinaigrette	Dessert fork (or asparagus tongs), finger bowl
Avocado	Vinaigrette, seafood, Roquefort dressing	Teaspoon, oyster fork, finger bowl
Cantaloup	Caster sugar, ground ginger	Dessert fork and spoon
Caviar	Sieved (separately) hard-boiled white and yolk of egg, chopped parsley, finely chopped onion. (a) hot toast, lemon or (b) blinis, sour cream	Caviar knife (or side knife or fish knife)
Eggs, wild, e.g. gulls, plovers	Brown bread and butter, oriental (spiced) salt	Small knife and fork, finger bowl
Escargot (snails)	Brown bread and butter or toast	Snail clasp, fork and teaspoon
Fruit cocktails	Possibly a liqueur or spirit (e.g. Cointreau, Kirsch)	Teaspoon or sundae spoon (and possibly small fork)
Grapefruit	Caster sugar	Grapefruit spoon or teaspoon
Herring, marinated	Sour cream and onions	Fish knife and fork
Herring, smoked	Buttered brown bread, oil and lemon	Fish knife and fork
Hors d'oeuvre varié	Oil and vinegar	Small knife and fork
Mussels, marinated	Sauce tartare	Fish knife and fork
Oysters, cold	Cayenne pepper and/or pepper-mill, brown bread, chilli or tarragon sauce or tarragon vinegar	Oyster fork, finger bowl
Oysters, hot (e.g. Rockefeller)		Oyster fork, finger bowl
Palm hearts	Mayonnaise, vinaigrette or preferred sauce	Small knife and fork
Pâté (firm, e.g. en croûte or de campagne)	Possibly gherkins, mustard	Small knife and fork
Pâté (soft, e.g. de foie)	Hot toast in a napkin	Side knife
Prawns, cocktail	Cocktail sauce, brown bread, lemon	Oyster fork, teaspoon
Salmon, smoked	Lemon, pepper-mill, cayenne pepper, brown bread and butter	Fish knife and fork
Taramosalata	Hot toast, lemon	Small knife (or fish knife)

Fruit cocktail (cocktail de fruit) Service of a fruit cocktail is similar to grapefruit (see below) except that they are served either in special cocktail coupes or in glasses. No finger bowls need be passed afterwards.

Grapefruit (pamplemousse) Grapefruit are prepared before the service, usually by waiting staff. Halve them and cut each segment of flesh separately. The half grapefruit is served (usually decorated with a cocktail cherry) in a special silver cup placed on an entrée plate with a teaspoon alongside the cup. Serve it from the left.

Grapefruit accompaniments Pass caster sugar immediately grapefruit is served. Leave on the table. A finger bowl is placed afterwards.

Melon (melon and cantaloup) Two kinds of melon are frequently served: cantaloup and honeydew. A cantaloup is a yellow-skinned, gourdlike melon. Honeydew is larger, usually greener and of a Rugby football shape. Lay a cover for guests of a fruit knife and fork placed across the plate, the tip of the handle of the knife resting on the prongs of the fork. An optional addition may be a sweet spoon laid across the plate with its handle to the right. The slice of melon is normally positioned on the plate at the sideboard, in the space formed between the crossed knife and fork. It is then placed before the guest with any accompaniments that are required.

Melon accompaniments Pass a silver flat with two bowls, one with caster sugar and one with ground ginger. In serving, place a couple of teaspoons of sugar neatly on the side of the guest's plate and a smaller quantity of ginger alongside it, according to the guest's request. Do not sprinkle sugar (or ginger) over the melon. Also place a sugar dredger on the table when melon is served. Melon, especially cantaloup, is often made into a melon cocktail, flavoured with port or other wine (see fruit cocktail service above). A thin slice of Parma ham is also sometimes served with honeydew melon. Melon is usually served as an hors d'oeuvre but can also be served as a sweet.

Pasta and egg dishes

Pasta

Macaroni, spaghetti, noodles (nouilles) and similar farinaceous early courses are served on entrée plates. The cover cutlery used traditionally consists of a joint fork only, and is placed on the right-hand side of the cover. Nowadays a dessert spoon (or even table spoon if not too large) is usually placed on the left.

For pasta, noodles and risotto (rice) when served au beurre or with tomato sauce, grated Parmesan cheese is offered.

Egg dishes

Omelets (omelettes) A fork alone is traditionally placed on the right-hand side. Today it is usual to set a meat knife and fork unless the omelette has a fish garnish (for example omelette Arnold Bennett), when a fish knife and fork should be laid.

En cocotte Place the cocotte on a medium-size plate (fish plate) especially where two eggs are served to each portion. Place a teaspoon on the right side of the cocotte(s).

Sur le plat Place the plat on an underplate with a dessert spoon and fork on each side of the dish.

Fish (poisson)

Sauced fish

When fish is covered with a sauce such as Mornay, Dugléré or Bonne Femme, no preparation is required before serving. Take care, however, not to break the fish. See that each person is given a complete portion with adequate sauce and a helping of the steamed or boiled potato which is usually served.

Unsauced fish

When fish is fried, shallow fried (meunière) or boiled, some preparation may be required before serving.

Use of guéridon and sideboard

All preparation of fish before serving must be done at the service table, or in the case of special dishes such as 'truite au bleu', on a guéridon in front of the customer; but never on the customer's table.

As a general rule, salt water fish are served without the head, fresh water fish with the head still on.

Fish dishes

Fish steak or tronçon For a steak of fish or 'tronçon', bones have to be removed and outside skin peeled off with a spoon and fork, taking care not to break the flesh. Place the bones and skin removed on a separate plate and on no account leave them on the dish as it is served.

Whole fish For a whole fish such as a Dover sole usually served grilled or meunière trim away small bones around the fish. Then lift each fillet separately from the spine bone with a spoon and fork. For other types of sole, trim off the small bones only; the centre bone remains in the fish as it is nearly impossible to remove without breaking the fish.

When sole is deep fried, small outer bones are removed before cooking. Fillets may then be removed by the waiter two at a time. Take out the centre bone and rebuild the fish on to the dish before serving.

Cold lobster (homard froid) Lay a fish knife and fork at the guest's cover. Half a lobster is the customary portion, dressed in the shell on a silver flat on a bed of shredded lettuce. Usual garnish is half a hard-boiled egg, tomatoes and slices of cucumber.

Should a guest wish to deal himself with a half lobster, then add to the cover lobster pick (fork), shell crackers and a finger bowl. Otherwise: first present the dish, then bring it back to the service table for preparing.

Place a little shredded lettuce on the guest's plate. Then using a spoon and fork, lift the flesh from the tail and cut away the shell part of the tail, leaving the flesh attached to the body of the fish. Place this portion on top of the lettuce on the plate. Next, using a clean napkin, pick up the claw in your left hand. Break the shell of the claw in half (this has been cracked previously in the larder) and, with the fork, ease the flesh out of the shell. Place this also on the plate. Next, using service fork and spoon, decorate the plate with half a hard boiled egg, tomato and cucumber. Having prepared all the plates in this way (when

Table 23 *Examples of fish services*

Type of fish	Accompaniment
Deep fried, egg and breadcrumbed (frit à l'anglaise)	Tartare sauce, lemon quarter, fried or plain parsley
Deep fried, in batter (frit à l'Orly)	Tomato sauce (hot or cold), lemon
Grilled (grillé)	Maître d'hôtel (or anchovy or similar) butter, a piquant sauce, e.g. Robert
Lobster, cold	Sauce mayonnaise, salad apart. See service notes
Lobster, hot	According to choice
Meunière	Lemon
Poached (poché)	Hollandaise sauce (or derivative), butter sauce, beurre fondu or egg sauce (or similar sauce)
Salmon, cold	Sauce mayonnaise, cucumber salad, mixed salad
Salmon, (poached) hot	Cucumber salad, sauce hollandaise, pommes vapeur (nouvelles)
Scampi, fried	Tartare sauce (or similar sauce)
Trout (truite au bleu)	Lemon, beurre fondu
Whitebait, fried	Cayenne pepper, moulin, lemon wedge, brown bread and butter

more than one person is being served) place them in front of each guest.

Cold lobster accompaniments Pass mayonnaise sauce separately in a sauceboat. An oil and vinegar cruet can be placed on the table.

Parsley with fish Fresh parsley sprigs served with fish are intended to give colour and are not usually served by the waiter unless by request of the guest. But fried parsley is part of the dish and should be served.

Entrée and main courses

Entrée

Table setting or cover required for an entrée is a joint knife and fork and an entrée plate. An entrée at dinner is complete in itself and is there-fore served on one silver dish, usually flat. Some light entrées such as a vol au vent may be featured as a preliminary course or a main course according to circumstances and portion size. A

Table 24 *Examples of entrée and main course services*

Dish	Accompaniment
Meats:	
Boiled, fresh beef, French style (boeuf bouilli à la française)	Grain or rock salt, gherkins, grated horseradish
Boiled leg of mutton (gigot de mouton bouilli)	Caper sauce (and purée of turnip)
Boiled salt silverside of beef (gîte à la noix)	Carrots, onions, dumplings
Braised ham (jambon braisé)	Spinach (épinard), Madeira sauce (sauce Madère) or peach sauce
Braised tongue (lange de boeuf braisée)	Florentine garnish, e.g. spinach, Madeira sauce
Calf's head (tête de veau), hot	Vinaigrette or gribiche sauce. (Some of the brains may be reserved to be mixed in the vinaigrette sauce)
Cold meats (assiette anglaise)	Mustards (English and French), pickle, chutney
Curries (kari)	Boiled rice, chutney, papadums, Bombay duck (Indian restaurants serve many other accompaniments) Dessert spoon and fork laid at cover
Grills	Mustard to be passed
Grilled ham (jambon grillé) or boiled, baked ham	Appropriate sauce on menu e.g. mustard, tomato, horseradish
Grilled steaks	Sauce Béarnaise (especially for Chateaubriand, fillets), maître d'hôtel butter, watercress
Haggis	Turnip purée, mashed potatoes (possibly hot oatmeal biscuits). Dessert spoon may be laid with knife and fork
Irish stew	Worcestershire sauce (soup spoon in addition to knife and fork laid at cover)
Jugged hare (civet de lièvre)	Red currant jelly
Lancashire hotpot	Pickled red cabbage
Roast beef (boeuf rôti)	Horseradish sauce, Yorkshire pudding, jus rôti (roast gravy unthickened)
Roast lamb (agneau rôti)	Mint sauce (sauce menthe) or mint jelly, jus rôti (roast gravy, unthickened)

spoon and fork is the required service equipment. At luncheon some entrées will have separate vegetable accompaniments.

Main course

For many main courses no preparation by a waiter is required (except in special cases for **carving à la carte dishes such as entrecôte double, Porterhouse steak, Chateaubriand, pheasant, grouse, etc.**). Service is straightforward. First pass the meat, then vegetables and finally sauce from the sauceboat.

Take care to give each person an equal portion and, if a dish is decorated with vegetables, potatoes, watercress, etc., see that you serve some of each to every guest. French and English mustards are nearly always required with this course, especially with grills. You should pass them to guests and not just leave them on the table.

For the following (and most main courses of meat, poultry or game) the cover laid is a large (meat) knife and fork. Where dishes such as curry or Irish stew require different or additional cutlery this is indicated. Moussaka and paella are sometimes thought to require a dessert spoon in addition to, or as substitute for, a knife. In other cases common sense should be applied;

Dish	Accompaniment
Roast leg of mutton (gigot de mouton rôti)	Red currant jelly or onion sauce, jus rôti
Roast pork (porc rôti)	Sage and onion stuffing, apple sauce, jus lié (thickened gravy)
Roast saddle of mutton (selle de mouton rôtie)	Red currant jelly or onion sauce
Roast shoulder of mutton (epaule de mouton rôtie)	Red currant jelly or onion sauce
Salmis of game (salmis de gibier)	Red currant jelly
Roast veal (veau rôti)	Savoury herb stuffing, bacon and jus lié (thickened gravy)
	Note: With beef, pork, ham, tongue, liver and kidneys offer French and English mustard
Poultry:	
Chicken Maryland	Horseradish cream
Roast chicken (poulet rôti)	Bread sauce, roast gravy (unthickened), possibly also grilled bacon or rolled bacon and sausage
Roast duck (caneton rôti)	Sage and onion stuffing (farce aux oignons), apple sauce (sauce pommes), roast gravy (unthickened)
Roast goose (oie rôti)	Sage and onion stuffing, apple sauce, roast gravy (unthickened)
Roast turkey (dindon rôti)	Cranberry sauce, savoury herb or chestnut stuffing, chestnuts, chipolatas, roast gravy (unthickened)
Game birds:	
Roast grouse	Bread sauce, fried breadcrumbs, roast gravy (unthickened)
Roast partridge (perdreau rôti)	Bread sauce, fried breadcrumbs, roast gravy (unthickened)
Roast pheasant (faisan rôti)	Bread sauce, fried breadcrumbs, roast gravy (unthickened)
	Note: Game chips usually accompany all roast birds. Each of the accompaniments is served in a separate sauceboat
Other game:	
Hare	Red currant or black currant jelly, chestnut purée, noodles
Rabbit, roast (lapin rôti)	Bread sauce, roast gravy (jus rôti) unthickened
Venison	Red cabbage, chestnut purée, Cumberland or poivrade sauce

for example when frog's legs are served (usually as a light entrée, introductory course) a small dessert knife and fork are customary.

Clearing the main course

When clearing after this course, remove side plates if no vegetable course follows and a sweet is next on the menu. Clear also cruets, sauce bottles and other condiments as well as toast Melba and butter.

When all is clear except for glasses, crumb down the table using a folded napkin and a plate. Then put on sweet spoons and forks or bring down (which ever is house custom) and put on sweet plates.

Vegetables

Vegetables as accompaniments   To accompany main courses (whether meat, poultry, game or fish etc.) many operations offer a selection of vegetables of the day. In up-market service a separate hot side plate is placed at the top left of the main course plate (10 to 12 o'clock). A separate fork is provided. Vegetables are served on to this side plate.

Vegetables, particularly finer ones, may be served as a separate course after the main course or, quite commonly today, as an introductory course.

Baked jacket potatoes (pommes au four)   Serve on small side plates with a fork on the side plate. Make an incision on one side of the potato, insert a pat of butter and sprinkle with cayenne pepper. (Sour cream and chives may be required instead of butter.)

Asparagus (asperges)   After laying the cover of a fork (and/or possibly asparagus tongs) place the guest's plate on the fork so that it tilts to his right. Serve the asparagus, the melted butter or sauce hollandaise (or mousseline). Set a finger bowl (with a slice of lemon in the water) for each guest.

Table 25   *Examples of vegetable accompaniments*

Item	Accompaniment
Artichoke (artichaut) globe, cold	Mayonnaise, vinaigrette or gribiche
Artichoke (artichaut) globe, hot	Hollandaise sauce, melted butter
Asparagus (asperge), hot	Hollandaise sauce, melted butter
Asparagus, cold	Mayonnaise sauce, vinaigrette or gribiche
Beets (betterave), cold	**Vinaigrette**
Broccoli (brocoli)	Hollandaise sauce
Cauliflower (choufleur)	Hollandaise sauce, melted butter
Corn on the cob (maïs)	Melted butter
Spinach (épinard), en branches	Cream, sometimes veal gravy

Salads

In restaurants offering high class service, a waiter prepares dressings 'in the room' and then dresses the salads before the guest.

Mode of dressing

For small quantities this dressing is often mixed on a plate or soup plate, for example by mixing by fork, mustard (French or English), a little pepper from the mill, and salt with a little vinegar – then whisking in the oil (for range of further dressings and details of procedure see below).

Dressings however elaborated are then best blended with leaf salads in the bowl. Then transfer the dressed salad to crescent-shaped salad plates. Place these together with a dessert fork by the top left-hand side of each guest's meat plate.

Customer-made dressing

Sometimes a customer prefers to make his own dressing. In this case place a salad bowl on the table above the cover, the required ingredients at the top left and a large plate with a large spoon and small fork in front of the customer. When he has dressed his salad it may be removed and arranged on salad plates by the waiter.

Service of salads

Place salads on the table immediately before the rest of the course is served. The plate position is at the top left (10 to 12 o'clock). The crescent or kidney-shaped salad plate should fit the meat plate just above the side plate. For shredded or broken salads, place a small fork on the side of the salad plate; for heart salads a small knife and fork.

Certain fruit salads, for instance those served in an orange or apple, need a teaspoon.

On the table all the salads should look uniform in size, design and position. It may be hard to find room for the last salad if they are not correctly placed. Move the cruet or an odd glass to make room. Such items as ashtrays, menus, table numbers, water jugs, etc., may be removed from the table.

Too often insufficient care is taken in salad service resulting in a few lettuce leaves garnished with pieces of tomato, cucumber and beetroot. Salad is as important as the rest of the meal and gives a waiter scope to show skill and willingness to give good service.

Types of salad

Leaf salad Lettuce leaves round (that is, cabbage lettuce), or cos, corn salad, chicory, endive, watercress, can be mixed as a 'composite' salad, or made individually as separate salads. Use vinaigrette dressing (see dressings below).

Heart salad **Good quality round (Webbs or cabbage lettuce), iceberg, cos or romaine lettuce with a tight heart. Serve in halves or quarters according to size.**

Both types are served with cold meats and can also be served with game or a grill on customer's request.

Fruit Chiefly used with game, or highly spiced or marinated dishes. Clean fruit flavour 'cuts' the richness of the dish.

Table 26 *Examples of dressings*

Dressing	Ingredients
American	Similar to English dressing with equal oil and vinegar and possibly sweetened with sugar
Acidulated cream	Fresh cream and fresh lemon juice seasoned with salt. Various other items are added according to salad. (Used mainly for fruit garnished salads)
English	Salt, pepper, English mustard and two parts vinegar to one of oil. Caster sugar as guest requires to taste. (Sugar offsets the vinegar's sharpness)
French	Salt, pepper-mill, French mustard and one part vinegar to three parts oil (nowadays preferred by knowledgeable English customers)
Lemon	Salt, pepper, fresh lemon juice and olive oil to taste, with caster sugar (popular with people who do not like vinegar)
Mayonnaise	Mayonnaise sauce thinned with vinegar and lemon juice to a dressing consistency
Sauce gribiche	Mayonnaise dressing with a garnish of chopped gherkins, capers, chervil, tarragon, parsley and strips of hard white of egg
Sauce ravigote	Vinaigrette with a heavy garnish of chopped chives, chervil, tarragon, capers and parsley
Sauce vinaigrette	Salt, pepper, one part vinegar to two parts olive oil, (also used for certain hot dishes e.g. calf's head). French or English mustard is often blended in additionally to guests' requirements
Thousand island	Mayonnaise dressing with a little chilli sauce, chopped red pimento, chives and green peppers

Cold cooked vegetables   Chiefly root (whole or sliced) arranged decoratively – carrots, turnips, onions, kohl-rabi, celery, celeriac, leeks, etc.

Raw vegetable salads   Shredded turnips, carrots, cabbage, celery, chicory, celeriac, spring onions, kohl-rabi, etc. Many variants and additions are possible. These and other ingredients can be combined in any mixed salad to a customer's wish and according to season. They can also be served separately as individual salads. (See below for a selection of salads.)

Salad dressings

In general, the English have a dry palate and are not fond of olive oil (corn oil and ground nut oils may be preferred). Continentals like olive oil. Americans who are big salad eaters have a sweet palate of a different nature. So dressings for salads should be balanced to appeal to customers' palates.

Some of the more popular dressings are shown in Table 26.

Method of dressing salads

At the appropriate time, present the salad and ask if customers would like it dressed and if so, their taste. Salads especially green salads should never be dressed until the last moment or their crispness will be lost. Mix the dressing on a dinner plate or soup plate. Measure out salt, pepper, mustard (possibly sugar), and vinegar and mix. Then add the oil. By moving the plate briskly back and forth with the left hand and whisking with a flat fork on the plate with the right hand, a creamy texture will form.

Never mix dressings in a silver sauceboat or dish: the silver will be badly scratched and be ruined.

Leaf salad   Pour dressing over the salad in its bowl and then remove any garnish on to a plate. With a spoon and fork lightly turn and twist the leaves in the bowl to impart a thin coating of dressing over the leaves. Place the leaves neatly on salad plates and decorate with the garnish which is also dressed.

Heart salad   Take care not to flood the salad with dressing. Lightly mask the open part with dressing, using a teaspoon, so that the dressing sinks between the leaves. Dress the garnish and arrange all on to the plates.

Fruit-type salad   Acidulated cream dressing is usually employed. Many such salads are already dressed, but some, where green salad is also used, need dressing at table. First arrange these salads on plates, then add the fruit, only lightly mask with the dressing.*

Desserts, sweets and puddings

Many customers conscious of 'U' words, avoid saying 'sweet' or 'dessert' in favour of using the word 'pudding'. Hence there may be confusion about how sweet items and courses should be described.

Originally, dessert appeared to mean whatever was brought to table after the table had been cleared (desservie) and could include other things besides fruit. Changes in eating style and the shortening of menus often now cause more traditional desserts to be bracketed with other kinds of sweets and puddings.

Waiters must thus accept that guests will use words like pudding, sweet and dessert indiscriminately, though purists may still believe that the term dessert should be confined to the fruits (generally fresh) presented after a table is 'desservie' and when the active service of foods by waiters has ended. Yet, paradoxically, the spoon and fork used for puddings are invariably called dessert spoons and forks.

---

*Further information on salads, salad dressings and special permutations (for example, Caesar salad) may be obtained from J. Fuller, *The Restaurateur's Guide to Guéridon and Lamp Cookery* (Hutchinson 1975).

Table 27 *Examples of salads with suggested dressings*

Name	Constituents	Dressing
À la française	Lettuce hearts, tomatoes, hard-boiled eggs. (Beetroot sometimes added but only at last minute due to staining)	Vinaigrette
Allemande	Diced apples, potatoes, gherkins, smoked herrings, onions, chopped parsley. (If decorated with beetroot see note on à la française)	Vinaigrette
Archiduc	Julienne of beetroot, endives, truffle and potato	Vinaigrette
Augustin	Cos lettuce heart with French beans, quartered tomato, hard-boiled egg, green peas	Mayonnaise
Carmen	Dice of pimentoes and chicken with peas, rice	Vinaigrette with mustard and chopped tarragon
Chicago	Tomatoes, asparagus tips, French beans, foie gras slice, julienne of carrots, mushrooms	Mayonnaise
Cressonnière	Sliced potatoes and hard-boiled egg, watercress leaves, chopped parsley	Mayonnaise
Dalila	Bananas, apples, julienne of celery	Mayonnaise
Demi-deuil	Lettuce heart with strips of truffle and potato	Vinaigrette
Eleonora	Cos lettuce heart garnished with artichoke bottom and asparagus points	Mayonnaise
Eve	Scooped out apple filled with dice of apple, pineapple and banana	Acidulated cream
Fanchette	Julienne of chicken, raw mushrooms, chicory, truffle	Vinaigrette
Florida	Lettuce heart with quartered oranges	Acidulated cream
Gauloise	Cos lettuce leaves with strips of fresh nuts	Mayonnaise
Indienne	Rice, asparagus, julienne of pimentoes, dice of apples	Curry-flavoured acidulated cream
Japonaise	Fresh fruit diced in acidulated cream (on bed of lettuce or within a scooped out orange half)	
Jockey-Club	Asparagus tips, julienne of truffle, lettuce hearts	Mayonnaise thinned with vinaigrette
Légumes (de)	Diced potato, chopped French beans, green peas and cauliflower	Vinaigrette
Lorette	Corn salad, beetroot strips, celery root	Vinaigrette
Louisette	Cos lettuce heart, quartered tomato, skinned, pipped grapes	Vinaigrette
Mimosa	Half lettuce hearts, garnish of orange segments, grapes, bananas	Acidulated cream
Niçoise	French beans, quartered tomato, sliced potato, decorated with anchovy fillets, olives and capers	Vinaigrette
Rachel	Celery, potato, truffle, artichoke bottoms in strips, asparagus points	Mayonnaise

Trolley service

At lunch time, cold sweets are usually presented on a trolley when service resembles that from hors d'oeuvre trolleys. Wheel the trolley round the table and serve each guest individually according to each guest's instructions.

Hot items

For hot sweets, use hot plates and place them before guests. Hold the serving dish in the left hand and serve the sweet with a spoon and fork or a spoon only, according to the type of sweet.

Coupes

For sweets served in 'coupes' place the coupe on a sweet plate with a teaspoon alongside the plate. For ice cream, pass wafers separately. Neatly arrange wafers on a doyley-covered silver flat. Never stick them in the ice cream. If a customer after taking a trolley sweet orders at the same time another sweet which is served in a coupe, then spoon the sweet from the coupe to serve it by the side of the other sweet on the same plate.

There has been an indication earlier (throughout Part Two) of the wide variety of cold and sweet puddings (entremets sucrés) that are available for service. Table 28 shows a few examples.

Service of sweet and savoury dishes together

Sometimes there may be a requirement to serve one (or more) guest with a sweet pudding and another (or more) with a savoury (see savouries on page 180) simultaneously.

For example, one or two guests may decide to have a bavarois (or ice cream) and the other a Scotch woodcock.

To prepare a table in readiness to serve these two items, clear away all unwanted plates and silver. Set a small knife and fork on the table for the one cover requiring the savoury; place cayenne pepper on the table. For the bavarois, bring down the dessert spoon and fork from the cover's top to the side position.

Table 28 *Examples of sweet course service*

Item	Accompaniment	Cutlery
Bombe Alaska		
Bombe glacée	Whipped cream	
Bombe Vesuvius	Flamed with warm brandy	
Fritters	Caster sugar, hot syrup-type sauces	
Gâteaux	Possibly fresh cream	All with dessert spoon and fork
Soufflés	Sabayon sauce or preferred sauce (possibly macédoine of fruit with cold soufflé)	
Soufflé pudding (pouding soufflé)	According to main flavouring: sauce sabayon (zabaglione), custard sauce	
Stewed fruit (compôte)	Fresh or whipped cream (crème Chantilly)	
Surprise omelettes	Sometimes flambé with warm brandy	
Coupes (ice cream)	Wafer biscuits	Sundae spoon
Fresh fruit	Caster sugar	Fruit knife and fork, finger bowl, grape scissors
Parfaits	Wafer biscuits	Parfait spoon

Should a guest choose an ice cream, remove the dessert spoon and fork. Do not place a teaspoon on the table for an ice cream but bring it on the side of the underplate bearing the coupe of ice cream.

Cheese (fromage)

Perhaps linked with a reduced interest by the weight-conscious in sweet items, cheese is increasingly popular and may be promoted as a special feature in many restaurants. Cheese boards and/or trolleys are used for this purpose. As with hors d'oeuvre, separate knives and forks must be used for each item.

Lay a clean side plate and side knife (and fork in most good class establishments) in front of each guest, a fresh dish of butter pats on an

Table 29 *Examples of accompaniments for cheese*

Item	Accompaniment	Cutlery
Firm cheese: **Cheddar, Cantal, Gruyère, Edam, etc.**	Non-sweet biscuits (except for digestive or wheatmeal style). Bread roll or French bread or other breads, butter, celery, radishes, spring onions, mustard	Small knife and fork
Soft cheese: **Brie, Camembert**	As above. (Occasionally chopped onion or cumin with munster may be requested especially by German guests)	
Petit suisse	A common form of service on the Continent is with caster sugar and fresh cream (crème fraiche) otherwise various biscuits and breads	Small knife and fork or dessertspoon and fork
Crowdie	Oatcakes may be served with crowdie	

underplate with a fork alongside in the centre of the table.

Set a dish or plate with a doyley containing a selection of cheese biscuits on the table. (Whole tins are sometimes presented, either wrapped in a napkin or in a specially made silver container.)

Present cheese, on a cheese board, to each customer. Cut a piece of the selected cheese with a special knife and place it on the customer's plate. Place also a glass containing sticks of celery on the table. Watercress may similarly be made available.

In different parts of the world (and even different areas of this country) there are variable tastes in what is eaten with cheese. Waiters may be asked for (and therefore be prepared to serve) other accompaniments from a crisp apple to pickled onions.

Cutting cheese

As cheese should be cut to yield portions satisfactory to the guest and in accordance with economy, it is inadvisable in restaurants to let customers help themselves.

For each cheese there is a special cut: a cut which conforms to its crust and preserves freshness. Figure 45(a) to (f) shows the different cuts for each type of cheese.

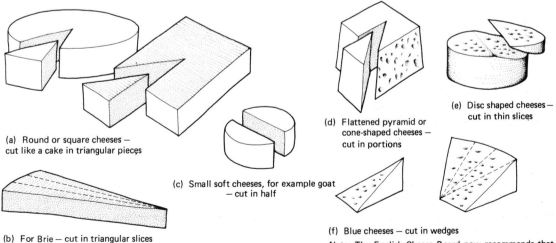

(a) Round or square cheeses — cut like a cake in triangular pieces

(b) For Brie — cut in triangular slices

(c) Small soft cheeses, for example goat — cut in half

(d) Flattened pyramid or cone-shaped cheeses — cut in portions

(e) Disc shaped cheeses — cut in thin slices

(f) Blue cheeses — cut in wedges

Note: The English Cheese Board now recommends that Stilton be wedge-cut, rather than scooped from the whole cheese. It is considered that this reduces waste and drying

Figure 45 *Methods of cutting cheese*

Savouries

For this course and with older styles of cutlery, small knives and forks were laid; when dealing with modern cutlery a guest may use joint knife and fork.

Put a hot plate in front of each guest. Place a plate covered with a folded napkin carrying salt and pepper, pepper-mill, red pepper and Worcestershire sauce on the table.

Add other sauces according to the nature of savoury. In some cases French and English mustard may appropriately be passed.

Fresh fruits

Place a finger bowl half filled with tepid water (possibly with rose petal or lemon slice added) on a fruit plate, a fruit fork to the left and a fruit knife to the right also on the same plate. The tip of the knife must rest on the prongs of the fork.

From the customer's left, place the whole cover in front of the guest and lift the finger bowl and place it above the plate.

Then present the fruit basket to the customer from the left. Carry the basket of fruit on your left hand. In the right hand hold a pair of scissors and finger bowl of cold water. If a customer wants an apple, an orange, a pear, etc., he helps himself from the basket. If a guest would like grapes, set down the finger bowl of water on the table, cut the stalk with the grape scissors and dip the grapes in the cold water. Serve the small bunch of grapes on to the customer's plate with the help of the grape scissors.

Coffee service

Coffee taken after luncheon or dinner is usually served at table by the waiter (though in some operations guests are encouraged to move to the lounge for coffee). Hence it is dealt with below as the concluding course of a main meal.

Preparing for coffee service

Prior to coffee service and when all guests have finished eating, clear and crumb down the table once again. Remove dirty and empty glasses. (Do not remove glasses not emptied without the guest's consent.)

In some cases, a small clean white slip cloth (napperon) is laid on the table to cover any stains which may have been made during the meal's service. A clean ashtray is then placed on the table.

Place a small warm coffee cup and saucer on a **china plate with the coffee spoon at an angle so that the handle points to the customer's right hand. Place this service from the right in front of each guest (though custom varies. Some favour** placement from the left as safer). Now set cream, if it is to be served, on the table (and, in some services, sugar also but see below). Make sure that coffee and milk to be served are really hot. (Pots and cups should be heated before serving.)

Serving coffee traditionally

The long standing procedure is for a waiter to carry on the palm of his left hand a salver covered with a cloth or doyley, or a plate with a doyley. On this is set the coffee pot, hot milk jug and sugar bowl.

Go to the guest's right and inquire 'Will you have black, sir, or with milk?' Then ask 'Do you take sugar, please, sir?' and if so, 'How many lumps' (or spoonfuls if brown).

Alternatively, you can serve sugar separately first and leave the bowl on the table. If you serve sugar from a salver you may rotate the salver to **bring the pot and jug nearer to the point of service (experienced waiters may complete coffee service without rotating the salver).**

Then fill the cup with coffee to about 6 mm (¼ in) from the brim. First serve the coffee by tilting the pot without lifting it from the silver flat; then do the same with the milk jug if required. In the best service, the coffee pot is inclined in a downwards position, making a pivot of the part of the pot exactly under the spout, but in such a way that this pivotal point does not leave the tray or plate. This requires a little practice. (Figure 46 illustrates this method). If fresh cream is preferred it may be left so that guests may help themselves, otherwise pour cream gently so that it floats on the coffee's surface.

When the service is completed, place the coffee pot and milk jug on the table at the host's right.

Modern deviations

Today, many believe the traditional practice to be dangerous, and encourage waiters to lift the pots or jugs one at a time, holding each firmly. Once again presentation, safety, speed and convenience have to be balanced one against the other. A service style will be decided upon by an establishment appropriate to its consumers' requirements, its staff capabilities and economic realities.

Alternative coffee service

'Speciality' coffee services such as filter, Turkish, Irish and brûlot are touched upon in Chapter 18.* One service method widely used, however, is with the 'Cona' coffee-maker.

Conas operate on the vacuum infusion principle. Made of heat-resistant glass, water is placed in a lower bowl. A glass infuser with a long tube is put on top with the tube passing into the lower bowl. Coffee is placed in the infuser and heat is applied to the water, which when boiling rises into the coffee filled infuser. The heat is removed and the infused liquid coffee now descends into the lower bowl again. (It may be infused a second time for additional strength if requested.)

*For greater detail of coffee services see J. Fuller, *The Restaurateur's Guide to Guéridon and Lamp Cookery* (Hutchinson 1975).

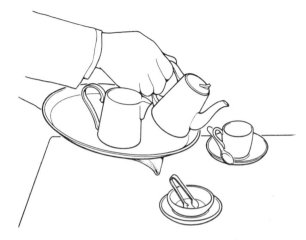

Figure 46 *Serving coffee traditionally*
The waiter inclines the pot downwards, making a pivot of the part of the base exactly under the spout. The pivot point remains on the tray

Conas are available in various sizes and combinations for use in a still-room (see Chapter 5) and also for making coffee 'in the room' on a sideboard or central service point for pour' n'serve service.

Table models for individual service to a guest's table are particularly popular in up market operations.

Once made in a table model the coffee may be served by the waiter direct from the glass bowl.

Cona machines are normally heated by electricity but the individual table service models are best used still with the small spirit heater as it is not practicable in most cases to connect to an electric point sufficiently adjacent to the table.

Also available for use with table models are candle warmers which keep coffee hot after brewing.

'White' coffee

It is preferable not to refer to coffee as 'white' for this is a slang expression. In any case, it is not always understood by visitors from overseas.

Liqueurs

Liqueurs are usually served into the glass. Carry

the filled glasses on a silver salver to the table, place them at the right of the coffee cup but not near the edge of the table. This procedure is appropriately varied if there is a liqueur trolley service in the room. (Further notes on liqueurs are found in Chapter 22.)

Tea in place of coffee

If a pot of tea is required by a guest, set a small tea cup, teaspoon and saucer on a side plate in front of him. Place a small salver or tray carrying a teapot, hot water jug, milk jug, on the guest's right-hand side to permit him to help himself whenever he judges that the tea is sufficiently infused. **Tea is never poured into the cup by the waiter.**

Chapter 18 deals further with the service of coffee and hot beverages on other occasions such as at breakfasts or on hotel floors or in lounges.

Presenting the bill

Except in 'popular style' operations where fast turnover of tables is the aim, do not present a bill until a customer asks for it. Always check a bill before presentation to ensure that it is correct. Shortages have already been mentioned and **management detest over-charging, for it is detrimental to an establishment's good name.**

Bills can be paid in two ways. Either by a customer to the waiter (and then to cashier) or by a customer on leaving, direct to the cash desk. The method adopted is determined by management (house custom).

Timing presentation

Prior to presentation, fold the bill from bottom to top with the right-hand corner turned back (the corner opposite the total, so that the total is not revealed). Then place the bill on a cash tray or plate.

The time for presenting the bill varies with the type of restaurant. In a higher priced restaurant more service may be required after a meal so the bill must remain open until asked for.

Do not lose any time in presenting the bill once it has been demanded. Never give a customer the impression that you are hastening his departure, either because other guests need the table or because the restaurant is nearly empty and you want to get home.

Receiving settlement

When the customer pays the bill, take it and the money to the restaurant cashier for encashment.

Place the receipted bill, with the change on the plate, on the table on the left-hand side of the host (though, again, right-hand placement is the custom in some operations). When returning the change on the plate or salver do not wait around for a tip even if a customer does not immediately collect his change off the plate. When a customer eventually takes his change do not remove the plate with the tip until the customer has left the table, unless the guest expresses in some way his desire for the plate to be removed.

Any tip left on the plate, no matter what size, should be picked up graciously with the plate and with a 'Thank you very much, sir'. Never show any disappointment even if (in your view) the amount is insufficient.

Bill procedure variations

Cash is less used in settling bills today in all kinds of circumstances. More hotels and restaurants accept cheques and credit cards in settlement of accounts. Waiting staff must familiarize themselves, therefore, with:

- General procedures regarding cheques and credit cards.
- House rules about which cards are acceptable.
- 'House' arrangements for accepting cheques and credit cards.

Credit cards

Credit cards can include that of the hotel or restaurant company itself, that of the British Hotels, Restaurants and Caterers' Association,

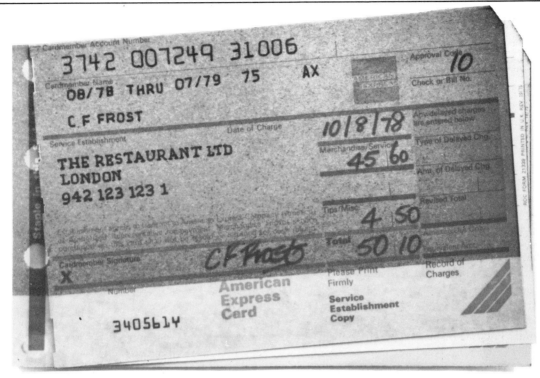

A typical voucher for charging a credit card account

principal UK bank credit cards (such as Access or Barclay), those of overseas banks, and internationally known credit card companies (for example American Express, Visa, Diners Club). There are many others.

A customer may ask which credit cards are acceptable. Be sure to know the answer. Often, without such inquiry, a guest may simply place his credit card instead of cash with the bill. Should his credit card not be among those acceptable to the restaurant then politely inform the customer so. Desirably make an alternative suggestion, such as that a cheque supported by a bank's card will be welcome. If you encounter any difficulties at this stage then refer the matter to the head waiter or restaurant manager.

Usually an acceptable credit card is proffered, in which case the cashier will prepare the billing pro forma in duplicate. Bring this with the bill and with a ballpoint pen for the customer to sign. Often restaurants enter the total amount of the bill without closing the entry on the account form so that a customer, should he so desire, may insert additionally any gratuity which he may wish to give.

When the form has been signed, separate the flimsy from the main copy, hand the customer's copy (usually flimsy) to the guest for his retention and return the credit card.

Cheque procedure

When a guest wishes to settle by cheque it is customary (unless the guest is extremely well known) to request the support of a bank card. These cards cover a cheque only up to a specified amount. When a guest proffers a cheque, if he does not also show his bank card, ask him courteously to do so. Take the cheque and the bank card (which carries the customer's specimen signature) to the cashier. Once the cashier has receipted the bill, return it to the customer in the usual manner.

Departure of guests

Service to customers ends only when they have left the restaurant and not when they have paid their bill.

When a guest rises from the table in order to leave, the waiter must immediately come forward. Usually hats and coats will be in a cloakroom, otherwise help guests with coats, hat and gloves. Check also that nothing belonging to a customer has fallen under the table or is hidden under a napkin.

If a tip is still on the plate, thank the customer sufficiently for him to hear, whatever the amount, just when he is ready to leave.

Bid 'Good day' or 'Good night' to guests and thank them for their patronage as they leave. (**Procedures for dealing with vacated tables once guests have departed are outlined in Chapter 12.**)

Complaints

All good waiters gain job satisfaction in completing service to a guest who is satisfied. Yet snags or hitches may arise.

Previous chapters have attempted to establish guidelines to help waiting staff minimize complaints, but complaints may arise at any stage during a meal and possible causes of complaint and methods of resolving them have been referred to in appropriate sections of previous chapters.

If any complaint has arisen during the service of a meal, a further apology (and possibly other action) is desirable before a customer leaves a restaurant. It may be appropriate, for example, to offer complimentary liqueurs with coffee; or to make a deduction from the bill; or in extreme cases to waive charges entirely for the meal. In any case, before a guest finally leaves further apology and assurance of future care from the maître d'hôtel or other responsible member of staff is likely to reassure a guest who might have had occasion to complain.

Naturally, no restaurant wants to have complaints and associates them with selling failure. In fact, complaints intelligently handled can often be turned to a restaurant's advantage. This is because any realistic customer is aware that even in the best ordered establishment something will occasionally go wrong. If this does happen then the opportunity can be seized for management and staff to show real concern for the guest, to take swift remedial action and to impress **the guest even more positively than where no** cause for complaint or misunderstanding might have arisen.

Most guests dislike complaining and are embarrassed by having to. If anyone has complained it is therefore important before the guest leaves the restaurant to re-establish warm and sympathetic relations. Make the guest feel that he will be really welcomed on any return visit and that the operation is alerted and concerned that there shall be no repetition in the future of what has caused complaint.

This chapter, and foregoing chapters, have outlined service action throughout a meal.

Table 30, which applies to 'silver service', is an aide memoire to the steps in serving a meal.

Table 30   *Service sequence checklist*

Stage of service	Action	Notes
Lay-up	Table preparation	Neat and aligned
Sideboard	Preparation	Tidy and organized
Mise en place done	Check lay-up. Collect rolls, butter and water	Cover jug
Guests arrive	Greet and seat Unfold guest's napkin Hand menus	Hold chairs On to laps Hold top
Guests studying menu	Serve water Serve rolls Place butter dish on table	*Pivot* from plate from *right* Unfold napkin on rolls From *left* on under- plate with doyley
Guests order	Using pad of folded service cloth for support, write carefully, *then* adjust covers using service plate	Split checks and take to: cashier; and kitchen still-room. Spike flimsy on sideboard
Prepare for starter course	Collect starter and plates	Check for cleanliness and heat
Serve starter	On to plate from *left*	Individual soup at table. Tureen and ladle at sideboard Hot hors d'oeuvres – *hot* plate Cold hors d'oeuvres – *cold* plate *Note:* Hors d'oeuvre accompaniments e.g. oil and vinegar
Prepare for main course	From kitchen collect plates and main course	Check plates are hot and clean. Place on sideboard. Put food on hot-plate
Clear starter from table	Stack empty plates and dishes as you go from left	Place stack on sideboard
Serve main course	Put on plates from *left* Serve from *left* main course dish	Long service cloth in left hand. Wipe each plate in turn Bring down dish close to, and parallel with, plate
Serve vegetables	Use spoon and fork as required	On salver with cloth underneath dishes Separate service gear for each vegetable

continued

Stage of service	Action	Notes
Serve gravy or sauce	From *left* on underplate	Sauceboat lip towards customer. Use ladle or spoon
Check	Garnishes	Ensure all accompaniments served and satisfactory
	Water and rolls, etc.	Replenish as needed
Main course clearance	When guests are finished remove unwanted items, e.g. cutlery, cruet. Clear and stack on sideboard	Use fork as bridge for knives
Prepare for sweet service	Crumb down	From left, use 'open end' of napkin to brush. Bring down dessert cutlery from cover top to side
	Hand menu	Write order. Split up checks
	Re-adjust cover if required	e.g. coupe/cheese. Use service plate to bring needed items
	Go to pastry	Collect sweet and plates
Serve sweet	Put on plates	From left, using cloth
Serve sweet/cheese	From the left	Check accompaniments biscuits, etc., all offered from left
	Check	Water, etc., as before
Take coffee order	Write check. Go to still-room and collect coffee, milk, sugar, cups, spoons, saucers	
Prepare coffee service	Assemble cups. Put on small underplates.	
Clear sweet/cheese course	Remove plates and stack on sideboard	
Serve coffee	Place coffee cups before guests from *right*. Request: 'Do you take sugar?' 'Do you wish black or with milk?'	Normally from right (but note house customs may differ): sugar; coffee; milk
	Check	Especially ashtray. Cover used ashtrays. clear, replace with new one
Bill presentation	Collect bill. Check it	Place folded bill on salver in front of client
	When requested collect money. Return to cashier Return bill, receipt and change. Place on table on plate	Leave on table
Assisting departing guests	When guests get up to leave help with chairs	Smile and say 'Thank you'

Part Four
Control, Functions and Other Services

16 Checking, control and the bill

Procedures for the presentation and settlement of a restaurant bill have to be supported. Waiting staff have specific tasks in checking and control arrangements. They not only serve food and drink 'in the room' but also prepare checks and pass them on. Service staff should understand their own part in any system but also appreciate what others do elsewhere to operate it.

Checking systems

As in all businesses, a checking system in hotels and restaurants is an essential part of the organization. Control, which implies checking at every stage enables food and drink to be co-ordinated with the aim of presenting a correct bill to each customer without delay.

To illustrate the purposes of control and checking basic manual forms are described in this chapter. Today, however, there is increasing application of mechanization (including microchip and similar) systems, especially in larger operations. At the other extreme in tiny, family-run restaurants control may be based on personal supervision. Under the constant eye of the proprietor (or a relative), checking may be much more rudimentary.

Supporting vouchers
Basically, all items, whether they are table d'hôte or à la carte dishes, wines, liqueurs, tobacco or coffee, are only obtained by a waiter on his presenting a check (or voucher) for items required.

This checking, fundamentally similar in all operations, varies in detail according to circumstances and the type of business for which an establishment caters. A check is written proof that a customer has been served with the items he has ordered, and if a dispute arises a mistake (if any) can be adjusted and the waiter, or department concerned, reprimanded.

If all orders to the kitchen or dispense were by word of mouth, utter chaos would result: bills would be made out incorrectly, disputes would arise, pilfering on a large scale would take place, and the business would go bankrupt through lack of control. Hence the need for checking.

One exception to this rule is that hotels with inclusive 'bed and breakfast' charges do not generally expect waiters to put in checks for breakfast dishes. It takes too long and wastes check pads. Control is obtained through the kitchen returns, for example 100 visitors – 100 breakfasts to be allowed for.

Types of checking
Two readily recognized types of checking are:

À la carte Where every dish on a menu is priced separately, so that every check order must state requirements and the price of a dish. These checks are just as important as if cash was passed, and if omitted on the final bill can account for loss of revenue and waiter's 'shortages' (short payment).

Table d'hôte Where a complete meal or set of courses at a fixed price is charged no prices need be mentioned, for example, 'Room 84, 4 lunches'.

If a meal deviates from a set menu, the check is expected to show the different dishes served and can be charged extra at the head waiter's discretion.

Detailed check pads

Some establishments operate menus which do not change. Steak operations, carveries and other speciality services are examples. In such cases checking and billing may be simplified. Check pads have full menu item details printed on them so that a waiter merely has to fill in the numbers required against the items wanted. The check (with carbon duplicate) can serve as a bill pad and as a receipt.

This bears some resemblance to a 'tea shop' system now out-dated in which at one time smaller establishments, such as cafés gave a waiter entire responsibility for taking his orders, collecting items and eventually making out his own bill.

The bill pads have carbon duplicates. The pads are already printed and cash entries are made only against those items the customer has consumed.

At the end of service the bill pad is handed to the control and the money is paid over. This system has many advantages vis-à-vis the restaurant and its control.

Carbon copies

Checks (in French 'bons de commandes' or 'bons') record an order, transmit it to the kitchen, provide an aide memoire for a waiter at his sideboard and the data from which later the cashier makes up a client's bill. Thus each waiter (chef de rang) is supplied with a check book. This may be used for ordering from all departments, or separate books may be supplied for still-room, dispense and so on. Check books are stamped with the waiter's number.

Triplicate, duplicate or single check systems may be adopted; but triplicate checks are virtually exclusively used now.

Single carbon
A single carbon with perforation is used for

Pate	Soup	Florida Cocktail	Smoked Salmon	Prawn Cocktail	Melon	£	p

Sole			Lamb Cutlets	
Halibut			Mixed Grill	
Fried Scampi			T-bone Steak	
Chicken Entree			Fillet Steak	
Steak Entree			Rump Steak	
Duck			Buffet	
Plat du Jour				

French Fried Pots.			French Fried Pots.	
Potatoes, S.B.			Potatoes, S.B.	
Grilled Tomatoes			Grilled Tomatoes	
Grilled Mushrooms			Grilled Mushrooms	
Peas			Peas	
Beans			Beans	
Carrots			Carrots	
Ratatouille			Ratatouille	
Salad			Salad	

Fruit Salad	Compote	Fruit Pie	Gateau	
Ice Cream	Water Ice	Cheese	Coffee	Tea
Bar/Cigarettes				

	No. of Covers	Table No.	Waitress
No. 24052			

Service not included – gratuities at customers' discretion.

Total includes V.A.T.

SALE OF MEALS
Total includes
V.A.T. at . . . . . %

No. 24052   **THE REGENT GRILL**

An example of a combined check, bill and receipt pad

table d'hôte or à la carte service with direct contact with the kitchen, one copy to kitchen and one copy on station or to restaurant cashier (house custom).

Double carbon

This is used where two copies are needed and is almost exclusively for full à la carte restaurants. The original is generally sent to the kitchen to obtain the goods, one carbon remains on station and one carbon goes to the restaurant cashier for preparation of the ultimate bill.

Triple carbon

The triplicate system involves one sheet of transparent paper (called a flimsy) so that the waiter has an original and two copies. To avoid two carbon papers in the triplicate system, double-sided carbon is used; the second copy is the flimsy tissue which takes the carbon impression of the reverse. The flimsy remains on the sideboard (or, more rarely, on the guest's table) to remind the waiter (and his commis) what is the next course to bring along. This system is used only in busy, high-class à la carte restaurants where four people at the same table may all order entirely different dishes.

Checking and the triplicate system

In the triplicate system, a waiter writes the order in his book or pad in which three consecutive pages carry the same serial number. Copies are clearly marked 1, 2 and 3 and generally state in print the meal (for example lunch, dinner). The waiter enters such information (according to house custom) as date, his own station number or letters, number of covers, table number and, if a guest is resident, the room number, and signs it. In traditional restaurants a waiter wrote the order in abbreviated French, no matter what country he was in.

Always write checks clearly and legibly to avoid mistakes and loss of time. The route of the checks is indicated in Figure 47.

Copy number 1, the original, is taken by the commis to the kitchen where the aboyeur may stamp it by stamp clock with the time of its receipt. Near the servery hot-plate (passe plats) and within the aboyeur's reach, is a numbered board (la table des bons) corresponding to the restaurant's table numbers. Each number has below it a spike on which the check is impaled.

Kitchen action

First, however, the aboyeur calls out the order loudly and distinctly (to be heard above kitchen clatter). For each item for a particular table he addresses the chefs de partie concerned, which is acknowledged (equally audibly) by the partie involved. Nearly every chef de partie is concerned to some extent with a customer's order. After the aboyeur's announcement of each new check, they (with their commis and apprentices) start to prepare the dishes ordered or adjust their work in hand to include them.

When the last item of an order has left the hot-plate, as shown by the aboyeur's copy, he will remove his copy from the spike and insert it through the slot of a locked box. The key to the box is kept in the control office (controlleur). Copies of orders provide important statistics to a catering operation or hotel and it is important that there is no opportunity for access to or tampering with checks.

Waiting station copies

The sideboard copy is retained for safe keeping by the chef de rang concerned at his table de service (sideboard or station table) on a spike file. Here the checks are consulted from time to time during the meal by the chef de rang and maître d'hôtel. Checks will be required in the event of a guest wishing to change his mind during dinner about a subsequent course. They are of use as advance information to the maître d'hôtel to have the carver (trancheur) in readiness (where separate carvers are employed) or for other trolley services.

A second copy is retained only during the meal's progress by the commis to guide him in his journeys between dining room and servery. It assists his memory, ensuring that he receives from the servery exactly what was ordered for a particular table number and that it is served to that table and not another.

Wine and other checking

Checks from dining room to kitchen do not constitute the whole checking system in a hotel or restaurant. They are also required for wines

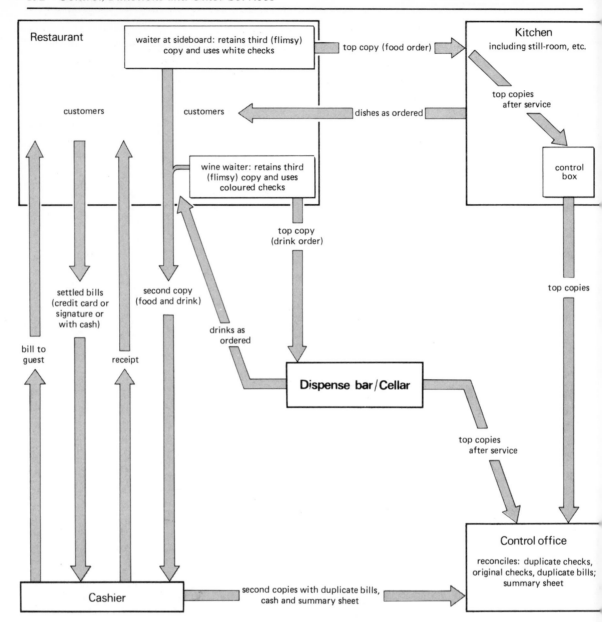

Figure 47   *Triple check route*

and liqueurs, to compile and render an accurate customer's bill and reduce pilfering.

Dispense bar and cellar checking
Checks from the wine waiter for orders from the dispense bar and cellar are usually made from pads of a distinctive colour. One copy is retained as an aide memoire by the wine waiter so that the correct number of bottles of the right wines reach the right table. One copy goes to the dispense bar or cellarman (caviste) to procure the wines ordered. One copy is returned to the

cashier where it is retained during the course of the meal. (Traditionally such checks were held in a thumb indexed blotting-type book under the table numbers.)

Shortly before the conclusion of the meal, information on the wine check is entered on the customer's bill (together with details provided by checks of other departments).

To prevent complications and mistakes, wines are usually given a 'bin number' in the cellar and that number is quoted on the wine list, so the wine waiter orders his wines by the number only (see Chapter 21).

Writing wine checks
An example of a wine check is shown below. The first figure denotes number and size of bottle, the second figure is the bin number, and, just underneath, is the total price.

	Table Number
	15
1 x 57	£9.40
Date	Sig. WO

If wines are returned to the cellar for any reason, a return check is made out, with the reason marked on the check ('unopened', 'corked', etc.), and signed by the person authorized to do so.

Checking for other drinks
Spirits by measure should be written as numbers of measures and total price, for example, 4 double whiskies @ 45p a measure, should read '8 whiskies 360p'. This method clearly indicates to the cashier how much to charge; saves time and error in making up bills; and prevents friction owing to the possibility of hurried accountancy causing 'shortages'.

If more than one item is written on the check, the total price should be written in and ringed.

Remember, well written, tidy checking avoids most of the shortages which irk waiting staff.

Minerals, beers and other open drinks should be checked for in the same way.

Checks for still-room and other services
Checks of other colours may be used by waiters for orders from the still-room (cafetier) for coffee and other hot beverages and other items, such as toast, for which the still-room is responsible.

Within the restaurant itself checks may be used for the supply of those items of a meal which are served from buffets or trolleys such as smoked salmon (or other items) from a cold table or roast beef from a carving wagon. This provides information for the cashier and prevents leakages (such as carving unauthorized portions for employees).

At the end of a meal a kitchen clerk or control clerk tallies all checks on remote service points with food returned to kitchen (or garde manger).

The 'return' check
For strict control of checking, once a check has been handed in it cannot be regained. If a commodity has to be returned for some reason, another check has to be made out marked 'return' and sent with the dish in order to cancel the transaction. To prove their legality to 'control', these checks should bear the head waiter's signature. The waiter then ensures that the item is taken off the bill by sending a copy to the cashier.

'En place'
On the table d'hôte a customer may wish for a slight change in a dish, so an 'en place' check has to be made, for example '4 soles frites "en place" fish du jour'. Although no money is involved, it should be signed by the head waiter to show that he has permitted an alteration from the fixed menu at no extra charge. Such a check is also used if a dish is replaced following a return.

'En suite' (or suivant)
Also used when serving a table d'hôte meal. In most establishments the meal order is taken up

to and including the main course. When the guest has eaten this dish and the plates have been removed, the menu is again presented and the order for the sweet is taken. This check which is headed 'en suite' shows the customer's choice as well as room or table number, date and waiter's signature or number.

Extra charge

Sometimes an extra charge is to be made, so the check could read: '4 @ £8.75 poulet Maryland extra £2.50.' The waiter must see that the extra charge is placed on the bill.

No charge

Sometimes a waiter requires ingredients from various sources to finish a dish (which has already been charged the full price). As checks are necessary for all items, to cover issue of stock, he makes a check, for example '2 Curacao for crêpes Suzette N/C' which is duly signed by the head waiter. Such a check may also be used for complimentary drinks (possibly following a complaint).

Cancellations

In many cases checks have serial numbers and every check must be accounted for. If a check is spoiled in any way, it has to be cancelled and sent to 'control'. The waiter writes 'cancelled' across the check and it is signed by the head waiter. On no account is it to be destroyed or thrown away.

Duplicates

If a check is mislaid, to save the customer waiting another check can be made with 'duplicate' written at the top. This is in case the first check gets through to control and the waiter is debited with two orders while only one is charged on the bill. This check requires the head waiter's signature to prevent dishonest usage. A duplicate check is also used to cover accidents to a dish.

(a) first and main course
    (*note line*)

(b) sweet check –
    continuing *or* include
    in menu price

(c) return and replacement

(d) supplement

Top ⟶ to issuing department
Flimsy ⟶ stays on station
Bottom ⟶ cashier

Examples of duplicate checks

The bill

Information which checks provide, supplemented by authorizations from head waiters, enables a cashier (un cassier) to make up a customer's account.

Cashier

A restaurant control system may be dependent upon a variety of control staff. Waiting staff may not ever encounter all the 'backroom' staff involved but they are likely to have dealings with a restaurant cashier.

The restaurant cashier receives money in payment of bills from the guests which is collected from the guests by waiters. In more popular operations the cashier may deal directly with customers. Whether dealing with waiters or public, a cashier needs to be alert and responsive, friendly, tactful, firm and honest. When working in the restaurant itself, the cashier should, like other restaurant staff, 'look good', that is, maintain a neat and clean appearnace at all times.

The cashier may stamp or otherwise code a bill for **non-residents** as 'chance'. **A resident** may sign the bill and it is then charged through the tabular sheet or hotel billing machine and recorded against the room number.

A cashier maintains a separate abstract or

RESTAURANT DAILY ANALYSIS SHEET

Service . . . .   Date . . . . , ...

Bill number	Table number	Number covers	Food					Drink							Total			Remarks
			Kitchen	Still-room	Total			Wines	Spirits	Liqueurs	Beers & minerals	Total			Credit	Cash		
					Credit	Cash						Credit	Cash					
Totals																		

I certifiy that all the above entries are correct . . . .

Figure 48   *An example of a daily analysis sheet used in a restaurant*

summary sheet of all sales subdivided into chance and cash sales. Wines, spirits, tobacco and other non-food sundries are separated from food sales.

In high class restaurants the caisse was traditionally situated 'off stage'. In the service area, cashiers wrote bills neatly in ink. Today, accounting machines enable restaurant staff to make their own bills so that the old tasks of cashiers change, decline or, in some cases, are entirely eliminated.

What the bill shows

The foregoing activity all leads to the presentation of a guest's bill. Whether by hand or mechanically produced a bill usually bears the name of the establishment as well as the VAT number.

RESTAURANT SUMMARY SHEET											
Bill number	Table number	Number covers	Food	Drinks	Sundries	Sub-total	V A T	Total	Cash	Credit	Room account

Figure 49   *An example of a summary sheet used in a restaurant*

An à la carte bill Shows the various courses with a section for wines, beers, minerals, coffee, etc. The bill is made up by totalling the checks for each course and entering the totals in the cash column opposite. Wines should be entered as ordered.

A table d'hôte bill Shows at the top the name of the meal with the other items, for example wines, beers, etc., underneath. An example of a table d'hôte bill is shown in Figure 50.

		£	p
	Breakfasts		
4	Luncheons @ £8.75	35	00
	Dinners		
	Suppers		
	Wines 1 × 57	9	40
	Minerals		
	Spirits	3	20
	Beers		
	Liqueurs		
4	Coffees	2	40
	Sundries: extra for Chicken Maryland.	2	50
		52	50
	Service 10%	5	25

W/L	Table number	Date	Total
A	15	9/3/84	£57.75

Figure 50 *A table d'hôte bill*

Hotel checking

In large luxury hotels the check system is further multiplied. On each floor, for example, there is a floor waiter (chef d'étage) with more check pads.These again are of different colours and in duplicate for use between departments concerned in supplying to a guest's room or suite any kind of meal and the accompanying items from the still-room, dispense or cellar.

When guests staying in a hotel take drinks in lounges or bars, they often prefer to have their orders placed on the 'house bill'. In basic procedures a waiter marks the check with a guest's room number and sends a copy to the 'bill office'. The waiter should politely ask the guest to sign the check (not forgetting to offer a pen on the plate or salver). This safeguards the **guest from inaccurate charges and also a waiter** if a guest queries an amount when he eventually pays. Should a guest refuse to sign, the waiter should ask his head waiter to initial the check as a witness against possible dispute.

Key card
Room number checking is now operated more thoroughly through several systems. For example, a guest may be required to produce his key card in order to charge any item to his accommodation account. A number of hotels code (by colour or mark) the key card of 'chance' guests, that is, those who have not pre-booked their rooms and are not known to management. These guests must pay for accommodation in advance and are not entitled to any credit from sales points.

Credit card system
Alternatively, a special internal credit card may be issued to a guest for identification when buying food and drinks to be charged.

Both the above systems require that details on the cards (either key card or credit card) be clear and unaltered especially the date of departure. This ensures the guest only charges amounts to his account while that account is still running.

Computer terminals

These have been installed into a number of hotels to allow the restaurant and the bar to charge the amount directly on to the guest's bill.

Control clerk

In restaurants which operate checking systems a control clerk (or his junior) collects the various checks from each service point at the end of each service period. Main control work often goes through the night. It is largely comparison and agreement in which original checks are compared with cashier's duplicates of the bills. These are clipped together. They should agree on menu selling price and number of persons served. Any shortage is entered into the shortage book and the waiter responsible may be made to adjust the payment. (Any procedure of this kind should be made clear in staff contracts of employment.)

Mechanized systems

Mechanization and microchip applications affect today's control procedures just as they do those of waiters and cashiers. In some mechanization systems there is an adaptation of the procedure whereby bills are settled by payment to the waiter who has his own till key.

Several firms have developed machines for restaurant billing and control. National Cash Register and Sweda are among the better known. Anker, a German company, have also developed restaurant registers. Several textbooks on control are available, therefore, this manual does not detail the minutiae of mechanized systems.

Waiters' registers (such as those developed by Anker) can, for example, with built-in memories offer silent, speedy recording and reliable accounting. They can also provide an end-of-day report together with sale scheduling and control. Departmental sales and waiters' sales can be distinguished. Departmental turnover can be specified and split up into a large number of items enabling a medium-sized menu with items numbered and priced to be stored. Internal turnover can be handled separately. Cancellations are exactly shown per waiter and a whole mass of other data can be automatically generated.

For the waiter operating a register of this kind several items can be recorded over single keys and many more by entry of a number, for example, from the menu. The register then performs automatically collecting the item price and/or number of items (possibly multiplied) in the respective item, department and waiter memorizes and selects and issues the kind of check format required.

A modern waiter, therefore, is likely to have in-house or 'on-the-job' training in manipulating registers or billing machines which are progressively becoming more sophisticated.

17 Functions and outside catering

The nature of banqueting is, like everything else in catering, continually questioned. This chapter does not attempt to deal with how to persuade customers to buy functions or with many aspects of marketing and organizing, but concentrates upon their service. Yet in so doing, it would be foolish not to note that changes mentioned elsewhere in this book also apply to function catering. Change is likely to affect banquet staff dress (especially extra waiters and waitresses), menus (especially 'cliché' dishes from Edwardian times), music, other entertainment and after-dinner speaking. Guidance to procedures which follow, therefore, should be read against a background of altering fashion and demand.

Banquets and other functions are today offered not only in hotels, conference establishments and function rooms but also in pubs, cafés and other operations at various market levels. Banquets may embrace dinners of great length, luxury and high cost but other functions can vary from friendly society lunches of modest character to hunt suppers. Functions include buffets, cocktail parties, weddings and silver weddings, twenty-first and eighteenth birthday parties, supper balls, business conferences and Rotary club lunches (these by no means exhaust possibilities).

Pre-banquet organization

The success of a banquet depends largely on its preliminary organization. Each member of staff taking part must similarly organize himself and his own section to fulfil adequately his own role in the function.

It will help a waiter to know something of the arrangements which precede the banquet as well as those which apply during it.

Banqueting briefing
Communicating information is vital to banqueting success.

This chapter is not primarily about selling functions and other managerial aspects, but much information for service staff stems from the selling activity. Information can be conveniently recorded on function order forms which note customers' requirements, and a banquet or function prospectus, which brings a catering establishment's functions to the notice of those with responsibilities for arranging and organizing the service of the function. Examples of these are shown in Figures 51 and 52 on pages 201 and 202. (See also Chapter 9.)

Banquet sales literature is usually developed beyond such simple basic forms. Derek Taylor, for example, recommends (in his *How to Sell Banquets*, Northwood Books 1980) a presentation book which incorporates pictures showing prospective clients all possible arrangements of function facilities as well as menu suggestions and other details.

Banquet management
In some operations, organizing and selling functions will be in the hands of an executive reporting to

the general manager and whose title might be conference and banqueting manager. Such an executive needs sound catering knowledge and function experience in substantial hotel operations.

Large hotels may also have a senior banqueting head waiter or function head waiter who reports to the banqueting manager. This head waiter will supervise other head waiters, wine butlers, waiters, bar, still-room staff and banqueting porters and engage extra casual waiting staff according to the demands of the business.

In America, banqueting head waiters in busy operations reach high salaries largely through their share of tips from all functions. Five per cent of such gratuities might be allotted to the head waiter and captains, with the head waiter receiving the larger share.

The following departments require prior notification of a function: kitchen, restaurant (banqueting or function manager), cellar, housekeeper, hall porter, still-room and plate-room.

Apart from the usual 'special business sheet' normally sent to all departments each week, further forms giving all necessary information to departments concerned may also be sent from the manager's office a few days in advance of the function.

Communicating to staff

Kitchen staff require the following information:

- Date and time of function.
- Number of services required and number of covers per service. (This information is supplied by the function head waiter.)
- Any other information which may be required from the service point of view.

Waiting staff (banqueting manager and/or function head waiter) require the following information:
- Date and time of function.
- Number to be served.
- Where to assemble.
- Where to serve.
- Menu detail.
- Plan of tables.

- List of guests.
- Drinks, apéritifs: wines, liqueurs, spirits and whether pre-ordered (booked) or cash.
- Cigars, cigarettes.
- Any other information.

Factors which affect these points include:

Number of covers
This is usually the number of guests expected, but it may not be the number who will actually be present. It is difficult, if not impossible, to add covers at the time of the function without disorganizing both kitchen and service, hence an accurate estimate must be received.

Where to assemble
Apéritifs and appetizers (nuts, crisps, canapés, etc.) are served in a reception room. A few chairs should be placed around the walls so that the elderly may sit down. Small tables, with ashtrays, for guests to deposit their empty glasses must be provided.

Where to serve
This information is supplied with the table plan.

Menu details
This consists of the menu for the actual function as served in the dining room and also information of any appetizers to be served during the reception, and perhaps tea, sandwiches and cakes later during the evening. Soup on departure may also be required or, in certain cases, breakfast. Notes and examples of menus are to be found in Chapter 8.

Quoting for functions
Normally a catering establishment's function prospectus takes care of many customers' need for detail and helps eliminate possible misunderstandings and queries. The function order form and banquet or function prospectus for the fictitious Polydor Inn, shown in Figures 51 and 52, are on opposite sides of the same sheet on the American form from which they are derived. The order form records the customer's demands; the prospectus details what is to be provided.

Brassington, Barchester **FUNCTION ORDER FORM** Telephone 044 73048

Organization . . . .

Address. . . . .

In charge . . . .

Telephone number . . . .

Function date . . . .

Day. . . . .

Starting time . . . .

Reception . . . .

Meal time . . . .

Vacated by . . . .

Guarantee

—————————
Guarantee figure

Guarantee means the number of meals to be served. We will be prepared to serve 10% more without delay. Should the number served be less than the guarantee, the minimum charge will be for 95% of the guarantee.

Banquet room

Menu

Starter. . . . .

Entrée . . . .

Potato. . . . .

Vegetable . . . .

Salad . . . .

Dessert . . . .

Coffee, tea, milk — rolls and butter
included with all regular meals

Price per cover £ . . . .

plus VAT and 15% gratuity

Lobby bulletin board posting

Tables and seating

Top table   yes ☐   no ☐

Number of persons at top table . . . .

Double set-up — separate tables   for meeting and dining

yes ☐   no ☐

Other instructions

Coffee breaks

	tea/coffee	rolls	biscuits
. . . . am			
. . . . pm			

Special needs

Movie screen ☐   Rostrum ☐

PA system. . . . .

Blackboard ☐   Piano ☐

Stages . . . .

Easels . . . .

Other. . . . .

Bar requirements

Portable bar   yes ☐   no ☐

Bill to . . . .

. . . .

. . . .

. . . .

Please sign

. . . .
Authorized representative   date

Return to . . . .
Banquet manager   date

Figure 51 *An example of a function order form*

BANQUET OR FUNCTION PROSPECTUS

Nature of function _____ Number _____

Date and day _____ Time _____ Room _____ Rent £ _____

Name of organization _____

Address _____ Telephone _____

Name of representative _____

Address _____ Telephone _____

Responsibility of party _____ Cash deposit £ _____ Credit approved _____

Price (per person) _____ Number expected _____ Number prepare for _____ Number guaranteed _____

Extras: wines   corkage   cigars   cigarettes   music   flowers   other

Menu	Buffet
	Wines
	Waters
	Liqueurs
	Cigars
	Cigarettes

Copies (original) to _____

Notify department heads _____

Remarks

Details and reminders

- ☐ Registration desk
- ☐ Collection of tickets
- ☐ Seating plans
- ☐ Table numbers
- ☐ Card room and tables
- ☐ Cards
- ☐ Tallies
- ☐ Lighting effects
- ☐ Spot light
- ☐ Platform
- ☐ Blackboard and pointer
- ☐ Checking stand
- ☐ Maid service
- ☐ Piano/organ
- ☐ Orchestra
- ☐ Food for orchestra

- ☐ Motion picture machine
- ☐ Slide lantern
- ☐ Radio
- ☐ Amplifiers
- ☐ Broadcast
- ☐ Cabaret show
- ☐ Exhibits
- ☐ House officer
- ☐ Printing tickets
- ☐ Printing menus
- ☐ Printing programmes
- ☐ Printing guest list
- ☐ Printing pass out checks
- ☐ Flags
- ☐ Favours
- ☐

Figure 52 *An example of a banquet or function prospectus*

Polydor Hotel,
LONDON.
W4

The Secretary,
The Meat Cleavers' Association,
LONDON.
NW22

6th November 1987

Dear Mr Carver,

Following our recent talk, I have pleasure in confirming that a tentative reservation has been made of the ballroom for your annual dinner dance for approximately 250 persons on Friday, 27th January, 1988.

Our ballroom will accommodate a maximum of 300 persons for this type of function.

I enclose menu samples for your consideration at the price levels (to   ) you indicated. The price quoted per head are exclusive of reception drinks which I gathered you wished served on a cash basis to all except official guests.

The charge includes hire of private accommodation, floral decoration, dinner, coffee and, at a set time later in the evening, light refreshment of a choice of tea, sandwiches, pastries and ices.

Ten per cent is added to the total of the account to include staff gratuities, with the exception of wine waiters who, where drinks are served on a cash basis, may receive gratuities at tables at the time of service at guests' discretion. Special cloakroom accommodation form part of the ballroom suite and will be available for guests, and this is included in the above charge.

We can supply and print menu cards similar to the enclosed sample at a charge of   per hundred. Should you need the services of a toastmaster, his fee will be   for the duration of the reception and dinner only, or until 11.30 p.m.

You may wish to make your own arrangements for an orchestra but, should you wish, we shall be happy to have our musical director quote to you.

We serve dinner to members of the orchestra and to the toastmaster at a charge of   per head.

I do hope we shall have the pleasure of catering for you. We shall spare no effort to ensure the complete success of the occasion.

Yours sincerely,

A. Merrythought
Banqueting manager

Figure 53   *A typical letter of quotation*

BANQUETING BOOKING FORM

To ensure that all arrangements for your function are to your complete satisfaction will you please complete the following details and return to us at least one month before the function.

We would be grateful for your written confirmation and £ . . . .   deposit as soon as possible. Deposits are not returnable if a function is cancelled within two months of the date it should have taken place.

Name of organization . . . .

Name of organizer . . . .   Address and telephone number

Date of function . . . .

Type of function . . . .

Venue . . . .

Time of arrival . . . .

Function close . . . .

Menu and cost . . . .

. . . .   Wines   cash / account

. . . .   Wines and liqueurs to be served

. . . .

. . . .

. . . .

. . . .

. . . .

Bar from . . . . to . . . .   cash / account   £   bar hire

Flowers   We can arrange at an additional cost   yes / no

Table plan   Top table with sprigs/informal/square/horseshoe/herring-bone
               Please let us have your table plan seven days before your function

Background music required during reception   yes / no   meal   yes / no

Band or Disco We can arrange at an additional cost   yes / no

Accommodation   Please inform us if you require any accommodation

Deposit paid . . . .   Other comments . . . .

. . . .

Signed . . . .

Date . . . .

The meal will be served promptly at the designated time. If guests are late thereby causing a delay we may have to proceed with functions in other venues before being able to continue with your service

Figure 54 *An example of a banqueting booking form*

WEDDING RECEPTION DETAILS

In order to ensure that all the arrangements for your function are to your satisfaction we would be grateful if you would complete the following details and return them to us one month before the date of your function.

We would appreciate your written confirmation and £ . . . . deposit as soon as possible. Your deposit is not returnable if your function is cancelled within two months of the date it should have taken place.

Name of bride. . . . .   Name of groom. . . . .

Name, address and telephone number for correspondence

. . . .

. . . .

. . . .

Date of reception . . . .   Venue. . . . .

Time of marriage. . . . .   Menu and cost. . . . .

Arrival at hotel . . . .

Time of meal. . . . .

Reception close. . . . .

Numbers . . . .
   (final numbers to be given five days before your reception)   . . . .

Table plan to be given seven days before your function

Flowers   Can be arranged to your requirements at an additional cost   yes / no

Bar   Open . . . . to . . . .   cash / account   £   bar hire

Background music required during reception   yes / no   meal   yes / no

Band or disco   Can be arranged at an additional cost   yes / no

Cake stand and knife   £ . . . . yes / no   Changing room   £   yes / no

Wine   cash / account   Details of wine and liqueurs to be served

Accommodation required

. . . .

. . . .

. . . .

Deposit paid . . . .   Other comments . . . .

. . . .

Signed . . . .

Date . . . .

The meal will be served promptly at the designated time. However, if guests are late thereby causing a delay it may be that we will have to proceed with functions in other venues before being able to continue with your service

Figure 55   *An example of a wedding reception booking form*

Mail confirmation

Lengthy letters should not be necessary where a good prospectus and order form are used. But should forms and standard literature not be available, then a letter of quotation or confirmation for a function should seek to cover all aspects. An example of a letter of quotation is shown in Figure 53.

Table plans

Usually a large hotel catering for all sorts of functions has ready three or four different standard seating plans for each one of the rooms used for this type of business. It is advisable to ask organizers to select one of those plans instead of using one of their own. This is because in arranging seating an organizer forgets to take into account such factors as doors, windows, pillars, etc., which affect the service.

'House' table plans (usually identified by numbers or letters such as A, B, C, D and so on) must all have been tested; either by careful calculation and planning or by actually putting the tables in position. Varying sizes of banqueting tables and table-cloths must be considered when drawing up plans, as must a room's size, shape and number to be accommodated.

Drafting plans

A scale plan of the room with card templates of tables to the same scale is useful in table planning, especially if guest numbers are near the room's maximum capacity. Cut templates to include both chair space and gangway space. If cut strictly to table size, you may put them too close together on plan and fail to allow for adequate service and access aisles. Moving real tables involves unnecessary time and labour; it is simpler to move templates until the best seating is achieved.

To be effective, a plan must show entries and exits and other factors related to room and seating such as pillars, alcoves and power points. Exits must be left unobstructed to meet local authority and safety requirements and service, and guest access aisles left clear.

Further sample forms

Figures 54 and 55 show two different booking forms used in an English provincial hotel. The banquet booking form indicates a style of arrangement while the second has been adapted specifically for wedding receptions.

Space for serving

Allow a minimum space of 132 cm (54 in) to 183 cm (72 in) between each table for chairs and for a space sufficiently wide for waiters to be able to serve. More space may be needed with awkward chair shapes.

Thus, for a 152 cm (5 ft) round table (seating ten covers) allow 3.53 m (11 ft) of floor space and cut your template to that size. M. R. Small (in *Catering for Functions,* Hutchinson 1976), points out that to the scale of 2.54 cm (1 in): 3.048 m (10 ft) a 10 pence piece is the right size, that is, 2.8 cm but, of course, other shapes and sprigging are usually required.

Side tables

For many buffet receptions such as weddings and birthdays additional tables are arranged round the sides of a room for service and convenience. Such occasional tables are not used for seating guests.

Cover tables with a white cloth, except when green baize is appropriate for a reception or registration table. Side tables are placed out of general traffic flow, where possible against a wall. A room's size and service methods determine how many side tables are needed and where to site them.

Registration, reception or display tables

Stand a registration table, equipped with register book and pens, near the entrance door or reception lines.

Tables for gifts may be needed for wedding or birthday parties. Position these near the entrance (possibly opposite a registration table). Many

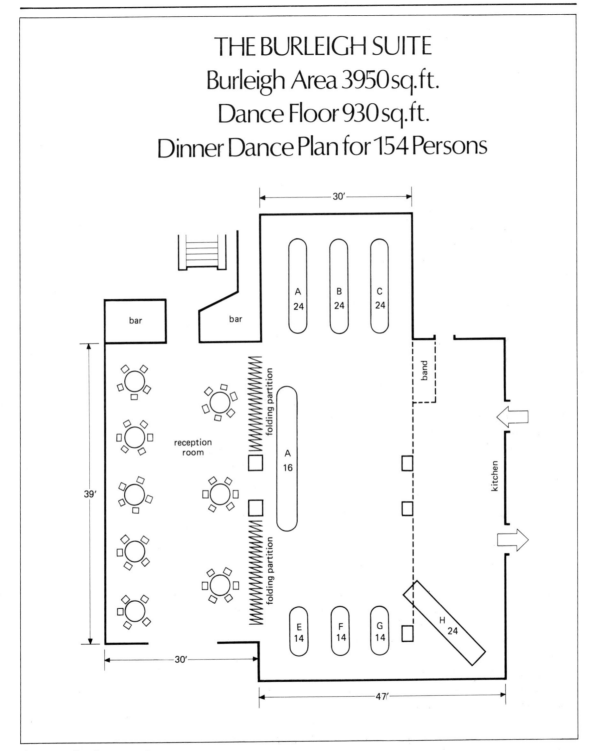

THE BURLEIGH SUITE
Burleigh Area 3950 sq.ft.
Dance Floor 930 sq.ft.
Dinner Dance Plan for 154 Persons

An example of a room plan

organizers may wish gifts to remain on display throughout a reception.

Types of plan

There are three main types of table plan: formal, informal and cabaret-style.

Formal layouts   Involve lines of long tables. In some of them, 'sprigs' run at right angles to a top table. Such sprigs may be flush against a top table but waiters can move and work more easily if space is left between them. Moreover, this facilitates draping and decorating the front of the top table.

Informal layouts   Seat guests at separate tables.

Cabaret layouts   Arrange smaller tables (round ten seaters are common) often leaving a centre space for dancing or entertainment.

Table plan display

One or two copies of the table plan must be displayed for guests in the reception room. For a large function, each table on the plan will carry either a letter or a number. Beside this plan a list of guests in alphabetical order indicates where a guest is seated by letter or number. Only in special circumstances are actual seats numbered at table, other than the top table. At the top table, each guest is informed of his place, usually by a name card at his (or her) seat. This information is previously advised by the organizers.

Sample layouts

Mention has already been made of the infinite variety of individual characteristics a room may have. Hence theoretical, 'ideal' table plans in a textbook are of limited use for they cannot always be fitted into banquet or conference halls of different shapes with obstructing columns, awkward exits and entrances and so on.

Each operation having developed its own 'house' table plans, these can be incorporated into a banquet and conference sales pack.

Drink arrangements

Wines, aperitifs and other drinks can either be paid for by those giving the function or paid for individually by each guest. In the first case there are two alternatives. Either an organizer may order beforehand what drinks are to be served and how many bottles, or each guest may order what he wants. The guest will sign the checks as well as the waiter serving the drinks.

In the second case, a guest orders whatever he wants and pays for it himself. This is referred to as 'cash drinks'. A limited wine list is often used for this type of cash drink business.

Reception drinks

As for aperitifs, organizers of functions may decide that a limited number of glasses will be paid for by them (usually one for each guest) and the rest to be on the cash basis.

A special reception bar is usually provided for a function of any size so as to facilitate the service. It is set up in or near the room where the reception is being held, with a barman or a wine waiter in charge. Stock for this bar is drawn directly from the cellars.

Other drinks and tobacco

Liqueurs and spirits can also be obtained, and these again can be paid for by the organizer or by individual customers.

The function head waiter must be informed as to what time a special licence, if any, has been obtained for this function. He is responsible for seeing that no drinks are served after the time limit has expired.

Cigars and cigarettes are sometimes provided by the organizers themselves and handed to the head waiter at the time of the function. These can also be ordered by the organizers when the function is first booked, in which case, the function head waiter will have to be notified. He may then draw his requirements on the morning of the function from the stores.

Cigar and cigarette service

Cigars are passed round in boxes by the wine waiters at a large function or by the function head waiter at a small one. Cigarettes in glasses or boxes (a dozen or so in each) are placed at intervals on tables after the loyal toast (of the Queen).

Numbers and staff

Sometimes a function organizer asks the head waiter to check on numbers present at the function and to notify him of that number as soon as possible during the meal, but the number of waiters and waitresses required both for the service of drinks and food will have to be decided well in advance on the basis of forecast numbers.

Service stations

Using silver service a waiter usually serves ten to twelve covers. A table seating such a number thus matches both the service dish made up in the kitchen and a waiter's station, but with tables of varying seating capacity in informal layouts, waiters should still serve similar numbers. At long tables waiters also serve similar numbers. Thus sprigs should be made up to seat guests in multiples of ten or twelve or whatever figure each waiter is to serve. Otherwise waiters work successively along rows of diners serving their allotted number. Waiters may serve more guests, up to sixteen or even more, when simpler services are introduced.

One wine waiter is allocated for each twenty-five guests or even more (up to forty) if wine is pre-ordered inclusive in the function.

Staffing examples

For a function for 300 in a high class hotel offering a four course dinner menu plus coffee, with table wines to include sherry with consommé, a white wine with fish, a red wine with the main course and brandy/liqueurs with coffee, pre-war staffing would have been in the nature of:

Banquet manager
Assistant banquet manager
Head waiter
20 waiters
10 commis waiters
9 wine waiters

Today, such a function might be staffed:

Banquet head waiter
Assistant banquet head waiter
20 waiters/waitresses
6 wine waiters

Toastmaster

If an announcer or toastmaster is required for the reception or for the dinner, a toast list will have to be provided for the announcer.

Ancillary sections

Instructions in the plate-room

The plate-room must be notified in advance of the date, time and place and total numbers attending the function. It is, however, advisable to give greater details to this department. They have to attend not only to the supply of silver for the kitchen but also to plates, cutlery and glasses.

They will, therefore, require to know details of menu, number of services required, how many on each service, or better still the sizes and types of silver for each course, if finger bowls are required, if special glasses must be made available to the glass pantry and any other information to suit the particular occasion.

Instructions to still-room

This department requires only information to provide adequately for rolls, butter, toast Melba, coffee and milk. All they generally need to know is date, time, place and total number.

On certain occasions, however, tea, sandwiches and cakes, or breakfast may be served later on during the evening or early hours of the morning. Then, the still-room will need advance notification as they, as well as the larder department, attend to this requirement.

Function furniture

Preliminary organization should ensure that adequate furniture and equipment for banqueting is available. Staff who serve at functions may not be involved in the selection and purchase of this furniture and equipment. They do have responsibilities for its handling and care. Knowledge of these items helps ensure an efficient environment, minimum maintenance, and smooth service.

Banquet furniture should:

● Be flexible.
● Complement function ambiance.

Function room and design

Function rooms involve use of partitions, link with kitchen, access to guest entry, location or floor level and other problems. Shape and size of doors, passages, lifts and storage rooms also affect the choice of furniture and equipment to go through them.

Movable partitions and room dividers can break a function room into smaller ones. Furniture choice and arrangement should also aid flexible room usage.

Moved about, set up and knocked down again, banquet furniture should combine mobility and folding features with ease of handling, durability and compact storage through stackability. Rounded runners on folding tables prevent damaging other table tops when stacking.

In folding furniture look for:

● Springs or clips that cannot easily break.
● Metal components of rust-proof or chip-proof finish.

Maintenance

Maintenance starts with good selection. Look for possible weakness in folding furniture such as easily broken hinges or springs. Furniture should be held securely but simply. Complicated locking devices can lead to human error and jeopardize guest and staff safety. Regular use involves frequent cleaning. Legs and other parts standing on the floor must be able to withstand knocks when vacuuming or polishing floors and should themselves be easily cleanable.

Mobility and handling

Equipment whether folding or knock-down should be easy to erect although lightweight furniture may not be the sturdiest. Wheeled carriers, dollies and trucks may help in moving but in selecting them, ensure they suit your furniture and your setting.

Storage

When not wanted, banquet furniture should be stackable compactly. One piece should not mark its neighbour nor should parts protrude.

Handling and storage can be reduced if function room furniture can serve more than one use. For example, a knock-down cabaret table permits interchangeable use of different tops on the same base, permitting varied use. Such multi-purpose use can reduce initial outlay, and reduce handling costs and storage space.

Tabling

Specialist firms offer banqueting furniture. Their tabling is often in modular units. Extensions and shape varieties facilitate permutation for different occasions. Folding (or knock-down) they are flexible and stackable. Special units also avoid the 'double legs' of two free-standing tables placed together. Another banquet-style leg, the 'Wishbone' maximizes banquet table seating, affording comfortable knee and foot room.

Banqueting tables vary in size and may be

made to individual specification, but rectangular ones usually accommodate three to six guests on either side. The space required for each cover is 61 cm (24 in) to 76 cm (30 in) maximum. The waiter may, therefore, have to work in a limited area.

Folding tables

Simple folding tables like 'schoolroom tables' are usually 46 cm (18 in) or 38 cm (15 in) wide. Thus two can be placed together to make either a 76 cm (30 in) or a 92 cm (36 in) wide table. This type of simple folding table is useful in meeting-room layouts where an audience sits on one side facing the platform. They can be used singly or in combination against a wall or in 'island' arrangement for buffets or displays.

One example of a flat-storing table (the Felton F2 from Primo Furniture) has a snap locking device. Its 36 mm (1½ in) thick top sits on a rigid under frame with square metal legs (in chrome or black stove enamel). It is available in widths 600 mm (24 in) or 750 mm (30 in) and lengths 1525 mm (60 in) to 2135 mm (84 in).

Circular and part circular tables

Other tables may have circular, semi or quarter-circular, oval, rectangular, serpentine or shaped tops. They may be of folding or knock-down type. Round tables 153 cm (60 in) in diameter seating ten covers are commonly selected as ten is a useful service unit for waiters. Knock-down or folding tables 153 cm (60 in) or 183 cm (72 in) long are usually chosen for straight layouts (longer ones tend to sag). These tables are usually either 68 cm (27 in) or 76 cm (30 in) wide.

Arc shapes or serpentine tables can constitute part of an open circle or if joined in reverse can be S-shaped. Serpentine permutations enable shapes such as circles, half-circles, U-shape and other buffet or top-table arrangements.

Linked with rectangular tops they round off buffets or sprig ends or make long, open ovals and other combinations.

Quarter-circle end tables round off a corner when two tables are placed at right angles. Half-circular end tables can round off a rectangular table. They can also make a raised centre for a semi-circular open buffet.

Other shapes and designs

A trapezoid shape has been developed for multi-purpose folding tables. Two trapezoids placed long side together make a solid hexagonal table. End-to-end six such tables placed together produce an open hexagonal table. Reversed side-by-side, they extend to make a long, straight line table for meetings, dining or display. Another combination can create a straight centre with two angled ends for display or buffet.

Traditional cabaret (or café) tables with fixed centre columns and substantial bases inhibit flexibility in use because they are heavy to move or cumbersome to store. Such tables are now made in which top, column and base may be easily separated. Different sizes and shapes can be interchanged on the same column base. Removing the top prior to dancing or a cabaret allows extra room space. Storable compactly, such tables can be brought in to use for extra seating at functions or in bars, coffee shop or restaurant.

Connecting and locking devices keep butted tables in position. Uneven floors can cause uneven table tops to sag when linking. Screw-adjustable legs at the bottom best corrects this. Alternatively, connecting devices at the top keep a level height on some types.

Once a folding table is erected do not drag or push it across the floor on its legs. This not only scratches the floors or damages carpet but also damages the tables, by forcing out dome glides or breaking crutch clips.

Table-cloths on folding tables

When table-cloths are to be used for banquet or dining, solid plywood (desirably baize-covered) is suitable for table tops as this allows legs and runners to be bolted through the top. A plywood top is more solid than those of thin surface in steel frames. For a neat fit, pin table-cloth drapes and mouldings.

Stackable chairs

Stacking chairs are prefered to folding ones because of appearance, durability (absence of moving parts) and ease of handling. But folding chairs may still be appropriate in some circumstances. In choosing stacking chairs consider:

● Lightness and ease of handling (liftable without effort to stack on the next chair).

● Absence of underside projection (which might mark the chair top on which it stacks).

● 'Wall-saver' legs (extension behind back, keeps them away from the walls).

● High stacking (whether on floor or dolly, desirably as high as a man can reach).

Receptions and preliminaries

Effective planning and the support of appropriate staff and equipment will help make smooth the conduct of the banquet and any reception preceding it. A banquet is usually preceded by a cocktail reception for which some of the function waiters may be required. Half an hour is normally allowed for the reception drinks.

Cocktails may include gin and French vermouth with a stoned olive on a cocktail stick (dry martini); gin and Italian vermouth with a cocktail cherry on a stick (sweet martini) but glasses of sherry are invariably among the choice of drinks offered to the guests. In certain cases other drinks may be offered or can be obtained on demand.

Small, savoury appetizers (such as cheese straws, game chips, salted peanuts, cocktail onions, canapés or other titbits), are arranged in small dishes around the reception room on small tables for guests to help themselves. These appetizers, however, are sometimes handed round by the waiters.

The table plan is usually displayed in the reception room to afford a guest maximum advance notice of where he is sitting.

On receiving the signal from the organizer or chairman, the toastmaster or announcer bangs his gavel three times and says, 'Mr Chairman, my Lords (or other titles in order of importance), Ladies and Gentlemen, dinner (or lunch) is served', in a loud, clear and formal tone of voice.

Dining room preliminaries

The banqueting hall doors are opened and the guests take their seats at table according to seating plan. In some cases, top table guests do not enter the banqueting hall until all other guests have found their places. Then the announcer will add, when announcing the dinner, 'With the exception of the top table, will guests kindly proceed to the banqueting hall'. On such occasions, all guests stand up when top table guests come into the hall and resume their seat only when everyone at the top table is seated.

During these preliminaries, waiting staff stand to attention at their respective stations.

The announcer now calls guests to attention by banging three times with his gavel saying 'Mr Chairman, my Lords, Ladies and Gentlemen, pray silence for the Reverend so-and-so (or Mr so-and-so) who will say grace'.

Once this has been done, the meal begins.

Mise en place

As banquet success hinges upon its organization, a complete mise-en-place of all material required is essential.

All cutlery must be on the table or on the waiter's service sideboard. This includes fruit knives and forks for dessert which are not set on the table until they are required. The various wine glasses that are going to be used must also be on the top table; except liqueur and brandy glasses which remain on the wine service sideboard until required.

Place setting

Cutlery and covers are laid as for table d'hôte

dinner (though usually a full range is required) but there are two ways in which glasses can be arranged:

● In a straight line across the top of the joint knife in the order in which they are going to be used, starting from the right with the sherry glass and finishing with the port glass.

● In the form of a triangle, the sherry glass being the pivot. Glasses to be used first are placed to the right, others to the left.

Banqueting service

A banquet menu may have four, five or more courses. Each waiter is allocated a number of covers varying from eight to sixteen according to the function's service style and importance. A wine waiter may serve up to forty covers. The function head waiter and the toastmaster or announcer normally stand behind the chairman during meal service and during the speeches following the meal.

Timing and movement

Waiters clear and serve together as a well-drilled team.

Station waiters should collect their food in prearranged sequence, the same sequence at every course. Top table is accorded priority but waiters with distant tables normally collect before those with stations near the servery to enable service to be simultaneous.

During meal service all staff movements are directed by the function head waiter. He gives necessary signals to the waiter serving the chairman to begin serving or clearing. Other waiters when not actually serving, stand at the foot of their stations constantly keeping an eye on the top table as well as their own station. They must not lean against walls, pillars or furniture. On no account must they enter into conversation with one another.

Wine waiters

Wine waiters enjoy greater freedom of movement than food waiters at functions. They need to go in and out of the room for customers' orders when drinks are on a cash sales basis. When wines are pre-booked, wine waiters receive one or two bottles of wine each of the first one to be served. They do not receive more of that wine, or of any other wines to be served, unless they return the first bottles they have received whether empty or not. Control on wines hinges on fresh bottles being supplied only on return of an equal number of empty or partly empty ones.

Toast procedures

At the meal's conclusion when coffee cups have been placed in front of guests, the toastmaster again calls guests to attention with his gavel. He announces, 'My Lords, Ladies and Gentlemen, pray silence for your Chairman who will propose the Loyal Toast'. As soon as this has been done, ashtrays must be placed on tables by the wine waiters. This toast is also an indication that the formal part of the meal is over and guests are now allowed to smoke.

When coffee has been served (immediately after the loyal toast), the food waiters have their coffee pots and milk jugs refilled. After a reasonable length of time, coffee is passed again. After this, coffee cups are cleared and food waiters leave the room for good. Only wine waiters now remain.

Speeches and replies follow from time to time each being announced by the toastmaster in the usual manner, 'Mr Chairman, My Lords, Ladies and Gentlemen, pray silence for Mr so-and-so who will propose the toast . . . .' (of the Association, for example) or 'Lady this-and-that who will give the reply . . . .'

Wine waiters during toasts

During this time, the wine waiters move quietly among the tables serving drinks. Glasses must never be empty during this period of toasting.

Waiters must change ashtrays frequently (covering the used ashtray with the inverted clean one, removing both together and replacing with the clean). Under no circumstances should a waiter go round with a plate on which merely to empty dirty ashtrays. At this stage, wine waiters have taken over from food waiters. They complete all the service that is required by guests.

Outside catering

High charges paid for outside catering reflect extra costs involved in, for example, transporting equipment, food and staff. These vary according to distance. Erecting a marquee or providing gas equipment can further add to costs.

Checking detail

All equipment must be checked out of store, checked at the function and again when returned to store if stock is not to decrease. Packing equipment so that it can be safely transported without crockery and glass breakage demands not only experience but also special boxes. Moreover, holding stocks of equipment to meet peak catering periods is also costly.

Several functions in one day can stretch equipment and staff to the maximum but on another day there may be no function at all or only one or two small ones. Active selling and planning is needed to keep turnover steady and to keep permanent staff and equipment employed. Some functions may be only marginally profitable but they help cover wages and are preferable to paying staff for no work or for tasks which normally command a lower wage rate.

Additional organization

Details of menus, numbers, date of the event have to be obtained from the organizer, as for any function. Additionally, the caterer (or his representative) should visit the function site preferably with the organizer to ascertain what space, cooking equipment, facilities for washing-up and furniture are available. He checks whether staff can have prior access to the premises for preparation, whether equipment must be removed immediately after and similar relevant details.

The day before a function, equipment needed is packed and checked against a list which accompanies it for subsequent checking. Similarly food and quantities to be allocated are carefully listed. An item inadvertently omitted can cause chaos during service. Organizing casual waiting staff often involves arranging transport either in the company's own vehicles or, if numbers and distance justifies it, by hired bus.

Casual or part-time staff

Problems of recruiting casual staff or jobbing waitresses are often associated with family ties; what days waitresses are able to work or accept work. Even prior agreements may be breached because husband or baby sitter may renege on an arrangement. Many who apply for waitress work do not realize what is involved and need rapid training. Building a team of reliable part-time waitresses is an important element in outside catering success.

Equipment, staff and space

Maurice Proserpi (writing in *Hospitality*, March 1980) recalled that for outside catering in marquees he used to allow 100 square feet (9.29 square metres) per eight persons (standard marquees are 40 feet (12.19 metres) wide or if butted 80 feet (24.38 metres) wide. When he catered for 700 persons under canvas for a banquet at a mill opening, in traditional style, he used ninety waitresses for food service, thirty waitresses for wines and reached a total of 200 staff (including head waiters, chefs, barmen, cloakroom attendants, porters and so on).

For 700 persons his furniture included:
90 x 6 feet (1.829 metres) oval tables
 700 chairs
6000 pieces of crockery
6000 pieces of cutlery
3500 glasses

plus culinary and service equipment, linen and other requisites. Today's aids in preparation and reconstitution of foods (including frozen or chill techniques) enable economies of staff to be achieved but the foregoing indicates some of the logistical problems and the magnitude of the task of setting up temporary function facilities in tents and furnishing them.

Outside catering equipment

For outside catering, equipment is often assembled in units to meet the needs of fifty guests and using boxes and packs appropriately sized. Crockery, silver, glass and linen requirements for restaurant use have been listed in previous chapters and can also help guide in function catering. For outside catering tasks, the following may additionally help.

Crockery for fifty
50 hors d'oeuvre plates
50 soup plates
50 fish plates
50 meat plates
50 sweet plates
50 side plates
50 dessert plates
50 ice plates
50 tea cups and saucers
 6 milk jugs
50 demi tasse cups and saucers
 6 sugar basins
 8 teapots, 8 dl (1½ pt) each
 8 hot water jugs, 5dl (1 pt) each
 8 coffee pots, 5 dl (1 pt) each
12 sauceboats

Cutlery for fifty
50 hors d'oeuvre knives and forks
50 soup spoons
50 fish knives and forks
50 large knives and forks
50 dessert spoons and forks
50 side knives
50 teaspoons
50 sundae spoons

30 pairs table spoons and forks, as servers
 6 sugar tongs
 6 mustard spoons

Glass for fifty
50 cocktail glasses
50 sherry glasses
50 Paris goblets
50 champagne glasses
50 small tumblers
50 port glasses
50 tumblers, 3 dl (½ pt) size
50 grapefruit glasses
 6 water jugs 8 dl (1½ pt) each
12 bowls (for salad and/or fruit)
 6 decanters
 6 each oil and vinegar bottles
 6 salt, peppers and mustards

Silver for fifty
12   entrée dishes or flats
12   vegetable dishes (or more if for self-help, family service)
 6   flower vases
 6   sugar sifters
 6   waiters' trays

Other items
Tabling: trestles and/or round
Chairs
Table linen, both long and square cloths
Linen or paper napkins
1 cake stand, pillars and cake knife
1 set carvers and steel, and cutting board
Ashtrays
Tea and coffee urns (insulated)
Ice cream scoops
Gas rings, tubing and adapters to possible butane gas
Water boilers and hose
Corkscrews and bottle openers
Wine and spirit measures
Wash-up tubs
Dish cloths and tea towels
Tool box (including drawing pins and string)
Water carriers
Cash till

DISPATCH LIST

Type of function.................................   Place of function......................................

Numbers to be catered ....   Date of function.....................................

Time of function...............................   Van departure time..................................

Menu			
Insert actual menu (with all items, e.g. coffee)			

Menu

Insert actual menu

(with all items, e.g. coffee)

Crockery, glass, silver	
Amount	Item
	grapefruit coupes
	hors d'oeuvre plates
	soup plates
	fish plates
	entrée plates
	joint plates
	sweet plates
	cheese plates
	fruit plates
	side plates
	ice coupes
	coffee cups and saucers
	coffee pots
	milk jugs
	sugar basins
	soup spoons
	fish knives and forks
	entrée knives and forks
	meat knives and forks
	side knives
	dessert spoons
	dessert forks
	coffee spoons
	ice spoons
	table spoons
	table forks
	salts
	peppers
	mustards and spoons
	vinegars
	oils
	water jugs
	cheese dishes
	butter dishes
	hors d'oeuvre raviers
	vegetable dishes
	entrée dishes
	silver flats
	service dishes
	glass dishes
	flower vases
	sauce boats
	cream jugs
	champagne glasses
	sherry glasses
	white wine glasses
	red wine glasses
	liqueur glasses
	wine coolers
	cocktail glasses
	pony glasses
	tumblers
	port glasses

Linen, etc.	
Amount	Item
	linen cloths
	small cloths
	linen serviettes
	paper serviettes

Commodities (food)	
Amount	Item
As demanded by menu	
plus staples such as	
	butter
	rolls
	biscuits
	coffee
	milk
	cream
	sugar, etc.

Other equipment	
Amount	Item
	tables and trestles
	chairs
	enamel jugs
	carvers
	cutting boards
	twelve-gallon urns
	eight-gallon urns
	ashtrays
	doilies
	menu cards
	tin openers
	bottle openers
	corkscrews
	ice servers
	stove (butane)
	spirits
	trays
	salvers

Figure 56   *An example of an outside catering van dispatch list*

```
┌─────────────────────────────────────────────┐
│              DISPATCH LIST                    │
├──────────────┬────────────────────────────────┤
│  Amount      │  Item                          │
│              │                                │
│              │  cups and saucers              │
│              │  small plates                  │
│              │  tea plates                    │
│              │  teapots (brown and silver)    │
│              │  milk jugs                     │
│              │  cream jugs                    │
│              │  sugar basins                  │
│              │  entrée dishes                 │
│              │  silver stands                 │
│              │  cake stand                    │
│              │  pillars                       │
│              │  cake knife                    │
│              │  cake vase                     │
│              │  flower vases                  │
│              │  tea knives                    │
│              │  pastry forks                  │
│              │  fruit plates                  │
│              │  ice plates                    │
│              │  teaspoons                     │
│              │  hot water jugs                │
│              │  glass jugs                    │
│              │  trays (large and small)       │
│              │  coffee jugs                   │
│              │  dessert spoons and forks      │
│              │  table spoons and forks        │
│              │                                │
└──────────────┴────────────────────────────────┘
```

Figure 57   *An example of a shorter dispatch list*

Transport check

In loading a van with equipment, commodities, etc., a check-list should accompany the load to ensure that all requirements are loaded and for subsequent checking for return after the function. Figure 56 indicates the type of form which may be devised.

The items listed in Figure 56 are examples only and are not intended to comprise an exhaustive list.

A separate or adapted form may be used for teas and similar receptions as can be seen in Figure 57.

Function costing

Banquets and other functions contribute importantly to profits and must be carefully costed and priced. Food commodities required to give effect to the menu must be identified and charged to the function together with staff costs, room costs and other overheads. A simple example of a basic function cost sheet is shown in Figure 58, and indicates the scope of such a costing.

Gauging function success

In order to evaluate the success of the catering effort at a function, a banqueting manager may well follow up the affair by asking the customer to complete a rating form. This also helps correct faults and improve future service.

Profitability and repeat business are the best indicators of success. Doing well in banqueting

POLYDOR HOTEL FUNCTION COST SHEET

Date . . . .   Serial number . . . .

Number of covers . . . .   Account to . . . .

Name . . . .

Menu	Commodities			Unit Value	Value	
	Quantity	Unit	Item		£	p
The actual						
menu is typed						
here						

Food cost		
add Wine cost		
* Total cost £		

Cost per person £

Quote per person £

Wine cost

Item	Unit value	Value	
		£	p

Total wine cost £

Overheads

Overtime		
Flowers		
Sundries		
Total £		

* Total food and wine cost

overheads

Total amount chargeable £

Figure 58   *An example of a function cost sheet*

GROUP BUSINESS RATING FORM

	Excellent	Good	Fair	Poor	Comments
Banquet					
food and beverage quality					
food and beverage service					
Meeting rooms					
appearance					
equipment.					
lighting					
air conditioning.					
Restaurants					
food and beverage quality					
food and beverage service					
Staff attitude					
banquet staff.					
sales staff.					
restaurant staff					
reception staff.					
telephonists.					
maids/room staff.					
porters.					
management					
Reception					
registration (hotel)					
registration (conference)					
accounting and billing					
Reaction of					
delegates					
speakers.					
conference officers					

Additional comments . . . .

. . . .

. . . .

. . . .

Name of group . . . .

Signature of official submitting report . . . .

Figure 59   *An example of a rating form which a manager might send to a customer*

cannot hinge on sales and organization alone. The quality of the product, value for money and the service staff who provide welcome and attention are important elements in building and maintaining good function business.

Food and service range

Menus largely determine the nature of catering and style of service and this is no less so in outside catering and functions held in hotels or banquet houses. Such menus have been considered in Chapter 8.

18 Breakfast, lounge and floor service

General rules of mise en place and of meal service apply to serving breakfasts and beverages but sometimes the importance of these in creating a favourable impression on guests may be overshadowed in a waiter's mind by the gastronomic interest of luncheons, dinners and banquets. It would be most unfortunate if waiters and waitresses should fail to give careful attention to breakfast service and that of the 'national' beverages tea and coffee.

Breakfast trends

Breakfast services are affected by changing customs and attitudes towards breakfast generally and also by hotel methods of charging.

From being a substantial meal in the Victorian period, including grills such as steaks and chops, and cold cuts from joints, breakfast has become steadily lighter in the Western World, though in Britain and America one cooked dish is still often provided at this meal.

What began in capital cities, such as London, of hotels charging for room only or including only a Continental breakfast has spread to the provinces and to resorts. This practice of charging for breakfast separately has begun to replace the inclusive charge for bed and traditional English breakfast.

Informal meals

In hotels, breakfast is an important meal because it is one that a customer invariably takes in the establishment itself. Nevertheless, service staff seldom need to guide a guest in choosing items from full, cooked breakfast. The simpler meals mentioned in Chapter 7 such as brunch, afternoon tea and high tea similarly do not present choice problems to the guest.

Composing menus for these meals is just as important and can present just as many difficulties as creating luncheon, dinner, supper and banquet meals. But as this manual is more importantly concerned with food service techniques it is not proposed, other than to outline breakfast pattern, to provide examples of informal menus.

Breakfast menus

Breakfast meals have been modified in recent years. It is possibly in hotels rather than in the home that a variety of cooked items for breakfast persist. The breakfast menus sequence in Table 31 indicate the possibilities but it is rare today for any guest to take more than one preliminary course, fruit/fruit juice or cereals and one cooked course followed by rolls, toast and preserves.

Breakfast composition

In the tables in this and Chapter 7, the left-hand column headed 'order of courses' has numbered headings, for example ten for breakfast, fifteen for lunch and so on. They appear in this order on a menu. They are not necessarily the number of courses available. At breakfast it is usual to serve any dish from numbers 1 and 2 (fruit and cereal) followed by 5 to 7 (eggs, fish, meats hot and cold). Finally a guest completes his meal with, say, toast (10) and marmalade (7). The beverages, although appearing on menus at number 3 are served directly after the first course but this is the only case where service does not follow the printed sequence.

In dividing dishes into courses when writing or laying out a menu, either a space is left between sets of dishes or a line ruled between them. Thus the selected dishes from 1 and 2 (fruit and cereals) would be separated by a space or line from those selected from 5, 6, 7 (eggs, fish, meats hot or cold) to form the first and second course. A dish need not be chosen from every heading. As few, as many, or none at

Table 31 *Breakfast menu sequence*

Order of courses		Dishes available	Notes
1 Fruits	(a)	Fresh: grapefruit, melon, juices	
	(b)	Stewed: compôte of figs, prunes, apples, mixed fruit. Cold baked apple	Cooked and served plain
2 Cereals		Cornflakes, shredded wheat, etc. Porridge Sometimes add the words 'milk' 'cream'	Hot and cold
3 Beverages		Coffee, tea, chocolate	
4 Bread		Rolls, croissants, brioche, toast, etc.	
5 Eggs		Scrambled, fried, boiled, poached, omelettes	
6 Fish	(a)	Grilled: mackerel, kippers, herrings, bloaters	Often printed without the word grilled
	(b)	Fish cakes, kedgeree, smoked haddock	
	(c)	Fried: plaice, sole, whiting	
7 Meats (hot)	(a)	Bacon (and egg), ham (and egg)	Usually printed without the word grilled
	(b)	Grilled: bacon, ham, gammon, sausage, kidney (lambs), calves liver	
served with		Potatoes: sauté, fried, bubble and squeak, mushrooms, tomatoes, black pudding, fried bread	
8 Meats (cold)		Ham, tongue, pressed beef (rarely poultry or butchers meat)	Salad is never printed on the menu
served with		Potatoes: sauté, fried or plain boiled	
7 or 9 Preserves		Marmalade, honey, jam	Desirably a whole fruit jam like cherry, strawberry, etc.
8 or 10 Dessert fruit		Apples, pears, bananas, peaches, grapes, etc.	Dressed in a basket

all can be chosen to suit the menu's requirement. For example, a Continental breakfast comprises only one course, usually headed by 4 (bread items), followed by 7 (preserves) and ending with 3 (beverages). Some full breakfast menus revert to this sequence and, therefore, this alternative is given below.

A full English breakfast

An old-style full breakfast menu was presented in the style shown in Figure 60.

It is, however, rare today for guests taking 'full' cooked breakfast to be offered more than one 'starter' course and one main course. Thus cereals (and porridge) are usually grouped with

BREAKFAST

Grapefruit
Fruit juice (orange, lemon, pineapple, etc.)
Tomato juice
Stewed fruit (plums, apples, figs, prunes, etc.)

Porridge or cereals

Steamed fillet of haddock
Fried fillet of sole
Grilled herring
Kedgeree

Fried egg and bacon
Poached egg on toast
Grilled sausage and fried egg
Mushrooms on toast
Grilled kidneys and bacon
Grilled tomatoes

Fresh fruits
(oranges, apples, pears, bananas)

Marmalade, honey, preserves

Toast, brioches, croissants, rolls, brown bread

Tea, coffee, milk, chocolate

Figure 60   *A menu for a full English breakfast*

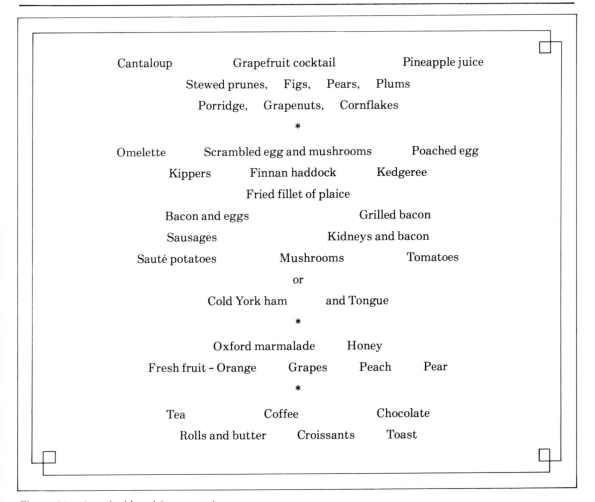

Cantaloup   Grapefruit cocktail   Pineapple juice

Stewed prunes,   Figs,   Pears,   Plums

Porridge,   Grapenuts,   Cornflakes

*

Omelette   Scrambled egg and mushrooms   Poached egg

Kippers   Finnan haddock   Kedgeree

Fried fillet of plaice

Bacon and eggs   Grilled bacon

Sausages   Kidneys and bacon

Sauté potatoes   Mushrooms   Tomatoes

or

Cold York ham   and Tongue

*

Oxford marmalade   Honey

Fresh fruit – Orange   Grapes   Peach   Pear

*

Tea   Coffee   Chocolate

Rolls and butter   Croissants   Toast

Figure 61   *A typical breakfast menu layout*

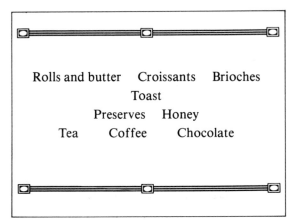

Rolls and butter   Croissants   Brioches
Toast
Preserves   Honey
Tea   Coffee   Chocolate

Figure 62   *A typical Continental breakfast menu*

the fruits and juices, and fresh fruit, if offered, similarly joins this section. Fish items are also merged with the bacon and egg group.

Today's full table d'hôte breakfast menu of three courses is therefore usually presented in the style shown in Figure 61.

In such a table d'hôte breakfast menu there are four sections but only three 'courses' as beverages and breads are served earlier in the meal.

For reasons already referred to, uncooked breakfasts are increasingly demanded and served. Such a menu is usually presented as shown in Figure 62. Fruit juice is often offered on Continental breakfast menus.

Breakfast preparation

For the two types of breakfast served in hotels – plain or Continental breakfast, and full or English breakfast – pre-preparation varies. A plain breakfast consisting of tea or coffee, rolls, toast (perhaps also croissants and rolls), butter and marmalade, requires only a modest mise en place.

Mise en place

A full English breakfast, despite modifications, remains a more elaborate meal and requires preparation in the dining room before service.

Grapefruits should be cut (this ought not to be done the previous night because of vitamin C loss, but some operations do pre-prepare grapefruit and cover them with clingfilm) and oranges squeezed.

In some cases the various juices, cereals, jugs of cream and of cold milk are arranged on a table (usually cold buffet table) in the dining room.

Services of jam, honey and marmalade are to be prepared but in many operations these (and butter) are prepackaged in individual portions.

Timing and tables

Though individual items may be simple in cooking and presentation breakfast can be difficult to serve because of timing and a table having to accommodate several items at the same time.

Tables also require much preparation as more items are set on them than at any other meal. Therefore, in order to be ready on time for breakfast service, as much as possible of the mise en place is done the previous night. This avoids confusion and panic in the morning and affords both staff and guests a good start to the

Figure 63   *English breakfast table setting for one person*
The fish knife and fork are positioned outside, the meat knife and fork inside. A dessert spoon for porridge or cereals is laid at the top of the cover. A small knife is placed on the sideplate to the right. The teapot, milk jug and hot water jug are positioned to the right. Note the angle of the handles for the guest's convenience

Figure 64
*Continental breakfast
table setting for one person*

day. If food and beverages are good and well-served a guest's impression of the hotel is improved. Badly served, his final impression can be marred.

Previous evening's preparation
The evening before, therefore, a clean table-cloth is laid on the table then the cover is set. A full breakfast cover consisted once of a medium-sized plate, a joint knife and a fish knife to the right, a joint fork and a fish fork to the left. In many establishments the fish implements are now omitted and brought only as a customer's order in the morning requires. In front, a sweet fork is placed, handle to the left and a dessert spoon, handle to the right but many operations leave out the dessert fork. On the left-hand side of this, a side plate is placed with a side knife on the right edge of the plate, in line with the other cutlery. Breakfast cups and saucers, if set the night before, are placed to the right beside the tip of the meat knife (or fish knife if laid) and with the cup upside down and with a covering cloth over. A slop basin, a cruet set and an ash-tray are positioned symmetrically on the table.

Morning preparation
Next morning, table waiters complete settings with: breakfast-size cups and saucers, tea spoons, table napkins (placed square on the medium-size plate). A bowl of soft sugar and one of lump sugar are then placed on each table, together with a jug of cold milk, a jug of cream and a service of preserves (marmalade, honey and jam usually in miniature jars or individual packs).

Checking covers
Head waiters or supervisors check that a full breakfast table setting finally consists of the following. Breakfast cups (or teacups) to the right of one of the covers, leaving space for beverage pots to be placed later. Sugar basin (with tongs or spoon), slop basin and tea strainer near the place earmarked for beverage pots. Cruet (salt, pepper) centrally placed. Preserve dish (marmalade/jam) within reach. Space near also earmarked for toast rack and butter dish. The cover itself (side plate, napkin and knife with cereal spoon, large knife and fork or fish knife and fork) should, with other items, all be neatly arranged.

Sideboard requirements

During this same mise en place time, waiters attend to sideboards, stacking cutlery, plates, cups, saucers, napkins, large and small tablecloths and anything that may be required during service. Prepare grapefruits (though as noted, some operations do this the evening before), orange juice, grapefruit juice, tomato juice, etc., and jugs of iced water. Assemble condiments to include fresh mustard, Worcestershire sauce, bottles of vinegar, etc.

Anything not required for breakfast should never be brought into the room nor kept on the sideboard. Unnecessary items will only hinder the waiter during service. Floral decorations are seldom used for breakfast.

Summary of morning preparation and mise en place

Kitchen
Porridge made
Bacon, sausages: batch grilling starts
Eggs available: prepare to order

Still-room
Coffee made in batches in advance (but Cona or
    similar services may be provided 'in the room')
Tea to order
Toast to order
Rolls warmed

Restaurant
For tables:
Milk on table
Preserves
Butters
Menu
No flowers

For sideboards:
Iced water (American guests)
Rolls/butter
Cream
Mustards, sauces
Extra covers

Breakfast service

Breakfast menus are presented to each guest by the head waiter or waiter and the order taken in the usual manner (Chapter 12). In coffee shops or other more modest services, menus may be already on the table. Instructions given by a customer regarding the preparation of his order (timing of egg, etc.) must be written on the check.

Breakfast service is fundamentally the same as for any other meal. Dishes from the various departments are brought to the sideboard, checked by the waiter for the correctness of the order and then served to the customer.

First class service of breakfast is done on silver, but many hotels adopt plate service to speed breakfast service. For plate service in grander operations with commis assistance the waiter usually collects orders from the kitchen and his commis attends to requirements from the still-room.

Hot beverage service

Customers appreciate prompt service of coffee, tea (or, more rarely, alternatives such as chocolate). Tea service presents few problems. There have been changes in coffee service.

Coffee
At breakfast there are two main alternative forms of coffee service. First, the traditional method is to place coffee, milk and sugar on the table in a coffee pot, milk jug and sugar bowl. Customers help themselves as they do in their own homes. When several people in one party occupy a table, place the coffee service on the right of the senior or eldest lady present.

Increasingly, however, coffee is now brewed on a sideboard or table in a Cona or similar machine. This with an accompanying jug of hot milk is carried from table to table by the waiter. ('Pour'n'serve' as it is sometimes dubbed.)

The method of serving coffee by the waiter after lunch and dinner is detailed in Chapter 15, but in many operations even after-dinner coffee may be similarly dispensed from a sideboard brew.

Freshness and timing

Toast, hot rolls, brioches and croissants are placed on the table at the same time as porridge or cereals unless a guest stipulates otherwise.

At breakfast time toast is always served in a toast rack. It must never be laid flat on a plate nor served in a pile as this makes it soggy and unfit to be served. Always see that tea and toast are freshly made and coffee and hot milk really hot. Remember customers rightly blame the waiter if they are not; for whether or not he caused the fault he is certainly responsible for checking that items are freshly made and hot.

Clearing and cover adjustment

When as a waiter you clear away the plate used for the main course, remove any spare (that is unused) silver left on the table. Also move the side plate directly in front of the guest. Similarly move the toast rack and service of marmalade and preserves nearer the customer. Then ask if more toast, coffee or a fresh pot of tea is required.

A customer must never be kept unnecessarily waiting between courses. Refer any delay in food service to the section head waiter. Investigate and seek to remedy any service hold-up and at once inform the guest, regretting the delay and explaining that you are seeking to overcome it.

Continental breakfast service sequence summarized

Present menu
Take order
Adjust covers
Serve starter (for example fruit juice)
Serve hot beverage. For tea check you have: strainer; slop basin; cold milk or dish of lemon slices and fork on side plate
At the last minute serve hot rolls (leave on table) and/or toast, butter and jam (on doyleys on side plates)

Full breakfast service sequence summarized

Present menu
Take order. Note guests' wishes – well-done bacon, etc. (possibly separate check for still-room)
Adjust covers
Collect starter
Place hot beverage, rolls, etc., unless customers indicate otherwise
Clear starter
Serve main course
Remove any unwanted items (for example sugar shaker)
Clear main course plate: adjust cover (move side plate to centre), place jam, etc., conveniently near guest.
Check toast, etc., for replenishment

Floor service

Luxury hotels may offer floor service (room service) of all the day's meals under the supervision of a head floor waiter with waiters working shifts. Other establishments may offer room service for breakfast only. Invariably hotels charge extra for floor service.

Floor waiters must be experienced in serving all types of meals and alcoholic beverages. They must co-operate with other departments such as housekeeping and kitchen to ensure smooth service.

Guests summon a floor waiter by push button/ lamp signal or by telephoning room service or reception, according to house custom.

Floor pantry

A floor waiter effects his own mise en place before meal service. The floor pantry from which he operates should be equipped with: sink unit, hot-plate, refrigerator, lift to main kitchen, salamander, gas ring, small still set or coffee-making machine. cutting boards, knives, storage space for china, silverware, cutlery, glassware, cruets, sauces, preserves, sugar, etc., linen, trays, salvers, trolleys, chafing lamps, suzette pans, wine service equipment and an internal telephone.

Ordinarily a waiter sends dirty plates down the lift but retains cutlery, pots and cups to wash himself, which are usually his stock and kept in his pantry.

For this reason, floor pantries are equipped with a sink, a lift to the still-room and the kitchen and facilities for boiling water and keeping coffee and milk hot. Normally a telephone or intercom is connected to the main kitchen and still-room. In some cases, tea and coffee are obtained from the still-room with the other part of the order, but usually dry tea and a supply of hot coffee and milk are sent up to the floor pantry.

Equipment and mise en place

Floor service crockery, cutlery and other equipment may be of a different design and/or colour, or marked distinctively from that used in restaurant or other departments to aid recognition and control. Stock should be no more than necessary to cover peak needs. A constant stock check is needed for floor pantries are susceptible to pilfering.

A floor waiter should arrange all his mise en place before the service of meals.

Floor checking

For control, triplicate checks are normally used for all meals, foods and beverages served. Check books for floor service are usually marked 'floor' and are a different colour from other departments (dining room, etc.). Room numbers must be carefully and clearly marked because of the extra charge customarily made for floor service. The original check goes to the kitchen or other issuing department to obtain the items, and a flimsy copy is retained in the floor pantry for reference. The guest should sign the duplicate which should then be passed immediately to control for addition to the house bill. On floors, customers sign bills which are then charged through the tabular sheet. Guests usually check out after breakfast, hence checks and bills must be passed promptly after service to the cashier.

Breakfast on floors

Because of the cost to hoteliers and consequent charges to guests, room service is less demanded than formerly.

Self-service

In motels and similar operations a customer's tray may be provided with disposable items, bag of rolls and/or croissants, wrapped butter portions, jam, coffee sachets, UHT milk portions (jiggers), wrapped sugars, paper napkins and a covered plastic beaker of juice. A customer can make his own breakfast when he wishes.

Refrigerators holding ice and cold drinks in bedrooms may also store butter, etc. for guest's breakfasts.

The amount of guest 'self-service' is determined by management's policy. More waiter service in rooms inevitably means higher prices and hence tends to be limited to expensive up market hotels.

Room service

Where breakfast room service is offered as in the restaurant, much is prepared the night before. Trays or trolleys are laid up and covered to protect from dust.

Room service in hotels of the highest class usually involves a trolley. This converts into a table with flaps. A trolley may even incorporate a heated compartment for a hot dish. Service in a suite (or bedroom) is similar to that in the restaurant except that the waiter does not remain throughout.

In most hotels, trays are used by floor service waiters. The night porter may similarly use a tray for very early breakfast floor service. In this case each customer has a tray. These are fully loaded before arriving at the guest's room. Food is kept hot in various ways, for example covers for plates, insulated jugs for coffee, tea cosy etc.

Floor breakfasts are usually ordered the previous night or given as a standing order (often by customers marking order cards to be hung on their outside door knob).

Trays in room service

For room service of a meal in bed the same lay-up applies to a tray as for a table (see below). In most cases the tray will be placed on the bed, or a trestle, as a table. Service in sitting rooms entails laying a table in the same style as in a restaurant.

Carrying a tray

Balance a tray on your outspread left-hand palm on a level with your shoulder so that in room service your right hand is free to knock on the door, and then to open it on obtaining permission to enter.

When a tray is to be carried, lay the heaviest dishes in the centre with glasses and lighter articles towards the edges. Place glasses upside down as they are more stable.

Do not take two hot courses in on the same tray, at the same time, to the same room, for the second course is likely to get cold while the first is being eaten.

Breakfast tray lay-up

For a full breakfast for one person, the tray should be covered with a tray cloth. The cover consists of the following:

Side plate and side knife and fork and/or fish knife and fork, dessert spoon (or alternatively dessert spoon and fork)
Breakfast cup, saucer and spoon
Sugar basin, caster sugar dredger, preserve dish and spoon
Cruet
Napkin

Because of weight and space factors, no underplate need be used for tray-served breakfasts and cutlery should be confined to what is needed for the particular order (which will be known either from a pre-order bedroom card or by telephone).

Serving

At the last minute, place the chilled butter and hot food and beverage on the tray or trolley and take it to the customer at the requested time.

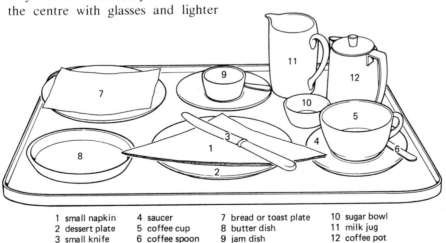

1 small napkin	4 saucer	7 bread or toast plate	10 sugar bowl
2 dessert plate	5 coffee cup	8 butter dish	11 milk jug
3 small knife	6 coffee spoon	9 jam dish	12 coffee pot

Figure 65 *A tray laid for breakfast with white coffee*

Knock at the guest's door and wait to be admitted. On entering, place the tray either on a special side table (only on the bed if the guest requests it). If a trolley is used, wheel it into the room and place it either in the centre of the room, by the window or by the bed at the request of the guest. Usually trays are used for single orders and trolleys for an order for two persons.

Show the dishes brought to the guest in case the order is incorrect or not to his liking. It can then be changed without the guest having to ring for the waiter again.

When you are about to leave, ask if anything else is required, otherwise do not enter the room again unless called for. Often a tray or trolley is left for the chamber maid to clear when she is cleaning the room. She will place it either in the passage or in the floor pantry for the waiter to clear later.

Lounge service

Lounge services in hotels have tended to contract in recent times because of demand and cost factors. Residents' lounges have either disappeared in city hotels or have been greatly reduced in area but, of course, some services of drinks and refreshment are still offered. In resort hotels, services such as morning coffee, afternoon tea and drinks either for holiday makers or for conference business have survived. Many hotels and restaurants also encourage guests to take coffee in the lounge after lunch or dinner in order to free restaurant tables for new seatings.

Lounge services may involve therefore:

'Morning coffee' which may include other beverages hot and cold including tea and chocolate. Biscuits are commonly served with morning coffee

Afternoon tea

Ice creams, sundaes, etc.

After meal coffee

Alcoholic and other cold drinks before, between and after meals

It is rare now for hotels to offer, or have demand for, other items (which may still be sought in cafés and popular restaurants) such as pastries including cakes, gâteaux and flans, yeast buns (Chelsea, Bath, etc.), scones, toasted items, sandwiches and ice cream items.

Afternoon teas

These are sometimes included in en pension terms in resort hotels and for conference business but are less offered to casual customers for they are seen to be uneconomic by many urban hotels. Items provided in good class resort hotels and similar operations might include:

Assorted sandwiches Thin brown or white bread, well-buttered, filled with egg, cress, tomato, lettuce, cucumber, fish and meat pastes, chicken, ham and, more rarely, foie gras, smoked salmon. Cut small and daintily.

Hot plate and yeast goods Buttered or toasted: scones, buns, tea cakes, Sally Lunn, Scotch pancakes, muffins, crumpets, toast.

Bread and butter White, brown, wholemeal, fruit, etc., sliced very thinly (sometimes rolled or curled).

Conserves Jam, lemon curd, honey, etc., but not orange marmalade at tea time.

Pastries Small afternoon tea pastries and gâteaux.

Tea Indian, Ceylon, China, Russian and iced.

In preparing a table for afternoon tea, the general guidelines for a breakfast lay-up may be followed except that teacups and saucers are usually of smaller size than breakfast cups (though for economy a 'standard' size may be used in some operations for both purposes), Check that cup handles are correctly positioned to the right of the guest, that the requisite silver is provided and that sliced lemon is included when China tea is ordered.

Other tea services

In addition to the conventional service of Indian, Ceylon and China tea in teapots with accompanying jug of hot water with milk or cream and/or lemon, tea may be served as:

Iced tea Prepared by chilling brewed tea and serving with ice and a lemon slice in Russian tea style.

Green tea Widely used in China and also popular in Northern India and Pakistan. It is served in this country in Chinese restaurants but is otherwise seldom seen in hotels and restaurants. Unlike black tea, the leaf is dried but not fermented. Green tea brews to a pale gold/green or green liquid and is served without milk (or, usually, lemon) accompaniments.

Lemon tea May be similarly served as Russian tea but many who take lemon in place of milk or cream are prepared to do so from a normal tea service with cup.

Russian tea Russians themselves take their tea strong and never with milk. Russian style in other parts of the Western World is to serve this tea in a glass tumbler which fits within a holding frame (traditionally silver plate). A slice of lemon accompanies it, usually provided separately on a small dish with small fork.

Other infusions

Apart from the foregoing other infusions are occasionally requested and served.

Tisanes

Probably as part of an interest in dieting and health foods infusions from leaves and herbs other than tea are more demanded than was formerly the case but still have nothing like the appeal of conventional tea. These brews of herbs are known as tisanes. These include:

Camomile The flower of that herb is infused like tea, served plain and is thought to aid digestion.

Ginseng From ginseng root for which healthful and aphrodisiac claims are made. Its taste is similar to liquorice.

Mint tea Widely served in the Middle East especially Morocco, is brewed from leaf mint. It is normally served in glasses garnished with a sprig of mint.

Tilleul Still quite widely appreciated in France, is brewed from dried lime blossom flowers.

Milfoil or yarrow Made from yarrow leaves and flowers.

Other infusions are more home health remedies than tea substitutes. They include such brews as:

Bergamot or oswega From the leaves and flowers of a border plant.

Raspberry From the leaf which is slightly reminiscent of the raspberry fruit.

Rosehip tea From wild rosehips.

Speciality coffees

Some 'special' coffees such as Turkish, Irish, or café brûlot may be served in the restaurant after dinner. Others may be served in the lounge.

These styles include:

Café Brûlé or Brûlot A flambé presentation in which a blend of brandy, sugar and crushed coffee bean is ignited in a large spoon and stirred into hot coffee.

Café Capuccino (or Kapuziner in Germany and Austria) A beverage for occasional (that is mid-morning or mid-afternoon) drinking made by blending chocolate into the coffee and topping with Chantilly cream.

Café Diable Is similar to but usually spicier than café brûlot.

Café Viennois Coffee with hot milk also topped with whipped cream.

Irish coffee Is served in a warmed 2½ dl (8 oz) glass goblet. Black coffee sweetened to guests' taste is reinforced with Irish whiskey and has double cream floated on the top by pouring over the upturned bowl of a spoon.

Other spirits and liqueurs have also been blended with coffee in similar types of service.

Turkish coffee Where coffee is made in individual pot or pan usually merchandised from a trolley.

Other French terms for coffee

Café crème or café à la crème Black coffee served with cream.

Café filtre   Filtered coffee. served in a variety of ways. One is by using an infusion pot fitted over a French-style (brown china ware) coffee pot. Boiling water is poured into the infusion and once it has passed through, the waiter replaces the infusion pot with a lid and serves the coffee in the usual way from his silver or service plate.

Café filtre may, however, be served in individual sized infusion pots which fit over the coffee pot. They are usually served complete to the guest but the waiter removes the infuser once all the boiling water has percolated through to the cup. A wider variety of filter pots including those with plungers to aid the passing through of boiling water are now available.

Café glacé   Is almost as much a soft coffee ice cream as a drink. One old recipe (from T. Fisher, *A Cup of Coffee,* Unwin 1883) adds one egg to six cups of sweetened black coffee, then mixed with cream. After freezing it should be 'the consistency of rich thick cream'. But modern versions vary. Some are as basic as chilled white coffee with a scoop of vanilla ice cream or coffee ice cream added.

Café au lait   Coffee served or diluted with equal or more amounts of hot milk. (For this the coffee is given a breakfast roast rather than the longer after-dinner roast.) Café au lait is not made by boiling coffee and milk together.

Café noir   Black coffee.

Mocha   After dinner coffee from the Mocha bean (see page 63). True Mocha has an acquired 'gamey' taste and the menu term is sometimes misleadingly used when only a strong after dinner roast has been used.

Lounge waiting staff

Lounge waiters are also members of the food and beverage service team who work outside the main area of service (that is, do not work in the restaurant/dining room, coffee shop or speciality restaurant).

In larger de luxe hotels, especially in resorts, lounges may be manned by a small brigade of **waiters. They work shift duties throughout the** day but not an early morning shift, for service to

lounges usually starts at 10 a.m. Light refreshments, afternoon teas and drinks are served.

Each waiter has a station in the lounge. This must be kept clean and free of used glasses, coffee cups and other items. (Magazines, newspapers, etc., must also be kept neat and ashtrays emptied throughout the service.) The lounge may have its own small still-room service for tea and coffee, toast, etc. Drinks are ordered from the dispense bar, sandwiches from the kitchen (garde-manger).

Most lounges close for waiter service at midnight. Service is not refused to any guest afterwards but is taken over by night porters. They do not 'man' the lounge but give service only as required.

Lounge checking

For control in the lounge, chance customers pay cash but residents, if they wish, may sign the check which must be immediately passed to reception/cash office. The checking system is similar to that used in the restaurant. (See Chapter 16.)

Hall porters and night porters

Hall porters are also provided with a check-book for use when they serve guests at times when normal service is not available. Night porters often provide a beverage and snack service (sandwiches, etc.) and serve early breakfasts in rooms. A porter may also be issued with a small stock of drinks and food for light snacks.

Continuing change

New types of customer, new social and economic factors continue to affect the provision of hotel and restaurant services at breakfast and on floors and in lounges. Moreover, mechanization is also developing means which allow guests more 'painlessly' to help themselves. Some of the foregoing services provided in the traditional way are now, because of costs and prices, decreasingly sought. Continuing shifts in demand **and new ways to satisfy guests are destined to be features of hospitality services.**

Part Five

Liquor and Tobacco

19 Table wine and wine lists

As more table wine is sold for consumption both at home and in restaurants much of the mystique about wines tends to disappear. Nevertheless, wine is a commodity which requires to be understood if it is to be successfully sold and served. In expensive restaurants there are specialist wine waiting staff headed by a sommelier (at least one American sommelier prefers to be called cellar master). In modest operations waiting staff may serve drinks as well as food.

To give waiting staff some background to beverage service, this part deals with drinks and tobacco, considers the nature of wine and wine lists and explains how to recognize and begin to understand wines.

Many books are devoted not merely to wine but to particular regions or aspects; so it will be obvious that an introductory treatment as given here, is aimed to provide a few basics from which waiting staff may proceed to further study.

Wine list

Just as a menu indicates the possibilities (and limitations) of food which a restaurant offers, so its wine list shows what alcoholic beverages for consumption at table are for sale. Selecting and purchasing wine is a skilled task. Notes here are intended only to give an idea of a wine list's nature. The range may be most modest (for example for use in steak bars or limited menu operations), being as little as two inexpensive red wines, two inexpensive white wines, supported by bar stocks of beers, spirits and liqueurs. But a fine restaurant's wine list may be an extensive one of several pages ranging over many countries.

Wine list sections

A wine list is divided into sections. Traditionally these were determined by the countries or regions of origin for example Burgundy, divided again into white and red sections.

Modern wine lists include wines from many more wine producing countries than once was the case and many shorter lists are balanced for commercial as well as gastronomic reasons, for example fish restaurants tend to feature more white wines. Above all, consumer taste for wine 'in fashion' (for example pétillant rosé wines) will be met irrespective of wine pundits' strictures on such popular but not 'gourmet approved' varieties.

Some operations find it convenient to allow a wine merchant to have exclusive supply rights and such merchants take much responsibility in constructing a restaurant wine list.

Today many lists, whether or not constructed in association with a particular merchant, are often grouped by wine style rather than by countries of origin, that is, dry white wines from whatever source will be listed as a section, but country or place of origin will also be indicated.

Some of the principal wines

The following is indicative of what may appear on a wine list (but with more detail of particular wines), and is not intended to be exhaustive. Light white wine is, for example, now produced in England and may be featured on British wine lists.

Red wines   Bordeaux (claret); Burgundy; table wines of other countries especially Italy (Chianti, Valpolicella, etc.), Spain (for example Rioja), Portugal (for example Dao), Australia*, Hungary and the Americas* may also be represented.

White wines   Bordeaux; Burgundy; Germany (Rhine and Moselle); Alsatian; wines from Yugoslavia, Hungary, South Africa*, etc.

Rosé wines   Anjou, Portugal, etc.

Champagne   Produced in the Rheims district in France.

Other sparkling wines   Sekt (from Germany), Asti Spumante from Piedmont, Italy) and from elsewhere in France.

Sherry   Deriving its name from the town of Jerez in Spain.

Ports   From the River Douro area of Portugal.

Madeira   From the Island of Madeira.

Liqueurs and spirits   especially Cognac (and **Armagnac**) brandies from France.

Before the war, table wine in first class restaurants came almost entirely from France and Germany. But today wines from America (North and South), Australia, South Africa and several European countries are usually featured. Not all of these wines can be discussed in detail in a book primarily concerned with restaurant service. Hence in this introductory treatment, emphasis is on 'traditional' French and German wines.

Identifying wine

The label on a bottle should help identify a wine. France, Germany, Italy and other countries have regulations regarding the designation and labelling of wine. A wine named after its place of origin carries such information as the precise name of the place (the commune or viticultural region), a trademark and the name of the producer or merchant who bottled it.

Since 1935 the French have regulated the naming of wines according to their place of origin and their system is outlined below. The Common Market (EEC) also has regulations which categorize wines as VQPRD or, if lesser quality, vins de table.

Germany's mode of identifying wine is also mentioned but the schemes of other countries (Italy for example) cannot for reasons of space be detailed. The advantage of nationally agreed standard descriptions are increasingly recognized by all wine-producing countries.

*Australia, South Africa, Cyprus and North and South America wines including those with characteristics similar to claret, Burgundy, hock, sherry and port.

French scheme

Fine French wines (and those of many other countries too) are named after the place they come from – their appellation d'origine. Under French regulations the appellation d'origine may only be used for wines made according to local practice in the place named on the label.

Appellation d'origine

The category 'appellation d'origine contrôlée' (AOC) guarantees origin and satisfies the production requirements as laid down by the INAO (Institut National des Appellations d'Origine).

Conditions apply particularly to:

Area of production.
Types of grape.
Pruning and cultivation methods.
Maximum yield per hectare.
Minimum alcoholic content before any enriching takes place.
Vinification and preservation methods.

The 1935 regulations have been progressively tightened for example the introduction in 1974 of analytical and organoleptic (tasting) tests for these wines.

VDQS wines (vins délimités de qualité supérieure)

VDQS wines constitute the second type of VQPRD wines (under EEC rules), the first being the appellation d'origine contrôlée wines.

VDQS wines are controlled by regulations similar to if less strict than AOC wines. These provide for a stamp of approval from a local viticultural syndicate when it is satisfied that a wine meets conditions laid down by the Ministry of Agriculture. These relate to :

● Area production.
● Type of grape.
● Minimum alcoholic content.
● Cultivation and vinification (yield) method.

Vins de pays

Vins de pays were defined in 1973 as table wines which have a geographical entity, but they must satisfy some quality criteria. They must be produced from noble grapes or recommended grapes grown in a certain department, zone or village and must bear the name of that area. (For example, vin de Pays des Côteaux du Vidourle.) Other conditions relate to minimum natural alcoholic content (10° for wines from the Mediterranean zone, 9.5° or 9° for other areas).

They must satisfy analytical tests bearing on the amount of sulphur dioxide or volatile acidity they contain and tasting tests of a commission appointed by the Institut des Vins de Consommation Courante, but unlike other wines of the vin de table category to which they belong, vins de pays do not have to show on their label the alcoholic content of the wine.

They can be given such names as Côte, Côteau, Mont, Val and in individual vineyards, Mas and Domaine, but must *never* be designated as Château or Clos.

If their quality and good reputation justify it, they may eventually be promoted into the VDQS category.

French and EEC descriptions

Apart from the fine, classified wines of France touched upon later in this chapter, merit listings are:

France	*EEC*
1 Appellation contrôlée (AC)	} VQPRD
2 Vins délimité de qualité supérieure (VDQS)	
3 Vins de pays	} Vin de table
4 Vins de table	

French wines

The following is an abbreviated introduction to French wine to aid waiting staff in interpreting bottle labels and understanding the nature of the wine. Remember that labelling is not always wholly consistent and each label should be read as an individual one.

Bordeaux

Both red and white wines are made on the clay, sand and gravel soils of the Gironde in the Bordeaux region. Important names include:

Red wines (claret)
On the left bank Médoc, Haut-Médoc, Margaux, Moulis, Listrac, Saint-Julien, Pauillac, Saint Estèphe, Graves.
On the right bank Saint Emilion, Pomerol, Canon et Côtes de Fronsac, Blayais, Bourgeais, Premières Côtes de Bordeaux, Côtes de Castillon.
Red Bordeaux wines Known in Britain as clarets, are full flavoured, yet light on the palate. They have bouquet and bright colour.

White wines
Dry Graves, Entre-Deux-Mers.
Mellow Premières Côtes de Bordeaux, Saint-Macaire, Graves de Vayres, Haute-Benauge, Sainte-Foy, Bordeaux, Blaye et Bourg.
Sweet and smooth Sauternes, Barsac, Cérons, Loupiac, Ste-Croix-du-Mont.

Dry Bordeaux wines are gentle in flavour, pale and slightly astringent. They are golden (which in a white Bordeaux generally indicates a sweeter wine) and have more body. Sweetest are Barsac wines, of full colour and an almost oily body. Sauternes and Barsac wines have noticeable bouquet.

Bordeaux and Bordeaux Supérieur

Ordinary Bordeaux wines are labelled Bordeaux or Bordeaux Supérieur indicating wine made from grapes from any part of Bordeaux and can be blended. A Bordeaux Supérieur must have an alcoholic content of more than 10.5 per cent, but the term supérieur does not mean that a wine otherwise is 'superior'.

District wines

A district wine is a wine grown in one of five major districts of Bordeaux:

Graves
The Haut-Médoc
Sauternes-Barsac
Pomerol
St Emilion

When labelled by district, all the wine's grapes were grown within the district named. If a good year, from a reputable shipper, such wine can be pleasant at relatively low cost.

Villages or communes

Ranking above district wines are village or commune wines. Most come from the Haut-Médoc, the most abundant source of fine Bordeaux. Villages such as Pauillac, St. Julien, Macau, Margaux, Cantenac and St. Estephe are among the better known. An appellation contrôlée St. Julien label, for example, indicates that all its grapes were grown within the St. Julien commune. This is the highest type of Bordeaux to be designated appellation contrôlée.

Châteaux

The finest Bordeaux must be made from grapes of a château's own vineyard and thus usually bear on the label the term 'mis en bouteille au château' (bottled at the château).

A château bottled wine bears its district or village appellation, for example Chateau Mouton Rothschild is labelled 'appellation Pauillac contrôlé'. (Pauillac village being that nearest the château.) Others bear a district one, for example Château Haut-Brion (appellation Graves contrôlée), or Château Cheval Blanc (appellation St. Emilion contrôlée).

Bordeaux classification

Some château bottled Bordeaux labels refer to a wine's classification such as Cru Exceptionnel, or Premier Grand Cru Classé, or Deuxième or Premier Cru, or Grand Cru Classé or similiar descriptions according to the wine's district. Red Bordeaux wines were first classified in 1855 based on what each had brought on the open market in past years. The sixty-two top-selling wines of the Haut-Médoc (with one from the Graves, Château Haut-Brion) were divided into five classes, or growths (crus), Pomerol, St. Emilion and Graves (with the Haut-Brion exception) wines were not then included.

But the Graves district developed a simple rating system in 1953 and accorded the term Cru Classé to the thirteen best reds and eight whites, leaving remaining Graves wines unclassified.

The following year, St. Emilion grouped its top wines into two classes: Premier Grand Cru and Grand Cru.

Pomerol classified their wines in four grades as: Premier Grand Cru, Premier Cru, Deuxième Premier Cru (or 'secondary' Premier Cru), and Deuxième Cru or 'second growth',

White wines of Sauternes-Barsac have also now been classified into three classes: Premier Cru Supérieur (only Château d'Yquem), Premier Cru and Deuxième Cru.

Even with the subsequent revision the classifications still leave something to be desired for they leave out other fine Bordeaux. Some wines of Bordeaux not in the five classes are designated cru bourgeois or cru bourgeois supérieur. These may be extremely good and some are thought to rival lesser wines of the five growths.

Burgundy

Burgundy, a famous gastronomic region towards the east of central France, produces some famous wines.

Chablis

In the north between Auxerre and Tonerre, is produced Chablis, a very dry white wine, light and heady, with greenish lights.

Côte d'Or

Burgundy's biggest wine-producing district stretches from Dijon to Santenay. It includes the Côte de Nuits and the Côte de Beaune.

Côte de Nuits

Produces wines which are left to mature such as: Chambertin (Gevrey), Musigny (Chambolle), Clos de Vougeot, Saint-Georges (Nuits), Romanée (Vosne) and Richebourg (Vosne).

Côte de Beaune

Further south in Burgundy from Ladoix to Chagny, both red and white wines are made. The reds mature more quickly than those from the Côte de Nuits. They include Corton, Pommard, Volnay, Savigny, Beaune.

White wines (Meursault and the various Montrachet wines) made from Chardonnay grapes have bouquet and elegance.

Mercurey or Chalonnais

This district is a continuation of the Côte de Beaune and its red wines (Mercurey, Givry) are of similar type.

Its white wines (Rully, Montagny) are less distinguished than those of Beaune.

Mâcon

This area from Tournus to Crèches also produces white and red wine. White Mâcon (from Pinot, Chardonnay grapes) includes the well-known Pouilly-Fuissé.

Red (and some rosé is made in the northern Mâconnais region from Gamay grapes.

Mâcon wines are generally regarded as sound rather than distinguished.

Burgundy characteristics

In general, red Burgundies, noted for firmness, are darker in colour and of more body than claret. Being heavy in tannin, astringency in a red Burgundy is probably not equalled by any other wine.

White Burgundies are comparable with white Bordeaux, both dry and sweet, but do not attain the sweetness of Sauternes. They can be almost greenish but the more common colour is pale straw, rather than pale gold. Some say they can achieve perfume as well as bouquet. Generally, they do not improve greatly after five or six years, and are for drinking relatively young.

Appellations

Certain famous Burgundian 'climats' such as: Romanée, Romanée-Conti, Richebourg, Musigny, Montrachet, Corton, Clos de la Roche, Bonnes-Mares are entitled to appellation contrôlée designations.

The name alone, for example Corton, is sufficient to indicate that a wine was harvested within the legal boundaries of its growth.

Communes or villages

Some areas consist of a commune or a 'village'. Such are Chambolle-Musigny, Vosne-Romanée, Aloxe-Corton, Chassagne-Montrachet, Gevrey-Chambertin, etc. A wine from any plot within a communal appellation area is entitled to that appellation. A label may carry the term 'AOC Gevrey-Chambertin' for example and also include the words:

'1er Cru'
'Clos Saint-Jacques'

To be a '1er Cru', the wine must be produced on vineyards or 'climats' classified 1er Cru. The words '1er Cru' alone signify wine produced from several 'climats' all classified '1er Cru'.

If the name of a 'climat' for example 'Clos Saint-Jacques' appears on a label, the wine (in this example an AOC Gevrey-Chambertin) is produced exclusively on the 'climat' 'Clos Saint-Jacques', itself classified 1er Cru.

Estate bottling

Terms 'mis en bouteilles à la propriété', 'mis en bouteilles au domaine' (corresponding to 'mis en bouteilles au château' for Bordeaux) and the rather ambiguous 'mise d'origine' signify that a wine was bottled where the grapes were harvested and where they were made into wine.

In Burgundy where vineyards are divided into many plots, merchants may own them in several appellations. Their wine therefore cannot carry the term 'mise à la propriété' because of the impracticality of having cellars and bottling plants on each plot. A merchant's repute is thus important in Burgundy, for he is responsible for the wine sold under his label whether he owns the vineyard himself or buys from a grower. Some famous names are Pierre Ponnelle, Bouchard Ainé et Fils, Joseph Drouhin, Louis Latour, Bouchard Père et Fils, but there are several others.

Good restaurants thus couple a merchant's name with that of the village. For wines bottled and sold directly by a grower, the latter's name always appears on a good list, for this is the Burgundian equivalent of a Bordeaux château.

Other Burgundy terms

Hospices de Beaune   Hospices de Beaune is not an appellation. The Hospices are a charitable institution owning a number of vineyards as a result of legacies. Their wines are auctioned annually on behalf of the Hospices' charities.

The famous name Hospices de Beaune indicates therefore that a wine is produced on the Hospices estate and not from an appellation area, 'Hospices de Beaune'.

Hospices de Beaune wines are not necessarily all from Beaune, for their estate spreads over several areas of the 'Côte': Beaune, Corton, Savigny, Pommard, Montrachet, and Meursault.

Cuvées such as Nicolas Rollin, Docteur Peste do not correspond to 'climats', but to plots named after either the founders or benefactors of the Hospices or after a donor of vines.

Thus, 'Hospices de Beaune' on a wine list is inadequate. The appellation, and if applicable, the name of the cuvée should follow, for example:

Corton – Hospices de Beaune – Cuvée Docteur Peste

Beaune – Hospices de Beaune – Cuvée Nicolas Rollin

'Aligote' Burgundy   Is a white wine named after the grape from which it is made.

'Passetoutgrain' Burgundy   Is a red wine made by fermenting two-thirds of Gamay grapes with on third of Pinot grapes.

Crémant de Bourgogne   Is a sparkling AC wine, light and pleasant.

Beaujolais

Beaujolais is a large wine-growing area in South Burgundy. Light in body but red and fruity, its wine is popular in Britain, and sells readily.

Along the river Saône as far as Lyon is produced the 'Beaujolais-Villages', each bearing the name of the village it comes from. For example, 'Beaujolais-Quincié'.

On the granite ridges to the North are nine great vineyards: Saint-Amour, Juliénas, Chenas, Moulin-à-Vent, Fleurie, Chiroubles, Morgon, Brouilly and Côtes de Brouilly.

When a label merely bears the word 'Beaujolais' with no other mention of growth it means that the wine comes from one or several different vineyards situated within the boundaries of the Beaujolais region.

Beaujolais appellations are: Beaujolais, Beaujolais Supérieur and Beaujolais-Village.

For the particular nine Beaujolais growths listed above the name Beaujolais need not appear on a label.

Primeur and Nouveau

Although a red wine, Beaujolais is not usually kept long in cellar but drunk young and cool. New or young wine is appreciated. There is general acceptance that if the new wine is released on 16th November rather than 15th December, it is more correctly described (for eleven weeks) as a 'Beaujolais nouveau – tirage primeur' and that for the following year this becomes 'Beaujolais d'année'. Although popular as a young wine a cru Beaujolais of a good year, once it is three or four years old, can resemble a good Burgundy with less body.

Alsace

The Alsatian vineyards stretch along the French side of the Rhine from Strasbourg to Thaun.

Alsace wines are appellation d'origine contrôlée. They are white, dry, fruity and fresh.

The grape variety from which they are produced is always named on the label. They are bottled in the 'flute d'Alsace' with a long neck (resembling a hock bottle) and which is reserved for them by regulations.

They are bottled young and drunk quite young. Since 1972 they must be bottled in their region of production to guarantee their authenticity.

Varieties

The seven grape varieties of Alsace are: Sylvaner, Pinot Blanc, Riesling, Muscat d'Alsace, Pinot Gris (or Tokay d'Alsace) Gewürtztraminer, and Pinot Noir.

Yugoslavia and Hungary, among other countries, produce wine similarly bottled, named after the grape and having some resemblance to Alsatian (and German) wines.

Champagne

True champagne comes only from three specified communes in the Rheims district, but it is widely imitated. Its name, however, is defended by the French government so that the word 'champagne' cannot (or should not) be used by sparkling wine of other countries or other regions. Hence genuine champagne does not need to carry the term appellation contrôlée. The word 'champagne' alone is sufficient.

Champagne is made beneath its native vineyards, in caves cut into the white chalk, twenty to thirty metres underground.

Methode champenoise

The 'methode champenoise' is famous and used for some other sparkling wines.

The first fermentation gives the wine its pale gold colour. The 'cuvées' or blending in vat of wine from different vineyards or vintages ensures its character.

The second fermentation, in bottle and under pressure (5 atmospheres) produces the sparkle.

Turning the bottles (for three months) and removing sediment which collects in the necks of the bottles gives champagne its clarity.

Dry and sweet

Champagne is dry by nature but liqueur (sugar and old wine) added determines whether it will be extra dry, dry, medium dry.

A bottle's label indicates degrees of sweetness (or dryness) thus:

Nature	no added sweetening
Brut	up to 1 per cent sweetening
Extra dry	up to 3 per cent sweetening
Dry or sec	up to 5 per cent sweetening
Demi-sec	up to 8 per cent sweetening
Demi-doux	up to 10 per cent sweetening
Doux (meaning 'soft' or sweet)	up to 12 per cent sweetening

Bottle sizes

In addition to quarter, half and bottle sizes, champagne may be bottled as:

Magnum	equivalent to 2 bottles
Jereboam	equivalent to 4 bottles
Rehoboam	equivalent to 6 bottles
Methuselah	equivalent to 8 bottles
Nebuchadnezzar	equivalent to 20 bottles

Naming champagne

Much champagne is sold under a brand name. Such wine may come from vineyards situated anywhere within the appellation Champagne.

Champagne firms blend the various cuvées (blancs de blancs and blancs de noirs) to their own proportions and a firm's blending skill maintains its particular style from year to year.

The champagne houses or firms' names are thus important. There are some twenty in Rheims and seven in Epernay. Famous names include Heidsieck, Mumm, Irroy, Krug, Lanson, Taittinger, Moet and Chandon, Pol Roger but, as indicated, there are others of great repute.

The words 'propriétaire-récoltant' under an owner's name indicates champagne made by the grower himself.

Vintage champagne   Is a blend of wines from different vineyards but all of the year named on the bottle. A 'vintage year' is one that has been so declared by the Institute Viticole. Usually only good or very good years are vintaged in champagne and marketed not sooner than three years later. Many brands do not show the vintage on the label itself (which is the same for the non-vintage champagnes), but on a secondary one placed above the first or else in a vignette on the ring round the neck of the bottle.

Brut champagne   Is the unblended product of one vineyard only. It may be vintage or non-vintage.

Non-vintage champagne   Is a blended wine that cannot meet the definition of vintage. It is not necessarily inferior to vintage ones but non-vintage champagne is usually lighter and less likely to stand up to the minimum three years ageing obligatory for vintaged wine. In short, they are champagnes which are ready earlier, light, pleasant and with finesse.

Premium blends
Some firms also blend wines of good vintages into special prestige cuvées such as Moet and Chandon's Dom Perignon or Taittinger's cuvée Grand Siècle. Some of these have distinctively-shaped bottles (either of, say, clear glass or of the old shape). Other firms may balance their non-vintage cuvées by blending a good over-rich year with a lighter one.

Blanc de blancs
This means 'white wine produced from white grapes' which is peculiar to champagne. But is often used for ordinary blended white wines from other regions obviously the product of white grapes even if they are hybrids.

Crémant
Another expression from Champagne, 'Crémant', signifies a wine with a light, almost creamy effervescence is now often employed for simple sparkling wines from other regions.

Veuve
The word 'veuve' (widow) is associated with the famous champagne house of Veuve Clicquot. Its use otherwise is meaningless as an indicator of quality.

Ageing
Except in the case of prestige cuvées, non-vintage champagnes are designed to be drunk as soon as marketed and not allowed to age. Vintage champagne is usually drunk not later than between six and ten years after the vintage. It can deteriorate with age. Some think that gas pressure in the bottles can create tendency to 'corkiness' with increased age.

Other French wine regions

Côtes-du-Rhône
The Côtes-du-Rhône vineyards lie between Lyon and Avignon on both sides of the Rhône. Variations in soil, climate, vine species and situation are reflected in the wines.

White wines   Are not numerous but those from the North have an individual character, for example Condrieu, Château-Grillet, white Saint-Joseph, Hermitage and Crozes-Hermitage, Saint-Péray.

The southern Côtes-du-Rhône white wines have fineness only if they come from light, sandy soils like Laudun and Lirac.

Rosé wines   Are more plentiful and include Chusclan, Lirac and above all Tavel.

Red wines   The Rhône valley is renowned for robust red wines, high in alcohol but varying according to soil, position and vine variety.

On the Côte-Rôtie in the North Red Hermitage and Crozes Hermitage from the granite soil near

Tournon can with age achieve the perfection of the great Burgundies.

In the South, the light, red wines of the Southern Côtes du Rhône are called after the commune in which they are produced and in some cases carry the name Côtes du Rhône Villages.

Côte du Rhône red wines for laying down have a marked tannin content. They are notable for their powerful bouquet. Some noteworthy wines are from Cairanne, Gigondas, Vacqueyras and Vinsobres (where rosé wines are also produced) and the famous Châteauneuf-du-Pape. This wine from vineyards between Orange and Avignon, on sun-baked pebbly soil is a perfect accompaniment to game.

Loire
The Loire valley yields light dry white wine such as Muscadet, Sancerre, Pouilly-Fumé popular with British consumers with fish. Medium dry white Vouvray is also produced in a sparkling variety. The area also produces rosé wine in Anjou and Touraine.

The reds (Touraine, Bourgeuil, Chinon) are less known on this country's lists.

Provence
These wines from the Mediterranean region tend to be stronger and sweeter. Their dry rosé wine often has a distinctive orange tint.

Languedoc-Roussillon
Similarly produces powerful reds, often purplish in colour, which furnish much of France's vin ordinaire.

South West
The sweet white Monbazillac comes from this area as do the sparkling wines of Gaillac. The red wines include Bergerac and the strong 'black' wine of Cahors.

French wine terms

Cru
Many terms used to describe wine are complicated by French regulations and restaurant wine lists, even in France, do not always reflect all the details of such regulations. The noun *cru* meaning growth is outlined below because it does often appear on bottles and lists.

Grand cru
'Grand cru' does not apply to private vineyards but is part of a controlled appellation. It is used collectively for wines from a designated area, for example:

Chablis grand cru The best growths only are entitled to this description as follows: Les Clos, Preuses, Vaudésir, Blanchots, Valmur, Bougros and Grenouilles.

Banyuls grand cru Designates a superior Banyuls regulated more severely than for Banyuls.

Saint-Emilion grand cru Saint-Emilion wines when approved by the tasting commission may be labelled 'Saint-Emilion grand cru' and accompanied or not by the vineyard name. Such Saint-Emilions do not come necessarily from the best vineyards, as in the case of Chablis and Banyuls.

Champagne grand cru Certain communes in Champagne, for example Crémant, Avize, Mailly, Verzenay, Bouzy, Ambonnay and Ay are entitled to use the words 'grand cru' but the term is not generally used in Champagne.

Pomerol grand cru No Pomerol grand cru exists since 1964 though on wine lists famous châteaux of Pomerol (and even others) are sometimes described as 'grand cru'.

Premier cru
Like 'grand cru' this term is not applied to private vineyards. Château Lafitte, for example, is not a 'premier cru' but a 'premier cru classé'. 'Premier cru' is used collectively for wines coming from a defined area within controlled appellations of **Burgundy**, for example Chablis, appellation

controlée communes of the Côte-de-Nuits and the Côte-de-Beaune, Rully, Mercurey, Givry and Montagny. There are no other 'premiers crus' anywhere apart from this region of Burgundy, not even in Bordeaux.

The words 'premier cru' are used with or without the name of the 'climat' (cru in Burgundy). The climat name alone may also be used with the appellation of origin. Examples of 'premiers crus' are: Chablis, Monts de Milieu, Gevrey-Chambertin, Clos Saint-Jacques, Beaune, Clos de Mouches, Meursault and Perrières.

Cru classé/premier cru classé/grand premier cru classé

The words 'cru classé' whether or not accompanied by any other term denoting origin from private vineyards in Bordeaux apply to:

● Controlled appellations in Saint-Emilion and Graves.
● There are in Saint-Emilion twelve 'premiers grands crus classes' and sixty-three 'grands crus classés'. The high number reflects the small vineyards, usually smaller than in the Médoc.
● Graves has only one category of 'crus classés': five for red wines, six for red and white, and one for white wines.
● The Pomerols are not so classified.
● Classified château wines of Bordeaux are divided into first, second, third, fourth and fifth 'cru classé'. The term 'cru classé' may be used alone on the label or accompanied by the number first, second, etc.
● The classified red wines are all Médocs except for Haut-Brion (a Graves).
● The whites are all Sauternes and Barsacs and are divided into three categories: 'grand premier cru classé' (only Château d'Yquem), 'premier cru classé' and 'deuxième cru classé'.

Réserve

Words like 'Réserve exceptionnelle' and 'Grand réserve' mean nothing.

Supérieur

A term added to certain Bordeaux, Mâcon, Beaujolais and Graves wines with a higher alcoholic content than the minimum for the appellation. It does not necessarily indicate superior quality. The term can be used for other areas but it is misleading to see Médoc Supérieur, Pomerol supérieur or Beaune supérieur on a wine list when the wine may be less good than one with a plain appellation.

'Grand', 'garantie réserve', 'grand réserve', 'cuvée' and 'cuvée réserve'

These terms are allowed by French regulations to be used alone or in addition to a trademark for non-appellation wines only if they cannot be confused with appellation controlled ones. As they can be freely used for appellation controlled wines, they add no additional guarantee for a customer.

'Haut'

May only be employed when part of an appellation, as in the case of 'Haut-Médoc'.

'Religious' names

Aristocratic and ecclesiastical titles mean nothing though terms such as 'Vin des moines', 'Réserve de l'abbaye', etc., both for appellation and non-appellation wines are often encountered. France's *Service de Repression des Fraudes* forbids the use of 'abbaye' unless a real abbey exists or there are authentic reasons for the word's use.

Mise d'origine or 'tirage d'origine'

'Mise d'origine' or 'tirage d'origine' are confusing and the terms 'château bottled' or 'estate bottled' are preferable. It is illegal under French regulations for non-appellation wines to be listed as 'Grand vin des caves X...mise d'origine' or 'Grand réserve...mise d'origine' as this deliberately misleads.

Other terms

Clos, Château, Domaine, Tour, Mont, Côte Cru, Monopole, Moulin, Camp and similar terms can only be used for appellation controlled wines coming from actual vineyards and which they exactly describe. But the word monopole is unofficially tolerated and the proliferation of 'châteaux' is well-known.

Pelure d'oignon (Onion skin)
These wines are non-appellation rosés.

Blanc de blancs
This simply means a white wine produced from white grapes.

Other words
Other descriptive terms seen on labels include:

Sec	dry
Demi-sec	medium dry (thus also medium sweet)

Doux	sweet
Domaine	a named vineyard
Negociant	a French wine dealer/shipper
Vin de table	table wine (ordinary wine)

Grape varieties
Well-known grape varieties, Sauvignon, Cabernet, Pinot Noir, Gamay and Muscat and other lesser known ones such as Pineau d'Aunis have been used for non-appellation wines for years. To avoid confusion with appellation controlled wines, such names should be preceded by the word 'variety' printed in the same size and colour. No regulations exist to control the use of these names on non-appellation wine labels.

German wines

Although some red and rosé wines are made in Germany, it is mostly white wine which is exported. German wines come in both green and brown bottles. Green bottles contain the light, delicate fragrant wines from the Mosel-Saar-Ruwer area. Brown bottles hold the distinctive Rhine wines. A flagon-shaped green bottle (Bocksbeutel) contains the more robust, and dry Franconian wines.

Designated regions
There are eleven designated regions for Germany's quality wine:

Ahr Northernmost region, noted for red wine.
Mittelrhein Vineyards on steep Rhine slopes; wines are hearty, stylish.
Nahe South of the Rhine, bordering one of its tributaries, wines are fresh and racy, made mostly from the Riesling.
Rheingau One of the world's famous viticultural districts. The Riesling wines are distinctive and elegant.
Rheinhessen A major wine-producing area. Wines are soft, aromatic, made mainly from Silvaner grapes.
Rheinphalz Another major producing area. Known historically as the 'wine cellar of the

Holy Roman Empire'. Wines are full bodied, rich and spicy.
Mosel-Saar-Ruwer Along the Mosel and its tributaries, the Saar and the Ruwer are some of the world's steepest wine terraces yielding fragrant and delicate wines which are made here primarily from the Riesling.
Franken Along the river Main, Silvaner vineyards produce robust, earthy and dry wines, sold in flagon-shaped bottles (Bocksbeutels).
Baden Southernmost region for wine in Germany marked by the Kaiserstuhl, an extinct volcano whose soil helps produce powerful and aromatic wines.
Württemberg Separated from Baden by the Black Forest. Thousands of small growers produce pleasant red and white wines.
Hessische Bergstrasse A very small region. Wines produced primarily for local consumption.

Of the above regions, those of the Rhine and Mosel (Moselle) are the best known and most frequently listed on wine lists outside Germany.

Rhine
Rhine wines are white wines, usually medium sweet to sweet in flavour, of fair body, full flavour and fine bouquet. They are classified by

area or origin, that is, Rheinhesse, Rheingau and Rheinpfalz. Rheingau wines are characterized by a certain hardness. The Rheinesse wines are softer than Rheingau and not quite so rich. The Rheinpfalz (Palatinate) wines are mainly table wines, and being made from more fully developed grapes, are usually rather sweeter. Examples of Rhine wines are: Deidesheimer; Niersteiner Domthal Riesling; and Hochheimer (hence the term 'hock').

Moselle

Similarly classified with Rhine wines are Moselle wines, which have a pleasant lightness, fragrance and dryness. They should be consumed young, as they also have a tingling taste, comparable with Alsatian wines. Examples of Moselle wines are: Piesporter and Bernkastler Doktor.

Categories

There are three categories of German wine: table wine, quality wine and specially graded quality wines.

Tafelwein (table wine)   Light, pleasant wines consumed mainly in Germany; made from approved grape varieties in Mosel (Moselle), Rhein, Main, Neckar and Oberrhein regions.
Qualitätswein (quality wine)   Quality wine of more body, made from approved grape varieties; must come exclusively from one of the eleven regions. Government panels taste and analyse all such wines before giving them control numbers, ensuring that they conform to requirements.
Qualitätswein mit Prädikat (specially graded quality wine)   The highest category of German wine, made from approved grape varieties are graded as follows:

> *Kabinett*   Lightest of these wines, usually dry, elegant and delicate.
> *Spätlese*   Late gathering. Wines have more body, a degree of pleasant sweetness.
> *Auslese*   Wines made from selected bunches of grapes.
> *Beerenauslese*   Wines from selected single berries from the ripest bunches, luscious, sweet.

> *Trockenbeerenauslese*   From individual grapes allowed to remain on the vine until dried, almost to raisins.
> *Eiswein*   Rare wines made from grapes harvested and crushed while still frozen.
> *Sekt*   Sparkling wine, reflecting characteristics of the Rhine and Mosel.

Interpreting labels

Although attractive, German wine labels are difficult for the uninitiated to understand. The sample label below provides information typical of (though of course not the same as) other bottles. It indicates:

Region from which the wine comes (see the eleven listed).
Vintage or year when the wine was made.
Village from which the wine comes. It becomes the name of the wine by adding an 'er' at the end (just as a man from London is a Londoner).
Vineyard where grapes were grown from which the wine was made.
Variety of grape used to make the wine; here a Reisling, Germany's premier grape. Other white varieties include Silvaner, Muller-Thurgau and Ruländer.
Special features of the grape, that is, Spätlese – late gathered after frost, or Trockenbeeren – grapes which have dried naturally on the vine.
Special features of grape choice, that is, Auslese – specially selected.
Name of producer or shipper.
Official quality testing number given by the government to wines passing rigid examination. This is found only on Qualitätswein and **Qualitätswein mit Prädikat**. (See above for explanation of these two grades of wine.)
Category of wine in bottle. (In the sample label a Qualitätswein.)

Liebfraumilch

The term Liebfraumilch really means nothing for any sound Rhine wine can be so named. Much Liebfraumilch comes from Rheinhesse but it does not have to. German wine law simply says that it must be 'a good quality Rhenish wine

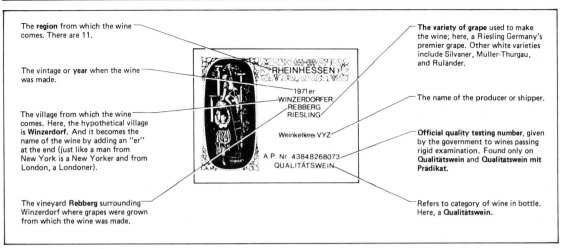

The region from which the wine comes. There are 11.

The vintage or **year** when the wine was made.

The village from which the wine comes. Here, the hypothetical village is **Winzerdorf**. And it becomes the name of the wine by adding an "er" at the end (just like a man from New York is a New Yorker and from London, a Londoner).

The vineyard **Rebberg** surrounding Winzerdorf where grapes were grown from which the wine was made.

The variety of grape used to make the wine; here, a Riesling Germany's premier grape. Other white varieties include Silvaner, Müller-Thurgau, and Ruländer.

The name of the producer or shipper.

Official quality testing number, given by the government to wines passing rigid examination. Found only on **Qualitätswein** and **Qualitätswein mit Prädikat.**

Refers to category of wine in bottle. Here, a **Qualitätswein.**

RHEINHESSEN
1971er
WINZERDORFER REBBERG RIESLING
Weinkellerei VYZ
A.P. Nr. 43848268073
QUALITÄTSWEIN

A basic German wine label
This hypothetical sample illustrates how to read the label's information

of a mild and pleasant character quality'. Although even this need not apply in Britain, leading brands clearly seek to establish that German standard. The term Liebfraumilch and brand names have been useful in promoting sales of German wine because relatively few wine drinkers outside Germany bother to master the somewhat complex label designations. A wine waiter's customers, if not the wine waiter himself, often feel comfortable with a widely promoted 'brand' of German wine and even feel 'safe' with the meaningless term 'Liebfraumilch'.

Brand names

A well known trademark on a bottle reassures customers that the wine will be consistent in 'style'. German, French and wines from other countries are often marketed in this way. In France, 'brand names' may be blended from those of various regions which a merchant selects in proportions of his choice and sold under his trademark. This is usually boldly printed on a label accompanied by the words 'marque deposée' (or registered trademark). But a French wine sold under a trademark may also be an appellation controlled one. For example a French grower entitled to use the simple appellation Burgundy can produce an AOC Burgundy from his own estate. Simple Burgundy may also be produced from declassified communal appellations or growths. Thus a Burgundy may bear a generic or regional appellation such as 'Appellation Bourgogne Contrôlée'; or it may also be sold under a trademark as 'Geisweiller Grand Vin' (registered trademark).

Because a merchant's premises are at Beaune a particular wine of his need not be a Beaune or even a Burgundy. A bottle may contain no Burgundy if it does not bear the words 'appellation contrôlée'.

Wines from other countries

As already indicated, there are many other wine countries. Some of these, though not considered in detail here, are important. Italy, for example, for a wide variety of table wines: Chianti, Valpolicella, Barbera and many other reds; sparkling white Asti Spumante, still whites such as Lachrima Christi, Soave and many others.

Spain (apart from sherry) has excellent red table wine especially Rioja. Portugal (apart from

Port) similarly has good table wines, for example, its Dao, and its extremely popular pétillants rosés and white vinho verde.

American, South African, Australian and other European wines increasingly appear on lists world wide as demand for wines increases. Former 'snobbery' about wine has given way to assessment on merit. All those wine countries have good products with which wine waiting staff should become familiar.

Age and appearance

The year of a vintage wine usually appears on a label on the neck. The cork also indicates locality and vintage.

White wine

White wines rarely benefit from age. Some of the best may improve with maturation in bottle but most are best drunk young.

Thus most German wines are drunk young for they can be enjoyed within a few years of bottling. However, top quality German wines (such as Spätlese or Auslese) retain their life for decades, maturing to the peak in bottle.

It is hard to tell a white wine's age by appearance. But one rule of thumb (which can be applied only if white wine is in a clear, plain glass bottle) is that dry wine is generally lighter in colour and sweet white is more golden. Thus, many white wines are golden yellow but some,

like Chablis and Moselle type, may be paler and even have a greenish tinge. Any brownish hue suggests poor keeping and early drinking.

Red wine

The age of red wine is usually easier to gauge. When held against the light, a red wine of about three years old will probably have a slightly bluish tint, even (at the edge of the glass) appearing almost purple. With age, the bluish tint gives way to a true red or deep ruby. Later still a brown tinge develops and becomes more accentuated with age.

Most wines lose hardness and roughness through ageing in bottle. They mellow and develop aroma and flavour. They hold this for a variable time until they begin to fade.

Wine product knowledge

The foregoing, chiefly concerned with wine identification, represents a beginning rather than an end of wine product knowledge. The wine waiter (or other waiters) is likely to become interested in wine knowledge for its own sake because it is, indeed, fascinating. Nevertheless, he should avoid the temptation to regard wine as a subject of either great mystery or mystique. He should rather harness knowledge of the product to his task of improving wine service and increasing wine sale in the restaurant.

20 Equipment and handling

Its complex nature demands that wine, especially fine wine, is properly selected, stored and served. Wine also requires appropriate equipment for these different aspects from purchasing to service.

Storing wine

A wine waiter should know the conditions that are desirable in a cellar and how the various wines should be stored.

Cellar temperature

Too cold a cellar inhibits the maturing of wine, too hot a cellar hastens ageing.

A wine cellar must be cool. Desirably between 10°C (50°F) and 13°C (55°F). Changes of temperature can spoil a wine's condition so keeping it constant is essential.

In cellars where both red and white wines have to be stored, red wines should be in the upper bins where it is warmer; and white wines in the lower or cooler temperature. Hoteliers and restaurateurs should be careful not to site a wine cellar near central heating boilers. If such proximity is unavoidable they should insulate against undue warmth and protect against vibration.

Storage conditions

Light adversely affects wine's colour and keeping quality, hence wine cellars are normally underground where it is dark.

A wine cellar must be clean and free from strong smells such as those from paint, paraffin (or other fuel oils), vegetables and vinegar. Dampness is not necessarily harmful for wine but over humidity can cause the labels to peel-

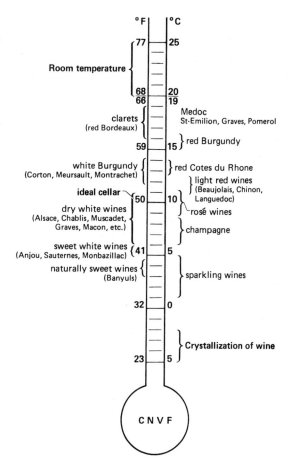

Figure 66   *Ideal temperatures of French wines*

off. Thus, a cellar should not be over dry (too dry a cellar may make corks porous and induce 'corkiness'). Satisfactory humidity is about 75 per cent.

As already mentioned, vibration, shaking or disturbing wine is harmful. Hence avoid proximity to traffic (busy roads or the hotel garage) and lifts. Bottles are stored horizontally in racks so that they cannot roll. This also keeps the corks moist and the bottles tight. (Spirits and liqueurs, on the other hand, are stored upright as spirit does not keep cork in good condition.)

Bin cards

Bottled wine, once binned, should not be disturbed until required for service; therefore each type of vintage must be stored separately, with each section of binning space correctly numbered to facilitate easy location of the wine. These numbers should correspond with those on the wine list.

Thus with each type of wine separately binned in its own section, a bin card should be affixed showing:

	Examples
Wine list number	23
Type of wine	Claret
Château (or other area designation)	Château Mouton Rothschild
Vintage year	1978
Stock position (that is, number of bottles remaining in bin)	44
Date of delivery	3–5–81
Date of stock check	10–8–82

Cellar book

A cellar master or sommelier may also find a cellar book a useful way to check wine stocks and movements, ensuring that he can quickly note fast moving (popular) items and slow less popular wines and prompts him to re-order. Such a book records:

● Name and type of wine
● Vintage year
● Shipper's/supplier's name
● Date and quantity of last order
● Date of delivery
● Date of last stock check
● A pencilled note of current stock position, that is, number of bottles left

Dispense cellar

Because restaurants have to serve wines at different temperatures at short notice as customers order them, immediate issue from the main cellar at the right temperature is obviously impracticable. Hence the need for dispense stocks or a 'daily cellar'. In such a room (normally at restaurant level) red wines may be kept at a constant room temperature and white and rosé wines in a cooling bin. 'Constant room temperature' and chill temperatures are, in many operations, achieved by thermostatically controlled racks.

Each wine should be laid in the racks with labels uppermost and an external bin card showing the wine list number.

All wines on a wine list must be available from dispense. Stocks of different types should accord with speed of sales as checked from the cellar book and the quantities served daily. A usual minimum of each wine is three bottles (for expensive ones) to a maximum of twelve bottles.

Dispense stocks should be made up daily to allow red wine time to reach correct temperature slowly and to afford an opportunity for the number of bottles sold that day to be checked.

Wine service equipment

Wine service staff may usefully later devote further study to all that is required to store and care for wine and to learn something more of equipment used prior to service for these purposes. The following notes, however, concentrate upon equipment used in the restaurant itself and by waiting staff during the ménage and service periods.

The following indicates numbers of items for restaurant service but is indicative rather than exhaustive. It does not, for example, include full cocktail bar requirements.

Approximate wine equipment quantities for a 100 seater restaurant

Wine service
25 champagne buckets
15 hock buckets
10 ice buckets
10 ice spoons or tongs
25 ice bucket stands
25 wine cradles or baskets
25 wine cradles or baskets (half-bottle size)
25 wine list covers

Glasses
100 Burgundy glasses
100 champagne flutes
 75 hock/Moselle glasses

 75 port glasses
100 red wine glasses
 75 sherry glasses
150 water glasses
100 white wine glasses

Other glasses and containers
75 beer tankards, 3 dl (½ pt)*
    (possibly beer tankards, 5 dl (1pt) may also be required)
50 carafes, (½ l)
50 carafes, (¼ l)
75 cocktail glasses
    (other highball, 'Old-Fashioned' glasses may also be required)
60 juice glasses, 1.25 dl (5 oz)
75 lager glasses, 3 dl (½ pt)
    (possibly lager glasses, 5 dl (1 pt) may also be required)
50 water jugs**

Glassware

Wine service equipment is made in a variety of materials. For example, metals (silver, EPNS and stainless steel) for buckets and stands, and basketware for wine cradles. Perhaps the most important material related to wine service is, however, glass; for though wine may initially be stored in casks, most of the wine that restaurateurs handle is in glass bottles and is subsequently poured into decanters and glasses.

Choice and purchase

A prominent glassware manufacturer, Squadron Leader James Rush, AFC, in noting the complexity of correctly using glass shapes and sizes for different types of drinks advises sommeliers and bar staff to study catalogues of specialized glassware companies (his own company James Rush & Co (Glassware) Ltd., has full descriptions and explanations of glass usage). He advises hotel and catering buyers to seek out a specialized glassware distributor (and to be wary of local cut-price merchants who merely cut prices with a limited range and give no service).

Glassware is usually bought in carton lots but most of the principal manufacturers have convenient carton packs containing an average of two to four dozen per carton. Do not try to buy glass in less than carton lots as inevitably you will have breakages and replacements will ultimately cost more.

Types

The importance of glass in relation to wine has been noted. Wine is appreciated by colour, aroma and taste. Shape and type of glass used helps considerably to enhance these characteristics.

A glass should be sufficiently thin for the lips to help the palate to enjoy the wine's flavour. Thick glassware reduces pleasure in wine drinking. In the past, restaurateurs chose machine-made glass over hand-made glass for economic

---

*Silver or pewter tankards may be provided for draught and bottled beer (other than lager beer) in some operations.
** Jugs may also be used for beer service in some establishments.

reasons but most customers dislike thick rims. Modern methods of cutting tops of glasses enable thin-rimmed glasses to be machine-made. These are costlier than thick-rimmed glass but still cheaper than hand-made. Thus in sophisticated restaurants elegant and distinctive demi-crystal ranges of glasses may now be considered rather than automatically manufactured ones. Here again a specialized company can help.

Colour

A wine glass should be of good clear glass. Only white German wines (or those of similar characteristics) should be served in coloured or smoked glass. In such cases it is preferable that only the stem and foot of the glass are coloured (brown for Rhine wines (hocks), green for Moselle).

The colouring of hock and Moselle glasses is reputed to have originated in former times when wine contained impurities or 'fliers'. Colour at the base of the glass was designed to obscure such flaws.

Size

Experience has determined the choice of different shapes and sizes of glasses for different purposes. Glasses should be sufficiently large to allow wine to be swirled in the glass to release the bouquet. Many establishments adopt a standard size of glass 1½ dl to 2¼ dl (6 oz to 8 oz) for all table wines.

Shape

A glass should be curved at the top so that the 'nose' (aroma) is trapped and the nose can appreciate the bouquet. Thus the tulip shape is most favoured; a 'standard' table wine glass usually has a capacity of six to eight glasses per bottle of wine (but see page 257). Larger bowls are preferred where swirling is particularly desirable to release aroma (for example Burgundy glasses), long stems are appropriate when wine is served chilled and so that guests' warm hands do not warm up the bowl (for example hock and Moselle glasses). Such factors have determined that red wine glasses have always larger bowls than white wine glasses. 'Big' red wines such as Burgundies often have 'bigger' than average bowls. Burgundy balloons of 3 dl (10 oz) capacity and over are often used.

Champagne glasses of the 'coupe' or saucer shape are sometimes used because guests like their festive associations. But for champagne, the bowl should not be large and open because of the danger of bubbles dissipating too quickly. Hence the old-fashioned champagne saucer is rejected by the knowledgeable and a flute shaped glass (or even a tulip) is the modern choice.

Good brandy is served in balloon glasses in many establishments but excessively large sizes are now regarded as pretentious and unnecessary. They have the additional drawback in restaurants of being more vulnerable to breakage.

Shapes of glass that custom and experience have determined are the most suitable for different wines are illustrated in Figure 69 on page 256.

Specifications

The Institut National des Appellations d'Origine of France have specifications for glass which aid organoleptic examination of wine samples (colour, clarity, bouquet, flavour) by all types of tests (simple tasting, profile analysis, etc.). Physical characteristics of the glass, its dimensions and other features are specified. In 1978, the British Standards Institute published specifications based on French requirements intended to help bring uniformity where variation existed.

Glasses used

The list shown in Table 32 includes the types of glasses commonly used in wine and drink service. Sizes are indicative. Variation may be encountered in cocktail and other glasses.

Glass

Glassware manufacture, James Rush, is quoted as saying in regard to glass purchase, 'Never store glasses in paper, especially printed paper. This causes paper stains which are almost impossible to remove. Glasses are best stored in their cellular cell cartons, loosely packed and stored in a dry atmosphere.'

Table 32 *Types and sizes of glasses for wines and drinks*

	Capacity		
	dl	*oz*	*Notes*
Sherry glass	¾–1	3–4	Often thistle or 'elgin'-shaped but tulip (that is, copita
Sherry schooner	1–1¼	4–5	style) is preferable. Similar to the old 'dock glass', the
Sherry copita	1–1¼	4–5	copita has a tulip bowl on a short stem and is widely used in Spain
Cocktail glasses, Manhattan	1⅛	4½	British cocktail glass sizes are often smaller than in America, but the trend is towards larger glasses
Water tumbler or goblet	2¼–3	8–10	
Water or wine goblet	2¼	8	Many establishments adopted a standard Paris goblet or tulip shaped glass (1½ to 2¼ dl (6 to 8 oz)) for all table wines but today 1½ dl (6 oz) is generally thought to be too small
Hock glass tulip shape on amber stem (for German Rhine wines)			Hock and moselle glasses are also available without colour but coloured or otherwise are also used for wines
Moselle glass tulip shape on green stem (for German moselle wines)			of similar character of other countries and regions such as Alsace, South Africa, Yugoslavia
Claret (red Bordeaux) glass	1½–2	6–7	Modern taste tends to regard the traditional 1½ dl (6 oz) as too small
Burgundy balloon	3	10	Larger sizes are to be found but are pretentious rather than practical
Champagne tulip	1½	6	Also used for other white, rosé and sparkling wines
Champagne flute			
Champagne coupe or saucers			Flat champagne 'saucers' are popular with some wedding patrons but frowned on by the knowledgeable
Port glass	1–1½	4–5	
Brandy balloon	1¼–3	5–10	Smaller ballons are more practical for functions. Even larger balloons are available but are regarded by the knowledgeable as unnecessarily pretentious and by restaurateurs as too fragile
Liqueur glass	½–1	2–3	The tiny liqueur glass is now less used than the small balloon or tulip (with a portion mark)
Beer glasses (bottled)	3¼	12	Many shapes available. Beer in 3 dl (½ pt (10 oz)) bottles is usually poured into 3½ dl (12 oz) glasses. Silver or pewter tankards may also be used for draught and bottled beer, other than lager. 5 dl (1 pt) measures may be appropriate in some operations
Lager glasses	3¼	12	Tall, tapered (but other variants now also used)
Fruit juice glass	1¼	5	
Tumblers, squash, etc.	3	10	
Iced tea glass	3¼	12	
Other containers			
Jugs, water	1½–1	2 pt	Sizes vary but 1¼ l (2 pt) is usual with retaining lip for ice. Jugs may be used for lager or beer service in some establishments
Carafes	½ l		Other metric sizes are used. Wide neck shape desirable for ease of washing

Figure 67   *A selection of bar and wine glasses*
From left to right − 10 oz beer mug, 20 oz beer mug, 6 oz tall wine glass, 2½ oz sherry(or liqueur) glass, 4½ oz schooner, 12 oz beer goblet, 8 oz goblet, 6 oz goblet, 8 oz spirit glass. Front − bar dish. Rear − 12 oz tumbler, 5 oz juice glass

Figure 68   *An Irish coffee glass*

Handling

Wine glasses are fragile and expensive yet many operations suffer up to 33 per cent breakage of glass per annum. Care in handling and selecting functional glass style is important. Of the three parts of a wine glass (bowl, stem and base), the bowl is exclusively the customers. Glasses should be handled by waiters as little as possible and never by the bowls. Usually they are handled by the stem and occasionally by the base.

In handling glasses, the rule in general is the reverse of those for plates and food. Plates are normally lifted and handled with the left hand; but glasses are charged with the right hand. This is chiefly because drinks are served from the right. Remember:

● Always lift a glass by its stem or at the base.
● Never pick up glasses with the rims between thumb and fingers.
● Remove broken glasses to the dustbin immediately.

Handling during mise en place

During the general setting of the room, the wine waiter is responsible for placing an all-purpose goblet or standard wine glass at each cover. Place the glass on the table at the right of the cover at the outside tip of the large knife; or if there is not a large knife then just where it would normally be placed. This glass normally remains on the table whether or not wine is ordered. When more than one glass is used, lay them on the cover in order of use. (See Chapter 11.)

When wine is ordered the appropriate glass is brought before wine service but the goblet remains for water. (Some customers, especially **Continentals, may order a spring or mineral** water. Americans may drink iced water.)

Prior to service, goblets are carried upside down between the fingers of the left hand or upside down on a tray but always by the latter method when guests are 'in the room'. In any case, always carry tumblers on salvers. Four glasses are a safe limit for the inexperienced to carry between the fingers. Loading and unloading glasses on to the hand carefully is essential to avoid breakages. Train yourself to carry glasses between the fingers in this way as it is quicker and safer when transferring them from pantry shelf to tables.

When carrying glasses any distance on a tray (say in outside catering), a slightly damp cloth on the tray helps stop sliding.

Handling during service

Procedures for handling glasses and bottles during service are dealt with in Chapter 21.

Washing glasses

Wash glasses in hot water, rinsing in hot, and then polish with a glass cloth. A glass should not merely be clean, but beautifully clean.

Modern glass-washing machines are usually efficient but care should be taken to ensure that glasses do not come into contact with each other when wet. This is when most chips and breakages occur. **Do not attempt to wash glasses loosely in water where glass rims and feet come into contact. Breakage from this source is phenomenal.**

A recognized sterilizing washing medium is helpful such as the Jeyes 'Superblend Glass Wash'. This will not only sterilize but also brings glasses up gleaming.

'Milton Sterilising Liquid' is also good, especially for decanters and carafes.

Washing decanters

Never use soap or soda when cleaning a decanter. Persistent stains may respond to lead shot, vinegar, egg shells, raw potatoes diced or other old fashioned aids.

A correspondent to *Decanter* (October, 1980) who, like many of us, find such remedies seldom effective recommended SDP, 'A product sold to home brewers for cleaning beer bottles available from Boots for a few pence a packet'. He found this dealt efficiently with a deeply stained Georgian decanter.

When using cleaning fluids, rinse thoroughly and allow the decanter to dry before using again. Keep stoppers off decanters after they have been washed in order to allow the inside to dry thoroughly.

Glass-washing machine

There are many mechanical aids to glass washing from simple one-at-a-time rotary washers in bars to machines which claim to cope with up to 1500 per hour.

Wine bottles

Apart from its label, the shape and colour of a wine bottle gives clues about its content. Chapter 19 touched upon wine identification but the following summarizes important aspects concerning wine bottle appearance.

Bottle recognition

The shapes of bottles delineated in Figure 69 are associated with the principal wines originally bottled in them. For example, both red Bordeaux (claret) and white Bordeaux wines are French wines in bottles that have a shoulder (as distinct, for example, from the sloping shouldered bottle of both red and white Burgundies). Other

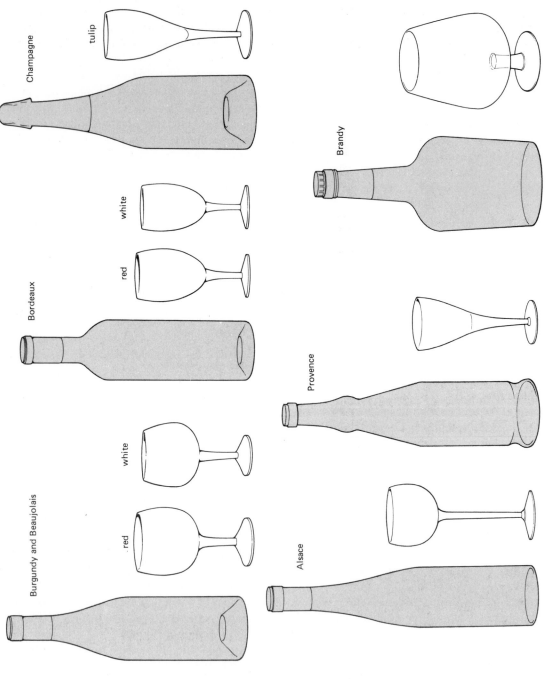

Champagne — tulip

Bordeaux — white, red

Burgundy and Beaujolais — white, red

Brandy

Provence

Alsace

Figure 69   *Types of bottles and glasses*

countries with wine made from similar grapes (or otherwise believed to have similar characteristics) tend to bottle in shapes 'classically' associated with them. Thus, Spanish wine believed to have Burgundy character or claret character will appear in bottles of those shapes. Wines of hock or Moselle type from many parts of the world similarly appear in bottles shaped like the tall, thin bottles associated with German wines.

Yield and servings

1 bottle (⅙ gal) or 7½ dl yields six servings when two thirds filling 2 dl (7 fl oz) Paris goblets or tulip glasses, but with 1½ dl (6 oz) glasses restaurateurs may allow for eight servings. At table, a half bottle per guest is a fair guide to consumption and if two wines, a white and red, are served allow a quarter of a bottle per person. Generally caterers average out aperitifs, sparkling or table wines at two servings per guest.

Consumption of wine and other drinks at parties and functions cannot, however, be fixed precisely. Quantities are affected by factors such as how many different wines are served at a dinner and the time allowed for reception drinks. At functions, waiters should not refill glasses,

Table 33 *Approximate bottle yields*

	Number of bottles	Number of servings	At functions or parties allow per person
Aperitifs			
Sherry, vermouth, Dubonnet, etc.	1	16	2 glasses
Champagne or white wine as aperitif	1	7	¼ – ⅜ bottle for formal parties
Vermouth, as mixer	1	32 in cocktails	2 glasses
Cocktails, mixed	1 eq	20	2 glasses
Main wine at dinner	1	6	¼ – ⅜ bottle at formal party*
First wine at dinner (dry white or light red)	1	6	½ bottle at formal party
Table wine, at meals	1	6 when two-thirds filling 2 dl (7 oz) glass	½ bottle – 3 glasses at main meal (especially dinner)
Hock or Moselle	1	6	
Hock or Moselle at stand-up wine parties	1	6–8	5–6 glasses 2–3 filling
Table wine included in set menu price	1	6	⅓ bottle per cover
Champagne	1	7	
Dessert wines (sauternes, trocklenbeerebauslese, etc.)	1	6	¼ bottle
or champagne	1	7	¼ bottle
Port	1	12–15	1½–2 glasses
Liqueurs	1	30–32	
Spirits	1	24 bar measures	
Spirits	1	30	
Cider	flagon	6–8	
Beers	pint	2	

*Allow more if decanted.

Table 34   *American bottle yields*

Size	Ounces	Dinner wine champagne	Aperitif or dessert wine
Fifth (4/5 qt)	25.6	8 servings	8–12 servings
Tenth (4/5 pt)	12.8	4 servings	4– 6 servings
Split	6.4	2 servings	
Quart	32.0	10 servings	10–14 servings
Pint	16.0	5 servings	5– 7 servings
Half gallon	64.0	20 servings	20–30 servings
Gallon	128.0	40 servings	40–60 servings

other than by a token pouring, of guests who appear barely to sip their wine. Nor should waiters be too assiduous in replenishing glasses of those guests who empty them too quickly.

Table 33 does not, therefore, lay down a precise basis but indicates reasonable bases for allowance.

Servings in America

According to the Californian Wine Advisory Board, average serving of dinner wine or champagne in America is 3 to 3½ fluid ounces; of cocktail or dessert wine, 2 to 2½ ounces. Various sizes of bottles yield servings approximately as shown in Table 34.

Practical attitude

The foregoing notes are intended to aid understanding of basic procedures in storing and handling wine and the nature of some materials associated with such handling, especially bottles and glasses. Naturally, those who serve should also seek to appreciate wines' qualities but as already indicated many books are devoted to the nuances of flavour and wine appreciation. Those who serve and sell wine should be competent in visually recognizing the commodity they are selling and capable of coping with it and its accompanying equipment at a strictly practical level.

21 Serving and selling

The word selling is included in this chapter's title to emphasize that service procedures for alcoholic beverages are intended to enhance wine so as to assist its sale. The chapter does not deal with wine selling from a managerial standpoint but rather indicates how restaurant serving staff can assist management in selling an important and profitable commodity.

In Chapter 20 it was noted how wine is stored and handled prior to service. Many of the factors (such as avoiding shaking and ensuring correct temperature) continue to affect waiting practice.

First, as in all forms of serving, it is important to be 'en place' or ready for service.

Glass

Table glassware (given general consideration in Chapter 20) is of prime concern. During mis-en-place, glasses are usually placed on tables upside down to avoid collecting dust in the bowls. Before a restaurant opens for service, lift them by the stem, polish and reverse them so that they are set the right way up.

When laying banquet covers, place three or more glasses, for example sherry, claret and/or hock and champagne in order of use, with the smallest glass to the right. Above them on the table place a port glass and a liqueur glass, as may be required. (See Chapter 11.)

Handling during service
Glass handling prior to the restaurant's opening was covered in Chapter 20. During meal service, however, never carry glasses in the hand. Always carry glasses the right way up on salvers (round trays 300 mm (12 in) in diameter, having a concave edge) whether they are being taken to or removed from a table.

At all times handle glasses by the stem (between thumb and fingers), or for the tumbler type, low down near the base. Never pick up glasses or clear them by putting your fingers inside. Only

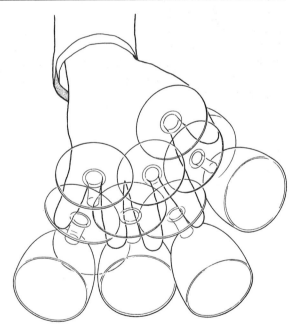

Figure 70 *The correct way to carry glasses*
Glasses should be carried by their stems between the fingers of the left hand. The right hand is then free to set them on the table. Seven glasses is the limit for safety – carry fewer until you have confidence and competence, and use a tray when guests are present

bring clean glasses into the room during service when they are required so that they can go straight on to the table. Remove dirty glasses on a salver or tray and, as they come off the tables, take them to the glass pantry. Always carry them on their own and never place them out of sight under a sideboard. Broken glass in a room can be dangerous hence be cautious in handling glassware.

Replacing glasses

If it is necessary to change a glass bring a fresh glass on a salver to the table. Exchange glasses by picking up the table glass on to the tray and placing the fresh glass in its place.

Always remove glasses from the table when empty; and always serve fresh wines (even if a second bottle of the same wine is ordered) and other drinks in fresh glasses.

In 'traditional' operations all glasses were removed from the table just before dessert course service and replenished by fresh ones. Even though a glass of proper shape and size was already on the table and had not been used, it was removed and another identical one brought in its place. Such labour and time-consuming rituals are seldom observed today.

Wine order

Wine sales are a source of considerable profit in licensed restaurants. In the class of restaurant where a meal is not complete without wine they are especially important. Most wine sales are initiated by the medium of a wine list. This should be presented at the proper time, that is, after the food order has been given, whether in the cocktail bar or at table.

		Table Number
		15
1 x 57		£7.40
Date 9–4–82		Sig. WO

Writing the check

A sommelier presents a wine list from the customer's left-hand side. Do not recommend a wine unless you know its qualities. When the guest has ordered, write out a cellar check. This is usually made out with two carbon copies; the original goes to the cellar or dispense to obtain the bottle, the duplicate to the cashier and the third copy is handed to the station waiter for reference and comparison with the bill when it is presented for payment.

As noted, wines are ordered by numbers in most establishments. In the wine list, to the right of the description of the wine, are two columns showing the price of whole or half bottles. Thus the check illustrated below, for an order taken by waiter WO, would read 1 x 57 or ½ x 57 according to the customer's requirements, the price being altered accordingly.

Presenting the bottle

When the bottle has been obtained, present it on a folded service cloth, as background, to the customer's right-hand side so that he can easily read the label. Mention the name of the wine and vintage, if any, for example 'Your Château Latour 1978, sir'. Take care not to shake the wine (for this may disturb any sediment), and not to shake any dust from the bottle on the table. Note you must *never* present an opened (uncorked) bottle. A bottle of wine must be approved by the customer *before* opening as mistakes can be costly to the restaurant, or even the waiter.

Drawing the cork

When the customer has approved the wine, leave the table, remove any wax or cut the tinfoil round the bottle's lip with the knife (sometimes attached to the corkscrew as in the 'waiter's friend' model), carefully wipe the lip of the bottle (or some sediment may drop in the glass later), and draw the cork.

Many wine waiters use either the lever or the French boxwood corkscrew. Correct use allows a cork to be drawn quietly and smoothly with no fear of breaking the neck of the bottle. Turn the screw clockwise, not right through the cork or pieces may fall into the wine. Now pull the cork to within 6 to 12 mm (¼ to ½ in) of the end and then withdraw it with a slight twist of thumb and fingers. This helps prevent any last minute jerk of the bottle and allows air to take the place of the cork more steadily. (In no circumstances should you hold a bottle between your legs when drawing the cork.)

Holding the bottle steady in your left hand, cover your right-hand forefinger with the corner of a clean waiter's cloth, insert it in the opening of the bottle neck and gently wipe inside. This is in case there is any vestige of cork there (see Figure 71(a) to (d). The wine may now be served.

The cork, removed from the corkscrew, should be presented to the host on a coffee saucer or small plate.

Corky wines (Goût du bouchon)

After uncorking and before serving a wine, smell the cork carefully. If you detect any unpleasant odour, indicating that a cork has gone musty and the mustiness has been absorbed by the wine, either replace the bottle by another at once or report the fact to the head waiter or manager. (Incidentally, most good wine shippers or merchants will replace such corky bottles.)

Opening chilled wine

When white or rosé wine is served from an ice pail, the opening of the bottle may be done in the cooler. Before service dry the bottle but never wrap it in a napkin for the label should always be uppermost and visible.

Serving the wine

First, pour a little wine into the host's glass. He will sample the wine to satisfy himself that it is in

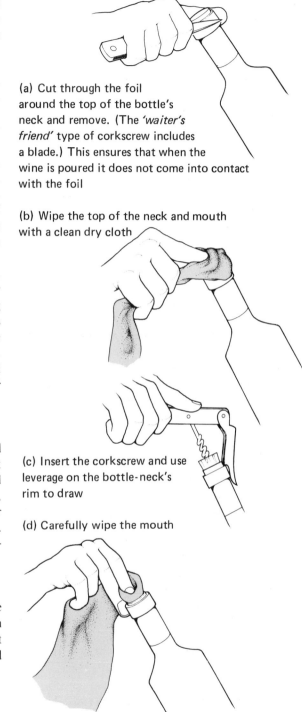

(a) Cut through the foil around the top of the bottle's neck and remove. (The *'waiter's friend'* type of corkscrew includes a blade.) This ensures that when the wine is poured it does not come into contact with the foil

(b) Wipe the top of the neck and mouth with a clean dry cloth

(c) Insert the corkscrew and use leverage on the bottle-neck's rim to draw

(d) Carefully wipe the mouth

Figure 71 *Uncorking a wine bottle*

good condition, at the right temperature, clear, without sediment and otherwise suitable to serve. The host may swirl the wine in the glass to release its ether, hold it up against the light to check clarity and sniff it for aroma.

Sequence of service

When the wine has been approved, continue to serve to the guests, beginning at the host's right with the ladies, then from the right again with the gentlemen until the host is reached and service thereby completed.

Technique of pouring

To fill a glass, stand on the right and bend sufficiently forward. Body balance is often aided by placing the left hand on your back.

Pour carefully and steadily. Hold the bottle label uppermost so that it can be read. Grasp the bottle, with the hand over it, thumb round one side, fingers round the other with the index finger lying up the shoulder (not on the neck). With the bottle's lip just over the edge of the glass, tilt downwards with a movement of the wrist until wine begins to flow. This keeps pouring under control.

Pouring can be stopped by moving the hand upwards again by pivoting from the wrist. A twist of the bottle to the right as each glass is poured helps avoid drips. At the end of each pouring remove possible drips by touching the lip of the bottle with a clean waiter's cloth folded into a pad.

Never pick up a glass from the table to charge it (except when possibly pouring bottled beer into a tumbler or tankard to avoid frothing over on to the cloth).

Serving white and rosé wines

Long experience has shown that wines always taste better when served at the correct temperature.

Temperature

Dry white wines and rosé wines are served chilled, not iced, generally between 6°–12°C (43°–54°F).

Filling glasses

Never pour more than to fill the glass two-thirds full only. Do not over-fill glasses (certainly never to the brim). Fill red wine glasses half full (some advocate that large Burgundy glasses (balloons) be only one-third filled. Fill white wine glasses half to two-thirds full. Stop pouring sooner if asked. Apologize if you inadvertently overfill a glass.

When all guests are served return to the host and fill his glass. This completion of pouring sequence is often forgotten by inexperienced waiters.

Placing bottles after serving

When all guests are served, return:

- White or rosé wine to its ice pail and place the folded napkin over the bottle's neck (when a white wine bottle is empty it is usual to turn it upside down in the ice pail before removal to indicate its emptiness to the host).
- Red wine or carafe wine to the side table unless requested (or house custom) to leave it on the customer's table.

When placing a bottle on the table it should be put just above and to the left of the host's wine glass, with the label facing him.

Replenishing glasses

Refill guests' glasses when the majority of them are low. Keep constant contact so as to refill glasses as necessary.

When a bottle is empty, politely inform the host that the wine is finished. The host can then order more wine if he thinks fit.

Dry fortified wines such as dry sherry, dry port, dry Madeira (Sercial) and similar aperitif wines are also served chilled. Chilling is best done slowly for all wines should change temperature gradually. Therefore, never put white wines in deep freeze (nor red wines in hot cupboards or boiling water). Semi-sweet white wines, champagne and sparkling wines are also served chilled (6°–8°C (43°–46°F)).

The French terms widely used for cooled wines are:

Rafraîchi Cooled (for still white or rosé wine).
Frappé Iced, but not frozen (for sparkling wines, or even sweet still wines).

Modern equipment allows dispense cellars to have wines including wines to be served chilled, at correct temperatures for service, but where this is not so or a customer wants his wine colder, despite the fact that over-chilling inhibits or kills bouquet, an ice bucket or wine cooler may be used.

Wine cooler

Wine coolers (pails or buckets) are, however, intended mainly for keeping cool the remainder of the wine after the first service.

Place the bottle in a wine cooler with water and ice just to the shoulder of the bottle. A deep receptacle is essential for properly cooling a bottle of white or sparkling wine.

Water mixed with ice lowers temperature quicker than ice used alone. If ice alone is used, it takes about 70 minutes for temperature to drop 10°C (50°F) as against about 23 minutes with ice and water. Cooling time may be further speeded by adding sea salt to the mix. Length of time 'on ice' in a cooler depends, as already indicated, on whether the wine is already at (or near) the right cooled temperature. A rough guide for minimum length of chilling time in an ice bucket is 15 minutes for white wine, 30 minutes for sparkling white wines. But for a bottle of champagne to be served very cool but not iced if not already chilled it is a good idea to put it into an ice bucket of ice and water two hours before serving.

Place the wine cooler in a stand at the side of the table, or on a large plate (covered by a folded napkin), which you may place on the table on the host's right-hand side.

After presentation, the cork can be removed with the aid of a lever screw without taking the wine from the cooler.

Checking service temperature

When offering the host a sample to taste, ask if the temperature of the wine is satisfactory. If the answer is that it is not cool enough, ask the host if he would like a little to be poured out at the moment or if he would prefer all the wine to be returned to the cooler for another few minutes.

Similarly, when the wine has been served, ask the host if he would like the wine which has been left in the bottle replaced in the cooler or left out as it may now be chilled sufficiently. Take care that wine is not over-iced for the aroma of the wine can then be masked or deteriorate. Never cool wine by adding ice to the glass.

With white wines, no more than two-thirds of a glass should be poured.

Place a napkin at the wine cooler for the purpose of wiping the bottle each time it is taken out. This napkin must not, however, be used for wiping the neck of the bottle when serving the wine.

Champagne and other sparkling wines

Sparkling wines are also served chilled. Many customers prefer them colder than the still white wines. After presentation (not forgetting to mention vintage, if any) the cork may be drawn.

Uncorking champagne

Remove the wire at the point indicated on the gold foil (generally a piece of twisted wire). Remove the cork with the right hand, by a slight twisting movement, holding the bottle in the left hand. Place a cloth over the hand gripping the bottle while the cork is extracted. Champagne bottles should be handled gently. Agitation of the bottle before opening causes increased effervescence, that is, 'fizz', which impedes good service. Do not allow a bottle to point in the guests' direction when drawing the cork.

Ensure you have quick access to the host's glass or wine will surge out of the bottle and 'fizz' over. By near access to the glass the bottle neck can be quickly inclined over the glass, and wine and fizz go into it instead of being spilt. However, the late Fernand Point (famed chef patron of La Pyramide, **Vienne**, and a great lover of champagne) used to show young waiters 'how to press a silver spoon against the open neck of the bottle to stop it bubbling over and to wait a few seconds before filling the glasses.'

Smell the cork for 'cork' before other guests are served. If a bottle is 'corky' remove the host's glass and the bottle and substitute another.

Serving red wines

Temperature for serving varies according to the type of red wine.

Temperature for light reds
In France, light and fruity red wines are served at wine cellar temperature: 10°–12°C (50°–54°F). This French practice of serving Beaujolais and similar light red wines cool is now almost universally followed in Britain and America. This is especially so in the case of Beaujolais nouveau and primeur.

There are, however, still those in Britain (to which some of the heavier, more fruity Beaujolais are shipped) who may prefer this wine to be served chambre (see below).

Sparkling reds
Sparkling red Burgundy (and similar sparkling reds) are also served chilled.

Red wine generally
In general, red wines are served chambre or at room temperature. As rooms vary this is usually about 18°C (65°F). In France red wines are served rather cooler than is customary in Britain. Many establishments have sufficient red wine stored in a warm dispense near the room or in display racks in the room itself.

Breathing
In any case, a red wine is improved by 'breathing' through uncorking prior to service (about an hour in advance if possible).

Rich, full-bodied red
In France, it is usually recommended that these wines are served as follows:

Bordeaux (Claret)	16°–18°C (61°–65°F)
Bourgogne (Burgundy)	15°–16°C (59°–61°F)
Côtes du Rhone	14°–15°C (57°–59°F)

These temperatures usefully apply to wines of similar character from other countries.

Warming red wine
Should a customer complain that a wine is not sufficiently chambré or 'roomed' and he requires it less cool, on no account immerse the bottle in hot water, **stand** it in front of a fire, or place it on a hot-plate. Such drastic action kills quality and bouquet, and can cloud the wine.

As the only safe method is to raise the temperature gradually, inform the head waiter. If a customer insists that something be done, the least drastic method is to warm a decanter and carefully pour in the wine so that it gathers warmth as it fills.

In residential hotels, a wine waiter will get to know his guests and take wine orders during a previous meal so that red wines can be placed in the room well in advance.

Another point in favour of this is that the cork can be drawn to allow the wine to breathe. This assists an old red wine, for it has been imprisoned for a long time.

Sediment
Old red wines 'throw' a sediment and therefore must be handled carefully, possibly decanted or cradled otherwise this sediment will be disturbed, cloud the wine, make it thick and impair its taste. Younger red wines have not had time to deposit sediment, but although they do not need decanting they should be handled with grace, rather than unnecessary elaboration, as should all wines.

Decanting

Decanting wine off the sediment is the best solution. Ideally this is done in the cellar to allow the least possible disturbance. Ordinary red wines of no great bottle age do not need ceremonious treatment but some restaurants will still use rituals (see Cradling below) even in merchandising common wine which does not justify it.

For finer and old red wines, a wine waiter should on receiving the order, recommend decanting. Some wine lists state that all red wines over a certain age will be decanted unless the customer wishes otherwise. Be sure politely to point this out to save repercussions if a customer is offended through having his wine opened before presentation.

At one time, decanting table wine was unfashionable. Today it is still controversial. Many connoisseurs contend, however, that decanting, apart from separating wine from its sediment, allows for maximum breathing or oxidation and this ensures development of its bouquet.

How to decant

Have a decanter at room temperature. Uncork the bottle on a firm surface without shaking it or disturbing the wine. Wipe the opening of the bottle carefully. Raise the bottle, rest its lip on the rim of the decanter or carafe, gently lift the bottle so that wine pours slowly inside. Watch the flow carefully and as soon as any suspicion of cloudiness approaches the clearness of the wine in the neck, stop pouring.

Wine is decanted over a light (candlelight traditionally) so that appearance of sediment in the neck may be readily seen. White wines are seldom, if ever, decanted except when inexpensive house wines may be served en carafe and that is for convenience (for example serving less than full bottles) rather than for wine care. (It was once fashionable for champagne to be served from jugs but this is no longer so.)

Before serving decanted wine, present the original bottle and cork to the customer to assure him that the wine he has chosen is, in fact, being served. When serving decanted wine

Figure 72 *Decanting*
Decant over (or against) a light so that sediment can be seen as it approaches the neck of the bottle. Any light will do but candles are traditionally used

it is customary to tell each guest what wine (château or domaine and vintage) he is receiving.

Heavy decanters are generally used for old port wine, whereas other wines are decanted into more delicate carafes so that their colour may be fully appreciated.

Cradles or baskets

An alternative is to serve red wine in the cradle or basket in which it has been brought from the cellar so that the wine never loses the almost horizontal position in which it is cellar-stored. It is unnecessary to cradle young wine. But 'grand' old wine needs handling with care without disturbing the sediment. Should a customer insist on a wine being served from the bottle, the cellar man places the bottle on a folded napkin in a wine cradle.

In the room take care not to shake the wine nor disturb the sediment. Present the wine in its basket to the host. Do not uncork until after this presentation. After approval, place the cradled bottle on a stable surface (either sideboard or guest's table) with a coffee saucer under the bottle's neck (to catch any spillage during opening).

Corks can become softened after years in the bottle, so draw them with care and without shaking the cradle. A lever corkscrew is recommended with the bottle remaining in the basket secured by holding with the right hand across the top. Once uncorked, serve carefully and speedily with the usual sampling for the host.

Take care not to pour too fast for the consequent bubbling in of air can disturb sediment. Be vigilant that the last wine served is clear. Leave clouded or muddy wine in the bottle.

When all are served, leave the wine basket on the host's right hand side.

Vintage and crusted port

In the case of old wines with heavy sediment and especially vintage and crusted ports, it is desirable, where possible, to allow bottles to stand for a day prior to opening. Thus port wine is normally uncorked from an upright position. For stability, place a clamp on the neck of the bottle and hold this with the left hand. Holding a napkin in the same hand to protect the hand from a possible breakage of the neck during opening, lift the right end of the waiter's friend, pushing down on clamp and neck in the left hand. If a cork is undrawable, use a sharp knife around the flange and tap off the top of the bottle. Alternatively, use red hot tongs then a cold bandage and snap off the top. Be sure to filter wine after these operations.

Wine serving summarized

All procedures outlined above are aimed to add service value to wine sold in a restaurant. They are not meant to be performed as empty rituals but assist the flow of serving and add to guests enjoyment. Main service points may be summarized as:

- Have correct glasses on table.
- Have wine at correct temperature.
- Have appropriate equipment (for example cradle or decanter for red, cooler for white).

- Present wine for approval.
- Remove top foil from neck.
- Wipe top.
- Gauging depth of cork, insert screw.
- Remove cork and inspect it.
- Wipe neck inside.
- Present cork to host.
- Pour taste for host.
- Serve other guests (usually two-thirds fill glass).
- Top up host's glass.
- Leave wine for later replenishment.
- Use clean glasses when serving a second bottle of the same kind of wine.

Order of wines with courses

Serving a different wine with each course is not a custom observed nowadays except on formal occasions. Today, a sherry may be served with the soup course, after which any one of the table wines mentioned in Chapter 19 may be served with the remainder of the meal.

Some indication is given below of what wines are commonly served during a meal's progress. But remember that wine choice is highly individual. 'Rules' should, therefore, be interpreted with caution. In the Sauternes area of France, it is not unusual for viticulturists to serve their sweet wines throughout a meal. Some Frenchmen will drink red wine with fish.

However, experience suggests that light and delicate wines should precede fuller bodied ones rather than follow them. This means serving the more simple wines first and progressing towards the more distinguished. It also usually means drinking young wines before old ones.

Generally, dry wines come first and sweet wines last; if a dry wine is served after a sweet wine it will taste too dry (that is, sour), whereas a sweet wine, coming after a dry wine will taste sweeter and more agreeable. The order of serving wine is:

- Dry white wines
- Red wine
- Sweet white wine

This sequence does not include all possible permutations and use, as has already been noted, of good wine from countries other than France and Germany. These can be introduced according to their character. There are sparkling wines other than champagne (Asti Spumante from Italy, Sekt from Germany for example), well-produced table wines from Spain, Portugal and other parts of Europe.

Wine and food partners

Apéritif Dry sherry, dry Madeira (Sercial), Vermouth (dry red, bianco, rosé). Cocktails. However, guests select widely and may choose to drink wine (especially champagne), Pastis (Pernod, etc.), Pineau de Charentes (grape juice with brandy added), 'cold duck' (term derived from kalte ende and blend of red wine with sparkling white) and many others.

Hors d'oeuvre No wine if food highly vinegary (some wine waiters suggest dry sherry or an undistinguished dry white wine).

Oysters Chablis, dry champagne, dry Rhine wine or other white wines (for example Pouilly fuissé, Chablis, Graves, Muscadet).

Smoked Salmon As for oysters.

Consommé Medium dry sherry or dry Madeira (Sercial) or Marsala.

Lobster Dry white wines, for example Chablis, Pouilly fuissé.

Fish Dry and medium white wines, Hock, Moselle.

Entrées Claret, (or rosés or possibly a dry white wine).

Table 35 *Matching French wine with food*

Wines	Short description	Food best suited
Graves, Muscadet, Pouilly-Fumé, Chablis, Mâcon, Alsace-Sylvaner, Sancerre, Loire White	White Dry and light bodied	Sea food Shell fish Goat's cheese

Wines	Short description	Food best suited
Alsace Riesling, White Burgundy, White Jura, Côtes de Provence White, Côtes du Rhône White	White Dry and full bodied	Fried fish Cold chicken
Anjou Rosé, Jura Rosé, Côtes de Provence Rosé, Côtes du Rhone Rosé, Burgundy and Mâcon Rosé, Bordeaux Rosé, Corbières Rosé	Rosé Medium dry	Hors d'oeuvre Cold meats Entrées Roast chicken Gruyère cheese
Sauternes, Barsac, Gewürztraminer, Côteaux du Layon	White Full bodied and sweet	Fish in sauce Foie gras Desserts
Beaujolais Loire Red, Mâcon Red, Bordeaux Rouge, Médoc, St. Julien, Margaux, St. Estèphe, Côtes de Beaune, Côtes du Rhône Red, Pauillac, Pomerol, Corbières and Minervois, Bergerac Red	Red Dry and light bodied	Grilled meats Roast meats Camembert, Brie Delicatessen meats Egg dishes
Côtes de Nuits, St. Emilion, Pomerol, Hermitage Red, Châteauneuf du Pape, Côtes de Beaune such as Pommard or Corton, Jura Red, Provence Red, Côte Rôtie, Fitou and Cahors	Red Dry and full bodied	Game Poultry in sauce Red meat in sauce Strong and sharp cheese
Champagne		Goes with every dish

White meats For blanquettes, fricassés, etc., dry or medium white wines.

White meat roasts and poultry Red wine but not too full bodied for example Bordeaux, Beaujolais or robust white wine.

Red meat, roasts and venison A more generous red wine, finer vintage wine: Burgundy, Bordeaux, or Rhone.

Fois gras A fine red wine.

Sweets Champagne, natural sweet wines (for example Sauternes or a German Trockenbeerenauslese).

Cheese Port, Madeira (Bual or Malmsey), Brown sherry (but cheese mates well with most wines).

Fruit Champagne, Sauternes, mellow wines.

Coffee Cognac, liqueurs.

French approach to partnering

In matching wine with food, the Comité National des Vins de France and SOPEXA, have suggested a basis for advising customers regarding French wines and this is detailed in Table 35.

German wine suggestions

The German wine producers' marketing authority make the following broad suggestion:

White Fish A wine from the Moselle or light Rhine wine.

With poultry and meat A full bodied Rhine wine.

Other countries, other tastes

In regard to all the above comments regarding partnering it is again stressed that: individual taste varies; and wine lists now carry items from other countries whose wines, when of similar character, are often substituted.

Selling

Selling drinks, including wine in a restaurant, primarily depends upon the approach and drive of management. An appealing and understandable wine list, a realistic pricing policy, staff training, are some elements necessary to increase liquor sales. As stated previously, this book does not seek to detail management responsibilities but to concentrate on waiters' serving and selling procedures. Nevertheless, one or two general points may be made.

Wine prices

Excessive mark-up on wine may inhibit sales, especially of more expensive types. A 100 per cent mark-up, or 50 per cent wine cost should suffice and will do more to generate sales than the 200 or 300 per cent mark-up tried out at greedier restaurants. For example, more champagne is sold when a bottle costing £5 is sold at £10 than when priced at £15 or over. As with food sales, actual margins of profit per item are more meaningful than percentages and a 50 per cent wine cost can seem highly acceptable when it is remembered that a table wine sale is an additional sale during a meal period when nothing else can be sold.

Sales promotion and literature

The wine list, like the menu is a piece of sales literature and should sell through its message. Managements today strive to keep wine lists understandable, to eliminate mystique and mumbo jumbo, and to carry a sales punch. Restaurateurs and their wine suppliers are, or should be, increasingly concerned to use other sales literature to sell wine including table tents and anouncements about house and other wine on the food menu. In America, drink sales are stimulated by displays, stirring rods, printed paper napkins and glasses.

Special promotions, 'sales offers' and general merchandising and 'packaging' should support waiters' sales efforts. Moreover, however attractive wine 'mystique' may be to restaurateurs, sommeliers and maîtres d'hôtels much wine has been popularized and sold through brand name wines, well-advertised.

Strand Palace Hotel
BANQUETING WINE LIST

A selection of aperitifs, other wines, spirits, minerals, and beers is also available

HOUSE WINES (Produce of France)

	¼ Bottle	Bottle	½ Bottle
Arc de Triomphe	98p	£3.75	£1.95
Réserve red, medium dry white, rosé			

Bin No.	RED	Bottle	½ Bottle
108	Beaujolais Cuvée de la Garelle Jaboulet-Vercherre 1978 (FB) Burgundy	£5.75	£3.00
189	Crozes Hermitage Jaboulet-Vercherre 1978 (FB) Rhone	£5.75	
391	Bardolino Bolla 1977 (IB) Verona	£5.75	£3.00
52	Mouton Cadet Selection Rothschild 1977 (FB) Bordeaux	£6.25	£3.25
106	Moulin à Vent David et Foillard 1979 (FB) Burgundy	£7.85	£3.95

Bin No.	WHITE	Bottle	½ Bottle
352	Moselblüemchen Blue Crest R. Langguth 1978 (GB) Moselle	£5.45	£2.85
318	Liebfraumilch Wedding Veil 1978 (GB) Rhine	£5.75	£3.00
211	Chenin Blanc J. Moreau 1978 (FB) Loire	£5.75	
210	Muscadet Cuvée Abelard Sevre et Maine 1978 (FB) Loire	£5.75	
146	Mâcon Blanc Villages Jaboulet-Vercherre 1978 (FB) Burgundy	£6.95	£3.60

Bin No.	ROSE	Bottle	½ Bottle
195	Mateus (EB) Portugal	£5.45	£2.85

Bin No.	SPARKLING WINES AND CHAMPAGNE	Bottle	½ Bottle
222B	Club Prestige Demi-sec (FB) France	£5.75	
230	Ayala, Château D'Ay Extra Quality, Extra Dry NV	£9.95	£5.15

	Port	Glass	Bottle
	Calem Vintage Character	50p	
	Cockburn 1970	£1.00	£10.00

When stocks of any particular vintage become exhausted, the best succeeding year is offered with every confidence.

Bottled at the Chateau (CB), Domaine/Estate (DB), in France (FB), in Germany (GB), in Italy (IB).

Prices include Value Added Tax

Yours faithfully

TRUSTHOUSE FORTE HOTELS

Training and product knowledge

However 'down to earth' a wine sales policy may be, training should aim to make all waiting staff aware of the nature of the commodity they sell so that they can respond to questions and, as necessary, make sensible recommendations. Such training on the job should support attendance at City and Guilds and other courses (mentioned earlier in Chapter 1).

This book is concerned with service at table rather than the details of viticulture and wine characteristics. Waiters (especially wine waiters) must nevertheless seek to acquaint themselves with all kinds of wine normally available in restaurants, that is, they should seek to have wide product knowledge. Fortunately there is a mass of books (possibly too many) about wine from which to gain information. The following books are just four good examples: L. W. Marrison, *Wines and Spirits* (Penguin 1970); Paul Breman, *Cheaper Wines* (Penguin 1976); Allan Sichel, *The Penguin Book of Wines* (Penguin 1976); P. Morton Shand, revised by Cyril Ray, *A Book of French Wines* (Penguin 1978).

Bartenders' and Sommeliers' Association

The United Kingdom Bartenders Association's *International Guide to Drinks* gives details of alcoholic drinks, but the Association itself and the Guild of Sommeliers both aim to promote vocational knowledge.

The Guild of Sommeliers is of interest to those who seek to specialize in wine service.

It does, however, have to be said that more and more wine is sold in restaurants without highly specialized wine waiting staff. As wine is seen to be an agreeable part of eating out, all waiters should appreciate the importance of wine as a profit potential as well as a meal enhancer and seek to master the relatively simple but effective methods of presenting and serving an increasingly widely used commodity.

An example of a function wine list

22 Drinks, licensing and tobacco

Waiting staff in restaurants are involved in serving table wines in conjunction with food, but they may also serve drinks before and after meals. Drink service may be in the lounge or at table. Lounge waiter's duties are touched upon in Chapter 18 but many of the following drinks are likely to be served by them.

Cocktails and other mixed drinks change in popularity. For some years short cocktails have been diminishing in favour as appetizers in Britain. But in any case this book does not seek to cover the duties of bar staff but rather to note examples of drinks and aspects of their service. For details of pre-meal alcoholic drinks, readers should refer to the United Kingdom Bartenders' Association's Handbook, *International Guide to Drinks*.

Aperitifs

Aperitifs or appetizer drinks are commonly taken before meals in a lounge or bar adjacent to the restaurant. Drinks favoured as aperitifs vary according to nationality. Cocktails are still on the whole more popular with, for example, Americans. In France sweeter aperitifs (including 'brand names' like Dubonnet, St. Raphael) and, even port, wines are favoured.

In Britain, sherry is probably the most popular pre-meal aperitif wine.

Sherry

Sherry is always a blended wine and styles range from extremely dry to sweet. The very dry wines are pale in colour, light bodied and of delicate bouquet. Sherry is 'fortified' with brandy, has a high alcoholic strength, and is thus an aperitif (or dessert wine) and not a table wine. Basically sherry is dry. Dark, sweet sherries are made by various blendings. One method is to boil down special wines to remove excess liquid and leave a dark essence, which is added to the blend.

Sherries are broadly described as 'dry', 'medium', or 'sweet', but are normally shipped under three types (which are given various trade names):

- Fino (pale, dry, delicate).
- Palo Cortado (distinguished, dry, darker than Amontillado).
- Oloroso (sweet).

There is also Manzanilla (dry – often thought to have a faint 'salt' taste). Amontillado (nutty, medium dry) and dessert sherries blended as 'creams' or 'milk'.

Sherry is fundamentally a white wine and hence (especially when served as an aperitif) is served chilled. However, dessert sherries are usually served at room or cellar temperature. Sherry shippers even advertise the possibility of serving sherry 'on the rocks' which at one time was unthinkable.

Other aperitif wines

Wines which are often taken as dessert wines, especially port and Madeira, also have drier versions (though they are seldom so dry as sherries can be) taken as aperitifs.

There is hardly any limit other than personal taste to what may be chosen as an aperitif. Many guests select champagne, dry white or rosé wines,

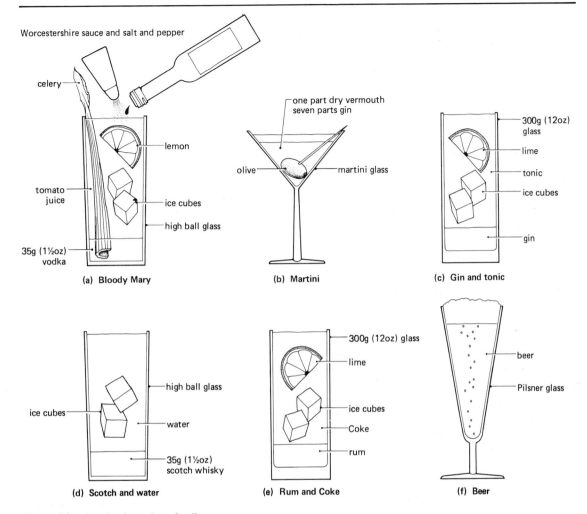

Figure 73 *A selection of cocktails*

vins jaunes or 'vogue' drinks such as Kir (Cassis with white Burgundy) or 'Cold Duck' (pink, sparkling wine made by blending red wine with sparkling white). Others prefer Dubonnet, Pastis (Pernod or Ricard), Marsala or other sweeter aperitif wines.

Cocktails

Mixing cocktails is a task for a trained and qualified barman but waiters should know the ingredients of a few of the more popular cocktails to help take an order; for they may find themselves on lounge service or assisting at a pre-function reception. These include:

Americanos Campari, Italian (red) vermouth.
Bacardi White rum, lime juice, sugar, Grenadine.
Bloody Mary Vodka, tomato juice, lemon juice, Worcester sauce, salt, pepper.
Brandy sour Brandy, lemon juice, sugar, cherry garnish.
Champagne cocktail Champagne, Brandy, bitters, lemon peel.
Coladas Cane spirit and/or rum-based drinks to which coconut and other flavourings are added.
Daiquiri As Bacardi (without Grenadine).
Gin and Dubonnet Gin with Dubonnet aperitif wine.

Gin and French   Gin with French vermouth.
Gin and Italian   Gin with Italian vermouth.
Gin and Lillet   Gin with Lillet aperitif wine.
Manhattan   Rye whisky, Italian vermouth, bitters.
Martini (dry)   Gin, French vermouth, olive garnish.
Martini (sweet)   Gin, Italian vermouth, cocktail cherry garnish.
Old Fashioned   Whisky, bitters, sugar, fruit garnish.
On-the-rocks   Any liquor served neat, poured over ice cubes.
Pink gin   Glass swirled out with Angostura bitters, before adding measure of Plymouth gin.
Rob Roy   Scotch whisky, vermouth, bitters.
Screwdriver   Vodka and orange juice on ice cubes.
Sidecar   Brandy, Cointreau, lemon juice.
Whisky sour   Whisky, lemon juice, sugar, cherry garnish.
White lady   Gin, Cointreau, lemon juice, dash egg white (optional).

Other spirit drinks

In addition to shorter cocktails used as aperitifs there are a number of longer drinks which may also be requested prior to a meal or generally during lounge service. These are often referred to as *Highballs*. The range of long drinks includes quite simple mixes such as whisky and soda, or gin and tonic (see page 271), or may be more elaborate ones such as John Collins, Rickeys, punches, juleps and shakes. These drinks are normally compounded by bar staff and their service follows the general rules outlined later in this chapter.

Inviting the aperitif order

An aperitif is enjoyed before a meal to stimulate the palate. It is usually taken in cocktail bars or lounges but in the restaurant a customer may like one at table.

Therefore, on seating a party, first ask the host if he would like a sherry, vermouth, cocktail or other appetizer. Serve these as quickly as possible so that they can be enjoyed even while the order for the meal is being taken.

Service of aperitifs in the restaurant

As these drinks are served in the glass, carry them on a cloth-covered wine salver in case of slight spillage during carriage. If the base of a glass is wet on arrival at the table, it can easily be cleared by rubbing off with a cloth-covered finger. Picking up a filled glass to wipe it can cause more spillage and possible accident. It is easier to change a cloth on the tray if it gets soiled. Place the glass on the table just below and to the right of the table glass, which should not be removed. When the drinks are finished, clear the glasses.

After dinner drinks

After dinner drinks fall broadly into three categories.

Dessert wines   Possibly taken with cheese or dessert fruit and which may even be thought to be effectively part of the meal itself.
Brandies or liqueurs   Normally served with coffee or at coffee time.
Longer drinks   Which are taken well after a meal has been consumed, for refreshment or as a continuation of a festive occasion.

Port wine

The principal dessert wine enjoyed in this country is port, often known as the 'Englishman's wine'. Port at functions is, because of its nature, often decanted and in military messes or gentlemen's clubs is subject to a degree of service ritual in that guests help themselves from the decanter and pass it only in a clockwise direction.

Ports are of four types: ruby, vintage, tawny and white. The first three are red wines, fortified with a special brandy early in the fermentation. This gives port a high alcoholic strength and permits a high sugar content (from the unfermented grape sugar in the wine for the added spirit inhibits further fermentation). They are stored in cask for eighteen months, two years, and three or more years respectively before bottling. The longer in cask the paler the colour of the wine, but nevertheless, not every year is a vintage year.

White ports are fortified after fermentation in the same manner, but are made from white grapes. Because of the special process of fermentation, ports are full bodied, full flavoured, sweet and of high alcoholic strength and colourful. Examples include: ruby ports shipped under brand names; vintage ports shipped under shipper's names, with vintage year; and tawny and white ports usually shipped under shipper's names, but sometimes under brand names.

Other dessert wines

Although port tends to take first place as a dessert wine, Madeira has also traditionally been favoured for dessert purposes by the English. As has been noted the dry version, Sercial, is often taken as an aperitif. So also is Verdelho though it is sweeter. The varieties Bual and Malmsey are sweeter still and are taken at the same stage of the meal as port.

Marsala from Italy is also sometimes chosen as a dessert wine. Both Madeira and Marsala are additionally widely used in cooking.

Liqueurs

Liqueurs were known in Roman times but developed in the Middle Ages through experiments with distillations of herbs, flowers and grape juice (brandy).

These ancient cordials were used as medicines; the secrets being passed down. The ingredients of some famous liqueurs of today remain secrets of monasteries after which they are named.

In modern times, many new liqueurs, often with a fruit basis, have been invented and marketed.

Liqueurs are thought to assist digestion, hence the taking of them after a meal.

Some liqueurs and their predominant flavours

Abricotine   Apricot
Advocat   Yolks of egg and brandy

Anisette   Aniseed
Apry   Apricot
Aurum   Orange
Benedictine   Herbs and brandy (DOM)
Calvados   Applejack and brandy
Chartreuse   Herbs (127) brandy (green or yellow)
Cointreau   Orange (white)
Crème de Cacao   Chocolate (served with fresh cream on top)
Crème de Menthe   Peppermint (green, white)
Curaçao   Orange (yellow, green, white and blue)
Drambuie   Herbs and Scotch whisky liqueur
Glen Mist   Irish Whiskey liqueur
Goldwasser (Danzig)   White spirit, herbs and gold leaf
Grand Marnier   Orange
Izarra   Mountain herbs and brandy (Basque)
Kirsch (Wasser)   Cherry kernels (bitter almond)
Kümmel   Caraway seed
Sambucca   Italian liquorice flavoured liqueur
Tia Maria   Coffee and rum
Van de Hum   (Van de Hum means 'Mister What's his Name' apparently because the inventor's name has been forgotten.) Herbs, bark, tangerine-orange
Vieille Curé   Herbs and brandy (Abbaye Cenon)

There are many more and, again, there are several specialist books on the subject.

Service of liqueurs

Liqueurs are usually served into the glass and carried on a silver salver to the table. As they are normally served at coffee time the glass is then placed at the right of the coffee cup but not near the edge of the table. Liqueur glasses vary in size and shape according to the preference of the establishment but have a line cut into the glass to mark the measure.

Service procedure varies if there is a liqueur trolley service in the room. In this case bottles are taken to the table by trolley, presented and the measure poured into the glass in front of the customer.

Liqueur cordials

Mention has been made of fashion in drinks. As well as served plain with coffee, liqueurs or other spirituous 'after dinner' drinks may also be served at other times, or in other styles for example 'on the rocks' or in mixed drinks simply as drinks even before meals. Coladas and cream-based cordials have been increasingly popularized for 'occasional' drinking in recent years.

Brandy

Many customers prefer a liqueur brandy after their meal. Brandy is a distillation from wine and is made in almost all wine-producing countries. Freshly distilled brandy is raw, fiery and colourless; but mellows and acquires its flavour and straw colour from years of maturation in cask. Spirit, unlike wine, does not mature in the bottle. As it is a spirit there is constant evaporation and therefore loss of stock. This, added to the fact that the years in cask tie up capital which cannot be used, explains the difference in price between young brandy and fine old ones.

In general, the longer a brandy is in cask the more mellow it becomes. Brandy made in France is considered the best and its finest comes from Cognac in the Charente area. Only brandy made in this area can be called Cognac.

Cognac description

The four districts of Cognac most esteemed are the Grande Champagne, Petite Champagne, Les Borderies and Les Fines Bois. Brandy from Grande Champagne is often designated Fine Champagne (this champagne area is not to be confused with the Champagne wine area around Rheims).

When introduced by Maurice Hennessy in 1869, the 'star' system for cognac was carefully applied. Today it is not considered to have the same reliability.

'Three stars' is a good quality everyday Cognac, the minimum age of any one brandy in a blend is thirty months, but it can be composed from cognacs of five to ten years old or even more, in varying proportions.

VO ('very old') and VSOP ('very superior old pale' a designation introduced in the last century to meet British taste for pale brandy) cognacs consist of older brandies: the youngest in any one is four and a half years, but in practice, they

consist of a large percentage of Cognacs aged ten, twenty, thirty or more years.

'Vieille Réserve', 'Grande Réserve', 'Royal', 'Vieux', 'XO', 'Napoléon', etc., apply to Cognacs which are older still and are of exceptional quality. At one time brandies of fine single years were matured in cask and bottled as vintage brandies but this practice of vintage years really no longer applies to Cognacs.

Note: There are distillations made from other fruits and labelled 'Brandy'; Cherry Brandy, Apricot Brandy, Peach Brandy, Prunelle (Plum) Brandy, etc. These are spirituous liquors not pure brandies and are served as liqueurs.

Armagnac and other brandies

Some Armagnac brandies are labelled 'Bas-Armagnac', 'Ténarèze' or 'Haut-Armagnac' when they come exclusively from one of these sub-regions. The simple Armagnac designation covers all brandies from the area or applies to a blend from the three sub-regions.

Labelling references (such as: stars, crowns, letters, etc.) may only be used for brandies at least one year old (three years old in Britain) and preserved in wood casks; the same is true for 'Monopole', 'Sélection de Luxe' and similar labels.

Such descriptions as 'VO', 'VSOP' and 'Réserve' apply to brandies which have matured at least four years in wood casks.

'Extra', 'Napoleon', 'XO', 'Vieille Réserve' and similar labels may be applied only to brandies having spent five years in wood casks.

A named year indicates an unblended brandy from one given year.

Serving brandy

As brandy is enjoyed as much by the nose as the palate it is usually served in a brandy goblet (see Chapter 20 regarding glasses). A large bowl (balloon) allows the glass to be wrapped by the hands to warm it through and release the bouquet. The narrow neck of a balloon traps aroma in the bowl and lets the nose gain full appreciation. When brandy is served, whether in a 'balloon' or liqueur glass, the name should be quoted, for example 'Your Bisquit Dubouché, sir (madam)'.

Warming brandy glasses

As stated, a slight warming is necessary to release the aromas. There is a practice of warming the glass before putting in the brandy and even gadgets exist for that purpose. Indeed, some customers ask for their glass to be warmed but this should never be done without customers' permission. Knowledgeable brandy drinkers prefer to use their hands, for if a glass is too warm, aroma is released too quickly and the brandy spoiled.

If, however, a customer requires his glass warmed, it should never be put over a methylated flame. Brandy is delicate, takes in ulterior flavours easily and can quickly gain the smell of methylated from a contaminated glass.

To warm a glass, if a guest insists, hot water should be used, afterwards wiping and polishing the glass thoroughly before pouring in the brandy.

On the other hand, in certain European countries, the goblets are iced before the brandy is poured in.

Spirits and dilutants

Although spirits are more popular in bars, they may be ordered at table instead of wine and taken with mineral water.

Whisky Scotch, Rye, Bourbon, Irish (Irish whiskey is spelt with the 'e'). Scotch whisky is preferred in this country, but Americans and Canadians have a liking for their own types of Rye and Bourbon. Most Scotch whisky is a blend of grain and malt whisky. Single malts, that is, unblended malt whisky from one distillery is more expensive. The finer, more aged malts, are often taken neat instead of brandy after a meal.

Gin 'London Dry' of various brands is the most popular. Other gins include: 'Plymouth', 'Hollands', 'Sloe' (Plymouth gin, which is less dry than London is the gin traditionally used for Pink gin (see the cocktail list on page 271).

Brandy Served as a long drink with soda water is usually a younger brandy than that listed as a liqueur brandy.

Spirits are usually served by measure, the customer ordering a 'single' or a 'double'. Many people demand a certain brand which, if in stock, should be served but if not available the customer should be informed and an alternative offered.

The most usual mineral waters asked for with spirits are:

For whisky Soda water or similar aerated water (for example Appollinaris ('Polly') or Perrier), ginger ale or plain water (which should be iced) (See further notes on mineral waters on page 276).

For gin Tonic water and slice of lemon, ginger ale, ginger beer or plain iced water.

For brandy Similar to whisky.

Spirit service

For service, check your order and obtain the spirits in glass and bottled mineral from the dispense. Carry the order to the table – glasses and bottles on a wine salver. Place the glasses on the table (see page 272) and ask the customer 'Would you say when please, sir (madam)'. Pour the mineral steadily until told to stop. Place the mineral bottle on the table if there is anything left in it.

Note: Ice should always be available.

Service of beers

Bottled beers are usually served from 3 dl (½ pt, 10 oz) bottles and poured into a 3¾ dl (12 oz) glass. They are served with a 'head' or 'collar' (froth). Serve without delay so that a full 'head' remains.

English draught (and bottled) beers are served at normal cool cellar temperature. Lager beers (including English) are always served chilled.

Draught beers served in half pints or pints must be served in glasses, mugs or tankards bearing the official crown marking and quantity and must be full to this mark.

Service of soft drinks

Fresh fruit drinks

Orange, lemon etc., or bottled squashes are frequently requested for younger guests. Place the measure of squash in a tumbler with ice and fill up with water or soda water, giving a light stir to mix properly. Drinking straws in a stand or in a tumbler should be placed on the table at time of service.

Fresh fruit squash

Such drinks, for example lemon squash, should be mixed at the table. In preparation, place on a wine salver the freshly squeezed juice in a glass (tumbler), a bowl of caster sugar, a bowl of ice with tongs (both on an underplate) and straw stand and then carry to the table with the soda water.

At the table put in sugar to the customer's taste and dissolve into the juice. Add the ice (when no tongs are available use service spoon and fork) and then slowly pour in the soda water, stirring lightly. Make certain the sugar is dissolved and that the soda is added carefully or there is liable to be an uncontrolled effervescence.

When plain water is required, use a lipped water jug so that ice is retained. Where no such jug is available, restrain the ice by using a large fork in the left hand, placing its prongs over the pouring lip.

Mineral waters

There are two types of mineral water: natural and manufactured.

Natural spring waters are bottled waters from the spas – some of the better known being Ashbourne, Vichy, Etat, Vittel, Contrexeville, Evian, San Pellegrino, Spa, Perrier, Malvern and Appollinaris.

Manufactured mineral waters include soda water, ginger ale, ginger beer, tonic water, lemonade, bitter lemon, etc.

Natural spring waters are not merely used as 'mixers' with spirits but are often ordered by guests to drink at table. Spring water may be chosen for its supposed medicinal properties or because some alkaline types offset any acidity from wine but chiefly because water is taken to quench thirst and clear the palate while an expensive wine is savoured.

For service, a quantity of mineral water is poured into the table glass and the rest placed on the table in the correct position.

Drink service

Lounge waiters and bar staff are those whose work concentrates on drinks service but all waiters have to cope with such service in the restaurant itself. Drinks before and after a meal are important sources of profit and also aperitifs help to create good first impressions of a restaurant while after the meal drinks can help to leave the good impression behind.

Because of possible consequences of drinking, the law in Britain, as in many countries, has developed to regulate alcoholic drink sale and service.

Licensing and legal aspects

Several books exist which deal specifically with law for the hotel and catering industry. In this chapter licensing law is touched upon only so as to give waiting staff some understanding of the legal framework within which they serve and sell wine. It is prudent for waiting staff to be aware of legal constraints and of how the law reflects society's views about drinking.

Licensing law affecting waiters' work

A waiter is not expected to know all the details of licensing law but should understand its application to his work. As ignorance of the law does not excuse breaking it, a careless waiter could unwittingly jeopardize his employer's licence.

Application of the law has tended to differ according to types of establishment, but since the Licensing Act, 1961, changes have been introduced to clarify licensing law and to eliminate anomalies. Differences still exist, however, between England, Wales and Scotland.

The type of licence held by an establishment is useful as a guide. Thus:

Hotels holding a full-on licence
Resident guests Can be supplied with alcoholic drinks at any time of the day or night, with or without a meal. Payment for these drinks can be made at time of service, or be added to the guest's hotel bill. A resident guest can also obtain drinks for his personal guests at any time, providing he pays for these drinks himself. It is illegal for non-resident guests to order or to pay for alcoholic drinks outside licensing hours, even if they are in the company of a resident guest.

Non-resident guests Can only obtain drinks during permitted hours. Drinks with a meal must be ordered during these hours. Up to thirty minutes after permitted hours are allowed for their consumption. If the drinks do not accompany a meal, only ten minutes 'drinking time' is allowed. At the end of these times, it is advisable for a waiter to request permission to remove the glasses. This must be done with tact, particularly if foreign guests are involved, as they are often unaware of the law.

Hotels holding a residential licence
In such establishments only resident guests can be supplied with alcoholic drinks with or without a meal. No specific times are laid down as to when these drinks can be supplied. Personal guests of resident guests can be served with alcoholic drinks, providing these are ordered and paid for by the resident guests.

Restaurant licence
This is sometimes called a table licence. Drinks in this case can only be supplied if they are to accompany a meal. Drinks must be ordered during permitted hours, and up to thirty minutes are allowed after permitted hours for their consumption.

Some establishments have a licence combining the facilities offered by the licences above. In England and Wales this is called a residential and restaurant licence (or in Scotland a restricted hotel certificate).

Restaurants holding a full-on licence
This is called a public house certificate in Scotland. Service of alcoholic drinks must take place during permitted hours. They can be supplied with or without a meal and the customary drinking-up time after permitted service hours is allowed.

Unlicensed restaurants
These establishments cannot under any circumstances sell alcoholic beverages. It is, however, permitted for managements to allow their staff to fetch and carry for their diners drinks obtained from licensed premises for consumption with a meal in their establishment. In this instance, certain conditions must be fulfilled:

1 Drinks must be obtained during permitted hours.
2 Guests must pay for the drinks when ordering.
3 Management must not derive any revenue whatsoever for this service.
4 Management is not allowed to hold stocks of alcoholic beverages for selling to customers.

In other words, it must be a non-profit making service introduced purely for the convenience of customers.

Supper licence
Establishments holding a full licence or restaurant or residential and restaurant licence, serving meals late in the evening, often have a supper licence. This also allows them to sell alcoholic drinks for an extra thirty minutes after permitted hours at lunch time until 3 p.m. (2.30 in Scotland on Sundays) from Monday to Saturday as well as for an additional hour in the evening after permitted hours on every day of the week.

Meals during extensions
These extensions only apply to drinks served with a meal, and thirty minutes consumption time is allowed in addition. The meal during an extension period must be one of a 'sustaining nature'. Unfortunately, it is not yet clearly established what a meal of a 'sustaining nature' should be. That knives and forks are used does not in itself determine whether the meal is sustaining.

The main factor appears to be that drinks are an accompaniment to a meal rather than the meal an excuse for drinking. This applies to establishments which can only supply alcoholic beverages with a meal.

Sunday drinking

Only establishments holding a seven day licence can supply alcoholic drinks on Sunday. The hours on this day differ from those applicable during the week.

Licensing terms defined

Licensing or permitted hours

The general licensing laws in England are:

Weekdays 11.00 a.m. – 3.00 p.m., 5.30 – 10.30 p.m. (11 p.m. in London)
Sundays 12.00 – 2.00 p.m., 7.00 – 10.30 p.m.

Local licensing justices have power to vary these times but permitted hours must not start before 10 a.m. nor end after 10.30 p.m. (or 11 p.m. in London). There must be a break of at least two hours in the afternoon and total permitted hours must not exceed nine (or nine and a half) hours.

In Scotland the hours are standard.

Weekdays 11.00 a.m. – 2.30 p.m., 5.00 p.m. – 10.00 p.m.
Sundays 12.30 – 2.30 p.m., 6.30 p.m. – 10.00 p.m.

Only hotels and restaurants can hold a seven day licence in Scotland.

Restaurant licence (table licence). Indicates that drinks can only be supplied with a meal.

Occasional licence

A permission valid for one occasion only, granted for serving drinks outside permitted hours (that is, functions) in the licensee's own premises, or for serving drinks during or outside permitted hours in some other place. Only a full-on licensee can be given this permission, and he must indicate date, time and place and reason on the application.

Supper licence

An extension of thirty minutes after closing time at midday during the week, and of one hour after closing in the evening for all days of the week including Sunday. During these extensions drinks can only be supplied with a meal.

Age for serving or consuming alcoholic drinks

The permitted age for consumption of alcoholic beverages is eighteen. Persons under eighteen but over sixteen can be supplied with beer, porter, cider or perry to accompany a meal.

No person under the age of eighteen can be allowed to dispense alcoholic beverages, nor be directly concerned with their service.

Weights and measures

Legislation which touches upon drink sale is widespread. Staff should keep themselves abreast of the most important, including that which regulates measures of bar drinks.

The Weights and Measures (Sale of Wine) Order, 1976 requires that wine when sold in a sealed bottle or 'by the glass', the capacity measurement need not be stated. When sold by other methods, that is, carafes, the carafe must contain either 25 cl, 50 cl, 75 cl or 1 l, or 10 fl oz or 20 fl oz.

Carafe sales

As wine sales by glass are not yet covered, terms like 'schooner' or 'glass' are not really meaningful. For carafe sales, however, to comply with this requirement, the wine list (or menu) must state that carafe wine is offered for sale by the litre or one of the subdivisions indicated above. When using government-stamped lined carafes, it is acceptable to fill the carafe simply to the measure line.

If using a wide mouth carafe, first ascertain the correct quantity by using a government-stamped measuring vessel decanted into the carafe. The line then merely serves as a guide to customers.

The most widely used carafe sizes are the ½ litre (50 cl) and full litre (100 cl).

False description

It will already have been noted that some wines, for example champagne have protected designations and waiting staff must be aware that it is an offence to attempt to 'pass off' alternatives to such protected designated wines.

Tobacco

Because of medical opinion about the health hazards of smoking, social attitudes towards tobacco in the restaurant have changed. Wherever food is served, smoking at table before and during a meal is considered undesirable. Pipes are taboo in good restaurants or wherever fine food is served, however modest the establishment.

Cigarette smoking at table is now widely regarded as antisocial and is likely increasingly to be viewed disfavourably.

At formal dinners the ritual of prohibiting smoking until the loyal toast has been drunk has long reflected the need to confine smoking till after all have finished eating.

There is less medical condemnation of smoking in which there is little or no inhalation. Hence cigars, which are usually enjoyed for their aroma and flavour, are still taken by many diners as a finale to a meal. Thus, waiting staff need to understand something of the nature of tobacco as a commodity which they sell and serve. Especially should they have some understanding of cigars.

Customers invariably order a brand of cigarette or tobacco that they know or like. It is only with cigars that a waiter may be asked to recommend or suggest a brand.

The following sections apply to all tobacco, whether in cigarettes, for pipes or as cigars.

Purchase

Hotels and restaurants usually buy tobacco from wholesale tobacconists (tobacco merchants, cigar merchants, etc.) or direct from manufacturers of particular brands (although this entails extra work, for more than one manufacturer's brands will have to be stocked).

Storage

Reliable merchants make sure that all tobacco they sell to a hotel or restaurant has been stored properly up to the date of sale. Tobacco is sensitive, easily absorbs moisture like a sponge and even takes on any strong smell near it.

Tobacco should not be exposed to extremes of heat and cold, or to wet or particularly dry air; otherwise the aroma is soon lost (particularly of cigars). A temperature of 18°C (65°F) with about 55 per cent humidity is the most suitable. Under ideal storage conditions in a humidor even cigars can remain in good condition for up to ten years.

Sale

As a customer nearly always knows what brand of cigarettes or tobacco he wants, it is only necessary to stock a sufficient quantity of the more popular brands. Those that are in less demand should be kept only in such quantities that they are sure to be sold before they lose their freshness.

Wherever a large quantity of tobacco (in any form) is sold, a hotel or restaurant will almost certainly have one member of staff who is responsible for ordering, storage, sale, records and passing invoices.

The work of a waiter is then restricted to taking customers' orders, obtaining the quantity required, and seeing that it is properly paid for.

The method will vary. In many establishments a waiter will give in a special order to whoever is in charge of tobacco and obtain it in a similar manner to his obtaining food from the kitchen; he will then enter the item on the customer's bill.

In other operations, and in most cafeterias, a customer is either required to pay cash at the tobacco kiosk or over the counter, or if a waiter takes the order he asks for the money and pays for it himself, without any record being made on his own check book.

Good cigars are expensive so a mark up of 50 per cent can bring worthwhile profit to a restaurant. If a mark up creeps higher there is always the possibility of customers bringing in their own.

The main types of tobacco for cigarettes and pipe-smoking are:

Virginian   By far the most popular. Grown in Virginia, the Carolinas, Kentucky and Tennessee and also outside America, for example, in Zimbabwe.

Turkish   From Asiatic Turkey, Balkans and Syria.

Egyptian   From the Nile Delta and Asia Minor.

Matches and offering 'a light'

A waiter must see that an ashtray (properly cleaned) is placed on the table for the guest at the right time and that a light (match, not lighter) is available should it be needed.

If a guest asks for 'a light' for a cigarette, strike the match (holding it away from the customer) and hold the flame to the cigarette.

Cigars

Good cigars are costly. Their service involves more ritual.

Cutting a cigar

Carry a cigar cutter. Connoisseurs of cigars prefer a cut end (either a deep V-cut or straight slice) rather than a pierced end. The good 'flue' provided by a cut ensures cool, free drawing of the smoke, whereas a pierced end tends to become 'tarry'.

If a customer requires you to cut his cigar, take care not to cut too deeply lest the cap is cut away allowing the wrapper leaf to unwind. Do not remove the decorative band or ring as doing this may also injure the wrapper leaf. (Customers may themselves choose to remove this band as some consider its retention while smoking 'vulgar'.)

Lighting a cigar

For a cigar, hand the guest the box of matches (not sulphur or wax vestas as they may spoil flavour). This is because the end to be lit is first warmed.

Cigar quality, strength and taste

The quality of a cigar depends on the tobacco. The best cigars are those which come from the Vuelta Albajo district, Number 1 in Cuba, where the tobacco is more aromatic in flavour than in any other part of the world.

Cigar smokers have different tastes. The majority like cigars to be mild. A cigar's strength is determined by the 'filler' which is the tobacco that makes up the main part of the cigar. This is held together by the binder tobacco round which the 'wrapper' or outer leaf (selected for appearance and texture) is rolled.

Blenders, therefore, make all cigars of a particular brand as uniform as possible. Mild and delicate blends are made of the finest and ripest leaf but full-flavoured ones are made of heavier leaf which has maximum body and aroma.

A dark wrapper does not necessarily indicate a strong cigar, and both light and dark wrappers may be bitter and strong if the tobacco has not been properly ripened and cured in the highly technical processes employed. Proper maturing takes from six months to three years.

Gauging quality

Knowledge of what constitutes a good cigar is acquired by experience and in smoking them. In addition to the fundamental data previously given, bear in mind the following.

Cigar ash gives some indication of quality. A first grade cigar produces a firm, greyish ash which lasts for a considerable time before falling.

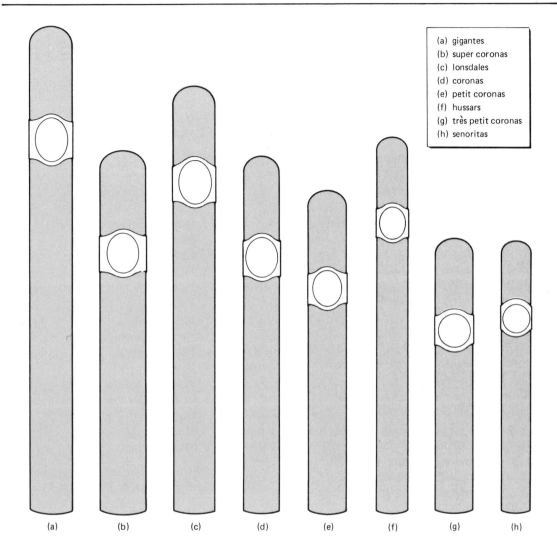

(a) gigantes
(b) super coronas
(c) lonsdales
(d) coronas
(e) petit coronas
(f) hussars
(g) très petit coronas
(h) senoritas

(a) (b) (c) (d) (e) (f) (g) (h)

Figure 74 *Examples of Havana cigar sizes*

It is not wise to put a cigar to the ear to crackle it. Although this will indicate whether it is dry (which is important), the crackling may break the leaf and damage the cigar. Press a cigar gently along its length with finger and thumb. Any hard spot may indicate a nub which may inhibit a full easy draw.

Cigars are usually sold in boxes of 25, 50 and 100. Cabinets are also provided, containing any number from 250 to 1000 usually assorted sizes.

Most sizes of cigars are also packed in metal tubes (cedar-lined for good quality) and these are popular for ease of sale and storage.

An attractive box or band does not necessarily mean a good cigar. Neither does, in fact, the cigar's wrapper leaf necessarily indicate that the important filler is of equal quality.

It is advisable to keep cigars in a service cabinet, in which there is say, a choice of three to six cigars, ranging from the good, moderate-priced cigar up to the more exclusive and higher priced ones. A guest should then be able to make a suitable choice.

A good cigar depends first and foremost on 'reputation', which indicates the quality of the filler and wrapper tobacco, its correct maturing, grading, rolling, storing and packing.

Countries of origin

Cigars are made in many parts of the world, for example Havana, Java, India, Burma, Manila and Mexico. Some good cigars are made in Britain (and of course in Holland and Switzerland), but they are from tobacco that is imported from Havana, Jamaica, Brazil, Java and America. Often the wrappers are leaf from Sumatra or Borneo, although Havana wrappers are also used on some brands.

Grades, brands and size

Some Havana cigars are graded (indicated on the underside of the box) by the colour of the wrapper:

Claro Light
Colorado Claro (or Col-Claro) A little darker (light medium)
Colorado Darker still (medium)
Colorado-Maduro Dark medium
Maduro Rich and very dark

Among brands of cigars sold in Britain, the leading ones are made in different sizes and shapes to suit individual preferences for example

Churchills, Lonsdales, Corona, Petit Corona, Half-a-Corona, Panatellas, Margaritas.

To check the authenticity of a Havana cigar, look for the green label affixed to every box as the Cuban Government's warranty.

Brand names

There are many brands of good cigars. Some of the famous names are:

Havana	Flor de Tabacos de Partagas (Partagas for short)
	Ramon Allones
	Romeo y Julieta
	Monte Cristo
	Cabanas
	H. Upmann
	La Corona
	Punch
	Bolivar
	Hayo de Monterrey
	Por Larranaga
Jamaica	La Invicta
	Flor de Nazenta
	El Trovador
Las Palmas	Flamenco
Manila	Manila Gold
	Manila Prince

A long-established and reliable importer (such as Hunters and Frankau in the City of London who have been shipping cigars since 1790) is not only a supply source for quality cigars but also of further information about their selection and enjoyment.

Conclusion

Restaurant sales of tobacco just as sales elsewhere will undoubtedly be affected by medical opinion about smoking and consequent social attitudes. Meanwhile, it is a commodity that restaurants sell. It is perhaps worth observing that following the example of many restaurants in America, restaurants may also extend their range of sales of other commodities quite apart from having any 'take-away' section. Waiting staff may not become greatly involved in other miscellaneous sales within a restaurant operation but their readiness to appreciate the changing nature of what services and commodities and what legal constraints surround them in food and beverage operations is a quality which they should cultivate. Selling and service of drinks, tobacco and other commodities is a developing rather than a static feature within the catering trade.

Index

trolleys – *contd*
  checking system, 191, 193
  cleaning, 79
  hors d'oeuvres served from, 167
  liqueurs served from, 182, 273
  mentioned, 17, 50, 75, 151, 182
  for room service, 228–9, 230
  sweet course served from, 177
tumblers, *253, 254*, 255, 259
tureens, serving soup from, 165–6

undercloths, 131
underdish, use of, 158, 159
underplates, 161, 165, 166, 178, 179, *186*
United Kingdom Bartenders' Association, 269, 270
Urbain-Dubois, chef, 156
urns, 61, 63

vacuum infusion machines, 63, 64, 181
VDQS wines, 237
vegetables
  cook, 30, *31*
  French terminology for, 112–3
  on menu, 86, 87, *90, 91, 94, 97, 99, 100*
  names of, 112
  salad, 176, *177*
  in season, 124
  service of, 174, *185*
  styles of, 112–3
vins de pays, 237
voitures *see* trolleys
VQPRD wines, 236, 237

wages, 20, 21, 22
waiters (waitresses), 17–43
  addressing guests, 38–9
  advancement, 18–19
  brigades, *16*, 23, 26, 27–9, 147, 152–3
  conditions of work, 20
  conduct, 40–1, 154
  conversing with guests, 41
  co-operation, 40
  courtesy, 39, 140, 154
  demand for, 15, 17
  dress, 29–30, 33–5
  friendliness, 18, 38, 39
  function, 200, 209, 213–4, 219
  furniture and equipment, responsibility for, 45, 57, 58
  health, 36
  honesty, 39–40
  hygiene, 36–8

  job seeking, 21–2
  knowledge required, 41, *42*
  ménage duties, 74–9
  operating restaurant registers, 198
  outside catering, 214
  personal qualities, 36–40, 42–3
  professionalism, 42–3
  restaurant design affecting, 44
  selling role, 17, 84, 105, 116, 259
  technical skill, 41, 42
  terms of employment, 20–1
  tools for service, 156–7
  training, 17, 19, 21, 269
  vocational interest, 21
  wages, 20, 21, 22
  see also floor waiter; functions: waiters; head waiter; lounge waiter; station waiter; wine waiter
washing-up, 65–8, 71–3, 255
water
  corrosive effect on cutlery, 72–3
  glasses, *133*, 251, *253*, 255
  jugs, 68, 129, 251, *253*, 276
  mineral, 275, 276
  serving, 143, *186*, 255
  staining by, 71
wedding receptions, *100*, 101, *205*
  see also functions
Wedgwood Hotelware, 67
Weights and Measures (Sale of Wine) Order (1976), 278
whisky, 272, 275
white wines
  age and appearance, 248
  as aperitifs, *257*, 270–1
  bottle yields, *257*
  chilled, 250, 261, 262–3
  decanted, 265
  food matched with, 267, 268
  French, 236, 237–8, 239, 241, 242, 243, 244, 245
  German, 245–7, 248
  glasses, 251, 252, *256*
  Italian, 247
  list of, 236
  Portuguese, 247–8
  serving, 262–4
    sequence of, 266
  temperature
    for serving, 250, 262–3
    for storage, 249
wine, 235–69
  age and appearance, 248